PERSPECTIVES ON OUR FATHER ABRAHAM

Marvin R. Wilson

PERSPECTIVES ON
Our Father Abraham

Essays in Honor of
MARVIN R. WILSON

Edited by

Steven A. Hunt

WILLIAM B. EERDMANS PUBLISHING COMPANY
GRAND RAPIDS, MICHIGAN / CAMBRIDGE, U.K.

Published 2010 by
Wm. B. Eerdmans Publishing Co.
2140 Oak Industrial Drive N.E., Grand Rapids, Michigan 49505 /
P.O. Box 163, Cambridge CB3 9PU U.K.

Paperback edition 2012

Printed in the United States of America

17 16 15 14 13 12   7 6 5 4 3

Library of Congress Cataloging-in-Publication Data

Perspectives on Our Father Abraham: essays in honor of Marvin R. Wilson /
    edited by Steven A. Hunt.
        p.   cm.
      ISBN 978-0-8028-6953-1 (pbk.: alk. paper)
      1. Abraham (Biblical patriarch)   I. Hunt, Steven A.   II. Wilson, Marvin R., 1935-

  BS580.A3P43   2010
  222′.11092 — dc22

                                                              2010003665

www.eerdmans.com

Contents

Contents

Foreword

It is a great privilege to introduce this volume celebrating Marvin R. Wilson, my longtime colleague and friend. Anyone who knows Marv even slightly is familiar with his remarkable memory and penchant for facts, even now that he has reached his mid-seventies. So let me tell you a few facts about Marv.

Between his eight years at Barrington College and his thirty-nine years at Gordon College, his illustrious teaching career is approaching the half-century mark. He has taught more than 9,000 students. In fact, at one time he taught at least one core course to every single student at Gordon. Many who have taken his Old Testament course count it as one of the most formative experiences of their lives. And, today, when I travel around the country and meet our alumni, Marv Wilson's is the faculty name I hear most often.

His passion for teaching is matched by his prodigious scholarship. In the 1970s, Marv was a translator and editor of the *New International Version*, which remains the best-selling English version of Scripture. His influential book *Our Father Abraham: Jewish Roots of the Christian Faith* (Eerdmans, 1989) has not only been through more than twenty printings but has been translated into Czech, Italian, and French. He has also coedited four books with Jewish scholars on evangelical-Jewish relations, one of his great passions. In 2001, Marv ventured out into new territory, or at least a new medium, by serving as the primary scholar for *Jews and Christians: A Journey of Faith*, a two-hour national public television program. More recently, he has planned and moderated several "Trialogues," public discussions among scholars from the Muslim, Jewish, and Christian communities. Thus, while his roots remain in the evangelical community, he has refused the comfort, as well as the isolation, of the evangelical "ghetto," preferring to remain open to "the other" and to the larger culture. In all of these respects — his passion for teaching, tireless scholarship, and cultural engagement — he serves as a wonderful model for younger faculty.

In the midst of all his accomplishments, Marv has always made time to listen and to be a counselor and friend to many, including generations of students and fellow faculty. He has also been a great friend to me. Our ties actually go back to Denver Seminary and our long association with Denver's esteemed former president and chancellor Vernon Grounds. When I came to Gordon College as a young dean of faculty in 1976, it was Marv who was the first faculty member to befriend me. He made a point of sitting with me at my first faculty retreat, inquiring after me and encouraging me.

During the past sixteen years, while I have been Gordon's president, Marv has scheduled an appointment with me each semester. He peppers me with questions written out in tiny script on a note card, brings me his point of view, and helps me find a balanced perspective on troubling issues. For an hour, sometimes two, we talk and pray. And Marv never uses these meetings to advance his own agenda. Instead, he is always concerned with the greater good of the college. Since he has a gift for sifting out the central issues from peripheral ones, I have found his counsel consistently moderate and wise.

Even in times of adversity, Marv and his wife, Polly, steadily affirm the goodness of God, and their unfailingly hopeful, faithful outlook has been inspiring to me and a great many others. Over the years, I have realized that there's a kind of holy music running just beneath the surface of their lives. If you listen closely, you can hear it. It's the ringing music of the ancient Hebrew Psalms and the great hymns of the church, as well as the lively Jewish folk tunes that Marv and Polly have sung so exuberantly with the generations of Gordon students who have taken Marv's course in Modern Jewish Culture. As Roger Green notes later in this volume, Marv sometimes evokes Tevye, the beleaguered hero of *Fiddler on the Roof,* who, in spite of everything, sings, "To life, to life, L'Chaim. L'Chaim, L'Chaim to life." It seems to me that Marv is all about heartily embracing life and its God-given goodness. For this and for all of his distinguished accomplishments, we gladly celebrate him.

R. Judson Carlberg, *President*
Gordon College
Wenham, Massachusetts

Acknowledgments

The seeds for this project were sown in a department meeting (without Marv!) at Gordon College early in the spring semester of 2007. We have come a long way since then. Special thanks to my colleagues at that meeting, each of whom immediately and enthusiastically supported the idea of honoring Marv on the occasion of his 75th birthday. If nothing else, their support for this project, not to mention the countless hours they put into researching and writing chapters for it, is a tribute to Marv's incredible reputation, devoted following, and enduring legacy at this small liberal arts Christian college on Boston's north shore. I am indebted to the administration too, especially President R. Judson Carlberg and Provost Mark Sargent, whose support for this project has been unwavering and substantial. I know the respect you both have for Marv and I'm grateful to have worked alongside you to bring this tribute to completion. Likewise, I would like to thank the members of Gordon's Faculty Development Committee, including our former Academic Dean, Dr. Kina Mallard, who saw fit to award a "top-secret" initiative grant for the project. It is gratifying indeed to be at a Christian institution that supports its faculty in their professional endeavors.

When I sent out the invitations for this volume, I had no idea how favorable the response would be. (In fact, this book is longer than I originally thought it would be — but everybody wanted to write a chapter for Marv!) What a delight it has been to work with all of the authors in this book. Their patience with me, my deadlines, my insistence that they follow publishing guidelines, and all my emails, etc., puts me in their debt. I'm glad also to have developed significant relationships with at least some of them during this process — one meeting in particular stands out, not least because of the delicious frappuccino under a clear blue Colorado sky!

I would be entirely remiss if I did not mention and thank my assistant, Jordan Montgomery, a senior triple-major at Gordon, whose long office hours, editorial skills, computer savvy, and dedication to this project have been greatly appreciated. I do not know that I could have hired a more capable assistant.

I'm grateful also for the team at Wm. B. Eerdmans Publishing who has been enthusiastically supportive of this project since its inception. I would specifically like to thank my former classmate, Michael Thomson, now acquisitions and development editor at Eerdmans. I'll see you next year at SBL!

Finally, I would like to thank and acknowledge those who missed me the most during the long hours that were spent working on this book. Bridget — you are the best. Where would I be without you? Who could have envisioned your journey from nanny to mother of four in the span of just a couple of years? Wow! Who does that? I love you and am so grateful for your presence in my life. And just so you know, I'm going to keep working on the adjectives and adverbs! Kids — Nathaniel, Jordan, William, and Lindsey — I am amazed at how you have handled the various traumas and transitions you have gone through in the last few years. "Resilient" does not even come close. . . . Thanks for sticking with me during our very dark time; thanks for giving me a reason to get out of bed in the morning; thanks for your love. I love you too.

STEVEN A. HUNT
Associate Professor of New Testament
Gordon College
Wenham, Massachusetts

Contributors

William B. Barcley, Pastor, Sovereign Grace Presbyterian Church, Charlotte, NC; Adjunct Professor, Reformed Theological Seminary

Rebecca Gates Brinton, Adjunct Professor, Gordon College, 2004-2007

R. Judson Carlberg, President, Gordon College

Roy E. Ciampa, Associate Professor of New Testament, Gordon-Conwell Theological Seminary

Gordon D. Fee, Professor Emeritus of New Testament Studies, Regent College

Roger J. Green, Professor of Biblical and Theological Studies, Gordon College

Ted Hildebrandt, Professor of Biblical Studies, Gordon College

Steven A. Hunt, Associate Professor of New Testament, Gordon College

David Klatzker, Rabbi, Temple Ner Tamid, Peabody, MA

JoAnn G. Magnuson, U.S. Project Coordinator, Christian Friends of Yad Vashem

David Mathewson, Associate Professor of New Testament, Gordon College

John N. Oswalt, Research Professor of Old Testament, Wesley Biblical Seminary

Elaine Phillips, Professor of Old Testament, Gordon College

A. James Rudin, Rabbi, Senior Interreligious Adviser, The American Jewish Committee

Mark L. Sargent, Provost, Gordon College

H. G. M. Williamson, Regius Professor of Hebrew, Oriental Institute, Oxford University

Lauren F. Winner, Assistant Professor of Christian Spirituality, Duke Divinity School

Edwin M. Yamauchi, Professor of History, Emeritus, Miami University

David J. Zucker, Rabbi, Shalom Park, Aurora, CO

The Life and Legacy of Marvin R. Wilson

Roger J. Green

Marvin R. Wilson. The name will be familiar to countless readers who pick up this book. The facts of his life only begin to tell the story, and so those facts must of necessity be followed by a look at the deeper meaning of his life and work and of the contributions that he has made to Christian higher education, to the broader Christian and Jewish communities, and to his family, friends, students, and colleagues. But it is impossible to study the man and his message without the biographical context, and so here is where we begin.

Marv is a true New Englander, born in Stoneham, Massachusetts, on July 17, 1935, the second child of Marion and Malcolm Wilson. Marion was a music supervisor in the school system in Providence, Rhode Island, among other places, and Malcolm and his brother worked in Boston for N. S. Wilson and Sons, a family business that manufactured and imported various products such as oils and chemicals and that had been first incorporated in 1916 by their father. Marion and Malcolm's first child, Malcolm, was three years older than Marv, and the two brothers grew up in a loving and supportive Christian family in Winchester, Massachusetts.

Public school was not for Marv. He wanted his high school education to be in a Christian school, and so his parents consented and Marv attended what is now known as Lexington Christian Academy. He was both a good student and an accomplished basketball player. He served as captain of the basketball team, and the pictures from those days clearly demonstrate his pride in being part of the team. His interest in sports would follow him throughout his life, in later years more as a fan than as a participant. His education at Lexington Christian Academy prepared him well for entrance into Wheaton College in Wheaton, Illinois, where he finally settled as a history major and received his Bachelor of Arts degree in 1957.

However, the love of his life would not be a Wheaton graduate, but a Gordon graduate, class of 1957. Pauline Rose Berfield, the eldest daughter of Rose and Lloyd, grew up in Revere, Massachusetts, was attracted to Gordon College, and spent half of her college life on the Fenway and the other half in Wenham, Massachusetts, after Gordon purchased the present property and moved to the latter location in 1955. Pauline's younger sister, Phyllis, followed her to Gordon and graduated in 1962. Marv and Pauline, who prefers to be called Polly, had known each other since about the age of eleven during Sunday school days at the Cornerstone Baptist Church in Cambridge, and their friendship matured. On June 15, 1957, one week after graduation, Marvin R. Wilson and Pauline R. Berfield were married in the church where they met. Their life together began rather inauspiciously by sharing work at a summer camp, Sandy Hill in Maryland, and they would continue to work at Brookwoods Camp in New Hampshire for the three following summers. Marv was being prepared to work with high school and college students even then.

Marv was clear about the direction in his life, and at the end of the summer he enrolled as a student in Gordon Divinity School, then located in Frost Hall on the campus of Gordon College. He received his Bachelor of Divinity degree in 1960, and then moved on to Brandeis University, where he received the Master of Arts degree followed by the Ph.D. in 1963. In the meantime a daughter, Deborah Ann Wilson (now called Tassa Rose), was born on November 21, 1961, and like her mother and aunt eventually became a graduate of Gordon College. Marv was ordained at the Cornerstone Baptist Church to the teaching ministry. During one of the summers while completing his degree at Brandeis, Marv worked for the Tavilla family. Marv could not have known how important that family would be to Gordon College many years later as one of the Tavilla sons, Stephen, served on the Board of Trustees of Gordon College from 1987 to 2004, with emeritus status from 2004 to 2008. Tavilla Hall, a lovely dormitory, stands on the campus of Gordon College as a living tribute by Stephen Tavilla in honor of his parents on behalf of the entire family. Marv was pleased to speak at the dedication of Tavilla Hall.

So by 1963 all was set for a new direction in the life of the Wilsons. The family was established, the degrees were all in hand, and Marv was ordained. The question remained, however, where to go. Marv could not possibly have realized at the time that a small Christian college in Barrington, Rhode Island, was looking for an Old Testament professor. As it turns out Marv was pursued by the president, Howard Ferrin, and especially by the dean, Terrelle B. Crum. The Wilsons packed their bags and moved to Barrington, Rhode Island, to begin teaching in the fall of 1963. Their commitment to that college was so strong that when they added a Saint Bernard dog to the family they named the dog Barrington.

Other colleagues joined Marv and Polly, and the time at Barrington College became special for all concerned. The family that was created there was a warm and supportive Christian community of learning that is still fondly remembered by faculty and students alike. Among those joining Marv on the faculty was Bill Buehler in 1964, recently returned from Basel, Switzerland, where he was the last American student to earn his doctorate under Karl Barth. And in 1970 — and here is where full disclosure is both desirable and critical — the writer of this chapter joined the faculty. Both Bill Buehler and his wife, Marlyn, became close friends and colleagues of Marv and Polly, as did I and my wife, Karen, whom I married in 1973, Marv officiating at that wedding along with my father. Other names bring back pleasant memories for those who knew Barrington College at that time — the Hummels, the Gregorys, the Fullams, the Oswalts, and others.

We taught and at times worshipped together, were all involved in a Sunday evening Bible study, and laughed and cried with each other. Our life together was fulfilling in every way. Outside of the college Marv and Polly found a wonderful place of worship at the Barrington Baptist Church, Pastor David Madeira and his wife, Annalise, becoming good friends. The Wilson membership remains in that church to this day. And in the midst of a very busy schedule Marv occasionally found time to preach and teach outside of Barrington College, and for a period of time was the interim pastor at the Warren Avenue Baptist Church in Brockton, Massachusetts.

Perhaps the most important influence that Bill and Marlyn Buehler had on Marv was to suggest that he see a movie that had recently been released entitled *Fiddler on the Roof*. They could not have imagined the impact the movie would have on Marv Wilson. His penchant for wanting to learn about all things Jewish may have begun while he was a student at Brandeis University, but it was greatly enhanced by seeing that movie. We have all lost count as to how many times Marv has seen the movie and/or the play (although Marv could easily provide that detail!), but it must be well into the twenties or thirties. Marv knows every song, every conversation, and every nuance of *Fiddler on the Roof.*

Marv initiated a new course while at Barrington College, and this course — still entitled Modern Jewish Culture — has been his signature course lo these many years. Marv decided to teach the course partly because as students in his Old Testament classes naturally asked questions about Jews and Judaism, Marv found himself constantly turning to his Rabbi friends to answer those questions. By his own admission, neither seminary nor graduate school had prepared him for the learning and research that was necessary for the construction and implementation of that course. But nothing has given Marv more joy than teaching Modern Jewish Culture. Stories abound to this day from students who have taken that course throughout the years, and it is probably fair to say that for most of them it was their first exposure to Judaism and their first opportunity to worship in synagogues of various Jewish traditions.

Marv has often recounted that he was a bit nervous at the maiden voyage of this course in summer school at Barrington College in 1964. As he entered the classroom on the first day, he learned that one of his students was a Jewish woman of Hasidic background. The irony was not lost on Marv, as this woman sat in his class learning about her own tradition from an evangelical Christian!

Marv's lifelong adventure of learning about Jews and Judaism and how to relate all of that to evangelical Christianity had begun — and what an appropriate beginning it was. If the Jewish proverb is true that "study is the highest form of worship," certainly no one better embodies that truth than Marv Wilson. His course in Modern Jewish Culture (as well as his countless other courses taught so passionately throughout the years) is a model for what Christian higher education is all about.

But those of us who taught with Marv at Barrington College were soon to learn that the days of our community life together with the Wilsons were about to come to an end. Little did we know that the dean of Gordon College, Richard Gross, had been trying to get Marv to leave Barrington and come to Gordon College since 1970. Truth be told, however, Marv did not want to leave Barrington. The teaching environment with colleagues was wonderful, the students were engaged, and the community was all that could be asked for, especially, for example, when Polly suffered a long illness and faculty, staff, and students alike rallied to support the Wilson family in ways still remembered today.

But in 1971 Marv was sure that it was the leading of the Lord to leave

Barrington and move to Wenham. Marv and I had adjoining offices separated by a door that was always kept open. The memory still lingers of the moment Marv came through that door and sat down with me to explain that he was leaving Barrington College. And as difficult as it was for the Barrington community to let go of the Wilsons, we all knew that it was best for them. And so the move ninety miles north of Providence took place in the summer of 1971, and Marv Wilson has served at Gordon College with distinction since then, surrounded by friends and family. In 1985 Barrington College merged with Gordon College, and beginning with that merger Marv's years at Barrington College were recognized as years of service to Gordon College. In 2008 Marv completed his forty-fifth year of service to Barrington College and Gordon College, and that was a good time to remember many of his accomplishments during his tenure at those two institutions.

It will come as no surprise that Marv and Polly made many lifelong friends at Gordon College, and the names of the Grosses, the Askews, the Bishops, and the Carlbergs come to mind, as well as countless others. And Marv has gladly and warmly welcomed new members of the department of Biblical Studies and Christian Ministries as the department has changed and expanded. When Marv moved to Gordon College, Harold J. Ockenga was the president of both the college and Gordon Divinity School, and when he resigned to become the president of the newly merged Gordon-Conwell Theological Seminary, Richard Gross became the president of the college. He was followed by Jud Carlberg. Both have spoken about what Marv's friendship and counsel have meant to them during their tenures as president. Happily for all concerned, as the years went by Marv was joined by two of his friends from the Barrington days. Bill Buehler was invited to teach at Gordon in 1981. And in 1985, at the time of the merger, the writer of this chapter gratefully accepted the invitation to join the faculty of Gordon. So the Wilsons, the Buehlers, and the Greens were together again, sharing both friendship and vocation.

Marv served as department chair for an unprecedented twenty-five years, eight years at Barrington College and then seventeen years at Gordon College until 1988. His outstanding teaching at the college has been recognized by students and colleagues alike as he has been awarded the Faculty of the Year award a total of five times between the two institutions. He was named the first incumbent of the Harold J. Ockenga Chair of Biblical and Theological Studies. He inaugurated Gordon College's Holy Land Pilgrimage and took fourteen trips to Israel with Gordon College alumni and other friends of the college. And in keeping with his delight in introducing Jews and Christians to each other for mutual conversation, he also traveled to Israel with Rabbi Sam Kenner and with both Jews and Christians to see the Holy Land together and through the eyes of the other. However, as was the case while teaching at Barrington College, Marv has been wholly engaged outside of the college with speaking and teaching, and for several years, as he had done while teaching at Barrington, he taught at the Evening School of the Bible at Park Street Church.

Marv Wilson is a prodigious writer, and this introductory chapter could not do justice to everything that he has written. However, two projects come to mind that are especially worth mentioning. First, Marv instituted, along with his friends Marc H. Tanenbaum and A. James Rudin, at that time both associated with the American Jewish Committee in New York, a series of conversations between evangelicals and Jews. What evangelical Christians and Jews have in common, especially with their mutual appreciation for the authority of the First Testament, perhaps surprised both the Christians and Jews at that first conference in New York City on December 8-10, 1975. Evangelicals at the conference were pleased with the appreciation that the Jewish leadership demonstrated for evangelicals, and the ice was broken with the Jews present at the conference when they discovered, to their amazement, that some of the Christian delegates were fluent in Hebrew, and that evangelicals had an abiding respect for the Hebrew roots of the Christian faith.

The Jews and the Christians ate together, prayed together, and studied together. However, genuine and serious dialogue includes differences, and the atmosphere of those conversations was such that differences, especially concerning Jesus Christ and his life, ministry, death, and resurrection, were not overlooked or ignored. Dialogue done in love became the hallmark of those discussions, and honest disagreements were acknowledged. Mutual respect allowed the conversations to continue, and several books have been published as a result of those conferences as Marv's conversations with the Jewish community have continued throughout his career. The title of the first book, *Evangelicals and Jews in Conversation: On Scripture, Theology, and History,* clearly demonstrates the breadth of Marv's interests throughout these many years.

However, Marv's great lifelong achievement that stands above all his other writing is his book entitled *Our Father Abraham: Jewish Roots of the Christian Faith,* now having exceeded twenty printings. Marv had been gathering a great deal of material for this book, especially from his several years of teaching his course on Modern Jewish Culture. And finally in 1987, while on a six-month sabbatical at Tyndale House at Cambridge University, he was able to write the text for this book, which he dedicated to Polly for the support that she had given those many years. Eerdmans published the work in 1989. The publishers get it right when they advertise the book as "personal and passionate." Still in print, the book has taken on a life of its own. The book is translated into several languages, and as recently as the fall of 2007 Marv was invited to speak in Florence, Italy, at the inauguration of the translation of his book into Italian.

Many stories abound about this book, but a favorite has to do with two young people whom the book brought together in marriage. Each was reading the book separately and one day noticed the other also reading it. They introduced themselves to each other and began to speak about the book and their common interests. Ultimately their interests led them beyond the book to marriage.

Marv received a phone call in his office one day, and Gordon College's *Stillpoint* records the call as well as Marv's reaction this way: "When the phone rang in Professor Marvin Wilson's office one day in 1995, a man on the other end of the line told him he loved his book *Our Father Abraham* and wanted to make a film about it. The caller laid out an impressive vision for the project. 'I thought the call was a joke from a colleague on campus,' Dr. Wilson says. 'That kind of offer doesn't usually happen in real life. It took more than an hour for me to be convinced that maybe it wasn't a joke.'" The caller was one Jerry Krell of Auteur Productions in Maryland. He and his friend, Meyer Odze, had produced programs for PBS, HBO, and the Arts and Entertainment Network. Jerry Krell convinced Marv that he really did want to produce a documentary for PBS based on some basic themes in the book, and eventually the project was entitled *Jews and Christians: A Journey of Faith.*

In turns out that the call from Jerry Krell was no joke after all. His associate producer, Cindee Jacobs, had handed him Marv's book. After reading the book three times, he was certain that this was a worthy product, and Jerry and Marv became fast friends as the project unfolded. After being approached about this possibility, Marv gave himself in true Marv Wilson fashion heart and soul to the production of this video. Funds had to be raised. Time had to be found. Speakers had to be contacted. About three hundred hours of taping were done for this two-hour video, both in the United States and in Israel. Marv relied on his friend in Israel, Halvor Ronning, to assist in setting up the production in Israel. Halvor, an evangelical Christian living in Israel with his wife, Miriam, had been the tour guide for Marv in many of his Gordon College Holy Land Pilgrimages, and stood ready and willing to give his invaluable expertise to the production of this video.

The video had its premier showing at Gordon College in 2000 and has been shown in several PBS markets since that time. Likewise, the video brought new life to Marv's book and to his life's work, and so continues to have an impact on both Christians and Jews today.

In spite of his commitment to teaching and to writing, he is ever ready to serve on boards, speak at various engagements, counsel students, or have dinner with friends and colleagues. The compassion of the man is exemplified, for example, in his service on the Committee of Church Relations and the Holocaust at the United States Holocaust Memorial Museum in Washington, D.C., as well as his ongoing commitment to the local Holocaust Center in Peabody, Massachusetts.

One would not want to leave the reader with the wrong impression of Marv Wilson, however. While a great teacher, a prodigious writer, an internationally acclaimed speaker and teacher, here is a down-to-earth person, with a twinkle in his eye and a generous smile. He can see the funny side of things even when the best-laid plans seem to go awry. Several stories about his good sense of humor could be given, but one will suffice. Many years ago Marv and I arranged a trip to New York City, Marv taking some students from Gordon College and I taking some from Barrington College. Marv picked us up in a clearly marked Gordon College van, and a happy group drove to New York. We parked the van on Park Avenue where free parking was available on the weekend and had a wonderful, adventurous weekend, among other things — and not surprisingly — attending some synagogues in New York. On Sunday morning, leaving our students in their accommodations, Marv and I went to get the van and then pick up the students and begin the journey home, planning first to drive through the Hasidic community in Brooklyn. With my familiarity with New York I knew exactly where we had parked the van, but I also knew that Marv was trusting in my recollection to find the van. As we turned the corner onto Park Avenue, I immediately saw that the van was missing, and I am not sure why I continued to walk with Marv for a couple of blocks, perhaps hoping and praying that the van would miraculously appear — but more probably trying to think of what I was going to tell Marv! But there was to be no miraculous intervention that morning, and I had to turn to Marv and confess that the van had been stolen and that we needed to make other plans to return home. I think that at that point we began to count the money that we had between us so that we could get the students home, perhaps by bus or train.

I did suggest, however, that first we needed to go to the local police precinct office and report that the van had been stolen. And so we walked to the police station, and as we neared the station what to our wondering eyes should appear but the Gordon College van parked in front of the police station! We walked in, and of course the hardened New York cops tried to convince us that some of our students had sneaked out in the middle of the night and had taken a drunken joy ride with the van around New York. Imagine the disbelief in the eyes of those cops (I think that I even detected that some eyes were rolling) when Marv tried to convince them that our students were from a Christian college and would never do such a thing!

But the conversation was going nowhere and what we were interested in was retrieving that van. In walked the night duty officer from the night before, who decided to give us our van, but not before telling us this story: a business manager from the West Side had given keys to his Spanish-only–speaking employee to go and pick up the company van that had been parked on Park Avenue. The van happened to be the same make and model as the Gordon College van, and the employee, not able to read the Gordon College sign on the van, put the key into the lock. The key worked! Then he put it into the ignition and it worked again! So he drove the van to the West Side, and his employer, greatly indignant, at least had presence of mind to tell his employee to return the van to the local police precinct. That is where Marv and I come back into the story. The van had been driven only a few miles (everyone who knows Marv knows that he is a stickler for details and so he knew the mileage on the odometer when we parked the van!). We picked up our students and drove merrily home in our Gordon College van. And lived to tell our story!

Marv's sense of humor remained intact during that entire experience, and that is only one of the traits of Marv Wilson that all who know him have come to appreciate. His humility, his putting others before himself, his pastoral approach to his teaching and his relationship with his students, and his love for his family and friends — all these characteristics are what endears this man to the hearts and minds of the many who have known him.

In spite of his reluctance to be in the spotlight, many honors have rightly been given to Marv Wilson from both the Jewish community and the Christian community as his teaching career has evolved. These, of course, are too numerous to mention here, but a couple will suffice. On Sunday, October 27, 2002, B'nai B'rith of the North Shore honored Marv with the Forty-First Person of the Year Award. Likewise, in 2004 he received the Leonard P. Zakim Humanitarian Award for his work on Christian-Jewish relations from the Anti-Defamation League at the annual North Shore Interfaith Seder.

However, perhaps the one that touched him most happened in April 2007. Betsy Gage Pea was a graduate from Gordon College, the class of 1979. She and her husband, Barry, wanted to honor Marv Wilson, and so they decided to endow the Dr. Marvin R. Wilson Award for Teaching Excellence in the Humanities. Betsy Pea well stated that "The strength of a college is in its professors. While studying at Gordon College I saw firsthand the impact Dr. Wilson had on the lives of the students." Literally thousands of students would add their amen to that.

The award is given annually to a faculty member in the Humanities Division or in the History Department, providing funding for professional study and development. At the convocation in which the award was acknowledged, President Carlberg remarked that "Generations of our students love Marv Wilson for his pastor's heart, his teachable spirit, and his commitment to growing Christian global leaders; and the gift from the Pea family acknowledges his contribution and helps pass his spirit to the next generation of faculty."

I am reminded of the text in Matthew 22:34-40, when Jesus was asked the question, "'Teacher, which is the great commandment in the law?' And he said to him, 'You shall love the Lord your God with all your heart, and with all your soul, and with all your mind. This is the great and first commandment. And the second is like it, You shall love your neighbor as yourself. On these two commandments depend all the law and the prophets.'" Marv Wilson knows his Hebrew Bible well, and he knows equally well how important it was for our Lord to capture the essence of the law in this conversation — love God and love your neighbor. Marv would never personally identify himself with this, but here indeed is a good summary of the life and ministry of this man — he has loved God with all his heart, soul, and mind, and he has loved his neighbor as himself. And for that many have risen up and called him blessed.

Tevya sings "If I Were a Rich Man" in *Fiddler on the Roof* and then imagines all of the things he would be able to do were this dream to come true. He could build a beautiful house and fill it with luxuries and fill his yard with poultry. In fact, the house would be so big that he would build a staircase "leading nowhere, just for show." His dreams get more serious as the song continues, but the humor of the song remains to the end. However, if Marv Wilson all of a sudden were to become a rich man, and even if he built a house with the kind of staircase that Tevye envisioned, he could not possibly enrich the lives of those around him any more than he has already done. He has been a loving husband to his wife, Polly, a loving father to his daughter, Tassa, and a loving grandfather to his grandson, Ian Zachary. He has been a trusted friend and neighbor, a respected teacher and student, an admired colleague, scholar, and mentor throughout these many years. Marv Wilson is already a rich man, and he has shared those riches without reserve. This book is a living tribute to such a truth.

Abraham in the Hebrew Scriptures

Abraham and Archaeology: Anachronisms or Adaptations?

Edwin M. Yamauchi

Adaptations?

The patriarchal narratives in general, and the story of Abraham in particular, as found in Genesis are ostensibly placed in the Middle Bronze Age (c. 2000-1500 B.C.E.).[1] The traditional association of the Pentateuch with Moses, whether one accepts the early or the late date of the Exodus, would take us to the Late Bronze Age (c. 1500-1200 B.C.E.). Scholars such as Cyrus H. Gordon, Ephraim Speiser, and William F. Albright had cited parallels from the Mari and the Nuzi archives as evidence of either an MB or LB date for the origin of these stories. Since the 1970s scholars such as Thomas L. Thompson and John Van Seters have pointed to alleged anach-

1. Based on an early date of the Exodus in 1446 B.C.E., Gleason Archer ("The Chronology of the Old Testament," in *The Expositor's Bible Commentary*, ed. Frank E. Gaebelein [Grand Rapids: Zondervan, 1979], vol. 1, p. 365) calculated Abraham's date as 2166-1991 B.C.E. Those accepting a late date of the Exodus would place Abraham's date two centuries later.

It is a great privilege to contribute an essay in tribute to Marvin Wilson, whom I have known for nearly fifty years since our graduate days, studying under Cyrus H. Gordon at Brandeis in the 1960s. (See Meir Lubetski and Claire Gottlieb, "'Forever Gordon': Portrait of a Master Scholar with a Global Perspective," *BA* 59 [March 1996]: 2-12.) We have kept in close touch since then. I have used his classic text, *Our Father Abraham*, for my senior seminar classes at Miami University. I have directed the graduate work of two of his students: John DeFelice and Jason Larson. My doctoral student, Scott Carroll, was his colleague at Gordon College from 1988 to 1994. Marv and I have been collaborating on a major reference work, *The Dictionary of Biblical Backgrounds* (Grand Rapids: Zondervan, forthcoming).

ronisms to judge these narratives as very late compositions, rendering these traditions wholly untrustworthy.

Conservative scholars in response have noted that in view of the fragmentary nature of our archaeological and epigraphic evidence, it is a fallacy for scholars to dismiss as inauthentic elements in the patriarchal narratives by the "argument from silence."[2] In view of the continuing need to make a transmitted tradition (whether oral or written) intelligible to later generations, there was the need to "modernize" or "update" terms, particularly the names of peoples and places. Bryant G. Wood observes: "Editorial updating of names that had gone out of use is not uncommon in the Hebrew Bible. Other examples are Bethel, named by Jacob in Gen 28:19, but used proleptically in Gen 12:8 and 13:3; Dan, named by the Danites in Judg 18:29 and used proleptically in Gen 14:14; and Samaria, named by Omri in 1 Kgs 16:24 and used proleptically in 1 Kgs 13:32."[3] So in some cases what appears to be an anachronism may be better understood as an adaptation.[4]

"Asia," a word derived from a Hittite Assuwa in the New Testament era, denoted a Roman province on the west coast of Turkey, not the Far East.[5] "Africa," a word derived from the Afri tribe, designated the Roman province around Carthage in what is today Tunisia, not the continent.[6] "Ethiopia," derived from a Greek word that meant "sun-burnt face," originally designated the region south of Egypt, known as Cush, today the Sudan, and not the modern country of Ethiopia on the eastern horn of Af-

2. For the fragmentary nature of these evidences, see Edwin Yamauchi, *The Stones and the Scriptures* (Philadelphia: J. B. Lippincott, 1972), ch. IV, "Fragments and Circles: The Nature of the Evidence."

3. Bryant G. Wood, "The Rise and Fall of the 13th Century Exodus-Conquest Theory," *JETS* 48 (2005): 479.

4. Numerous words in the King James Version (1611) are either no longer intelligible or convey altogether different meanings today, e.g. "reins" (literally kidneys, now translated "heart"), "pitiful" (now translated "compassionate"), "corn" (referring not to maize but to grain), etc. See Ronald Bridges and Luther A. Weigle, *The Bible Word Book: Concerning Obsolete or Archaic Words in the King James Version of the Bible* (New York: Thomas Nelson & Sons, 1960). Some thirty years after the publication of the New International Version (NIV) in 1973, the Committee on Bible Translation felt that a revision was necessary, resulting in the TNIV (Today's New International Version), with the publication of the New Testament in 2002 and the Old Testament in 2005.

5. Edwin Yamauchi, *New Testament Cities in Western Asia Minor* (repr. Eugene, OR: Wipf and Stock, 2003), p. 15.

6. Edwin Yamauchi, *Africa and the Bible* (Grand Rapids: Baker Academic, 2004), p. 40.

rica.[7] "Kittim," a name derived from the Mycenaean colony of Kition on Cyprus, designated Greeks in the Old Testament but Romans in the Dead Sea Scrolls.[8] "Sepharad" in the Old Testament originally designated the city of Sardis in western Turkey, but today the Sephardic Jews are those who originated from Spain and North Africa; "Ashekenaz" in the Old Testament originally designated Scythians, nomads from Russia, but later became associated with Germany, hence the designation of Ashkenazic Jews as those with European origins.[9]

The parallel case of Homeric traditions, which preserved many LB or Mycenaean elements in a framework of an eighth-century composition, may be illuminating.[10] A penetrating and persuasive analysis by E. S. Sherratt demonstrates that there are certain elements of the transmitted tradition that are preserved intact, whereas there were also adaptations to make these traditions intelligible to later audiences or readers.[11]

Anachronisms?

In the narratives about Abraham and Isaac, there are three elements in particular, which are considered glaringly anachronistic by critical scholars. According to Maynard P. Maidman, "There are, indeed, significant parallels between the Genesis patriarchs and the ancient Near East, but these appear to be Iron Age parallels, in just the time period Wellhausen places the authorship and editing of Genesis. Thus, for example, the patriarchs' camels, Chaldean Ur and Philistines in Palestine are all Iron Age — *not* Bronze Age — realities."[12]

7. Yamauchi, *Africa,* ch. 6, "Why the Ethiopian Eunuch Was Not from Ethiopia."

8. David W. Baker, "Kittim," in *The Anchor Bible Dictionary* [hereafter *ABD*], ed. David N. Freedman (New York: Doubleday, 1992), vol. 4, p. 93.

9. Edwin Yamauchi, *Foes from the Northern Frontier* (repr. Eugene, OR: Wipf and Stock, 2003), p. 63.

10. Edwin Yamauchi, "Homer and Archaeology: Minimalists and Maximalists in Classical Context," in *The Future of Biblical Archaeology: Reassessing Methodologies and Assumptions,* ed. James K. Hoffmeier and Alan Millard (Grand Rapids: Eerdmans, 2004), pp. 69-90; for an abridged version, see Edwin Yamauchi, "Historic Homer: Did It Happen?" *BAR* 33 (March/April 2007): 28-37, 76.

11. E. S. Sherratt, "'Reading the Texts': Archaeology and the Homeric Question," *Antiquity* 64 (1990): 807-24.

12. Maynard P. Maidman, "Abraham, Isaac and Jacob Meet Newton, Darwin and Wellhausen," *BAR* 32 (March/April 2006): 63.

In a very influential monograph, *Abraham in History and Tradition,*[13] John Van Seters sought to overturn the earlier positive assessment of the patriarchal narratives by Albright, Gordon, and Speiser[14] by focusing on just these three anachronisms.

As for camels, Van Seters wrote: "A special comment is necessary on the mention of camels. Most scholars, even those who argue for an early date for the patriarchal traditions, regard the mention of camels as an anachronism."[15]

As for Philistines who are mentioned in Genesis 21 and 26, Van Seters commented, "many scholars who argue for the antiquity of the patriarchal traditions are prepared to admit that this reference to Philistines is an anachronism."[16]

As for Ur of the Chaldees, Van Seters noted: "The reference to Ur of the Chaldeans and its association with Harran and a route to the West reflect the political circumstances of the Neo-Babylonian period."[17] He asserted that there is nothing that points "to the Amorite migration of the early second millennium B.C."[18]

The linkage between Ur and Haran, which was prominent in the reign of Nabonidus, the last Neo-Babylonian king,[19] led Van Seters to conclude: "The present study has argued that the Yahwistic version of the tradition dates to the exilic period."[20] Van Seters considers the Yahwist an "antiquarian historian" like Herodotus,[21] and disputes the common critical scholarly consensus on redactors or editors.[22]

13. (New Haven: Yale University Press, 1975).

14. Van Seters justifiably criticized some of the parallels with the Nuzi practices adduced by Gordon and Speiser. For a more balanced, but still positive assessment of Near Eastern parallels for the patriarchal narratives, see M. J. Selman, "Comparative Customs and the Patriarchal Age," in *Essays on the Patriarchal Narratives,* ed. A. R. Millard and D. J. Wiseman (Leicester: Inter-Varsity Press, 1980), pp. 93-138.

15. Van Seters, *Abraham,* p. 17.

16. Van Seters, *Abraham,* p. 53.

17. Van Seters, *Abraham,* p. 121.

18. Van Seters, *Abraham,* p. 38.

19. See Paul-Alain Beaulieu, *The Reign of Nabonidus, King of Babylon (556-39 B.C.)* (New Haven: Yale University Press, 1989); Edwin Yamauchi, "Nabonidus," in *The International Standard Bible Encyclopedia,* ed. G. W. Bromiley (Grand Rapids: Eerdmans, 1986), vol. 3, pp. 468-70.

20. Van Seters, *Abraham,* p. 310.

21. John Van Seters, *Prologue to History: The Yahwist as Historian in Genesis* (Louisville: Westminster/John Knox, 1992).

22. *The Edited Bible: The Curious History of the "Editor" in Biblical Criticism* (Winona Lake: Eisenbrauns, 2006).

Camels

Camels in the Near East were the one-humped dromedary *(Camelus dromedaries),* a marvelous beast of burden that could go three to four days without drinking, carry over 400 pounds, and travel 20-25 miles in a day. The camel, which appears 54 times in the Old Testament, is mentioned in the accounts of Abraham (Gen. 12:16), Isaac (Gen. 24:10), and Jacob (Gen. 31:34). The date of their domestication has been disputed. W. F. Albright, who believed that camels were not domesticated before 1200 B.C.E., believed that Abraham was a donkey caravaneer.[23]

But scattered osteological and iconographic evidences convince other scholars that camels, at least on a limited scale, had been domesticated much earlier.[24] M. M. Ripinsky placed the date of the domestication some time in the fourth millennium B.C.E.[25] R. W. Bulliet traces the domestication of the camel in stages. The first stage occurred in southeastern Arabia in the fourth or third millennium B.C.E. and then spread to southwestern Arabia. The second stage, some time after 2000 B.C.E., involved the use of camels to transport incense from southwestern Arabia north.[26] Oded Borowski therefore concludes: "the presence of camels in the Patriarchal stories can be defended, and the story can be treated as primary evidence of camel use without disputing Albright's contention that camel-breeding nomads did not exist in Syria and northern Arabia until later."[27]

23. W. F. Albright, "The Historical Framework of Palestinian Archaeology between 2100 and 1600 B.C.," *BASOR* 209 (1973): 12-18. His conclusions were similar to those of R. Walz, "Zum Problem des Zeitpunkts der Domestikationsproblem der altweltlichen Camelidae," *ZDMG* n.s. 101 (1951): 29-51; R. Walz, "Neue Untersuchungen zum Domestikationsproblem der altestenlichen Camelidae," *ZDMG* n.s. 104 (1954): 45-87.

24. See John J. Davis, "The Camel in Biblical Narratives," in *A Tribute to Gleason Archer,* ed. W. C. Kaiser and R. F. Youngblood (Chicago: Moody, 1986), pp. 141-52; Joseph P. Free, "Abraham's Camels," *JNES* 3 (1944): 187-93; K. A. Kitchen, "Camel," in *The Illustrated Bible Dictionary,* ed. J. D. Douglas (Leicester: Inter-Varsity, 1980), vol. 1, pp. 228-30; K. A. Kitchen, *On the Reliability of the Old Testament* (Grand Rapids: Eerdmans, 2003), pp. 338-39.

25. M. M. Ripinsky, "The Camel in Ancient Arabia," *Antiquity* 54 (1975): 297.

26. R. W. Bulliet, *The Camel and the Wheel* (Cambridge, MA: Harvard University Press, 1975). See also Paula Wapnish, "Camel Caravans and Camel Pastoralists at Tell Jemmeh," *JANES* 13 (1981): 105.

27. Oded Borowski, *Every Living Thing: Daily Use of Animals in Ancient Israel* (Walnut Creek: Altamira, 1998), p. 114.

Ur of the Chaldees

We read in Genesis 11:27-28 (NIV): "This is the account of Terah. Terah became the father of Abram, Nahor and Haran. And Haran became the father of Lot. While his father Terah was still alive, Haran died in Ur of the Chaldeans,[28] in the land of his birth." The association of Abraham's Ur with the Chaldeans is problematic because the Chaldeans, a tribe who lived in southern Mesopotamia, who produced the kings of the Neo-Babylonian era, such as Nebuchadnezzar, were first attested in Assyrian sources in the early first millennium B.C.E.[29] This phrase may be best understood as an explanatory gloss to differentiate this Ur from other cities with similar names.

Cyrus H. Gordon favored identifying Abraham's home with a northern Ur, that is with Ura' (modern Urfa' or ancient Edessa), fifteen miles northwest of Haran.[30] But most scholars identify Ur with the famous Sumerian city in southern Mesopotamia, which flourished in the third millennium B.C.E.[31]

The site of Tell al-Muqayyar was identified correctly as Ur in the middle of the nineteenth century, and then excavated by C. Leonard Woolley from 1922 to 1934 in an expedition sponsored jointly by the British Museum and the University of Pennsylvania. Woolley uncovered a great flood pit, which he identified with Noah's flood, and royal graves of the Early Dynastic period with marvelous treasures and also grim evidence of the sacrifice of scores of servants.[32]

---

28. The phrase "Ur of the Chaldees" appears in Gen. 11:28, 31; 15:7; Neh. 9:7.

29. Edwin Yamauchi, "Chaldea, Chaldeans," in *The New International Dictionary of Biblical Archaeology,* ed. E. M. Blaiklock and R. K. Harrison (Grand Rapids: Zondervan, 1983), pp. 123-25. The later association of the Chaldeans as astrologers may have given rise in the Hellenistic era to the practice ascribed to Abraham in Jubilees 12:16: "Abram sat up during the night on the first of the seventh month, so that he might observe the stars from evening until daybreak so that he might see what the nature of the year would be with respect to rain."

30. Cyrus H. Gordon, "Abraham and the Merchants of Ura," *JNES* 17 (1958): 28-31. See also Barry J. Beitzel, *The New Moody Atlas of the Bible* (Chicago: Moody Press, 2009), map 30, p. 99.

31. H. W. F. Saggs, "Ur of the Chaldees," *Iraq* 22 (1960): 200-209; Alan R. Millard, "Where Was Abraham's Ur?" *BAR* 27 (May/June 2001): 52-53, 57.

32. C. Leonard Woolley, *Ur of the Chaldees* (New York: W. W. Norton, 1965); Julian Reade, "The Royal Tombs of Ur," in *Art of the First Cities*, ed. J. Aruz and R. Wallenfels (New York: The Metropolitan Museum of Art, 2003), pp. 93-132.

Ur was a great city of the Sumerians, who were the first literate civilization and who spoke a unique agglutinative language.[33] They flourished particularly in the so-called Ur III period, with such great rulers as Shulgi and Gudea. But at the end of Ibbi-Sin's reign (2029-2006 B.C.E.) the city of Ur was destroyed by the Elamites from southwestern Iran,[34] as recalled by the doleful "Lamentation over the Destruction of Ur."[35]

Now it is clear from his name Abram (Abraham) and his association with the Arameans (see below) that the patriarch was not a Sumerian. S. Spero raises the interesting question, "Was Abram Born in Ur of the Chaldees?" as we are not explicitly told this, coupled with the fact that the area of Haran is implied as his birthplace (Gen. 24:4, 10; 28:2, 10).[36] It is possible that Abram was born in Haran and migrated with his family to Ur, and then returned to his original homeland. Both Ur and Haran were centers of the Sumerian moon god (Nannar = Akkadian Sin), and Terah's name has been associated with the Hebrew word for moon.[37] As Van Seters has pointed out, there were strong connections between Haran and Ur in the Neo-Babylonian period insofar as Nabonidus's mother was a devotee of the moon god of Haran, and Nabonidus restored the ziggurat at Ur. But the Neo-Babylonian era was not the only period of close contacts between southern Mesopotamia and the north Syrian region. Since 1974 discoveries at Ebla in northwestern Syria not far from Haran have revealed strong trade contacts with Ur. According to F. Pinnock, "The relations between the two centres, therefore, may have been continuous between the mature Early Syrian period (= Early Dynastic IIIb in Mesopotamia) and the Third Dynasty of Ur."[38] Therefore close relations between Ur and Haran in northern Syria existed in the early second millennium B.C.E., and not just in the Neo-Babylonian era (sixth century B.C.E.).

33. S. N. Kramer, *History Begins at Sumer* (Garden City, NY: Doubleday & Co., 1959); S. N. Kramer, *The Sumerians* (Chicago: University of Chicago Press, 1963); A. Parrot, *Sumer* (London: Thames and Hudson, 1960); Walter R. Bodine, "Sumerians," in *Peoples of the Old Testament World*, ed. A. J. Hoerth, G. L. Mattingly, and Edwin Yamauchi (Grand Rapids: Baker Books, 1994), pp. 19-42.

34. Edwin Yamauchi, *Persia and the Bible* (Grand Rapids: Baker Book House, 1990), p. 288.

35. S. N. Kramer, "A Sumerian Lamentation," in *ANET*, pp. 455-63.

36. Shubert Spero, "Was Abram Born in Ur of the Chaldees?" *Jewish Bible Quarterly* 24 (July/September 1996): 156-59.

37. A. Parrot, *Abraham et son temps* (Neuchâtel: Delachaux et Niestlé, 1962), pp. 32-35.

38. F. Pinnock, "Ebla and Ur: Exchanges and Contacts between Two Great Capitals of the Ancient Near East," *Iraq* 68 (2006): 94.

A Wandering Aramean

Deuteronomy 26:5 exhorted, "Then you shall declare before the LORD your God: 'My father was a wandering Aramean.'" Abraham's relatives Bethuel and Laban are identified as Arameans (Gen 25:20; 31:20). In Genesis 31:47 Laban speaks in Aramaic. Van Seters considers the patriarchal associations with the Arameans quite anachronistic.[39]

The earliest attestation of Arameans, called Ahlamu, was believed to be in Assyrian texts of the twelfth century B.C.E.[40] Moreover our earliest Aramaic texts are dated about 900 to 850 B.C.E.[41] In 1979 in northern Syria at Tell Fekherye a remarkable statue was discovered with a bilingual inscription in Old Aramaic and in Akkadian, which is dated between 850 and 825 B.C.E.[42]

But Aram does occur as a place name as early as the twenty-third century B.C.E., and as a personal name in Mari texts (eighteenth century B.C.E.) and at Alalakh (seventeenth century B.C.E.).[43] The patriarchs had much in common with the Amorites,[44] Semites from northwest Syria, who infiltrated into Mesopotamia in the early second millennium B.C.E. and took over Mari, Ashur, and Babylon. Roland de Vaux, after a thorough discussion of the evidence, concluded: "All the same, the term 'Proto-Aramaeans' has the great advantage of showing that there was a continuity between the Amorites of the patriarchal age and the Arameans of the eleventh and tenth century B.C."[45]

An archive of 20,000 cuneiform tablets, including more than 4,000 letters, was discovered at Mari, a major site on the Euphrates River, exca-

39. Van Seters, *Abraham,* p. 30.

40. Wayne T. Pitard, "Arameans," in Hoerth, *Peoples,* p. 208.

41. Edwin Yamauchi, "Aramaic," in Blaiklock, *Dictionary of Biblical Archaeology,* pp. 38-41.

42. Ali Abou-Assaf, Pierre Bordreuil, and Alan R. Millard, *La statue de Tell Fekherye et son inscription bilingue assyro-araméenne* (Paris: Editions Recherche sur les civilizations, 1982); Pierre Bordreuil and Alan R. Millard, "A Statue from Syria with Assyrian and Aramaic Inscriptions," *BA* 45 (Summer 1982): 135-41.

43. A. Malamat, "The Aramaeans," in *Peoples of Old Testament Times,* ed. D. J. Wiseman (Oxford: Clarendon, 1973), p. 134.

44. Against the cavalier dismissal of the Amorite background of the Patriarchs by Van Seters, see the response by D. J. Wiseman, "'They Lived in Tents,'" in *Biblical and Near Eastern Studies: Essays in Honor of William Sanford LaSor,* ed. G. A. Tuttle (Grand Rapids: Eerdmans, 1978), pp. 195-200.

45. R. de Vaux, *The Early History of Israel* (Philadelphia: Westminster, 1978), p. 209.

vated by the French from 1933 to the present.[46] As Mari was destroyed by Hammurabi (eighteenth century B.C.E.), all these texts come from the Middle Bronze Era. Though the major part of the archive was found between 1934 and 1937, the laborious task of collating the cuneiform copies and translating them keeps bringing new information to light.

Van Seters denied that the description of the patriarchs as pastoralists had anything to do with the second millennium B.C. But as Daniel E. Fleming notes, "The Mari archives give us a picture of how Bronze Age tribal peoples lived, along with their herding communities, and the Genesis stories are entirely appropriate to that portrayal."[47]

Dominique Charpin, one of the two principal translators (with Jean-Marie Durand) of these texts, has published a most important article, which highlights the second millennium B.C.E. background of the patriarchal narratives and counters the skepticism of Van Seters. She reveals that from publications in 1991 and 1994 we now have attestations of the Ahlamu/Arameans in three Old Babylonian texts that date to the eighteenth century B.C.E.[48]

Abraham and his descendants are called Hebrews (e.g., Gen. 14:13) either by outsiders or in conversation with outsiders. The discovery of the Amarna Letters in Egypt in 1887 when published contained references to marauders in fourteenth-century B.C.E. Palestine called the *Habiru* in Akkadian (*'apiru* in Egyptian), whom scholars such as John Garstang were quick to equate with the Hebrews, an equation which is still accepted by some of the advocates of the early date of the Exodus. However, the wide distribution of the Habiru cannot support such a simple identification with the Hebrews.[49]

As to Van Seters's objection to having Abraham called a "Hebrew,"[50] the Mari texts contain the verb *habārum*, which means "to emigrate," that perfectly corresponds to the designation of "Abram the Hebrew."[51] Com-

---

46. Gordon D. Young, ed., *Mari in Retrospect* (Winona Lake: Eisenbrauns, 1992).

47. Daniel E. Fleming, "History in Genesis," *WTJ* 65 (2003): 260. See Victor H. Matthews, *Pastoral Nomadism in the Mari Kingdom* (Cambridge: American Schools of Oriental Research, 1978).

48. Dominique Charpin, "'Ein umherziehender Aramäer war mein Vater': Abraham im Lichte der Quellen aus Mari," in *"Abraham, unser Vater": Die gemeinsamen Wurzeln von Judentum, Christentum und Islam,* ed. R. G. Kratz and T. Nagel (Göttingen, 2003), p. 43.

49. See Edwin Yamauchi, "Habiru," in Blaiklock, *Dictionary of Biblical Archaeology,* pp. 223-24.

50. Van Seters, *Abraham,* p. 54.

51. Charpin, "Abraham im Lichte," p. 44: "Ein hābirum jener Zeit war demgemäss ein 'Emigrant', ein Zustand, der sehr gut die Situation Abrams beschreiben könnte."

menting on one of the major tribal groups of the Mari texts, Fleming observes: "Among the Binu Yamina only, however, the herding groups were called 'ibru(m), from the fact that they did not share the settled homes of their tribespeople. This noun shares the exact pattern of the word 'Hebrew.'"[52] Therefore the phrase "a wandering Aramean" appropriately describes Abraham's ancestral background.

Philistines in the Patriarchal Age at Gerar?

According to Genesis 20–21 and 26, Abimelech, the king of Gerar, dealt both with Abraham and later with his son Isaac. Gerar was in the western Negev, northwest of Beersheba. The stories in which both Abraham and Isaac dissimulate to protect themselves and their wives are quite reminiscent of Abraham's disreputable behavior in Egypt (Gen. 12:10-20). Many scholars therefore view the later stories as merely literary doublets, but there are some differences between them.[53] Through Yahweh's intervention, the patriarchs were saved from harm, swore a covenant with Abimelech, and dug the well of the "oath," namely Beersheba.[54]

Abimelech's name, which means "My father is king," is clearly Semitic, whereas the name of his general, Phicol, is not. Cyrus H. Gordon regarded this as evidence that the Philistines were "already Semitized by the time of the Hebrew Patriarchs," whom he was inclined to place in the Amarna Age (early fourteenth century B.C.E.).[55] Many scholars, including Van Seters, regard these references as gross anachronisms.[56] Others, such as Victor Matthews, believe that these accounts may reflect genuine historical conflicts which have been retrojected earlier: "it seems plausible that the story of Isaac's difficulties with the 'Philistines' is in fact a reflection of later historical events when the Israelites were being pressed southward by Philistine aggression."[57]

52. Fleming, "History," p. 261.

53. For an exacting analysis of these stories, see T. Desmond Alexander, *Abraham in the Negev: A Source-Critical Investigation of Genesis 20:1–22:19* (Carlisle: Paternoster, 1997).

54. For an illuminating study, see J. K. Hoffmeier, "'The Wives' Tales of Genesis 12, 20 & 26 and the Covenant at Beer-sheba," *TynBul* 43 (1992): 81-99.

55. C. H. Gordon, "The Role of the Philistines," *Antiquity* 30 (1956): 22.

56. Van Seters, *Abraham*, p. 52.

57. Victor H. Matthews, "The Wells of Gerar," *BA* 49 (1986): 124.

Excavations at Gerar and Beersheba

When writing on this subject in 1972, I had expressed the hope that excavations at Gerar might be able to cast some light on the problem of Philistines there. The great pioneer archaeologist, Sir Flinders Petrie, had identified the mound of Tell Jemmeh as Gerar.[58] Petrie was led by his conviction in the accuracy of the biblical account to believe that there must have been earlier Philistines who were traders and not invaders.[59]

In 1956 Yohanan Aharoni identified Gerar with the site of Tell Abu Hureira (Tel Haror).[60] Eliezer Oren, who excavated Tel Haror from 1982 to 1990, notes that Gerar was one of the largest MB settlement sites in southern Canaan, covering an area of about 40 acres. It was occupied in the MB II period (eighteenth-sixteenth centuries B.C.E.).[61] Near an altar with hundreds of offering vessels was "an elegant carinated chalice on a high foot with Minoan-type tall handles."[62]

Beersheba ("The Well of the Oath") has been identified with a huge mound, Tell es-Saba´, at the base of which was a well-preserved, stone-lined well. The excavations at the site from 1969 to 1976 by Y. Aharoni and Z. Herzog uncovered no evidence of occupation earlier than Iron Age I, the end of the twelfth century B.C.E.[63] These results led Aharoni to consider the patriarchal narratives as anachronisms.[64] Aharoni's conclusion is cited by T. L. Thompson as one of the chief arguments for rejecting the patriarchal narratives.[65] But as Alan R. Millard points out, Aharoni's conclusions may be challenged: "First, there is no evidence that the mound now called Tel Beersheva was ancient Beersheba. . . . Secondly, the assumption

58. Margaret Drower, *Flinders Petrie: A Life in Archaeology* (Madison: University of Wisconsin, 1995), pp. 364-69.

59. T. and M. Dothan, *People of the Sea* (New York: Macmillan, 1992), p. 64.

60. Y. Aharoni, "The Land of Gerar," *IEJ* 6 (1956): 26-32; cf. Y. Aharoni, *The Land of the Bible: A Historical Geography,* rev. ed. (Philadelphia: Westminster Press, 1979), p. 435.

61. E. D. Oren, "Gerar," in *ABD*, vol. 2, pp. 989-91.

62. Eliezer D. Oren, "Haror, Tel," in *The New Encyclopedia of Archaeological Excavations in the Holy Land,* ed. Ephraim Stern (New York: Simon & Schuser, 1993), vol. 2, p. 581.

63. See Y. Aharoni, "Beersheba, Tel," in *Encyclopedia of Archaeological Excavations in the Holy Land,* ed. Michael Avi-Yonah (London: Oxford University, 1975), vol. 1, pp. 160-68; Dale W. Manor, "Beer-Sheba," in *ABD*, vol. 1, pp. 641-45.

64. See Y. Aharoni, "Nothing Early and Nothing Late," *BA* 39 (1976): 55-76; Z. Herzog, "Beer-sheba of the Patriarchs," *BAR* 6 (November/December 1980): 12-28.

65. T. L. Thompson, *The Historicity of the Patriarchal Narratives* (Berlin: W. de Gruyter, 1974), pp. 2-43.

that the excavated well is Abraham's well is groundless. . . . Thirdly, the Genesis narratives do not imply that Beersheba was a town in Abraham's day."[66]

Philistines in the Age of the Judges and Early Monarchy

The Philistines, who occupied a pentapolis of five cities (Ashdod, Ashkelon, and Gaza on the coast, and Ekron and Gath inland), gave their name to the land of Palestine. They were bitter rivals with the Israelites over possession of the Shephelah, the foothills between the coast and the Judean hills. Conflicts between the Philistines and Samson, Saul, and David are among the most familiar stories from the Bible. The excavations of all of the pentapolis save for ancient Gaza, which rests under the modern city, have yielded an abundance of informative materials. Trude Dothan and R. L. Cohn provide this summary: "There are over 250 references in the Bible to the Philistines, most of them in the books of 1–2 Samuel and those parts of it utilized in 1 Chronicles, though there are scattered references to the Philistines in the Pentateuch and the Prophets. Their appearance in the biblical account of the rise of the monarchy in Israel thus accurately reflects their historical encounter with the Israelites during the eleventh and tenth centuries B.C.E."[67]

The earliest extra-biblical reference to the Philistines *(peleset)* occurs in a famous text of Rameses III at his mortuary temple of Medinet Habu,[68]

---

66. A. R. Millard, "Methods of Studying the Patriarchal Narratives as Ancient Texts," in Millard, *Essays,* p. 56. See also Mervyn D. Fowler, "The Excavation of Tell Beer-Sheba and the Biblical Record," *PEQ* 114 (1982): 7-11.

67. T. Dothan and R. L. Cohn, "The Philistine as Other: Biblical Rhetoric and Archaeological Reality," in *The Other in Jewish Thought and History* (New York: New York University Press, 1994), p. 61. A recent thorough summary of both the biblical and archaeological data on the Philistines is Peter Machinist, "Biblical Traditions: The Philistines and Israelite History," in *The Sea Peoples and Their World,* ed. E. D. Oren (Philadelphia: University Museum, 2000), pp. 53-82. See also L. E. Stager, "Biblical Philistines: A Hellenistic Literary Creation?" in *"I Will Speak the Riddles of Ancient Times": Archaeological and Historical Studies in Honor of Amihai Mazar on the Occasion of His Sixtieth Birthday,* ed. A. M. Maeir and P. de Miroschedji (Winona Lake: Eisenbrauns, 2006), pp. 375-84; S. M. Ortiz, "Rewriting Philistine History: Recent Trends in Philistine Archaeology and Biblical Studies," in *Critical Issues in Early Israelite History,* ed. R. S. Hess, G. A. Klingbeil, and P. J. Ray, Jr. (Winona Lake: Eisenbrauns, 2008), pp. 191-204.

68. See Richard H. Wilkinson, *The Complete Temples of Ancient Egypt* (London:

in which he describes an invasion of assorted "Sea Peoples"[69] whom he defeated in his eighth year (c. 1175 B.C.E.).[70] According to the Papyrus Harris, the pharaoh then settled some of the Sea Peoples as his subjects.

Caphtor and the Origin of the Philistines

According to Amos 9:7 the Lord declared: "Did I not bring Israel up from Egypt, the Philistines from Caphtor?" Caphtor, from whence also came the Caphtorim (cf. Gen. 10:14; Deut. 2:23; Jer. 47:4), is generally recognized to be the island of Crete in the southern Aegean, which was called Keftiu in Egyptian and Kaptara in Akkadian.[71] With Arthur Evans's discovery of the palace of Minos at Knossos in north central Crete, the splendid palatial Minoan civilization, which dominated the island during the Middle Bronze Age (2000-1450 B.C.), was brought to light. Among its distinctive features were frescoes depicting youths somersaulting over bulls. The Minoans used a script called Linear A, which Cyrus Gordon deciphered in 1962 as a northwest Semitic dialect — though his decipherment has not been accepted outside the circle of his students.[72] The Minoans influenced Myceanae, the Aegean islands, and such Anatolian sites as Miletus.

During the Late Bronze Age, from 1450 to 1200 B.C., Knossos was occupied by the Mycenaean Greeks from the mainland, as the decipherment of Linear B by Michael Ventris in 1952 demonstrated. The collapse of the Mycenaean world around 1200 B.C. triggered the mass movement of the Sea Peoples eastward.

The buildings, graves, gods, and especially the pottery of the Philis-

---

Thames & Hudson, 2000), pp. 193-99. Artistic representations of scenes from this temple may be found in Yigael Yadin, *The Art of Warfare in Biblical Lands in the Light of Archaeological Discovery* (London: Weidenfeld and Nicolson, 1963), pp. 332-41.

69. N. K. Sandars, *The Sea Peoples: Warriors of the Mediterranean* (London: Thames and Hudson, 1981).

70. John A. Wilson, trans., "The War against the Peoples of the Sea," in *ANET*, pp. 262-63.

71. Gary A. Rendsburg, "Gen 10:13-14: An Authentic Hebrew Tradition Concerning the Origin of the Philistines," *JNWSL* 13 (1987): 89-96. John Strange, *Caphtor: Keftiu: A New Investigation* (Leiden: Brill, 1980), has argued unpersuasively that Caphtor was Cyprus.

72. See C. H. Gordon, *Evidence for the Minoan Language* (Ventnor: Ventnor Publishers, 1966). For a list of his journal articles, see "Bible World and Near East Bibliography of Cyrus H. Gordon," in *The Bible World: Essays in Honor of Cyrus H. Gordon,* ed. Gary Rendsburg et al. (New York: KTAV Publishing House, 1980), p. 293.

tines — including their monochrome pottery, which was derived from Mycenaean IIIC pottery — all attest that the Aegean roots of the Philistines were Mycenaean,[73] and point to the fact that during the penultimate stage of their journey eastward some of them had settled initially on Cyprus.[74] It is quite striking that Goliath is described in 1 Samuel 17 wearing armor, including greaves (shin-guards), which were typical of Homeric heroes, and which have been corroborated as accurate traditions by the discovery of Mycenaean examples.[75]

Linguistic evidence may indicate an Anatolian element among the Philistine population. In 1985, when J. F. Brug wrote his monograph on the Philistines, there was as yet no decisive evidence of their language.[76] Scholars have speculated that the Philistine name Achish (1 Sam. 21:10) could be compared with Trojan Anchises, and that Phicol (Gen. 21:22) might be Anatolian.[77] Then in 2005 at Tell es-Safi, which has been identified as Gath, the hometown of Goliath, a tenth- or early ninth-century B.C.E. potsherd was uncovered with two non-Semitic names, *alwt* and *wlt*, inscribed in Proto-Canaanite letters. They seem to be similar in form to Goliath (1 Sam. 17:4), a name that has been compared to the Lydian Alyattes in form.[78]

---

73. Dothan and Cohn, "The Philistine as Other," pp. 61-73; Jane C. Waldbaum, "Philistine Tombs at Tell Fara and Their Aegean Prototypes," *AJA* 70 (1966): 331-40; Trude Dothan, "The Philistines Reconsidered," in *Biblical Archaeology Today* (Jerusalem: Israel Exploration Society, 1984), pp. 165-76; Amihai Mazar, "Some Aspects of the 'Sea Peoples' Settlement," in *Society and Economy in the Eastern Mediterranean,* ed. M. Heltzer and E. Lipinski (Leuven: Peeters, 1988), pp. 251-60.

74. F. M. Cross and L. E. Stager, "Cypro-Minoan Inscriptions Found at Ashkelon," *IEJ* 56 (2006): 129-59.

75. Edwin Yamauchi, *Greece and Babylon: Early Contacts between the Aegean and the Near East* (Grand Rapids: Baker Book House, 1967), p. 45.

76. J. F. Brug, *A Literary and Archaeological Study of the Philistines* (Oxford: British Archaeological Reports, 1985), p. 200.

77. I. Singer, "The Origin of the Sea Peoples and Their Settlement on the Coast of Canaan," in Heltzer, *Society and Economy,* p. 243; J. D. Ray, "Two Etymologies: Ziklag and Phicol," *VT* 36 (1986): 355-61.

78. News releases include: "Giving the Philistines Their Due: Inscription Found at Gath," *BAR* 31 (November/December 2005): 19; "Gath Inscription Evidences Philistine Assimilation," *BAR* 32 (March/April 2006): 16. Frank Moore Cross, however, is highly critical of Aren Maeir's reading: "Moreover to identify the putative ʿalwt with the name glyt (deemed a namesake of biblical Goliath) is linguistically bizarre." Cross and Stager, "Cypro-Minoan Inscriptions," p. 152. So we will need to reserve judgment on the evidence of this one sherd.

Minoan Proto-Philistines?

Scholars have responded to the allegations of anachronism in the case of Philistines at Gerar in the patriarchal age with two solutions, which are: (a) the explanation of a later updated adaptation of the name Philistine for an earlier population, often combined with (b) belief in the possibility that there might have been earlier "proto-Philistines"[79] related to the Minoans of Crete.[80]

Some tantalizing lines of evidence have been pursued in this regard.

The Phaistos Disk is a clay disk which was discovered in southern Crete at Phaistos, in a Middle Minoan IIIb context (1700-1600 B.C.E.). It is imprinted in spiral fashion on both sides with impressed signs, one of which is a man's head with what appears to be a "feathered" headdress quite similar to that worn by Philistines depicted by Egyptians.[81] Because of its unique character, the Phaistos Disk has defied all attempts to decipher it.

In an article published in 1995, Clyde E. Billington drew attention to what appears to be a striking correspondence between a Minoan temple (c. 1700 B.C.E.) discovered by Greek archaeologists in 1979 at a mountain site in central Crete called Anemospilia, near Arkhanes,[82] and a Philistine temple from Ekron (c. 1100 B.C.E.).[83] However, as Billington's two-dimensional

79. "Minoan Proto-Philistines" is a useful designation used by Edward E. Hindson, *The Philistines and the Old Testament* (Grand Rapids: Baker Book House, 1971), p. 47.

80. Brug, *Study of the Philistines,* p. 43; Neal Bierling, *Giving Goliath His Due* (Grand Rapids: Baker Book House, 1992), p. 24; Edward Hindson, *The Philistines and the Old Testament* (Grand Rapids: Baker, 1971), p. 47; David M. Howard, Jr., "Philistines," in Hoerth, *Peoples,* pp. 237-38; K. A. Kitchen, "Philistines," in Wiseman, *Peoples,* pp. 56-57; Kitchen, *On the Reliability,* p. 341: "Thus it is conceivable that Abimelek and his retainers (especially Phicol) may also once have been Kaphtorians or even Kerethites, before 'Philistines' later became a blanket term for non-Canaanite, Aegean people in that part of southwest Canaan." See also O. Margalith, *The Sea Peoples in the Bible* (Wiesbaden: Otto Harrassowitz, 1994), pp. 27-28, 42-43; Eugene H. Merrill, *Kingdom of Priests* (Grand Rapids: Baker Book House, 1996), pp. 41-42; T. C. Mitchell, "Philistines," in *IBD,* vol. 3, p. 1222; Gordon Wenham, *Genesis 16–50* (Dallas: Word Books, 1994), pp. 188-89.

81. R. W. Hutchinson, *Prehistoric Crete* (Baltimore: Penguin Books, 1962), pp. 66-70; Simon Davis, *The Decipherment of the Minoan Linear A and Pictographic Scripts* (Johannesburg: Witwatersrand University, 1967), ch. 7, "The Arkalochori Bronze Axe and the Phaistos Disk."

82. Y. Sakellarakis and E. Sapouna-Sakellarakis, "Drama of Death in a Minoan Temple," *National Geographic* 159 (February 1981): 204-22.

83. Clyde E. Billington, "Did Abraham Learn Human Sacrifice from the Philistines? A

plan of the Minoan temple is his reconstruction from the three-dimensional artist's representation in *National Geographic,* an exact comparison is not assured.

During the Middle Minoan period (MB), Crete exported beautiful Kamares Ware,[84] which has been found in Egypt[85] and the Levant. A rim fragment of a classical Kamares Ware cup was found at the earlier stratum of what later became Philistine Ashkelon.[86]

The most spectacular new evidence of a Minoan presence in the eastern Mediterranean has been the surprising and almost simultaneous discovery of Minoan frescoes in Egypt and in Palestine. Manfred Bietak, an Austrian who had been excavating since 1966 at the eastern Delta site of Tell el-Deb'a (ancient Avaris), found in 1987 at Ezbet Helmi the remains of Minoan frescoes, including bull-leaping scenes,[87] in an Eighteenth Dynasty palace (sixteenth century B.C.E.).

Also in 1987 the Israeli archaeologist Aharon Kempinski found Minoan frescoes in a Middle Bronze Age palace at Tel Kabri in western Galilee. These frescoes, together with those found earlier in palaces at Mari and at Alalakh in northern Syria, provide evidence that guilds of Minoan artisans were dispatched from Crete to the Eastern Mediterranean,[88] just as Cyrus H. Gordon had emphasized the location of the craftsman god, Kothar-and-Khasis in *Kptr* — that is, Crete — in the Ugaritic myth of Anat (14-26).[89]

Comparative Study of Two Temples, One Minoan and One Philistine," *Near East Archaeological Society Bulletin* 39-40 (1994-95): 22-30.

84. Reynold Higgins, *Minoan and Mycenaean Art* (New York: Frederick A. Praeger, 1967), p. 28.

85. See Yamauchi, *Greece and Babylon,* p. 29.

86. Lawrence E. Stager, J. David Schloen, and Daniel M. Master, *Ashkelon I: Introduction and Overview (1985-2006)* (Winona Lake: Eisenbrauns, 2008), p. 231. I owe this reference to Daniel Master. Cf. T. Dothan, S. Zuckerman, and Y. Goren, "Kamares Ware at Hazor," *IEJ* 50 (2000): 1-15.

87. Manfred Bietak, *Avaris: The Capital of the Hyksos* (London: British Museum, 1996), p. 71. See also Bryant G. Wood, "New Discoveries at Rameses," *Bible and Spade* 21 (January 2008): 31.

88. Barbara and Wolf-Dietrich Niemeier, in Aharon Kempinski, *Tel Kabri: The 1986-1993 Excavation Seasons* (Tel Aviv: Emery and Claire Yass Publications in Archaeology, 2002), pp. 270-85. I owe this reference to Daniel Master.

89. Cyrus H. Gordon, *Before the Bible: The Common Background of Greek and Hebrew Civilizations* (New York: Norton, 1965), pp. 194, 236.

Conclusions

Alan R. Millard maintained, "the Philistine group may have resided in the area long before their name is found in other written sources."[90] While it is true that the presence of the Medes, for example, is attested by archaeological evidence six centuries before they are first mentioned in the texts of the Assyrian king Shalmaneser III (ninth century B.C.E.),[91] it is unlikely that the appearance of the Medes, for example, in "The Table of Nations" (Gen. 10) can antedate this reference.

In 1973, in a review essay of Edward E. Hindson's book *The Philistines and the Old Testament,* I remarked: "Though I would be the first to agree that evidence for contacts between Palestine and the Aegean is constantly multiplying, I am still not as sanguine as the author in holding that these contacts justify our understanding the 'Philistines' in the patriarchal narratives as earlier representatives of the Aegean Philistines."[92] After thirty-five years of new archaeological evidence, I am afraid that the occasional Minoan import and even the presence of Minoan artisans does not add up to an immigration of Minoan "proto-Philistines" at Gerar.

In 1972 I had written: "On the basis of the present evidence I would suggest that the term 'Philistine' in the patriarchal narratives is a name which has been substituted for an earlier, no longer comprehensible term."[93] Commenting on the expression "land of the Philistines" found in Genesis 20:32 and 34, Peter Machinist writes: "The twofold mention, one might then suggest, was added to bring the story 'up-to-date' and situate it more clearly geographically for a later audience to whom the region was Philistine territory."[94] In regard to the use of the term "Philistines" in these narratives, Fleming comments: "Such details are not out-of-place anachronisms, but are part and parcel of the Israelite landscape that needs no apology for the early readers."[95] I would agree with his conclusion: "Gene-

90. Millard, "Abraham," p. 39.

91. Yamauchi, *Persia,* pp. 34-47.

92. Edwin Yamauchi, "Archaeological Evidence for the Philistines: A Review Article," *WTJ* 35 (1973): 321-22.

93. Yamauchi, *The Stones,* p. 46.

94. Machinist, "Philistines," p. 55. James K. Hoffmeier (*Israel in Egypt* [New York: Oxford University Press, 1997], p. 202) notes that there are similar issues of the "anachronistic" use of the term "Philistia" in the Song of Moses (Exod. 14:1-18), which can be explained in two ways: "1. It reflects the time of writing the poem from its earlier oral form. 2. It points to later editorial glossing or updating after the arrival of the Philistines."

95. Fleming, "History," p. 259.

sis shows that the Bible was capable of preserving the crucial story of Israel's ancestry, without recourse to eyewitness documentation. . . . God has surely provided what is necessary to understand what he accomplished when he called Abraham to an unknown promised land."[96]

96. Fleming, "History," p. 262.

Abraham's Experience of Yahweh: An Argument for the Historicity of the Patriarchal Narratives

JOHN N. OSWALT

What is the significance of Abraham in the Old Testament and, indeed, in the Bible as a whole? And what implications does that significance have for the question of the historicity of Abraham and the rest of the patriarchs? These questions and their answers will be the foci of this brief study.

We are perhaps too familiar with the figure of Abraham. Apart from his centrality in the book of Genesis, he occurs another 113 times in the Bible: 41 times in Exodus through Malachi, and 74 times in Matthew through Revelation. So we tend to say, "Oh, yes, the story began with Abraham," and move quickly on. But how does the story begin with Abraham? What place does he hold in the story (or the meta-narrative, to use current academic jargon)? Is he analogous to Confucius, or Buddha, or Muhammad? That is, is he the founder of a religion, the inspired genius who taught, or at least is thought to have taught, the fundamental principles of that particular understanding of reality? Surprisingly, the answer is no. Abraham did not found a religion in the way that those persons are thought to have done. So far as we know he never wrote anything, never proclaimed anything, never taught anything. To be sure, the Bible would clearly have us believe that he passed some things on to his descendants, but those things

---

It is both a privilege and a pleasure to offer this study in honor of Marvin Wilson. Dr. Wilson, in his capacity as chairman of the Department of Religion and Philosophy at Barrington College, offered me my first faculty position and was a faithful mentor to me as I began my work as a teacher. I have followed his career since those days with appreciation and admiration. His friends and students rise up to call him blessed.

were not in the way of teachings. They were the accounts of experiences that he had had with a god who obtruded himself into Abraham's (or Abram's) life and would not let go. *In other words, the entire significance of Abraham as "the founder of Israel's religion" lies in what it is claimed that he experienced in the context of time and space.*

Let me make that last point more explicitly. The veracity of what Confucius, or Buddha, or Muhammad taught about the nature of reality has nothing to do with whether those persons actually lived or not. That veracity rises or falls on other grounds entirely. If it could be shown conclusively that none of them ever lived, that would have no material effect on what is taught in their writings. To be sure, we may argue that it was because of various experiences in the lives of these great religious figures that they came to their insights. But be that as it may, the teachings are entirely independent of whatever those formative experiences may have been or may not have been.

But that is not so with Abraham. His experiences *are* the religious teachings of Genesis 12–24 and everything that follows that block of material and is dependent upon it. The same is true for Isaac and Jacob, the other two "fathers" regularly referred to in the Bible. The claim, whatever we do with it, is that certain unusual, if not to say unique, experiences with this god, who was later revealed to be the One Creator, Yahweh, led to understandings of reality that contradicted everything that was taught and believed elsewhere in the ancient Near East. This means that if in fact there were no such persons who had such experiences, there is absolutely no means of verifying what their lives are supposed to have taught them, and their descendants, and us. But even more to the point, there is then no satisfactory explanation for where those understandings actually came from, and still further, where the very idea of religious truth emerging from unique encounters with Yahweh in time and space came from.[1]

Before considering these points further, I want to review what the Bible teaches on the basis of Abraham's supposed experiences with the One who is Reality about reality. First of all, it teaches us that Yahweh is absolutely trustworthy. He came to Abram and Sarai and offered them things

---

1. It was reported to me by a friend who grew up in India that when the American missionary E. Stanley Jones, who was a close friend of Mahatma Gandhi, challenged Gandhi to accept the Christian faith, Gandhi replied that he could not believe the Bible was divine because it was mostly composed of stories. That is precisely correct. Whereas other holy books are composed of divine pronouncements, this one is largely the report of the encounter of humans with Yahweh. It stands alone.

that were neither spiritual nor transcendent. They were almost crushingly mundane: a baby, a homeland, a reputation (Gen. 12:1-3). There is nothing "religious" here at all. There is no offer of forgiveness of sin, or of special favor with the divine, no promise of a blissful afterlife. Nor is this promise made only once. As the narrative continues, those promises are repeated in one way or another seven more times.[2] What is happening? Yahweh is beginning at the beginning again. The serpent had based his appeal to Eve upon Yahweh's supposed untrustworthiness: he was "playing his own game" and did not really care about his creatures' well-being. The experience of Abraham tells us that that claim is a lie; God wants for us the things we long for, and he can be trusted to provide them in better ways than we can ever provide them for ourselves.

Not only does the experience of Abraham teach that God is trustworthy, wanting the best for us, it also teaches us that God is reliable; he is faithful. Genesis 15 makes that point. The only genuinely "right" thing we humans can ever do is to stake our lives on, to act on, the reliability of God, something Eve and Adam refused to do. They would not believe that what God said was reliable, true. But Abraham, having experienced God's trustworthiness to that point, was willing to believe that what God said, even if frankly incredible, could be depended upon. This, of course, was correctly appealed to by the Apostle Paul in Romans 4 and in Galatians 3. There can be no relationship with a transcendent God that is not based on a conviction of that God's trustworthiness (the goodness of his intentions for us) and his reliability (the consistency of his character). Ultimately then, it is not our performance that makes it possible to have a relationship with him, but his performance and our response to it.

That same experience recorded in Genesis 15 taught something further that sealed the previous two points: Yahweh, the Creator, will voluntarily bind himself to his responsive creatures in a unilateral covenant. It may be argued that there is a covenant implicit in Eden, and there is certainly an explicit covenant not to destroy the world with water in the Noah narrative, but it is only in the experience of Abraham that we find God binding himself in a personal way, making his trustworthiness and reliability a matter of legal adjudication. The torch and the firepot passing through the split halves of the sacrificial animals is expressive of Yahweh's putting himself under a curse, as the writer to the Hebrews understood (Heb. 6:13). This covenanting character of the Holy One tells us something

---

2. Gen. 12:7; 13:14-17; 15:1, 18-19; 17:1-8; 18:10; 22:15-18.

about his innermost being. Although he is a God of *mishpat*, of unchanging balance and order, Yahweh is also a God of self-giving, self-denying, undeserved love. Beyond simply responding in faith to God's trustworthiness and reliability, Abraham was not required to commit himself in any way to Yahweh. It is all from Yahweh's side. To be sure, Yahweh seeks a mutual commitment, as becomes clear in Genesis 17, but his loving favor is not dependent in any way upon a prior commitment from Abraham.

That Abraham understood these implications about the nature of God comes to us in an indirect way, in the account of the search for a wife for Isaac. Students of the Hebrew of the Old Testament know that the word *khesed* is so far unique to Hebrew.[3] Yet it occurs some 250 times in the Hebrew Bible with the majority of the occurrences being in reference to Yahweh. As is well known, the range of meanings which the term can have is very broad, ranging from "kindness" to "mercy" to "passionate devotion." The most recent studies have challenged the older position that the term was primarily a covenantal one.[4] Certainly it appears in covenantal contexts (see 1 Sam. 18:3-4 and 2 Sam. 9:1) but it is not limited to them (see Ruth 3:10). But the first place where the word occurs with any frequency in the Bible is in Genesis 24, where Eleazar, Abraham's servant, is calling on God for assistance in his search for a wife for Isaac. He asks God to show *khesed* to his master (vv. 12, 14) by leading him, Eleazar, to the right woman. When it seems that this has taken place, he blesses "Yahweh, the God of my master Abraham, who has not forsaken his steadfast love *(khesed)* and faithfulness *('emunah)* to my master" (v. 27). Then he calls on Laban and Bethuel to respond to this divine activity by doing the same things (v. 49).

It seems clear to me that the text is intending that we the readers should understand that Eleazar has come to look on his master's God in the same way that his master looks on God. Abraham has learned in some fifty years of dealing with this God who has broken into Abraham's life

---

3. Attempts to link the Hebrew root with terms having the same three consonants in other Semitic languages have been unconvincing. See H. J. Stoebe in E. Jenni, and C. Westermann, *Theological Lexicon of the Old Testament,* 3 vols., trans. M. Biddle (Peabody, MA: Hendrickson, 1997), vol. 2, p. 449.

4. See F. I. Andersen, "Yahweh, the Kind and Sensitive God," in *God Who Is Rich in Mercy*, ed. P. O'Brien and D. Peterson (Grand Rapids: Baker, 1986), pp. 41-88; G. R. Clark, *The Word 'Hesed' in the Hebrew Bible*, JSOTSup 157 (Sheffield: JSOT Press, 1993); K. D. Sakenfeld, *The Meaning of 'Hesed' in the Hebrew Bible: A New Inquiry,* HSM 17 (Missoula: Scholars Press, 1978).

that he is characterized by a love that is unconditional and a dependability that is without limits. And Abraham has communicated that understanding of God to his servant. Thus in a moment of need Eleazar does not engage in divination or in some other kind of magical manipulation of divine power. Instead, he simply casts himself upon what he now regards as the proven character of God. In some ways the theology of this passage is the more compelling because it is inferential. We the readers are invited to ask ourselves where this remarkable estimation of the character of the Divine has come from. The answer to the question is surely not that a great religious leader intuited these things and made it his life work to teach them, but rather that this understanding simply emerged from the crucible of intimate experience with Yahweh and became the modus operandi of the life not only of the patriarch, but also of all those associated with him.[5]

The trustworthiness, reliability, and self-giving love of Yahweh are seen in another experience of Abraham with Yahweh. This is the remarkable incident reported in Genesis 18. Yahweh is about to destroy Sodom and Gomorrah. As Creator of the universe he hardly needs ask anyone's permission to do this. Yet, Yahweh decides to take Abraham into his counsels on the matter. Genesis 18:17-19 reports the divine reasoning:

> Then Yahweh said, "Shall I hide from Abraham what I am about to do, since Abraham will become a great and mighty nation and all the nations of the earth will be blessed because of him? For I have chosen him so that he will command his children and his household after him to keep the way of Yahweh by doing righteousness and justice, so that Yahweh may bring to Abraham what he has promised him."

What is significant about this statement and the interchange that follows it is that it is not a didactic moment in which truths about God and reality are taught. To be sure, it *is* a teaching moment, but the teaching takes place in the context of experience. Yahweh has called Abraham so that through what he has learned about God all the nations can be blessed, which means that they will learn to walk in his way, living according to what he declares is right and according to the pattern of life that he has established (i.e., they will allow him to determine what is good [*tob*] and evil [*ra'*]). But what is the pattern (*mishpat*) by which Yahweh lives? Is it simply a matter

---

5. I cannot claim that these thoughts originated with me. I first learned them from Dr. Dennis F. Kinlaw. They appear in the forthcoming *Lectures in Old Testament Theology* under our joint authorship.

of "majority rules"? Is he a purveyor of "steel-trap justice" in which one misstep is immediately rewarded with destruction? What would Abraham think of Yahweh if he woke up some morning to find the cities of the plain a pile of cinders? What happened? Is it that finally 51 percent of the inhabitants of the cities have become wicked, with only 49 percent of them now remaining righteous, so that the 49 percent are made to pay for the sin of the 51 percent? Is Yahweh really characterized by that trustworthiness, reliability, and self-denying love that he thought was so? Or has Abraham been mistaken?

So Yahweh stood in front of Abraham,[6] inviting him to respond to the news of the imminent destruction, almost forcing Abraham to ask God to justify himself. So Abraham, with his heart in his hands (v. 27), dares to pray for the righteous in those places, challenging Yahweh with proportions that are almost ridiculous. Would Yahweh look the other way concerning the sins of thousands so as not to treat a handful of righteous persons wrongly? While Abraham may have been thinking of his nephew Lot and his family, the text does not say so but suggests that the issue is a broader one. The upshot is that we learn that for this God it is not "majority rules." In fact, for him almost the slightest provocation will be grounds for the showing of *chesed*. For the sake of only ten righteous this God would show mercy to thousands of the wicked.

I said above that while God offered a unilateral covenant to Abraham if he would only accept it, God was not going to be content with that over the long run. God wanted Abraham in a committed relationship with him, as he wants all of us, according to the Bible. The reason for this is that we were made for dependence on God and can only find our truest selves in that dependent relationship. Just as a tree that has been uprooted from the ground cannot survive, neither can we survive unless we are rooted in our Creator.[7] But Yahweh did not ask for that level of commitment from the outset. Abram did have to trust God to the extent of leaving the familiar and the known to obtain the promises, but Yahweh did not ask for any re-

---

6. This seems to be what the original text said. It is one of a handful of *tiqqune hassopherim*, places where the scribes admit that they changed the text because they could not believe that what was before them was correct. The altered text says that Abraham still stood before the Lord, and one can see why that change would have been made: surely the Lord never stands before anyone as a supplicant.

7. Jesus uses a slightly different metaphor in John 15. He is the vine and we are the branches. We are alive and we produce fruit (which the vine does not produce by itself), but we only do so by reason of being inextricably attached to the vine.

ciprocal commitment from Abraham. When one is establishing one's bona fides one does not make a lot of demands, even if one is God! It is only after the debacle with Ishmael, in which Abraham trusted his own understanding and ability to fulfill the promise of God (Gen. 16), that God asks for one sign of returned commitment from Abraham to Yahweh. It is the mark of circumcision. Commentators point out that this was by no means a unique practice in the ancient world, and tend to look for cultural explanations for the practice. I wonder what it is that prejudices us against the biblical explanation, which is very clear in the context. In the ancient world the erect penis was a symbol of reproductive power. Here was the surging, thrusting power of life, which the strong person could harness for his own purposes. That is exactly what Abraham had tried to do by means of Hagar. It may have been too late for Sarah, but not for him! He had the strength to supply what he needed and in so doing fulfill the purposes of God. Surely it is no accident that after the birth of Ishmael, the very next incident reported in Genesis is Yahweh's appearance to Abraham in which with incredible *chesed* he reaffirms his earlier promises. But he prefaces it with an important statement: "Walk before me and be *tammim*." Like the sacrificial lambs to which the term *tammim* is most commonly applied, be complete, be whole, be all that you were meant to be as a human being in the image of God. Here is where Yahweh had been headed all along. We can only become what we were meant to be in a walk with God.[8] But such a walk is only possible when we have renounced our ownership of the power of our lives and handed it over to God. That is what the sign of circumcision was intended to symbolize: a surrender of our right to use our earthly power for the achievement of our own goals. But it was only a symbol, as the Old Testament knows perfectly well, and, like all Old Testament symbols physical circumcision is quite meaningless unless the corresponding reality exists in the life. What is needed is a circumcision of the human heart, the core of the personality (see Deut. 10:16 and Jer. 9:25-26).

We could go further still in analyzing the theological content that emerges from the experiences of Abraham with Yahweh. But these are enough to illustrate the basic point. The Bible makes some remarkable affirmations about the Creator of the Universe, the only Holy One. It says that he is good, he is true, he is right, he is just (in the broadest possible

---

8. See Eph. 5:1-2: "Therefore, be imitators of God and walk in love as Christ also has loved us and given himself for us, an offering and a sacrifice to God for a sweet-smelling aroma." Is it accidental that the opposite of what those verses express is "fornication" (v. 3)?

sense of that term), he is pure (in the sense of being one thing), and he is unfailing love. And all these are the characteristics of a transcendent Person. Furthermore, this God invites his people into a covenant relationship in which they abandon their efforts to conceptualize this world in such a way as to make it subject to their control. Rather, they live in trusting reliance upon God, showing that reliance by living lives which mirror his own. Now where does this understanding, which cannot be found in most of its details, and certainly not in its totality, anywhere outside the Bible come from? How did it emerge in Israel and when did it emerge? Who was the first to intuit these things, and how did he (or she) manage to convince his (or her) thoroughly pagan family members of these features of deity which would have been utterly foreign to those family members, not only in detail, but especially as a whole?

The Bible says to us that no one "intuited" these concepts, and that no one had to move a pagan Israel from one belief system to another (some time after the exile). The Bible insists that these concepts go right back to the very origins of the nation in the *experience* of the "fathers" of the nation: Abraham, his son, and his grandson. They did not "emerge" over long years of development. Rather, they were the logical inferences of unique experiences of humans with God in time and space. To be sure, this understanding was radical enough, and required a radical enough renunciation of one's own control of one's life, that Abraham's descendants were always succumbing to the lure of paganism with its comfortable "this-worldly" gods who could be conceived of in such a way as to make them subject to human control. But that movement was always a deviation from what had been known about Yahweh from the beginning, so that the grounds were always there for the voice of the prophets calling upon them to "turn around" (i.e., repent).[9]

So the foregoing presents us with two issues. First, the Old Testament argues that its fundamental theology goes directly back to "the fathers," springing full-blown as it were from them. Second, it argues that the theology was not the result of intuition, or speculation, or religious genius. Rather, it was the result of their experiences with Yahweh. It was inferential, not speculative. Clearly, this presents us with problems, and again,

---

9. So Jeremiah does not suggest that he is wanting to introduce his people to a better conceptuality of deity than they have known before. Instead, he ejaculates in horror about this unheard-of thing: that a people should abandon the God they have always known for some god they have not known previously. Even pagans don't do that, he says. See, e.g., Jer. 44:3.

they are twofold. First, things like these do not happen today (God does not make very specific verbal promises to people; he does not come walking down the road with two friends to have supper; he does not ask us whether we agree with his next steps in ordering his world; he does not make 99-year-old women get pregnant; etc., etc.). That being so, given the principle of uniformitarianism to which science has let itself fall captive, *these things could not have happened.* That leads to the second problem. Where and when did the Hebrew people come up with the idea that they did? But more than that, where did the Hebrew people get the idea that God reveals himself in unique human historical experiences? And still further, if the Israelites did not derive their understanding of Yahweh from these experiences, where did they get them? And further still, why did they claim to derive it from these experiences?[10]

Let me press these issues further. The Israelite concept of God is unique, there is nothing like it anywhere else. No place else is God thought to be a transcendent Person, utterly different from his creation. The Greek philosophers stretched for the idea but could never quite get to it, and eventually they fell back into the grossest paganism. Ultimately, this concept of transcendence is the "bottom line": is this world self-explanatory, containing within itself everything that is, or does it take something that is *not* this world to explain this world? The Bible alone (and thought derived from it, such as Islam) says God is not this world. Where did that idea come from? But beyond that, whence came the idea that God is utterly self-consistent, utterly dependable, utterly reliable, and wholly love? The Bible offers us an explanation. It tells us that while God is consistent, he is by no means locked into the small-mindedness of uniformitarianism. It tells us that the Creator of the Universe, who sits above the circle of the earth, can do brand-new things (see Isaiah 43:15-19). It tells us that God incarnated himself into human life, not first with Jesus Christ, but rather climactically with him. The Bible insists that no one discovered or created this religion, because that would assume that God is somehow inherent in the recurring cycles of nature and is somehow discoverable in them. The Bible insists that the God who is not this world broke into it and revealed himself to us in unique, non-recurring

10. John Van Seters's *Abraham in History and Tradition* (New Haven: Yale University Press, 1975) has seemed to many to forever lay to rest the historicity of Abraham and the rest of the patriarchs. He showed convincingly that previous attempts to use archeology and form criticism to argue for that historicity were deeply flawed. However, he did not address the arguments from the content of the texts themselves.

interactions with unique human beings. Our question is whether we will admit that possibility or not.

If we will not accept the possibility, then we are at a loss to explain both the Bible's world view and its theology.[11] If Abraham did not have the experiences recorded of him — indeed, if there was no Abraham — we are at a loss to explain the source of the incredible theology. We ask the Bible where it got its remarkable understandings. But when it answers us, we say that such things are impossible, that the text must be concealing the truth about its origins. The Bible must have arrived at its understanding of reality in the same manner as everyone else: speculation on the basis of the cosmos as we perceive it. And if the Bible alone seems to come out at a diametrically opposite place as all the rest, that is only an appearance — it is not really distinct. Is this not to skew the evidence to agree with our preconceived notions?

In the end, I believe the most serious argument for the historicity of Abraham is the fact that the Bible claims to have derived its fundamental understandings of reality from the human-historical experiences of this man and his immediate descendants. They were the "fathers" upon whom the entire superstructure of biblical faith is made to stand. If they were not historical, then who of the biblical characters were? The Bible will not admit of a piecemeal approach. Just as Mary did in her Magnificat (Luke 1:54-55), the biblical narrative keeps taking us right back to "the fathers" if we wish to understand the significance of its teachings. In the end, the entire superstructure falls to the ground. It will not do to say that the patriarchs are characters in a fictional narrative created to be the vehicle for the purveying of religious speculations. Where else was anything like this done? These are not epics like Gilgamesh or Homer. In both structure and content the patriarchal narratives are radically different from the epics of the ancient world.

I recognize that what I have been arguing is a species of the "either-or" argument, which can lead to fallacious conclusions by ignoring good alternatives to the supposed polar opposites. But what are the alternatives? If the biblical teachings are unique, and they are, and if those teachings are said to have originated in the human historical experiences of certain per-

---

11. What has happened increasingly since 1960 is that, since we will not accept the plausibility of the Bible's explanation of its unique theology and worldview, we have then been forced to deny that those understandings *are* unique. See, e.g., the several recent works of Mark Smith, the most recent of which is *The Memoirs of God: History, Memory, and the Experience of the Divine in Ancient Israel* (Minneapolis: Fortress, 2004).

sons, we are forced to conclude that those persons did indeed exist and experienced those things. If we argue that those persons did not exist and did not experience those things, then we cannot explain where those biblical concepts came from. That the Israelites were no different from their Ammonite or Edomite neighbors in their religious understandings, but that a small cadre of fanatics created out of whole cloth a new theology, as well as a fictional national history to embody it, and were able to foist the entire creation on the rest of the nation after the exile — this is not a workable alternative.[12]

12. See W. G. Dever, *Did God Have a Wife? Archaeology and Folk Religion in Ancient Israel* (Grand Rapids: Eerdmans, 2005), pp. 276, 299, etc.

A Song of Our Father Abraham: Psalm 105

TED HILDEBRANDT

An "Abrahamic" Psalm in a Davidic Psalter

Psalm 105 is unique as the only psalm that refers specifically to the patriarch Abraham himself and does so not just once but three times (Ps. 105:6, 9, 42). The only other psalm to even mention Abraham is Psalm 47:9, where it refers to the "God of Abraham." This emphasis on Abraham in Psalm 105 stands in stark contrast to the absence of any reference to David, who is the major figure in most of the book of Psalms.

Much of the Psalter is reflective of the story of David. His name is found in the titles of 73 psalms, especially in the early chapters of the book (see the titles of Pss. 3–41 and 51–70).[1] "Historical" titles further link some psalms to particular events in David's life, such as "when he fled from Absalom" (Ps. 3; cf. Pss. 18, 51–52 et al.).[2] Book II of the Psalter concludes,

---

1. B. S. Childs, "Psalm Titles and Midrashic Exegesis," *Journal of Semitic Studies* 16 (1971): 137-50; Bruce K. Waltke, "Superscripts, Postscripts, or Both," *JBL* 110 (1991): 583-96; and Gerald H. Wilson, *Psalms: From Biblical Text to Contemporary Life,* vol. 1, The NIV Application Commentary (Grand Rapids: Zondervan, 2002), p. 20.

2. Gerald H. Wilson, *The Editing of the Hebrew Psalter* (Chico, CA: Scholars Press, 1985), pp. 170-71.

It has been a great privilege for this writer to have spent the last decade at Gordon College with Dr. Marv Wilson and his resilient wife, Polly. What a legacy this father "Abraham" has left in my life, as well as the lives of his colleagues, Jewish friends, and many generations of students!

"Here end the prayers of David son of Jesse" (Ps. 72:20) — even though Davidic Psalms continue well past this "ending" colophon (see Pss. 108–110, 138–145). It is not surprising that the addition of Psalm 151, in both the Greek Septuagint (LXX) and the Hebrew Dead Sea Scroll 11QPs[a], is an autobiographical psalm of David and his battle with Goliath.[3] Moreover, the "Davidizing" of the Psalter is manifest in the Greek Septuagint, which has repeatedly added Davidic headings not found in the Hebrew Masoretic text (see Pss. 33, 93, 95–99, 104).[4] This is particularly noticeable in Psalm 33 (LXX 32), which is an orphan psalm, bearing no title in the Masoretic text, yet is found in the midst of a solid Davidic collection (Pss. 3–41). The Septuagint added a Davidic title to this psalm ("A Psalm of David"), although it may reflect an early Hebrew *Vorlage* similar to that found in the Dead Sea Scroll 4QPs[q], which also contains the Davidic title.[5] This nexus between David and the Psalms is also recognized in the *Midrash Tehillim* on Psalm 1:1, which comments that "Moses gave Israel the Five Books, and David gave Israel the five books of Psalms."[6] The New Testament continues the process of expanding attribution of psalms to David when Acts 4:25-26 quotes the words "Why do the nations rage . . . against his Anointed One (Messiah)" from Psalm 2:1-2, which is an untitled psalm in both the Hebrew and Greek texts yet is identified in Acts as from "the mouth of your servant, our father David" (cf. Heb. 4:7; citing Ps. 95).[7]

Why, then, is God's "servant," our father Abraham, highlighted in the concluding historical psalm pair of Book IV (Pss. 105–106), while David is never mentioned? Is it not odd that neither David nor Zion is cited at all when Psalm 105:1-15 is a verbatim parallel to a hymn given during David's installation of the ark in Jerusalem as recorded in 1 Chronicles 16:8-22? Why does the psalmist return to Abraham and avoid any reference to the Davidic king, covenant, and city that were so renowned internationally that even the Babylonian captors requested that the exiled Jews sing "one of the songs of Zion" (Ps. 137:3)?

---

3. Klaus Seybold, *Introducing the Psalms* (New York: T&T Clark, 1990), pp. 13, 16.

4. Derek Kidner, *Psalms 1–72* (Leicester: The Tyndale Press, 1973), p. 34; and Gerald H. Wilson, "The Structure of the Psalter," in *Interpreting the Psalms: Issues and Approaches*, ed. David Firth and Philip S. Johnson (Downers Grove: InterVarsity Press, 2005) p. 241.

5. Peter Craigie, *Psalms 1–50*, Word Biblical Commentary 19 (Waco: Word Books, 1983), p. 270; Wilson, *Editing*, pp. 174-75.

6. Seybold, *Introducing the Psalms*, p. 16; William G. Braude, *The Midrash on Psalms* (New Haven: Yale University Press, 1954), line 5; Wilson, *Psalms*, p. 77.

7. Wilson, *Psalms*, p. 20.

Current scholarship has identified the editorial framework that structures the book of Psalms into five books or collections, each marked off by a concluding doxology (Bk. I: 1–41; Bk. II: 42–72; Bk. III: 73–89; Bk. IV: 90–106; Bk. V: 107–150; cf. Midrash citation above).[8] The presence of duplicate psalms confirms that these "Books" once were separate collections and later concatenated (see Ps. 14 [Bk. I] = Ps. 53 [Bk. II]).[9] Surely within the "Books" there are mini-collections from other authors, such as the choir directors Asaph (Pss. 74–82) and Korah (Pss. 44–48). There is even one psalm attributed to Solomon (Ps. 72) and one to Moses (Ps. 90). While Books I and II are dominated by Davidic headings, Book III features Davidic contemporaries in the songs of Asaph (Pss. 73–83), Korah (Pss. 84-85, 87-88), and Ethan (Ps. 89). It is Ethan's Psalm 89 that concludes Book III with the penetrating, accusatory question: "Where is your former great love, which in your faithfulness you swore to David?" (Ps. 89:49).

Book IV opens, not with a Davidic response to Ethan's question, but with the only psalm attributed to Moses (Ps. 90). Furthermore, Book IV concludes with a psalm-pair featuring Abraham (Ps. 105) and Moses (Ps. 106). Book V returns eschatologically to a Davidic king (Ps. 110), with a Zion-centric doxology concluding the whole Psalter (Pss. 145–150). This raises the question: Why does Psalm 105 uniquely focus on God's promises to his anointed (Messiah's) servants (note the plural), Abraham and the patriarchs, with no mention of God's servant David, the Davidic covenant, the coming "anointed" Son of David, or his kingly rule from Zion?

New Methodologies and New Questions

This study examines Psalm 105:1-15 from both canonical and intertextual perspectives. While drawing on insights gained from a more traditional approach that explores the unique sounds, words, images, themes, lines, and structures, with a particular eye to semantic/syntactic parallelism as well as rhetorical and literary features, this study explores their significance within a new intertextual and canonical framework.[10] It does not

---

8. Tremper Longman, *How to Read the Psalms* (Downers Grove: InterVarsity Press, 1988), p. 43; and Wilson, "Structure," pp. 229-34.

9. Craigie, *Psalms 1–50*, p. 28.

10. Some core books that describe Hebrew poetry are: Robert Alter, *The Art of Biblical Poetry* (New York: HarperCollins, 1985); Adele Berlin, *The Dynamics of Biblical Parallelism* (Bloomington: Indiana University Press, 1985); James Kugel, *The Idea of Biblical Poetry: Par-*

pursue the profitable genre analysis promulgated by Gunkel, Mowinckel, Westermann, and others, which focuses on each genre as arising from a conjectured historical or cultural *sitz im leben* whether in the cult (sacrifices/feasts/Temple/priests), the king's royal court, or the editorial sage's wisdom circle (see Ps. 1).[11] Yet an intertextual comparison has been made of Psalm 105, as a historical psalm presented in hymnic style,[12] with other historical psalms such as Psalms 78, 106, and 135, and has revealed lexical and thematic overlaps between them as a genre. This intertextual comparison is largely limited to the second section (Ps. 105:16-45) and will be treated elsewhere.[13]

Recent scholarship has moved to the consideration of the meaning of a particular psalm to its context within the canonical setting shaped by later editors who assembled the psalms into collections and finally into a completed book. Though each individual psalm was written/recited by an author in light of an original audience and setting and was formatted in the style of a particular literary genre, yet these separate individual psalms were later placed together into a canonical text by editors who, in the construction of the book, have shaped each psalm and seated each psalmic jewel into its present canonical literary setting. Thus it behooves the modern reader to read the psalm in light of its canonical context within the book of Psalms in order to recapture that editorial layer of meaning. The works of G. Wilson, Howard, McCann, Zenger, and others have highlighted editorial principles of collection, connection, and meaning within the canonical book of Psalms.[14] They have gained new insights into the

---

allelism and Its History (New Haven: Yale University Press, 1981); M. O. O'Connor, *Hebrew Verse Structure* (Winona Lake: Eisenbrauns, 1981); and W. G. E. Watson, *Classical Hebrew Poetry,* JSOT Sup. 26 (Sheffield: JSOT Press, 1986).

11. Anthony R. Ceresko, "The Sage in the Psalms," in *The Sage in Israel and the Ancient Near East,* ed. John Gammie and Leo Perdue (Winona Lake: Eisenbrauns, 1990), pp. 217-30.

12. Hans-Joachim Kraus, *Psalms 1–59: A Commentary* (Minneapolis: Augsburg, 1988), p. 308.

13. See my website: http://faculty.gordon.edu/hu/bi/ted_hildebrandt/index.cfm.

14. Many of these writers and others present their cases in J. Clinton McCann, ed., *The Shape and Shaping of the Psalter,* JSOT Sup. 159 (Sheffield: Sheffield Academic Press, 1993). Robert L. Cole, *The Shape and Message of Book III: Psalms 73–89,* JSOT Sup. 307 (Sheffield: Sheffield Academic Press, 2000), applied these insights to Book III. Zenger and Davis worked on Book V: E. Zenger, "The Composition and Theology of the Fifth Book of Psalms, Psalms 107-145," *JSOT* 80 (1998): 171-81; Barry C. Davis, "A Contextual Analysis of Psalms 107–118," Ph.D. dissertation (Deerfield: Trinity Evangelical Divinity School, 1996). Creach, Zenger, Howard, and Goulder have examined Book IV: Jerome Creach, "The Shape of Book

message of Psalms as a book because of an analysis that takes seriously each psalm's relationship to its neighbors, and its function within the clearly marked five "books" (Bks. I-V) that comprise the book of Psalms as a whole. A canonical reading shows Psalm 105's relationship to neighboring psalms as well as its function in Book IV. Beyond a psalmic canonical reading, an intertextual method is utilized to help in the exploration of Psalm 105:1-15 and its shared expression with 1 Chronicles 16, both of which may have drawn on a common oral/written original that pre-dated both texts.[15]

New methodologies provoke the reader to ask and answer new questions. What is the relation of Psalm 105 to its neighbors (Ps. 104 and Ps. 106)? How does Book IV answer the demise of the Davidic covenant raised at the end of Book III in Psalm 89, after facing the destruction of the Temple, the defeat of the Davidic king, and the humiliation of Mount Zion when its inhabitants were helplessly exiled to Babylon? How is the meaning of Psalm 105:1-15 — which is a nearly verbatim parallel of 1 Chronicles 16:8-22 — shifted when taken from that historical context and placed into the book of Psalms at the close of Book IV? What do the slight variations between 1 Chronicles 16 and Psalm 105 reveal about the direction the artistic bricoleur was going when he authored Psalm 105? How is the story told in historical narrative altered when the same events are recited in poetic form (cf. Exod. 14/15 [The Song of the Sea], Judg. 4/5 [The Song of Deborah]; 1 Sam. 31/2 Sam 1 [David's eulogy for Saul])? How does the change of medium, from narrative to poetry, change the message? Why is Abraham brought in at this point in the Psalter and how does he help respond to the lack of divine deliverance experienced as the Babylonians triumphed over Zion? If the sages who edited the Psalter paired psalms (9/10; 42/43; 105/106; 111/112), is it possible that they paired proverbs as well (cf.

Four of the Psalter and the Shape of Second Isaiah," *JSOT* 80 (1998): 63-76; M. D. Goulder, "The Fourth Book of the Psalter," *Journal of Theological Studies* 26 (1975): 269-89; E. Zenger, "Israel und Kirche im gemeinsamen Gottesbund: Beobachtungen zum theologischen Programm des 4. Psalmenbuchs (Ps 90–106)," in *Israel und Kirche heute: Beiträge zum christlich-jüdischen Dialog — Für Ernst Ludwig Ehrlich,* ed. M. Marcus, E. W. Stegemann, and E. Zenger (Freiburg: Herder, 1991), pp. 236-54; David M. Howard, *The Structure of Psalms 93–100,* Biblical and Judaic Studies vol. 5 (Winona Lake: Eisenbrauns, 1997). G. Wilson's *Editing,* his Yale dissertation, was one of the early works that began this productive thread of research in 1985.

15. Koptak, to the contrary, has 1 Chronicles 16 being based on Ps. 105. Koptak, "Intertextuality," in *Dictionary of the Old Testament: Wisdom, Poetry and Writings,* ed. T. Longman and P. Enns (Downers Grove: InterVarsity Press, 2008), pp. 325-26.

Prov. 26:4, 5)?[16] Though a complete exegesis of Psalm 105 is beyond the scope of this paper, these questions will provide direction for the exploration of this psalm of Abraham and its role as the close to Book IV.

Intertextuality: Reading Psalm 90 as an Opener for Book IV

This present study explores two layers of meaning. It focuses on the types of understandings derived from an intertextual and canonically sensitive reading. These methodologies were used to examine the psalm line-by-line and word-by-word. A baseline usage of every word in Psalm 105 was set in comparison to its frequency of use in the whole book of Psalms. Each word was specifically examined to see whether it was found in neighboring psalms in order to discover whether proximity or juxtaposition were factors used by the editors in fitting adjacent canonical psalms together. The individual psalm was then analyzed in terms of its function in the larger collectional structure of Books I-V. Psalm 105's relationship with its parallel in 1 Chronicles 16 was also carefully scrutinized.

Tanner suggests the notion of bricolage — a collage of elements in an artistic creation — as a model for understanding the multifaceted mosaic of texts interacting with one another. Part of a text's meaning is produced via quotations, allusions, and text-to-text interaction.[17] She cites five categories of text-to-text interaction: (1) intertextuality — the relationship of a text to imbedded texts, whether quoted or alluded to (bricolage); (2) paratextuality — the relation of the text to titles in a work (i.e., psalm titles); (3) metatextuality — the relationship of commentary to the text being elaborated (as in this current study); (4) architextuality — the relationship of a text to texts of a similar literary type or genre (historical psalms, laments, hymns, etc.); and (5) semiotextuality — the relation of a text to how the current reader actually comes to decipher its meaning.[18] While Tanner calls this final type "hypertextuality," it is better to reserve that term for the digital, non-linear interaction of linked texts displayed on a screen as opposed to static text on a printed page.[19]

---

16. Ted Hildebrandt, "Proverbial Pairs: Compositional Units in Proverbs 10–29," *JBL* 107 (1988): 207-24.

17. Beth L. Tanner, *The Book of Psalms Through the Lens of Intertextuality* (New York: Peter Lang, 2001), pp. 6, 16.

18. Tanner, *Psalms Intertextuality,* p. 27.

19. Janet H. Murray, *Hamlet on the Holodeck: The Future of Narrative in Cyberspace*

Tanner's intertextual treatment of Psalm 90, the opening psalm in Book IV, of which Psalms 105 and 106 are a closing pair, illustrates the multiple meanings a poem may have as its echoes are heard in different historical contexts. She cites the following well-known poem by Walt Whitman:

> O Captain! My Captain! Our fearful trip is done;
> The ship has weather'd every rack, the prize we sought is won,
> The port is near, the bells I hear, the people all exulting,
> while follow eyes with steady keel, the vessel grim and daring;
> But O Heart! Heart! Heart!
> O the bleeding drops of red, where on the deck
> My Captain lies fallen cold and dead.[20]

These vivid images describe the death of a sea captain who has weathered the turbulent seas yet lies slain on the bloodied deck of the boat that he had just guided safely into port. The poetic text of the death of a beloved captain takes on a new layer of meaning upon discovering that it was written in the historical context of the assassination of President Lincoln in 1865 at Ford's Theatre in Washington, D.C., just after the conclusion of the Civil War. Further nuance was added for this writer when he realized that Whitman had served under Lincoln as a nurse in that same bloody conflict. Like many poems that capture a moment in history, its image came to life once again when the boat deck was bloodied in the 1963 assassination of John F. Kennedy. Similarly, the biblical poems echo down through history. Thus Psalm 90 can be understood as a plum, square, and level description of the ephemerality of human life, which quickly passes and returns to dust. But it takes on "new" meaning when it is read intertextually with the Song of Moses, in Deuteronomy 32, as Moses considers his own imminent death. The meaning shifts once again when Psalm 90 is read in the context of the Babylonian exile.

Going one step further, a totally different perspective is gained by reading this same Psalm of Moses (Ps. 90) canonically as the opening to Book IV and as a response to Psalm 89, which closes Book III. McCann and G. Wilson observe that Psalm 89 reflects the failure of the Davidic monar-

---

(Cambridge, MA: MIT Press, 1999); George P. Landow, *Hypertext 2.0: The Convergence of Contemporary Critical Theory and Technology* (Baltimore: Johns Hopkins University Press, 1997); and Andrew Glassner, *Interactive: Techniques for Twenty-first Century Fiction* (Natick, MA: A. K. Peters, 2004).

20. Tanner, *Psalms Intertextuality,* p. 85.

chy during the devastating time of the exile to Babylon in 587 B.C.E.[21] Psalm 90 fits well as an answer to the demise of the Davidic covenant in part by shifting the focus from Yahweh's refusal to help, to Israel's rebellion. Their unfaithfulness, not God's, was the source of the real problem (Ps. 90:13).[22] Thus Psalm 90 wrestles with the disorientation of exile by looking to Moses. It reconceptualizes the Babylonian exile in terms of a Mosaic framework — seeing the exile as a new "wilderness experience" where the chosen community becomes land-less, Temple-less, ark-less, and monarchy-less.[23] In Psalm 90 those who have experienced the collapse of the Davidic covenant in the Babylonian exile turn back to Moses as their lives fade, and in hope they embrace the Abrahamic covenant (Pss. 105/106) with its promise of land and the multiplication of the chosen seed in spite of the humble beginnings of the patriarchs as land-less, Temple-less sojourners.

Word	Frequency in Psalms	Books I-II	Book III	Book IV (only 17 chs.)	Book V
Moses משה	8x	—	77:21	90:1; 99:6; 103:7; 105:26; 106:16, 23, 32	—

Surely pure randomness does not account for the number of times that Moses is found in these psalms. Of the eight times he is mentioned in the Psalter, seven are in Book IV, which opens with Psalm 90, uniquely titled "A prayer of Moses the man of God," and closes with the pair of Psalms 105/106 that contain four references to Moses (Pss. 105:26; 106:16, 23, 32). He is never referred to in Book V, which returns to an eschatological perspective of King David (Ps. 110), a focus on the triumph of Zion (Pss. 125–126, 128–129, 146–147, 149), and the Psalms of Ascent (Pss. 120–134), which provide songs to be sung by festive pilgrims as they ascend the steep slopes of Mount Zion.

History and Poetry: A Reflection on Psalm 105

The intertextual approach has opened a question of the relation of historical narrative to poetry. In what way does the poet refashion the data of the

---

21. J. Clinton McCann, *The Book of Psalms*, The New Interpreter's Bible, vol. IV (Nashville: Abingdon Press, 1996) p. 1034.

22. Wilson, *Editing*, p. 215.

23. Tanner, *Psalms Intertextuality*, p. 98.

historical narrative when he crafts them into poetic expression? The following is not meant as an exhaustive detailing of how poetry and narrative interact but as an initial reflection of how a bricoleur poet reshaped historical events to create Psalm 105. The image is of the poet as a master craftsman (bricoleur) shaping and fitting fragments of colored glass into a beautiful stained glass window.

The first technique used by the poet is *selection*. Out of all the events of the first Passover and the mighty acts of God as the Israelites left Egypt, the bricoleur of Psalm 105 selects for mention the Egyptian gifts of silver and gold (Ps. 105:37; cf. Exod. 11:2).

The second technique observed is *compression* (cf. Ps. 105:14). The psalmist compresses three stories from Genesis into a single pair of poetic bicola by describing Sarah's/Rebekah's coming under possible harm from foreign kings as a result of Abraham's/Isaac's claiming that his wife was his sister (cf. Gen. 12, 20, and 26).

> He allowed no one to oppress them;
>> for their sake he rebuked kings.
> Do not touch my anointed ones;
>> do my prophets no harm. (Ps. 105:14)

A third poetic technique is *reordering* historical events to fit the poet's point. In Psalm 105 the poet cites the Egyptian plague of darkness first when actually it was ninth of the ten plagues listed in Exodus (cf. Ps. 105:28; Exod. 10). Perhaps, as Clifford suggests, the poet was contrasting the darkness of the first plague against Egypt with the first act for Israel in the desert with God's cloud lighting up the night, rather than following a strict historical sequencing of events.[24]

The fourth transformational technique is *attribution,* where the poet attributes agency and motives that were not found in the original historical narration. Thus it was God who ordered the famine in Canaan that necessitated the patriarchal clan to seek refuge under the tutelage of Joseph in Egypt (Ps. 105:16; cf. Gen. 41:56).

---

24. Goulder, "Fourth Book," pp. 288-89, opines that the psalmist is using a Genesis 1 model, moving from the darkness to light, connecting Ps. 105:28 and verse 38. The connection with Genesis 1 is more suited to Ps. 104 than Ps. 105, however. Cf. Archie Lee, "Genesis 1 and the Plagues Tradition in Psalm CV," *VT* 11.3 (1990): 259. Clifford's suggestion seems more tenable given the context in Psalm 105. R. Clifford, "Style and Purpose in Psalm 105," *Biblica* 60 (1979): 426.

A fifth technique, *image enhancement,* may be seen in Psalm 105:18, where the description of Joseph's enslavement is enhanced by images of shackled feet and a yoke of iron although these were not present in the original account in Genesis (Gen. 37:28).

A sixth technique is *interpretive addition,* in which the poet adds his interpretation of the original event that was simply recorded in the historical narrative. For example, in Psalm 105 the patriarchs are understood as "anointed ones" and "prophets" (v. 15), whereas the term "anointed" (Messiah) is not present in the patriarchal narratives but is used later of kings and prophets — although in Genesis 20:7 Abraham is identified as a prophet by the Philistine king Abimelech. Further illustrations are found in Psalm 105:39 in the descriptions of the divine cloud as a *protective* covering and the fire as a *guiding* light in the night, in contrast to the Exodus account of the cloud as an instrument of *guidance* and the fire providing *protection* from the Egyptians (Exod. 13:21; 14:19-20).

Seventh, there are times when the poetry *concatenates disparate events* into a new stream of meaning. In the closing verses of Psalm 105 (vv. 42-44) the Abrahamic covenant (Gen. 12, 20) is juxtaposed with the exodus from Egypt (Exod. 15) and the conquest under Joshua (Josh. 1–8) to illustrate God's keeping his promise to Abraham.

Finally, the poet may make a *perspective shift.* In the original narrative Moses' intercessory pleas result in the LORD's provision of bread from heaven and water from the rock, whereas in Psalm 105:40-41 the context is shifted away from the people's rebellion and Moses' intercession to a simple, sovereign act by God in direct response to the people's request.

> They asked and he brought them quail,
>   and satisfied them with the bread of heaven.
> He opened the rock, and water gushed out. (Ps. 105:40-41a)

Similarly, in the description of the plagues in Psalm 105:28-36, the perspective is strictly divine, with none of the interaction between Moses and Pharaoh that is extensively detailed in the Exodus narrative (cf. Exod. 7–12).

These are some of the techniques employed by the poet to craft the historical material into poetic form in Psalm 105. All these poetic methods create a focus in this psalm on the absolutely sovereign movements of God and give historical support to the major theme of Book IV: the LORD reigns.

Hearing Psalm 105 in an Intertextual Context

This historical psalm, like other historical psalms (Pss. 78, 106, 135) — a rather infrequent type — selectively and creatively reflects on the history of Israel to support and declare its messages. Even Mowinckel, who emphasized the cultic nature of most psalms, allowed for the non-cultic nature of the historical psalms. The didactic flavoring of Psalm 105, reflecting a wisdom perspective (cf. Ps. 105:22, 45), also leads away from a priestly/temple/feast setting to a more sage/instructional *sitz im leben*.[25] Ironically, 1 Chronicles 16:8-22 is paralleled nearly verbatim in Psalm 105:1-15; yet the historical setting in Chronicles is clearly cultic as David, with great ceremony, ritual, and innumerable sacrifices, brings the ark into the sacred tent he had raised for it in Jerusalem. This festival was overseen by the Levites and priests, particularly Asaph, one of the Levitical choirmasters to whom David delivered this psalm. In Chronicles, the narrative's purpose was to lead the people in worship in the presence of the long-awaited and newly installed ark at Jerusalem following its exile among the Philistines (cf. 1 Chron. 15:17-19, 25-29). Thus this "historical" psalm reflects a cultic (ritual, ark, priests) origin as well as didactic wisdom crafting (Ps. 105:22, 45).

Psalm 105:1-6: Summons to Praise

Give thanks to the LORD, call on
    his name,
    make known among the nations
       what he has done.

(Ps. 105:1)

Give thanks to the LORD, call on
    his name,
    make known among the nations
       what he has done.

(1 Chron. 16:8)

The psalm begins with a hymnic "summons to praise (Ps 105:1-6)"[26] using imperative verb forms to exhort worshipers to sing praise to the LORD, to declare his mighty acts, and to "seek" his presence (בקשׁ [seek, 3b]/דרשׁ [seek, 4a]/בקשׁ [seek, 4b]; two Hebrew words both translated "seek"). The repeated plural verb forms indicate that this call to worship is

25. Clifford, "Style and Purpose in Psalm 105," *Biblica* 60 (1979): 420; cf. Mowinckel, *The Psalms in Israel's Worship*, vol. 2 (Nashville: Abingdon, 1962), pp. 111-12.
26. Leslie C. Allen, *Psalms 101–150*, Word Biblical Commentary (Waco: Word Books, 1985), p. 40.

directed to the whole community rather than to a lone individual. The delayed explicit reference to the addressees in verse 6 clearly identifies them as the descendants of Abraham and Jacob and focuses attention, in the first five verses, on the praise of the LORD (cf. Pss. 104:35; 105:1 (LXX 104:1), 45; 106:1, 48 — each adjacent psalm of this triad begins and/or ends with a "hallelujah"). The audience before whom the declaration of Yahweh's mighty deeds is to be made is "the peoples" (Ps. 105:1). The repetition of the word "peoples" six times in this psalm emphasizes its importance as a key word. The shift in the LXX from ἐν λαοῖς ("among the people," i.e., Israel) in the parallel text of 1 Chronicles 16:8 to ἐν τοῖς ἔθνεσιν ("among the nations") supports the idea that the audience is foreign "peoples" (cf. Ps. 105:1, 13, 20). This contrasts with the nationalistic use of "people" in the later section of this psalm as "his people" (Ps. 105:24, 25, 43).

The object of what is to be declared among the peoples provides an inclusio for this section, which begins with making known his deeds (v. 1) and wonderful acts (v. 2) and closes with the piling up of "wondrous works," "his miracles" and "judgments" (v. 5). The phonetic aesthetics of the repeated "*rû* + *lo*" (v. 2a/b) and concluding pronominal "יו" sounds that end both verses 1 and 2 draw focus to "*his* deeds" (v. 1) and "*his* wonderful acts" (v. 2). The recital and remembering of the LORD's "wondrous works" manifest the theme of the incomparability of God's kingship, as demonstrated by his mighty acts of deliverance in history and their relevance to the present crisis of the exile. This reinforces the major theme of Book IV, which revolves around the Yahweh Malak (the LORD reigns) psalms (Pss. 93, 96, 97, 99). Verse 6 is a janus, or literary hinge, looking back to identify those called to worship in verses 1-5 and looking forward to the next section of God's promises in the Abrahamic covenant confirmed to Jacob in verses 7-11.

O descendants of *Abraham* his servant,	O descendants of *Israel* his servant,
O sons of Jacob, his chosen ones.	O sons of Jacob, his chosen ones.
(Ps. 105:6)	(1 Chron. 16:13)

The intertextual comparison of Psalm 105 with Psalm 89 and 1 Chronicles 16 yields two insights. First, the variation between the texts of Psalm 105 and 1 Chronicles 16 aids the hinge function of verse 6 by facilitating its link with verse 9. The parallel passage in 1 Chronicles 16:13 says, "O descendants of *Israel* his servant." The bricoleur of Psalm 105 craftily substitutes "O descendants of *Abraham* his servant" (v. 6). The shift to "Abraham" away from "Israel" enhances the janus by looking forward to the next section (Ps. 105:9), where the covenant with Abraham becomes dominant.

Second, it is of great significance that the term "chosen" (v. 6) is plural, thereby identifying the descendants of Jacob as "chosen ones." The noun "chosen" occurs just five times in the Psalms, two of which are in an inclusio opening Psalm 105 in verse 6 and closing it in verse 43. The rarity of this term and the proximity of fourth and fifth usages in Psalm 106:5 ("chosen ones") and Psalm 106:23 (Moses, chosen one) clearly show that Psalms 105 and 106 join together as a pair. The only other place this noun appears in the Psalms is in Psalm 89:3 (Heb. 4), with reference to David who is labeled God's "chosen one" and his "servant." These are the exact designations that Psalm 105:6 applies to the descendants of Abraham and Jacob. G. Wilson claims that, in closing Book III, Psalm 89 references the Davidic covenant as failed and laments how long the LORD will be in restoring the benefits of the Davidic monarchy.[27] Psalms 105/106, concluding Book IV, respond by projecting these very special Davidic terms ("chosen," "servant") back onto the descendants (plural) of the patriarchs Abraham and Jacob. It is a return to Abraham that will allow the exilic community to move beyond the collapse of the Davidic monarchy and reunite in their position as chosen descendants of father Abraham.

		Book III		Book IV	
Word	Frequency in Psalms	Ps. 78	Ps. 89	Ps. 105	Ps. 106
chosen בחיר	5x	v. 70 (verb) = David	v. 3 = David	vv. 6, 43 = nation	vv. 5, 23 = nation, Moses
servant עבד	57x	v. 70 = David	vv. 3, 20, 39 = David	vv. 6, 42 = Abraham, 26 = Moses	v. 36 they served idols (verb)

This insight comes only as a result of a canonical reading of Psalms 105/106 as the conclusion of Book IV, and intertextually against the backdrop of Psalm 89 as the conclusion of Book III. This outlook is confirmed by an intertextual comparison with Psalm 78, which is another psalm of historical genre at the center of Book III that in many ways parallels Psalm

27. Wilson, *Editing*, pp. 213-14.

105 in Book IV. Psalm 78 states, "He chose [verb form] David his servant" (v. 70). Here again, parallel terms are used to identify David as the chosen servant, in contrast to Psalm 105, which extends the "chosenness" to the people and the exceptional servanthood to Abraham, thus moving away from the exclusive identification with David found in Book III.

Psalm 105:7-11: God's Confirmation of the Abrahamic Covenant

In Psalm 105:7-11 God is the subject of every verb as he remembers/confirms his covenant with Abraham, Isaac, and Jacob concerning the promised land.[28] This change of subject from the second-person direct address "you" (vv. 1-6) to God as the subject in verses 7-11 was overlooked by the NIV translators who put the strophic division after Psalm 105:7 rather than correctly inserting it after verse 6.

Phrase	Frequency in Psalms	Book I	Books II & III	Book IV	Book V
Lord our God יהוה אלהינו	10x	20:8	—	94:23; 99:5, 8, 9 105:7; 106:47	122:9 123:2

Seven out of the ten times that the title "the Lord our God" is used in the Psalms are in Book IV. This phrase links Psalm 105:7 with its neighbor Psalm 106:47, which itself echoes back to 105:1-3 through its references to giving "thanks," his "holy name," "glory," and "praise." There is a significant shift, however, from an imperatival command to praise that opens Psalm 105 to the petition from those scattered "among the nations" for regathering that closes Psalm 106.

Word	Frequency in Psalms	Book I (41 chs.)	Book II (31 chs.)	Book III (17 chs.)	Book IV (17 chs.)	Book V (44 chs.)
land/earth הארץ	60x	9x 0.2/ch.	18x 0.6/ch.	4x 0.2/ch.	24x 1.4/ch.	5x 0.1/ch.
land/earth ארץ	190x	31x 0.76/ch.	43x 1.4/ch.	31x 1.8/ch.	44x 2.6/ch.	41x 0.9/ch.

This strophe on the covenant provides the basis of the "wondrous works" that are seen worked out in the "historical" section of this psalm

28. McCann, *Psalms*, p. 1105.

(12-45).[29] The land aspect of the Abrahamic covenant is highlighted by the repetition of the term "land" (אֶרֶץ) ten times in this psalm. Adjacent psalms also emphasize this word with seven usages in Psalm 104 and five in Psalm 106, totaling twenty-two times in Psalms 104–106 in Book IV. The term "land" binds Psalms 104–106 together. Psalm 104 describes God's universal reign over and care of the land in creation. Its promise in the Abrahamic covenant is developed in Psalm 105; its pollution by those rebelling against the covenant of the LORD and its removal as a result of divine judgment are underscored in Psalm 106. Though the LORD had promised this specific "land" to the patriarchs, yet his sovereign rule extends universally well beyond it to "all the earth" (Ps. 105:7), which will be the point of much of what follows in the patriarchs' experience as sojourners in Canaan, Joseph's descent into Egypt, and Israel's later deliverance from Egypt.

| He remembers his covenant forever, the word he commanded, for a thousand generations. (ESV) (Ps. 105:8) | [*You*] Remember his covenant forever, the word that he commanded, for a thousand generations. (MT, ESV) (1 Chron. 16:15) |

An interesting divergence occurs between the Masoretic text of 1 Chronicles 16:15, which reads "*You* remember his covenant," and Psalm 105, which reads "*He [God]* remembers his covenant forever."[30] Psalm 105 features God's actions and commitments as the sole sovereign who reigns and who protects his people without dependence on human response. Howard's canonical analysis has suggested that "The LORD Reigns" or YHWH Malak Psalms (יהוה מָלָךְ), which dominate Book IV (vid. Pss. 93:1; 96:10, 97:1, 99:1), are fleshed out historically in the closing pair of this book (Pss. 105/106).[31] A similar historical perspective is taken in Psalms 135 and 136, with an exclusive focus on God's steadfast love (חֶסֶד). This hymnic praise stance contrasts with the negative historical outlook of Psalms 106 and 78 that expose Israel's rebellion and covenant violation as reasons for the disasters experienced by Israel. Thus "he remembers" (Ps. 105:8) the covenant and Israel too should "remember" so that it may go well with

29. McCann, *Psalms*, p. 1105.

30. Some LXX manuscripts have "He remembers" in 1 Chron. 16:15, which is also followed by the NIV, RSV contra NRSV, NJB, ESV, NET, NASB.

31. Howard, *Psalms 93–100*, p. 182.

them (Ps. 106:13; 1 Chron. 16:12 = Ps. 105:5). The focus of Psalm 105, however, is on God's acts — not on Israel's rebellious response.

Word	Frequency in Psalms	Ps. 78	Ps. 89	Ps. 105	Ps. 106
covenant ברית	21x	vv. 10, 37 unfaithfuness	vv. 4, 29, 35, 40 David	vv. 8, 10 Abraham	v. 45 deliverance

The "covenant" (בְּרִית; 21 times in Psalms) plays a major role in the conclusion of Book III (Ps. 89:4, 29, 35, 40 — the only psalm using the term 4 times) as well as in the conclusion of Book IV (Pss. 105:8, 10; 106:45). There is an important shift between Books III and IV, however, in the use of this term. In Book III (Ps. 89) the initial three references are to God's making his covenant with his "chosen" "servant" David (Ps. 89:3) and his stated commitment to keeping it, saying, "my covenant with him [David] will never fail. . . . I will not violate my covenant or alter what my lips have uttered" (Ps. 89:28, 34). Nonetheless these early promissory statements about the Davidic covenant give way to the psalmist's later grappling with the devastation of the exile voiced in the concluding covenantal lament: "You have renounced the covenant with your servant [David] and have defiled his crown in the dust" (Ps. 89:39-46). Some suggest that it is to this accusation of the failure of the Davidic covenant at the end of Book III to which the editors of the book of Psalms are responding in the conclusion of Book IV. They return, with hope, to the Abrahamic covenant (Ps. 105). In Psalm 106, the poet cites covenantal violation as the reason for the exile, and the covenant's eternality provides the basis for the petition for Israel's regathering (Ps. 106:47). In the heart of Book III, Psalm 78 (vv. 10, 37) also uses the term "covenant" in the context of Israel's unfaithfulness and covenant violation, thereby providing a basis for divine judgment.

To moderate this stark contrast of covenants, Howard correctly suggests that the major motif of Psalms is "Yahweh reigns" and that "this theme manifests itself in the dual expression of YHWH's divine kingship and the mediation through the human Davidic kings, both of which find their earthly expression at Zion."[32] Nonetheless, Book IV seems to focus on the divine kingship side whereas Book V returns to the Davidic king (Ps. 110) and Zion (Pss. 132–135 et al.).

---

32. Howard, *Psalms 93–100*, p. 207. Cf. James Mays, *The Lord Reigns: A Theological Handbook to the Psalms* (Louisville: Westminster John Knox Press, 1994).

The "cutting" (כָּרַת) or making/solemnizing of a covenant verbally links back to Genesis 15:18, where the original Abrahamic covenant was "cut," and to Genesis 26:3, where the covenant of inheriting the land was reiterated to Isaac. Seeking to make sense of the exile, the psalmist returns to the sure, "forever" foundation of the covenant made with Abraham that promised the land as the gathering place of the community. It is ironic that the word "forever" (עוֹלָם) is found most frequently in Psalm 89 (7 times) in reference to the eternality of the Davidic covenant. God's commitment to the Davidic covenant, however, was called into question by the author of Psalm 89 after the devastation of the exile (Ps. 89:49). There will be a new appeal to another "forever" covenant at the end of Book IV (Ps. 105:8, 10; cf. Ps. 106:1, 31, 48 [bis]).

Word	Frequency in Psalms	Ps. 105	Ps. 106	Ps. 135
Canaan כְּנַעַן	3x	v. 11 promised land	v. 38 idols of	v. 11 kings of

In Psalm 105:11 the psalmist ends this strophe (Ps. 105:7-11) by citing a conversation between God and Abraham from Genesis 17:8. The word "Canaan" occurs only three times in the book of Psalms; yet this very rare term is found in the adjacent Psalms 105 (v. 11) and 106 (v. 38; cf. Ps. 135:11), thereby providing another lexical link bonding these two psalms into Book IV's concluding pair. Note also that in the Genesis parallel the pronominal references are to "give to you and to your descendants . . . all the land of Canaan" (NASB). However, the initial singular "you" gives way in Psalm 105:11 to the plural "as your portion for an inheritance," thus reflecting the pluralizing *tendenz* of this psalm. This use of the plural personalizes and identifies the psalmist's present exilic audience with the statement in Genesis 17 concerning Abraham's descendants' future inheritance of the land. Allen is correct in suggesting that the shift from singular "you" Abraham to plural "you" descendants is well in keeping with the movement in this psalm of the covenantal promises from Abraham to his descendants, who are caught in an exile and scattered outside the promised land.[33]

---

33. Allen, *Psalms*, p. 37.

Psalm 105:12-15: Patriarchal Sojourners Protected

Having reiterated the covenantal promise of the land, the psalmist turns to the actual patriarchal experience in the land of promise. The poet focuses on three factors: the patriarchs were few in number when they first came into the land; they arrived after wandering from one nation to another; and they were protected by God from the kings who already occupied the land. Each of these themes would resonate with the exilic and post-exilic communities. Both strophes, Psalm 105:5-11 and 12-15, end with divine speech acts in which God directly addresses the patriarchs concerning the promise of the land in the former and the rulers of that land in order to protect the patriarchs in the latter (v. 11 — promise; v. 15 — protection).[34]

The infrequent term "few in number" used in verse 12 is also found in the complaint of Jacob, in Genesis 34:30, describing his situation of conflict with the inhabitants of Shechem. Such sentiments could surely be shared by the post-exilic community, who, being few in number as they returned, were facing opposition from Sanballat, Tobiah, and Geshem — the inhabitants of the land (Neh. 4, 6). The undersized number is matched by their lack of status: they are "sojourners" (ESV) or "resident aliens" (NET) in the land of promise.

Verse 13 depicts the patriarchs' sojourning in the promised land as wandering between nations (cf. Gen. 15:18-19). "Nation" (גּוֹי) is used repeatedly in both Psalm 105 (vv. 13 [bis], 44) and 106 (vv. 5, 27, 35, 41, 47). In Psalm 106, "nations" is used as the cause of Israel's seduction into covenantal violation (v. 35), as an instrument through which judgment comes on Israel (v. 41), and as a place of scattering of an Israelite community longing to be regathered (vv. 27, 47). Psalm 105 reverses the use of the term "nations" by showing it instead as a place of divine protection (Ps. 105:12-13) and the land as a gift fulfilling the Abrahamic covenant (Ps. 105:44). The rare reference to "kingdoms" is paralleled with another historic psalm's explicit mention of this term as it relates to the Mosaic conquest of the transjordan kings Og and Sihon (Ps. 135:11).

---

34. Warren, "Modality, Reference, and Speech Acts in the Psalms," Ph.D. dissertation (Cambridge: Cambridge University, 1998). See also my website, where this dissertation on the Psalms as well as those by Barry Davis and Gerald Shepherd are freely available (Google "Ted Hildebrandt Psalms").

He allowed no one to *wrong* them;	He allowed no one to *oppress* them;
for their sake he rebuked kings.	for their sake he rebuked kings.
(LXX)	(NIV/MT)
Ps. 105:14 [MT]/104:14 [LXX]	1 Chron. 16:21

Verse 14 has two features of particular interest. First, while the Hebrew is exactly the same in Psalm 105:14 and 1 Chronicles 16:21, the Greek translation of this psalm, which is 104:14 in the Septuagint, changes the infinitive "to oppress" (δυναστεύω; 1 Chron. 16:21), which fits well with the Hebrew and the post-exilic perspective, to another infinitive, "to wrong" (ἀδικέω; Ps. 105:14), which is more descriptive of the Genesis wife-sister encounters with foreign kings (Gen. 12:10-20; 20:3-17; 26:7-11). Second, Book IV is permeated with the "Yahweh Malak" (LORD reigns) psalms, but in Psalm 105 all three usages of "king" (מֶלֶךְ; *melek*) are in reference to foreign kings (Ps. 105:14, 20, 30). The Israelite forefathers are portrayed as resident aliens wandering about, while the hand of the divine king stays the power of each foreign king so that "no one oppressed" his servants. Such sheltering of the little band of sojourners clearly finds echoes in the hoped-for care of the post-exilic community under Ezra and Nehemiah as they faced antagonistic inhabitants of the land.

"Do not touch my anointed ones;	"Do not touch my anointed ones;
and do my prophets no harm."	do my prophets no harm."
Ps. 105:15	1 Chron. 16:22

Two pieces of evidence point to a solid connection of this present strophe (Ps. 105:12-15) with the text of Genesis. First, it shares with the Genesis accounts the same divine protection of Sarah/Rebekah, using the verb "touch" in Psalm 105:15 as well as in all three wife/sister incidents in Genesis (Gen. 12:17; 20:6, 11; 26:29). Second, while the use of the term "prophet" is rare in the Psalms, Abraham is identified as a "prophet" (Ps. 105:15b). Only Genesis 20:7 labels Abraham as a prophet in God's rebuke of Abimelech in the same context as the wife/sister story alluded to in Psalm 105:14-15.

Word	Frequency in Psalms	Ps. 89	Ps. 105
anointed משׁיח	10x	vv. 28, 51 (singular) David, rejected?	v. 15 (plural) patriarchs, protected

Verse 15 uniquely labels the patriarchal sojourners as "anointed ones" (messiahs; מְשִׁיחָי, χριστῶν). Although one might expect the term "anointed one" (messiah) to be frequent in Psalms, it is used just ten times. Psalm 89 is the only psalm that uses it twice (vv. 38, 51 [Heb. 39, 52]). In both instances the "anointed one" appears in the context of a lament over divine abandonment. So Psalm 89:38, closing Book III, complains:

> But you have rejected, you have spurned,
>> you have been very angry with your *anointed one*.

The lament continues in verse 51:

> The taunts with which your enemies have mocked, O LORD,
>> with which they have mocked every step of your *anointed one*.

Both bicola clearly identify the "anointed one" as David (cf. Ps. 89:35, 49). Psalm 2 contrasts the "kings of the earth" who take "their stand against the LORD and against his Anointed One" (Ps. 2:2). Yet in both Psalms 2 and 89 the reference is to David or David's divinely installed successor (cf. also Ps. 18:51). Psalm 105:15, however, transfers the "anointed one" away from David and applies it to the patriarchs Abraham and Isaac as "anointed ones."

Two things are unique in the Psalm 105 statement: "Do not touch my anointed ones" (v. 15). First, Abraham is given the title "anointed one." Kraus expresses his bewilderment that such a title would be used of the patriarch.[35] Anderson says, "It is unlikely that the Patriarchs were actually anointed with oil" and suggests that it is being used in a secondary sense, simply as one called and equipped by God.[36] Allen provides a hint at the solution, which is confirmed by an intertextual analysis. He states, "The psalmist is transferring to the patriarchal period a term especially associated with the Davidic monarchy."[37] The unique pluralizing of the form ("anointed ones") also shifts this regal term away from David to a more democratized identity with God's sojourning people as the "anointed ones" whom he protects from the hands of oppressive foreign kings.

The above becomes even more intriguing upon noting the very clear *tendenz* of the Chronicler to transform the narrative in favor of David and

35. Hans-Joachim Kraus, *Psalms 60–150*, A Continental Commentary (Minneapolis: Fortress Press, 1993), p. 311.
36. A. A. Anderson, *Psalms*, vol. 2, New Century Bible (Greenwood, SC: The Attic Press, 1972), p. 729.
37. Allen, *Psalms 101–150*, p. 38.

away from patriarchal or Mosaic history. This is clearly seen through a comparison of the great prayer of Solomon dedicating the Temple as recorded in 2 Chronicles 6:41-42 and 1 Kings 8:50-53. In 1 Kings the Solomonic prayer of Temple dedication ends with "just as you declared through *your servant Moses* when you, O Sovereign LORD, brought our fathers out of Egypt." In 2 Chronicles 6 the same prayer concludes with "O LORD God, do not reject your anointed one. Remember the great love promised to *David your servant.*" There is no mention of Moses or the exodus. Dillard posits that the Chronicler has substituted an ending drawn from Psalm 132:8-10 in which the "anointed one" is palpably David.[38] Thus, identifying the sojourning patriarchs as "anointed ones" in Psalm 105:15, with no mention of David, reinforces our thesis that Psalm 105 (Book IV) is answering the lament of the demise of the Davidic covenant (Book III; Ps. 89) by returning to the Abrahamic promise. The avoidance of any reference to the Davidic kingship, while utilizing Davidic terminology in a song the Chronicler cites as being given by David to Asaph to be sung at the installation of the ark in Jerusalem, demonstrates the unique Abrahamic perspective of this psalm in its use of patriarchal history to declare "The LORD reigns."

Finally, it is with Psalm 105:15 that we bid the parallel with 1 Chronicles 16:8-22 adieu. The first fifteen verses open Psalm 105 with a nearly verbatim replication of 1 Chronicles 16:8-22, and Psalm 106 closes with a doxology paralleled in this same song recorded in 1 Chronicles 16:35-36. As we have argued repeatedly, together these two psalms form a psalm-pair; an inclusio binds the beginning of Psalm 105 to the end of Psalm 106 via their parallel recorded in 1 Chronicles 16.

Save us, O LORD our God,	Cry out, "Save us, O God our Saviour,
and gather us from the nations,	gather us and deliver from the nations,
that we may give thanks to your holy	that we may give thanks to your holy
name and glory in your praise.	name and glory in your praise.
Praise be to the LORD, the God of Israel	Praise be to the LORD, the God of Israel
from everlasting to everlasting.	from everlasting to everlasting."
Ps. 106:47-48	1 Chron. 16:35-36

38. Raymond B. Dillard, *2 Chronicles,* Word Biblical Commentary (Waco: Word Books, 1987), p. 51. Cf. Gerald Shepherd, "The Book of Psalms as the Book of Christ: A Christo-Canonical Approach to the Book of Psalms" (Ph.D. dissertation, Westminster Theological Seminary, 1995), p. 485.

This doxology closes Book IV (Ps. 106:47-48) in the same manner that doxologies close the other four books of the Psalms (Bk. I: 41:13; Bk. II: 71:9; Bk. III: 89:52; Bk. V: 145–150). This shared relationship of the poem recorded in 1 Chronicles 16 with two psalms in the Psalter (Pss. 105/106) gives some insight into how psalms ripple through history into new contexts (cf. "O Captain, My Captain" supra). The bricoleur poet crafted a poem that fit not only the installation of the ark at Jerusalem but also the story of the sojourning patriarchs and then resonated with the hopes of the exiles returning from Babylon. The editor's use of an inclusio-bonded pair of psalms (105:1-15/106:47-48) to conclude Book IV is reminiscent of the inclusio-bonded pair used by the editor to open the Psalter (Pss. 1:1; 2:12).

Conclusion

This essay has examined the historical hymn Psalm 105:1-15 as a unique Psalm of Abraham. The question was asked: How does a poet craft historical events into poetry? From Psalm 105 it was observed that the poetic bricoleur employed eight methods when working with historical data: (1) selection, (2) compression, (3) reordering, (4) attribution of agency and motives, (5) image enhancement, (6) interpretive addition, (7) concatenation of disparate events, and (8) perspective shifts.

The intertextual and canonical methodologies helped raise several questions, such as: Why are David, Zion, and the Temple, which predominate so much of the Psalter, never mentioned, yet Moses and Abraham, who are rarely mentioned in the Psalms, are repeatedly featured in Psalm 90, which opens Book IV, and in the closing pair, Psalms 105/106 (Pss. 105:26; 106:16, 23, 32)? The question was only heightened by the fact that Psalm 105:1-15 is paralleled nearly verbatim with 1 Chronicles 16:8-22, which is clearly set in the ceremony of David's installation of the ark in Jerusalem. Wilson and McCann have raised the following canonical question. How does Book IV answer the penetrating question raised by Psalm 89 at the end of Book III: "Where is your former great love, which in your faithfulness you swore to David?" The question posed by Psalm 89, lamenting the demise of the Davidic covenant, is "resolved" by a return to the land-focused Abrahamic covenant (Ps. 105). Tanner's intertextual approach to Psalm 90, beginning Book IV, was employed to confirm that Psalm 105 closes Book IV with a patriarchal framework used by the Babylonian exiles to see a new sojourning of the chosen community who, like the patriarchs, were land-less, Temple-less, ark-less, and monarchy-less.[39]

The lexical links and divergences between Psalm 105 and Psalm 89, Psalm 106, and 1 Chronicles 16 were explored, yielding both points of connection and departure. For example, there is a significant shift in Psalm 105:6 to "Abraham" compared to 1 Chronicles 16:13, which has "Israel." This bonds the psalm to the Abrahamic covenant and allows Psalm 105:6 to function as a janus, tying the two initial strophes of Psalm 105 together.

Psalm 105 is joined to both Psalms 89 and 106 by the use of the term "chosen," which occurs only five times in the Psalms, all of which are in Books III and IV. In Psalm 89 it refers to the chosenness of David, while in Psalms 105/106 it refers to the nation and Moses. The great historical center of Book III, Psalm 78, uses the verb form "chose" to again refer to David. Similarly the term "servant" is used repeatedly in Psalm 89 (vv. 3, 20, 39) and Psalm 78:70 in reference to David, but Psalm 105 shifts this Davidic designation to Abraham and Moses, with no mention of David (Ps. 105:6, 26, 42). The word "covenant," used frequently in reference to the Davidic covenant in Psalm 89 (vv. 4, 29, 35, 40), is repeated in Book IV in Psalms 105 and 106, but here the reference is to the Abrahamic covenant of the promised land. "Canaan" is used only three times in the Psalter. It bonds Psalms 105 and 106 together, as do the ten usages of the word "land" in Psalm 105 and five in Psalm 106. Psalm 104 also refers to the land seven times. Each of these three psalms, however, uses the land for a different purpose; yet all use it to support the major theme of Book IV that "Yahweh reigns." Each psalm in this triad (Pss. 104–106) ends with the exclamation "hallelujah."

The term "king" is used all three times in Psalm 105 to refer to foreign kings. Yahweh is portrayed as the sole sovereign, whose reign protects his people from these foreign kings. The word "anointed" *(messiah)* is pluralized, moving it away from its normal Davidic connection and applying it instead to the descendants of Abraham as a community of "anointed ones" (Ps. 105:15).

Thus the psalmist employs these shifts in terminology to develop themes with which he binds together two sojourning communities, Abraham and the post-exilic returnees, who are separated by over a millennium. Both are protected from foreign kings by God's sovereign hand. The exilic community would find hope as they, like Abraham, sojourned and were in desperate need of God's protection from foreign inhabitants of the

39. Tanner, *Intertextuality*, p. 21.

land. This expression resonated from the narratives of patriarchal history, through the Davidic installation of the ark (1 Chron. 16), and into the post-exilic community via the poetry of Psalm 105, even as Whitman's poem echoed from the sea captain to Lincoln to Kennedy.

Dr. Marv Wilson has highlighted our father Abraham as a bridge once again between communities — only this time it is between the Jewish and Christian communities. Then, as now, Abraham provides sojourners with hope. Dr. Wilson, in selecting Abraham as the connecting conduit, has himself become a new "Abraham" who is fathering a generation of Christians with a greater sensitivity of shared history with our Jewish friends. He has shown how Christianity is grafted into the root of Judaism.

Marv concludes his chapter on "Hebrew Thought" with quotes well suited to the historical Psalm 105's return to Abraham: "This is our foundation: to know the God of history, Israel's history (cf. Heb. 11)" and "to recite his magnalia (mighty works)" — an invitation also echoed in the opening of Psalm 105.[40] He finishes with ideas drawn from the deep well of Rabbi Abraham Heschel. "We are not alone. The future is secure. God is alive, at work, and in control." We join with Rabbi Heschel, Dr. Wilson, and the psalmist in proclaiming, "Yahweh reigns!" Hallelujah — praise the LORD (Ps. 105:45).

---

40. Marv Wilson, *Our Father Abraham: Jewish Roots of the Christian Faith* (Grand Rapids: Eerdmans, 1989), pp. 161-62.

Abraham in Exile

H. G. M. WILLIAMSON

It is a striking fact that, despite the centrality of Abraham in the opening chapters of the history of the people of God in Genesis, he rather disappears from view so far as the literature of Israel is concerned until the period commonly known as "the Exile." It was evidently when part of the remnant of the small southern kingdom of Judah was deported to Babylon by Nebuchadnezzar in the early part of the sixth century B.C.E. that the narratives of the patriarch, who had himself come, of course, from "Ur of the Chaldees" to Palestine, once again caught the imagination of his successors in the faith.

It is clear from the texts that have survived, however, that it was not only the Babylonian exiles who drew inspiration from the patriarchal narratives. The community that remained behind in Judah also turned to these traditions for reassurance and reorientation. The purpose of the present chapter, therefore, is to outline the reception history of the material during those decades with the aim of inquiring which of the varied aspects of the Abrahamic tradition spoke most loudly to these two traumatized communities.[1] To do so in a volume happily designed to honor a dear friend may seem appropriate, but of course I am acutely conscious that he knows more about Abraham than I shall ever know, and I can only express the hope that my few remarks will bring pleasure, even if not instruction.

---

1. Outside the Pentateuch and the passages explicitly discussed in this chapter, there are references to Abra(ha)m only at Josh. 24:2-3; 1 Kings 18:36; 2 Kings 13:23; Isa. 29:22; Jer. 33:26; Mic. 7:20; Pss. 47:10; 105:6, 9, 42; 1 Chron. 1:27-28, 32, 34; 16:16; 29:18; 2 Chron. 20:7; 30:6. These are mostly genealogical, formulaic, or else clearly of later date than the exile. For the few exceptions, too many uncertainties surround them to make sensible use of them in the present context.

The earliest passage in our exilic corpus that refers to Abraham occurs in the book of Ezekiel. Here, when the news of the final defeat of Jerusalem is brought to Ezekiel in Babylon, where he had already been exiled during Nebuchadnezzar's first campaign ten years earlier (cf. Ezek. 1:1-3), the word of the LORD through the prophet reveals that those left behind in Judah were saying: "Abraham was one, and he inherited the land; but we are many; the land is given us for an inheritance" (33:24). In sentiment, this is very close to the earlier record of what more or less this same group had been saying: "Get you far[2] from the LORD; unto us is given this land for a possession" (11:15).[3]

Although there is an allusion at 33:24 to the promise that Abraham would be the ancestor of many, the element of the promise that is uppermost is, of course, the gift of the land.[4] At first sight, this might seem somewhat surprising, given the fact that the purported speakers were not those who had been exiled to Babylon but rather those who remained behind. It is likely, however, that their insistence reveals the different ways in which the recent catastrophic events were interpreted in each center. Those who were left in Judah are said to have been generally the poorer and less influential members of society (e.g., 2 Kings 25:12). As might have been expected, the ruling and other leading echelons of society seem to have been those whom the Babylonians were most concerned to remove into exile, the reason presumably being in part to prevent the possibility of further rebellion against them.[5]

2. So MT; many understandably revocalize as a perfect, "They have gone far away." For a recent discussion of this phrase, see Alejandro F. Botta, "רחק in the Bible: A Reevaluation," *Biblica* 87 (2006): 418-20.

3. According to Daniel I. Block, *The Book of Ezekiel Chapters 25–48*, NICOT (Grand Rapids: Eerdmans, 1998), pp. 258-59, 11:15 will have derived from the community that survived the first deportation in 597 B.C.E., whereas 33:24 postdates the final deportation in 587 B.C.E.; see similarly Paul M. Joyce, *Ezekiel: A Commentary*, LHB/OTS 482 (New York and London: T&T Clark, 2007), p. 193, and also Gershon Brin, "The Date and Meaning of the Prophecy against 'Those Who Live in These Ruins in the Land of Israel' (Ezekiel 33:23-29)" (Hebrew), in *Texts, Temples, and Traditions: A Tribute to Menahem Haran*, ed. Michael V. Fox et al. (Winona Lake: Eisenbrauns, 1996), pp. 29*-36*.

4. With others, Matthias Köckert, "Die Geschichte der Abrahamüberlieferung," in *Congress Volume Leiden 2004*, ed. André Lemaire, VTSup 109 (Leiden: Brill, 2006), pp. 103-28 (106), stresses that there is no actual reference to the promise as such in Ezekiel 33, which he would have expected had that already been part of the narrative tradition.

5. Cf. Oded Lipschits, *The Fall and Rise of Jerusalem: Judah under Babylonian Rule* (Winona Lake: Eisenbrauns, 2005), pp. 79-84.

Furthermore, it is clear from the majority of the written records that have survived that the dominant religious tradition of Judah was viewed as being continued primarily among those who had been deported, not by those who remained behind. With history being written in this case as most others by the eventual victors (i.e., here, the descendants of the exiled community), it is not surprising, therefore, that we have tended to lose the voice of interpretation by those who were not among them.

A moment's thought will bring to mind, however, the strong possibility that those left in the land will have seen things very differently.[6] After all, this was not by any means the first time that the people in the land had suffered severe defeat, as many examples throughout the historical books could illustrate, and in normal circumstances those killed or deported would have been understood as the ones directly in the line of God's judgment. Any who remained — who were spared — will reasonably have believed that they were vindicated as blameless and that the future lay with them. Why should the present defeat be any different? Against the ultimately prevalent opinion as put forward by Jeremiah, Ezekiel, and many other later writers that the stream of tradition was carried forward by the exilic community, it is entirely understandable that the Judean community should have seen the situation the other way round and so have appealed to the great promise to Abraham their father in favor of their continuing inheritance of the land.

At this point, therefore, I turn to draw in another voice that supports this conclusion, surprising at first sight, but nevertheless deriving, in my opinion, from the same circles as those cited by Ezekiel. And incidentally, if this is correct, it will mitigate against any suggestion that the words reported in Ezekiel are somehow to be discounted in light of the fact that Ezekiel himself clearly rejected the claims that he was reporting. It might theoretically be supposed that since he was himself a prominent member of the exilic community he cannot be trusted to report faithfully the self-presentation of the group in Judah with whom he was in such obvious disagreement. But the alternative testimony that I now add indi-

6. For recent studies and surveys, see, for instance, Rainer Albertz, *Die Exilszeit: 6. Jahrhundert v. Chr.*, Biblische Enzyklopädie 7 (Stuttgart: Kohlhammer, 2001) (ET, *Israel in Exile: The History and Literature of the Sixth Century B.C.E.*, Studies in Biblical Literature 3 [Atlanta: SBL, 2003]); Oded Lipschits and Joseph Blenkinsopp, eds., *Judah and the Judeans in the Neo-Babylonian Period* (Winona Lake: Eisenbrauns, 2003); Jill Middlemas, *The Troubles of Templeless Judah*, Oxford Theological Monographs (Oxford: Oxford University Press, 2005).

cates that in fact his report was fair, even though the wider contexts in which his words occur show how clearly he himself disagreed with the position he was reporting.

The passage I have in mind is the great prayer included now in Nehemiah 9. In its present setting it serves as a prayer uttered by some Levites in the compilation comprising the reading of the law in Nehemiah 8, the prayer of confession and appeal in chapter 9, and the renewing pledge of obedience in chapter 10, the whole being put together to give the overall shape of a covenant renewal process. As has frequently been observed, there are a number of literary tensions in this compilation that make it questionable whether this sequence should be interpreted in a straightforwardly chronological, historical manner,[7] but that does not really affect my current concern. As I have sought to argue in greater detail elsewhere,[8] the whole ethos of this prayer is clearly that of the community who remained in Judah and were not removed to exile in Babylon. Only such a setting makes sense of the presentation of the Babylonian victory, and it is against that background that the urgent appeal for aid with which the prayer concludes makes most sense of the wording and outlook. It is, I believe, a tribute to the ongoing theological value of this community's insights that the prayer was adopted by members of the returning exilic community as expressive also of their deepest sense of political and economic need.

An important element of this prayer is the historical review of Israel's history with its God, from which important lessons for the present are drawn. While this starts with creation, it then moves immediately to the Abraham narrative in verses 7-8. Here, although Abraham's origins in Ur are acknowledged, the main focus is on the covenant between him and God. In this he was promised the land of the Canaanites and others — a promise to Abraham himself and to his descendants that is said to have been fulfilled

7. See my commentary, *Ezra, Nehemiah,* WBC 16 (Waco: Word Books, 1985), pp. 275-340; Michael W. Duggan, *The Covenant Renewal in Ezra-Nehemiah (Neh 7:72B–10:40): An Exegetical, Literary, and Theological Study,* SBLDS 164 (Atlanta: Society of Biblical Literature, 2001).

8. "Structure and Historiography in Nehemiah 9," in *Proceedings of the Ninth World Congress of Jewish Studies. Panel Sessions: Bible Studies and Ancient Near East,* ed. M. Goshen-Gottstein and David Assaf (Jerusalem: Magnes, 1988), pp. 117-31, repr. in H. G. M. Williamson, *Studies in Persian Period History and Historiography,* FAT 38 (Tübingen: Mohr Siebeck, 2004), pp. 282-93; see further, with only slightly differing conclusions in respect of our present concerns, Mark J. Boda, *Praying the Tradition: The Origin and Use of Tradition in Nehemiah 9,* BZAW 277 (Berlin: de Gruyter, 1999).

because God is righteous. This sets the main theme for the remainder of the prayer as a whole, and it speaks elegantly once again of the importance of this promise of land to those who survived the fall of Jerusalem by remaining in Judah during the following decades. The close link with the sentiments of this same group as reported by Ezekiel are obvious and support the conclusion that this was indeed the element of the Abraham stories that spoke most powerfully in those particular circumstances.

A final possible reference to Abraham by this same community occurs at Isaiah 63:16. In the context of an extended lament in 63:7–64:11 (ET 12), the speakers affirm that, despite their present miserable situation, God remains their father and redeemer. The passage is unusually difficult to date or to interpret, however, so that it is best noted as merely a possible parallel and certainly not the core of the argument in the first place.

The first uncertainty concerns the lament's date. On the usual view that Isaiah 56–66 is post-exilic, it might initially be assumed that the passage is somewhat too late for us to consider within a discussion of "Abraham in Exile." Furthermore, there are a few, mainly following the studies of Steck, who would date the lament even later — in the Hellenistic period.[9] I have elsewhere sought to add strengthening arguments to the case held also by others, however, which regards this lament as much earlier, in fact precisely as a product of the Judean community during the exilic period.[10] It may be noted, for instance, that this was the only possible period for which we have direct evidence that the sanctuary had been trodden down by enemies (63:18) and burned with fire (64:10 [ET 11]) or when Jerusalem/Zion was a wilderness and a desolation (64:9 [ET 10]). Suggestions that this might refer to some later catastrophe, such as Ptolemy I's Judean campaign in 302-301 B.C.E., or even to the Maccabean period,[11] are completely speculative; there is no evidence of such destruction at those times. In addition, it is often attractively maintained that the bulk of chapters 65–66 was written explicitly as a response to the various points of complaint included in the lament.[12] In that case, unless these chapters too are dated late

---

9. See most recently and with abundant bibliography, Johannes Goldenstein, *Das Gebet der Gottesknechte: Jesaja 63,7–64,11 im Jesajabuch*, WMANT 92 (Neukirchen-Vluyn: Neukirchener Verlag, 2001).

10. "Isaiah 63,7–64,11: Exilic Lament or Post-Exilic Protest?" *ZAW* 102 (1990): 48-58.

11. For the former, see Goldenstein, *Gebet*, pp. 246-47; for the latter, with regard either to the whole of the passage or to some later additions included within it, see Karl Marti, *Das Buch Jesaja*, KHAT 10 (Tübingen: J. C. B. Mohr [Paul Siebeck], 1900), p. 400, with refs.

12. See especially Odil Hannes Steck, *Studien zu Tritojesaja*, BZAW 203 (Berlin: de

(for which again there is no additional evidence), it seems more plausible to remain with the view that the lament itself was written somewhat earlier and then was included here as the basis for the author's further arguments in these concluding chapters.

The second uncertainty relates to the interpretation of the specific verse in question. In the Revised Version it reads: "For thou art our father, though Abraham knoweth us not, and Israel doth not acknowledge us: thou, O Lord, art our father; our redeemer from everlasting is thy name." Since it is difficult to imagine that any possible group of speakers would have surrendered their claim to the use of the name Israel (as some have occasionally implied), it is likely that the references to Abraham and Israel are to the patriarchs themselves rather than their heirs. But how, then, can one understand a group of speakers emphatically asserting that God is their father even though the patriarchs do not acknowledge them? An allusion to failed necromantic practices has occasionally been suggested in the past,[13] but though possible, it seems unlikely. More usually it is held that the references to the patriarchs are included in order to underline the speakers' sense of hopelessness: nothing is going right for them, but nevertheless they cling to their faith in God as father and redeemer.[14] Finally, as a refinement of this latter view, Blenkinsopp has most recently proposed that the introductory particle *kî* might be construed not indicatively, "for/because," but counterfactually, "if" (cf. GKC §159 *aa, bb*), hence: "Were Abraham not to know us, Israel not to acknowledge us, yet you, YHVH, are our Father."[15] Either way, the important point to note is that the positive emphasis is on God as father rather than the patriarchs, and it is indeed to this that the lament returns as it moves toward its summarizing conclusion (64:7 [ET 8]): "But now, O Lord, thou art our father. . . ."

Despite these very real uncertainties over the date and sense of the la-

Gruyter, 1991), pp. 221-25, followed, for instance, by Lena-Sofia Tiemeyer, *Priestly Rites and Prophetic Rage: Post-Exilic Prophetic Critique of the Priesthood*, FAT 2. Reihe 19 (Tübingen: Mohr Siebeck, 2006), pp. 60-63; similarly, though with more redactional complexity, Klaus Koenen, *Ethik und Eschatologie im Tritojesajabuch: Eine literarkritische und redaktionsgeschichtliche Studie*, WMANT 62 (Neukirchen-Vluyn: Neukirchener Verlag, 1990).

13. See, for instance, Bernhard Duhm, *Das Buch Jesaia*, HAT 3/1 (Göttingen: Vandenhoeck & Ruprecht, 1892), p. 439.

14. For instance, R. Norman Whybray, *Isaiah 40–66*, NCB (London: Oliphants, 1975), p. 261.

15. Joseph Blenkinsopp, *Isaiah 56–66: A New Translation with Introduction and Commentary*, AB 19B (New York: Doubleday, 2003), p. 263.

ment generally and of the significance of the reference to Abraham in 63:16 specifically, it nevertheless seems to me most probable that we here have another reference to the significance of Abraham for the Judean community in the exilic period (or very shortly thereafter). It is unlike the other passages we have noted so far, in that it does not so much tie in positively to one of the promises recorded as having been granted to Abraham as rather indicate that somehow, even if the patriarch no longer "knows" this community, they retain their firm faith in God himself. Furthermore, the fact that Abraham is here used in parallel with Israel (Jacob) suggests that it is this rhetorical point that is uppermost rather than some focus upon the Abrahamic narrative in detail. Nevertheless, the point still stands that the focus of the lament generally is upon the poor physical conditions in which the community are living rather than upon the decimation of their population or their role as a source of blessing or cursing among the gentiles. Without my wishing to press the point too strongly, therefore, it seems that this reference may also fit with the others that we have seen deriving from this community and that it may refer to the same element in the Abraham account.

I conclude, therefore, that so far as the Judean community was concerned during the exilic period, the revivification of the significance of Abraham was due to the fact that God had promised him the land. Although this community was still physically present in the land, yet they felt alienated from its full enjoyment by the deprivations they were experiencing and the sense of alienation brought about by the Babylonian conquest and occupation.

Against this consistent position, I turn now to two passages that refer to Abraham in the second part of the book of Isaiah, namely 41:8 and 51:2. As will be well known, there is considerable dispute at present about where these chapters were written. Following the widespread acceptance of the conclusion that they could not have been written by Isaiah of Jerusalem, there was initially quite a variety of opinions on offer as to their possible place of origin. Thereafter, during most of the twentieth century there was a general and usually undefended consensus that they were to be located among the exilic community in Babylon. Led by Barstad, however, a forceful challenge to this consensus has arisen more recently,[16] and in particular

---

16. See, for instance, Hans M. Barstad, *A Way in the Wilderness: The "Second Exodus" in the Message of Second Isaiah*, JSS Monograph 12 (Manchester: University of Manchester Press, 1989); *The Myth of the Empty Land: A Study in the History and Archaeology of Judah during the "Exilic" Period* (Oslo: Scandinavian University Press, 1996); *The Babylonian Captivity of the Book of Isaiah: "Exilic" Judah and the Provenance of Isaiah 40–55* (Oslo: Novus Forlag, 1997).

Tiemeyer has now made use of these very references to Abraham to urge that the author must be part of the same community as the one we have discussed already.[17] In reviewing the passages, therefore, it will be interesting to see how far they are in close agreement with those we have studied already.

Isaiah 41:8-13 is a classic example of what is generally labeled an oracle of salvation.[18] In such passages it is usual for the prophet to allude in the introductory address to material with which we are familiar from the psalms of lament before going on to reassure listeners that they need not fear because God will be with them and help them in their distress.

In the present passage, the reference to Abraham comes as part of the initial address: "But thou, Israel, my servant, Jacob whom I have chosen, the seed of Abraham my friend. . . ."[19] Here we should take note of several points. First, the sequence "Israel, Jacob, and Abraham" is unique in the Hebrew Bible.[20] We are familiar, of course, with such sequences elsewhere in the Bible as "Abraham, Isaac, and Jacob," and elsewhere in Isaiah 40–49 it is common for Jacob and Israel to stand in synonymous parallelism.[21] It is noteworthy, however, that here we have the unusual order of Israel first, whereas elsewhere the reverse order usually pertains. Despite the somewhat casual appearance of this reference to Abraham,

17. Lena-Sofia Tiemeyer, "Abraham — A Judahite Prerogative," *ZAW* 120 (2008): 49-66.

18. See, for instance, Joachim Begrich, *Studien zu Deuterojesaja,* BWANT 77 (Stuttgart: Kohlhammer, 1938), p. 6; Claus Westermann, *Isaiah 40–66: A Commentary,* OTL (London: SCM, 1969), pp. 67-69; Antoon Schoors, *I Am God Your Saviour: A Form-Critical Study of the Main Genres in Is. xl-lv,* VTSup 24 (Leiden: Brill, 1973), pp. 47-58; Karl Elliger, *Deuterojesaja: 1. Teilband, Jesaja 40,1–45,7,* BKAT 11/1 (Neukirchen-Vluyn: Neukirchener Verlag, 1978), pp. 133-36. For a discussion of more recent doubts about this categorization, with references to further literature, see John Goldingay and David Payne, *A Critical and Exegetical Commentary on Isaiah 40–55,* vol. 1, ICC (London: T&T Clark, 2006), pp. 154-59.

19. For allusions to Abraham throughout this chapter, see John Goldingay, "'You Are Abraham's Offspring, My Friend': Abraham in Isaiah 41," in *He Swore an Oath: Biblical Themes from Genesis 12–50,* ed. Richard S. Hess, Philip E. Satterthwaite, and Gordon J. Wenham (Cambridge: Tyndale House, 1993), pp. 29-54. For a discussion of "who loves whom" in the word translated "my friend," see the survey of opinions and analysis in Peter Höffken, "Abraham und Gott, oder: wer liebt wen? Anmerkungen zu Jes 41,8," *Biblische Notizen* 103 (2000): 17-22, repr. in *"Fürchte dich nicht, denn ich bin mit dir!" (Jesaja 41,10): Gesammelte Aufsätze zu Grundtexten des Alten Testaments,* Beiträge zum Verstehen der Bibel 14 (Münster: Lit, 2005), pp. 139-45.

20. Ulrich Berges, *Jesaja 40–48,* HThKAT (Freiburg: Herder, 2008), p. 190.

21. Cf. 40:27; 41:14; 42:24; 43:1, 22, 28; 44:1, 5, 21, 23; 45:4; 46:3; 48:1, 12; 49:5-6.

therefore, it is clear that it is accompanied by unusual features that suggest that attention is being drawn to some aspect of the content. And given the striking appearance of Abraham last in the list, it is tempting to suppose that it is the reference to him, in fact, to which our attention is being particularly drawn.

Second, it is clear that in this verse, as often elsewhere in these chapters, Jacob and Israel are used as titles for the community being addressed and not for the patriarchs as individuals in their own right. What is more, the same is effectively the case with the reference to Abraham, given that it is not the patriarch who is being addressed but "the seed of Abraham," meaning his descendants and so, by obvious implication, the listeners to, or readers of, these words.

Third, by referring to his audience specifically as the seed of Abraham the prophet surely has the use of "seed" in the Abraham narratives in mind. As might be expected from the word itself, its focus is on the promise that God would increase Abraham's family to the point where they would become a "great nation" (Gen. 12:2). This is clear from such a cardinal passage as Genesis 15, where Abram initially laments that he has "no seed" and that his heir is in that sense an outsider (v. 3), to which God responds first that one of Abram's own descendants will be his heir and second that, as he looks at the number of the stars, so numerous will his seed become (v. 5). Of course, such a promise cannot be wholly divorced from the promise of a land in which this seed would dwell (e.g., 12:7), but the main focus is on the promise of descendants.

In the present passage in Isaiah it would seem that the same focus is paramount. It is true that the immediately following clauses go on to remind the reader that the seed of Abraham is one "whom I have taken from the ends of the earth and called from the corners thereof," but this leads not to an emphasis on the promise of land, as might initially be supposed, but to God's choice of them as servant and then that God will strengthen and uphold them against the threats of external opponents. In other words, the concern is with community rather than with territory.

What accounts for this emphasis on community rather than land? Before putting forward a possible answer to that question, let me observe that the emphasis is comparable to the other place where there is a reference to Abraham in these chapters, namely 51:2: "Look unto Abraham your father, and unto Sarah that bare you: for when he was but one I called him, and I blessed him, and made him many." This verse comes at the start of what I regard as an extended poetic composition constructed as two panels, each in three sections (51:1–52:2).[22] In such a long passage it is clear that there will be scope to include more than one major element, and in the present instance this certainly includes references to the restoration of Zion, something, indeed, that occurs as early as the very next verse after that just cited: "For the LORD hath comforted Zion: he hath comforted all her waste places, and hath made her wilderness like Eden. . . ." Nevertheless, that is far from being the only concern in the passage, and indeed it is noteworthy that the first panel (51:1-8) is addressed to "you that follow after righteousness, you that seek the LORD," and that this same theme is resumed in the address of the third section (verse 7): "you that know righteousness, the people in whose heart is my law." Clearly, therefore, alongside the restoration of Zion (not the land), the issue of the formation of the character of the community is also prominent, and it is primarily with this, it may be suggested, that the reference to Abraham is concerned.[23] The progress from one to many is the first feature of the narrative to which attention is drawn, and this fact also explains the inclusion of Sarah at this point, an element not paralleled in the other passages we have analysed.

It thus seems that these two references in Isaiah 40–55 have the same element of the promises to Abraham uppermost in mind, and that is the one of a large family — of seed rather than of land. The contrast with the references surveyed earlier in this essay is obvious.[24]

The reason for this seems to me likely to be due to their origin in communities in different circumstances and conditions. The question this raises is therefore clearly whether these latter two references can be sensibly associated not with the community in Judah but with that in Babylon. While the matter can obviously not be proved, there are reasons to believe that it is probable. Against what might first be thought, the uppermost concerns of this community might not have been the issue of land, which from

22. See more fully my analysis in *Variations on a Theme: King, Messiah and Servant in the Book of Isaiah* (Carlisle: Paternoster, 1998), pp. 156-65.

23. Indeed, Risto Nurmela, *The Mouth of the Lord Has Spoken: Inner-Biblical Allusions in Second and Third Isaiah,* Studies in Judaism (Lanham: University Press of America, 2006), pp. 59-60, finds the reference here to be directly dependent on Gen. 22:17, which refers to God making Abraham's seed numerous.

24. See similarly Köckert, "Geschichte"; see too Hayim Tadmor, "The Origins of Israel as Seen in the Exilic and Post-Exilic Ages," in *Le Origini di Israele* (Rome: Accademia Nazionale dei Lincei, 1987), pp. 15-27, and Christof Hardmeier, "Erzählen — Erzählung — Erzählgemeinschaft: Zur Rezeption von Abrahamserzählungen in der Exilsprophetie," in *Erzähldiskurs und Redepragmatik im Alten Testament: Unterwegs zu einer performativen Theologie der Bibel,* FAT 46 (Tübingen: Mohr Siebeck, 2005), pp. 35-55.

their point of view had been lost, but rather the maintenance of their community as a cohesive unit in the face of all the pressures to assimilate and hence to disappear from history, as had happened much earlier in the Assyrian period to the exiled members of the northern kingdom of Israel. Our knowledge of the circumstances in which this exiled community lived are not anything like as clear as we might wish, but recent work has pointed to the importance of strategies for social maintenance and cohesion,[25] and the promise of numerous progeny from slight beginnings seems to fit that portrait quite naturally.[26] The differences between the two groups of texts seem more compelling in separate social contexts than the elements that almost inevitably unite them. Thus, in short, for the Judean community the promise to Abraham about land confirmed them in their view that they were the ones through whom God would continue to work following the fall of the state, whereas for the community in Babylon the promise about seed reassured them of a future as a viable society, despite their loss of land.

In conclusion, it is clear that the Abraham narratives, which came to renewed prominence in the exilic period, are of an obvious richness. If the proposal is correct that various elements of the narrative were appropriated in different ways by different communities, it follows as a probability that they already existed in some shape or form prior to the exile,[27] and were not first invented in the exilic period, as some have recently proposed. More important, like so much of Scripture, there is in these narratives a wealth of variety that can be applied to and can nourish communities in very differing circumstances and with very different perceptions of the meaning and direction of history. While Scripture is not so open that it can mean whatever a reader chooses to find there, it is flexible to an inspiring extent in the range of human experience that it can address. Abraham in exile, it seems, can address many different sorts and conditions of people.

25. See especially Daniel L. Smith, *The Religion of the Landless: The Social Context of the Babylonian Exile* (Bloomington: Meyer Stone, 1989).

26. I have drawn attention to this factor from quite a different angle in "The Family in Persian Period Judah: Some Textual Reflections," in *Symbiosis, Symbolism, and the Power of the Past: Canaan, Ancient Israel, and Their Neighbors — from the Late Bronze Age through Roman Palestina*, ed. William G. Dever and Seymour Gitin (Winona Lake: Eisenbrauns, 2003), pp. 469-85.

27. See more fully Ludwig Schmidt, "Väterverheißungen und Pentateuchfrage," *ZAW* 104 (1992): 1-27; Antje Labahn, *Wort Gottes und Schuld Israels: Untersuchungen zu Motiven deuteronomistischer Theologie im Deuterojesajabuch mit einem Ausblick auf das Verhältnis von Jes 40–55 zum Deuteronomismus*, BWANT 143 (Stuttgart: Kohlhammer, 1999), pp. 107-60.

Abraham in the Christian Scriptures

And the Word Became Flesh — Again?
Jesus and Abraham in John 8:31-59

Steven A. Hunt

Introduction

This paper intends to bring the modern tools of literary criticism to bear on the text of John 8:31-59. We hope to show through the reading that emerges that the narrator uses several important details in this text to build on and concretize earlier Christological claims about the deity and pre-existence of Jesus. Far from being simply analogous or abstract, Jesus' statements in the text intend to convey that, as an earlier manifestation of the pre-existent Word, he was the one who appeared to Abraham in Genesis. This reading, supported by modern literary critical methods, corresponds to understandings of John from which many early Christian interpreters would not flinch.

A Note on "the Word" in the Prologue

The author of the Gospel of John speaks of the pre-existent Word in the first phrase of the first verse — "In the beginning was the Word." We learn also

What a pleasure it has been to work alongside Prof. Marvin R. Wilson, and what a real delight it is now to dedicate this chapter to him on the occasion of his 75th birthday. Happy Birthday, Marv! I wish for you many more years of health and happiness. Thanks so much for your decades of service to Gordon College in general and the program of Biblical Studies in particular. Both are better off owing in large part to you and your tireless efforts on their behalf.

that "the Word was with God and the Word was God" (1:1). This statement, which distinguishes between the Word and God, ends, paradoxically, by speaking of the Word as God. The second verse reiterates the Word's pre-existence "in the beginning" and the proximity of the Word "with God." The Prologue speaks to the Word's creative activity in the beginning too: "All things came into being through *him*" (1:3); indeed, the "world came into being through *him*" (1:10).[1] The Word's deity, pre-existence, proximity to God, and relationship to the creation are some of the primary themes of the Prologue. That his activity as the Word "in the beginning" relates so obviously to the beginning as described in Genesis, goes without saying. It is important for our purposes only to note that in the Johannine theological worldview, the Word has been involved with this world since "the beginning."

Important also to the Prologue is the decisive manifestation of the Word who became flesh and lived among his creation (1:14). Some rejected him (1:10-11), but others received him (1:12-13) and in turn saw his glory (1:14), the very glory of God which had never been seen before in fullness. The Prologue concludes, "No one has ever seen God. It is God the only Son, who is close to the Father's heart, who has made him known" (1:18). In addition to the obvious allusion to the theophany on Mt. Sinai (Exod. 33–34), we note only that here the Son's deity and proximity to the Father are highlighted yet again.

These themes are a major part of the story of Jesus too. For example, the theme of pre-existence pervades the narrative in various ways, running like a thread throughout the remainder of the Gospel and reaching a climax in Jesus' prayer in John 17 (while clearly alluding to the Word in the Prologue):

> So now, Father, glorify me in your own presence with the glory that I had in your presence before the world existed. . . . Father, I desire that those also, whom you have given me, may be with me where I am, to see my glory, which you have given me because you loved me before the foundation of the world. (vv. 5, 24)

Because the pre-existent "Word became flesh" (1:14), that is, the Word becomes Jesus in the narrative which follows, so many of the sayings of and

---

1. Note the masculine pronouns in the Prologue, anticipating the man Jesus would become. In addition to the numerous references in the Gospel to the "Son of Man," Jesus is referred to by both friends (4:29; 9:11) and foes (5:12; 7:46; 9:16, 24; 10:33; 11:47, 50; 18:14, 29; 19:5) as a "man." Most importantly, in 8:40 Jesus refers to himself this way.

about Jesus take on a new urgency. So, for example, while John the Baptist can be said to have been "sent from God" (1:6; cf. 1:33), the same language to describe Jesus, the Word in flesh, means so much more.[2] Thus, John the Baptist's being "sent from God" refers only to his mission, not his origin; for Jesus, it refers to both. This becomes especially clear when the word "sent" is linked with καταβαίνω in 6:38 when Jesus says, "I have *come down* from heaven not to do my own will but the will of him who *sent* me."[3] His having come down from heaven relates both to his being "from above"[4] as well as to his "ascending" (ἀναβαίνω) into "heaven" (3:13) and to "the Father" (20:17) where he was "before" (6:62).[5]

Jesus' pre-existence is seen too in the simple fact that he has "come." The verbs ἔρχομαι and ἐξέρχομαι, so frequent in the Gospel,[6] are used any number of times to communicate that Jesus has come "from God" (3:2; 8:42; 13:3; 16:27, 30),[7] "from the Father" (16:28), "from above" (3:31), "from heaven" (3:31),[8] or, as Jesus says when praying, "from you" (17:8); similarly, Jesus has come "into the world" (1:9; 3:19; 9:39; 11:27; 12:46; 16:28; 18:37); come in his "Father's name" (5:43; cf. 12:13); come "to his own" (1:11); come

---

2. The author uses the important verbs πέμπω and ἀποστέλλω in the Gospel to make clear that Jesus has been "sent" from the Father: on πέμπω, see 4:34; 5:23-24, 30, 37; 6:38-39, 44; 7:16, 18, 28, 33; 8:16, 18, 26, 29; 9:4; 12:44-45, 49; 13:20; 14:24; 15:21; 16:5; 20:21; cf. a more ambiguous usage in 13:16; on ἀποστέλλω, see 3:17; 5:36, 38; 6:29, 57; 7:29; 8:42; 10:36; 11:42; 17:3, 8, 18, 21, 23, 25; 20:21; that they are virtually synonymous verbs is seen clearly when they are juxtaposed, e.g., in 20:21 (cf. 17:18), or when they are alternately used to describe John the Baptist's being sent (1:6, 33; 3:28).

3. Eight of the 17 uses of the word καταβαίνω in John refer to Jesus' descent "from heaven" (3:13; 6:33, 38, 41-42, 50-51, 58); another refers to the Spirit's descent "from heaven" (1:32).

4. The author uses both ἄνωθεν (3:31; cf. 19:11; should one include 19:23 in this list too?) and ἐκ τῶν ἄνω (8:23) to indicate Jesus' place of origin.

5. See also Jesus' claim to be "before" (πρὶν) Abraham in 8:58; cf. also John the Baptist's twice repeated testimony that emphasizes that Jesus came "ahead" (ἔμπροσθεν) of him because Jesus was "before" (πρῶτος) him (1:15, 30; cf. 10:4). See further Raymond E. Brown, *The Gospel According to John I–XII*, The Anchor Bible (New York: Doubleday, 1966), pp. 63-65.

6. The former verb is used 157 times in the Gospel and the latter 30 times.

7. John uses three different prepositions to communicate "from" (ἀπό, ἐκ, παρά) — all are virtually synonymous and ought not to be pressed into theological debates. Cf. Leon Morris (*The Gospel According to John,* rev. ed., The New International Commentary on the New Testament [Grand Rapids: Eerdmans, 1995], p. 410, n. 85), who writes: "we must bear in mind John's penchant for slight variations in vocabulary without real difference in meaning."

8. Cf. the idea already in the writings of Paul (1 Cor. 15:47).

and "spoken to them" (15:22), so that in his coming "they may have life" (10:10); and while Jesus knows where he has come "from" (8:14), among others, there are a number of discussions whence he comes (6:14; 7:27, 31, 41-42).

Related to his coming is his "going." To be sure, the words ὑπάγω and πορεύομαι are used synonymously in some instances (see esp. 14:28 where they are in juxtaposition). But the words themselves take on multi-layered meanings depending on the context in which they are found.[9] Jesus' "going" then proves quite intriguing: on the one hand, Jesus says that he is going to the one who "sent" him (7:33; 16:5), to "God" (13:3), or to the "Father" (14:12, 28; 16:10, 17, 28), presumably meaning simply that he is returning to where he was before. And surely this is correct in one sense. But there is another layer of meaning here when these words are understood specifically within the context of Jesus' death. Especially in the sayings found in 8:21-22 and then again in the related passage of 13:33, 36, Jesus' "going" refers more immediately to his death than to a return to the Father.[10] Still, we should not lose sight of the former sense even in these texts. Understood in light of the Prologue's assertion that the Word was in the beginning with God (1:1) and then became flesh (1:14), having been sent from the Father, Jesus' going to the Father in these later texts implies a *return,* which in turn requires his pre-existence.[11]

To sum up, as rightly noted by so many, the Prologue (1:1-18) sets the stage for the author's Christology in the Gospel. Everything in the narrative related to Jesus, the Word made flesh, takes on a new vibrancy, a new urgency in the overwhelming, sometimes blinding light of the Prologue. That Jesus was sent from God does not denote just his mission, it denotes his origin too. That he comes from above, comes from the Father, and is

9. See further on this important topic Paul Anderson's fine essay, "From One Dialogue to Another: Johannine Polyvalence from Origins to Reception," in *Anatomies of Narrative Criticism: The Past, Present, and Futures of the Fourth Gospel as Literature,* ed. Tom Thatcher and Stephen D. Moore (Atlanta: Society of Biblical Literature, 2008), pp. 93-119.

10. The parallel structure of the two texts with οἱ Ἰουδαῖοι in the first and Peter in the second repeating Jesus' word, as well as Jesus' comment in 13:33 referring back to 8:21, demonstrates that they are to be read together. Indeed, to complicate the matter further, both of these texts need to be read in light of 7:33-36. In addition to the texts mentioned above, cf. also the use of the verbs in 3:8; 8:14; 10:4; 14:2-3; 16:7.

11. Cf. Edwyn Hoskyns (*The Fourth Gospel,* ed. F. N. Davey [London: Faber and Faber, 1947], p. 349), who concludes, "The story of the life and death of Jesus is the story of the descent of the Word of God; and His resurrection is not an ascent to the Father, but a return thither."

going to the Father again where he was before, all suggests that Jesus existed in some sense prior to the time when his disciples saw his glory (1:14) and he finally and decisively made the Father known (1:18). His preexistence, therefore, should be given its due weight in every Johannine narrative or discourse which speaks either explicitly or implicitly of Jesus prior to his coming into the world.[12]

Hospitality in the Fourth Gospel

Another theme introduced in the Prologue, which links to his preexistence, is the world's negative reception of the Word. The Prologue makes clear that the Word "came to what was his own and his own did not receive him" (1:11). Chapters 2–12, then, detail the rejection of Jesus, the Word in flesh, and prepare the reader for his crucifixion at the hands of "his own people" in chs. 18-19.[13] His rejection, seen routinely in his opponents' inhospitable reception of his word, becomes a major motif providing the spark for several of the confrontations in the discourses of the Gospel, especially between Jesus and οἱ Ἰουδαῖοι (hereafter "the Jews").[14]

12. See, for example, the way a number of Pauline scholars deal with Paul's statement in 1 Cor. 10:4 when referring to the Israelites in the wilderness who drank from the spiritual rock, "and the rock was Christ." Gordon Fee writes, "it seems far more likely that [Paul] uses the verb 'was' to indicate the reality of Christ's presence in the OT events than that he sees him there simply in a figurative way" (*The First Epistle to the Corinthians*, The New International Commentary on the New Testament [Grand Rapids: Eerdmans, 1987], p. 449). So also Hans Conzelmann, *1 Corinthians*, Hermeneia (Philadelphia: Fortress Press, 1975), p. 167; Anthony C. Thiselton, *The First Epistle to the Corinthians*, The New International Greek Testament Commentary (Grand Rapids: Eerdmans, 2000), pp. 729-30; C. K. Barrett, *The First Epistle to the Corinthians*, Harpers New Testament Commentaries (Peabody, MA: Hendrickson Publishers, 1987), p. 223; and Ben Witherington III, *Conflict and Community in Corinth: A Socio-Rhetorical Commentary on 1 and 2 Corinthians* (Grand Rapids: Eerdmans, 1995), p. 221.

13. "His own people" in 1:11 should not be delimited to οἱ Ἰουδαῖοι. Not only did Pilate hand Jesus over to be crucified (19:16) while Roman soldiers oversaw the process (19:23-25a), but, more importantly, 1:11 is balanced by the broader assertion that "the world did not know him" in 1:10.

14. I am keenly aware of the way in which the Gospel of John has been used and continues to be used as a weapon against the Jewish people. I use the term "the Jews" (in quotes), therefore, with reluctance, and only as a means of referring to this identifiable group within the Gospel. In the spirit of a volume dedicated to Prof. Marvin Wilson, a man who has devoted the better part of his life to attempting to foster understanding, dialogue,

The discourse that follows the healing of the sick man on the Sabbath in 5:16-47 is especially instructive: the narrator notes in v. 16 that, angered at his healing of the man on the Sabbath, "the Jews started persecuting Jesus"; interestingly, it is only after Jesus speaks the word to them directly in v. 17 that the situation escalates and we read for the first time that "the Jews" seek to kill him (v. 18). The tightly constructed narrative at this point leaves little doubt as to the narrator's likely intention: while Jesus' signs in the Gospel may be troubling, in the end it is his signs as they are accompanied and interpreted by his word that will get him killed.

The rejection of Jesus' word also explains the dispute between Jesus and "the Jews" during "the bread of life" discourse (6:25-59). But in this text his rejection is not limited to "the Jews"; in fact, the story here comes to its climax with some of his own disciples rejecting him and his word (6:60-72). Some of them said: "This teaching is difficult. Who can accept it?" (6:60).[15] The narrator then concludes ominously: "Because of this

---

and respect among Jews and Christians, one may only hope for a time when uninformed or ill-informed Christians will read John more appropriately. An anti-Semitic reading, I strongly believe, is an abuse of John's Gospel. My own view comports well with Andrew T. Lincoln, *Truth on Trial: The Lawsuit Motif in the Fourth Gospel* (Peabody, MA: Hendrickson Publishers, 2000), p. 398: "if we accept the widely held definition of anti-Semitism as hatred of the Jewish people as a group because they are Jewish, then this Gospel itself is certainly not anti-Semitic." Elsewhere, in his discussion of John 8:44, considered by some "the *locus classicus* of Christian anti-Semitism," Lincoln demonstrates point by point that virtually every indictment Jesus levels at "the Jews" in John 8 is paralleled by an indictment YHWH or the prophets leveled at Israel in the Old Testament. Thus one views this material in John properly only when one views it through the lens of "intra-Jewish polemics" (*The Gospel According to Saint John*, Black's New Testament Commentary [London: Continuum, 2005], pp. 272-74). See also D. Moody Smith, *The Theology of the Gospel of John*, New Testament Theology (Cambridge: Cambridge University Press, 1995), pp. 169-73; D. F. Tolmie, "The Ἰουδαῖοι in the Fourth Gospel: A Narratological Perspective," in *Theology and Christology in the Fourth Gospel*, ed. G. Van Belle, J. G. Van Der Watt, and P. Maritz, BETL 184 (Leuven: Leuven University Press — Peeters, 2005), pp. 377-97; on the subject generally, see the essays in Reimund Bieringer, Didier Pollefeyt, and Frederique Vandecasteele-Vanneuville, eds., *Anti-Judaism and the Fourth Gospel* (Louisville: John Knox Press, 2001), especially the "Select Bibliography" contained therein, pp. 293-314.

15. The words translated "teaching" here in the NRSV are ὁ λόγος, a favorite expression of the author (40 times in John), owing no doubt to its prominent, albeit different use in the Prologue (1:1, 14). Interestingly, the author employs the singular form in reference to the sayings or teachings of Jesus in every instance (e.g., 2:22; 4:41, 50; 5:24, 38, *passim*) save three. In each of these exceptions, the plural refers either to the division created over his "words" (7:40; 10:19) or to those who do not love him and therefore do not keep his "words"

many of his disciples turned back and no longer went about with him" (6:66).

Still, not everyone rejects Jesus in the Gospel. Some receive him too; that is, they show him hospitality by welcoming him and his word. Such reception by individuals and groups punctuates the Gospel here and there throughout.

So, for example, consider the Samaritan woman and her village in John 4:4-42. Traveling from Judea to Galilee and being tired from his journey during the heat of the day (v. 6), Jesus sat down by a well in a Samaritan village called Sychar. He encountered a lone Samaritan woman, requested a drink, and then engaged her in a broad-ranging conversation. After he revealed himself to be the Messiah (v. 26), she returned to her town and invited the townspeople to come and meet Jesus too (v. 29). Upon doing so, they invited Jesus to remain with them and he ended up staying with them for two days (v. 40). After relating the fact that many Samaritans believed, literally in Greek, "because of the word of the woman testifying" (διὰ τὸν λόγον τῆς γυναικὸς μαρτυρούσης; v. 39), the narrative concludes: "And many more believed because of his word (διὰ τὸν λόγον αὐτοῦ). They said to the woman, 'It is no longer because of what you said that we believe, for we have heard for ourselves, and we know that this is truly the Savior of the world'" (vv. 41-42). Their warm reception of Jesus should be understood at one level through the lens of hospitality, an important virtue in the ancient world. Accordingly, they received a tired stranger from a foreign land and welcomed him in their town. That they receive Jesus' word, however, crystallizes this hospitality, focusing it in a distinctively Johannine fashion.

Likewise the following story when Jesus was in Cana of Galilee for a second time. After a transitional scene where the author details the Galileans "welcome" (δέχομαι; 4:45) for Jesus, a scene clearly in keeping with the broader theme of hospitality in the Gospel, in Cana he is approached by a royal official whose son was at the point of death in nearby Capernaum. After begging Jesus to come and heal his son, Jesus responds telling the man, "Go; your son will live." The narrator succinctly reports that "the man believed the word that Jesus spoke to him and started on his

---

(14:24). On the other hand, the author consistently uses the plural form of ῥῆμα to refer to Jesus' "words" in the Gospel (3:34; 5:47; 6:63, 68; 8:20, 47; 10:21; 12:47-48; 14:10; 15:7; 17:8). That these two expressions are used virtually synonymously is seen most clearly in their juxtaposition in 12:48: "The one who rejects me and does not receive my word (τὰ ῥήματα) has a judge; on the last day the word (ὁ λόγος) that I have spoken will serve as judge."

way" (v. 50). The reception of Jesus' word is the climactic moment in the narrative, as it is precisely the moment when the son recovers, even though the father does not learn of the boy's recovery until the next day. The narrative concludes noting that the official's "whole household" believed as well (4:53). In the broader context of Jewish hostility to and rejection of Jesus in Jerusalem, a scene which focuses first on Jesus' sign in the Temple (2:13-25), and then on Nicodemus who completely misunderstands Jesus' word in 3:1-10, the immediately juxtaposed scenes related to the Samaritan woman and her town, the Galileans, and the royal official in Cana and his household and their subsequent reception of Jesus, particularly his word, are telling.

This kind of hospitality becomes a major motif in the narrative, as the author uses a cluster of words to talk about reception, favoring the word λαμβάνω which gets employed mostly with the sense of receiving Jesus (1:12; 5:43; 6:21; 13:20) or his word (see, e.g., 3:11, 32-33; 17:8).[16] Importantly, both concepts are combined in 12:48, the structural conclusion to his public ministry: "The one who rejects me and does not receive my word has a judge."

The reception of Jesus is not only stressed at the level of vocabulary, but in terms of characterization too. Repeatedly men and women show this kind of hospitality to Jesus in the Gospel: Jesus' disciples; the man born blind; Mary, Martha, and their brother Lazarus; Mary Magdalene; and others too all receive Jesus and his word in ways commensurate with their role in the narrative.

Abraham and Hospitality

The paradigm for hospitality in Jewish thinking is, of course, Abraham, who went out of his way to receive three special visitors in Genesis 18.[17] Jewish tradition expands on this story in various ways so that Abraham's hospitality ultimately becomes legendary. Consider *The Testament of Abra-*

---

16. The author also uses παραλαμβάνω (1:11) and δέχομαι (4:45), both in reference to receiving Jesus. Reception of the Spirit/Paraclete in like manner surfaces in 14:17 and 20:22.

17. Whether these three visitors were men, angels, or God was a significant matter of debate in early Jewish and Christian writings as well as later Rabbinic texts. See Andrew Arterbury, "Abraham's Hospitality among Jewish and Early Christian Writers: A Tradition History of Gen 18:1-16 and Its Relevance for the Study of the New Testament," *Perspectives in Religious Studies* 30.3 (2003): 359-76.

ham, a Jewish work typically dated to the end of the first century C.E.[18] Abraham's hospitality is one of the most prominent themes in the text, understood as a key measure of his righteousness. The first two verses of the book say it very well:

> Abraham lived the measure of his life, 995 years. All the years of his life he lived in quietness, gentleness, and righteousness, and the righteous man was very hospitable: for he pitched his tent at the crossroads of the oak of Mamre and welcomed everyone — rich and poor, kings and rulers, the crippled and the helpless, friends and strangers, neighbors and passersby — (all) on equal terms did the pious, entirely holy, righteous, and hospitable Abraham welcome (1:1-2).[19]

Christians too were fond of referring to Abraham's incredible hospitality. Both the New Testament and early Christian literature refer to Abraham in this regard. So, for example, the letter to the Hebrews alludes to Abraham's reception of the three visitors in Genesis 18 in order to support the admonition to show hospitality: the author writes, "for by [showing hospitality] some have entertained angels without knowing it" (13:2).[20] The church fathers refer to Abraham's hospitality also to encour-

---

18. See E. P. Sanders's introductory comments to the document in James H. Charlesworth, ed., *The Old Testament Pseudepigrapha: Apocalyptic Literature and Testaments* (New York: Doubleday, 1983), p. 875.

19. See also 1:5; 2:2; 3:7-9; 4:1-4, 6, 9; 17:7; 20:15 (the final text here is a later Christian interpolation). Many Jewish texts celebrate Abraham's hospitality. Putting the matter succinctly is *Genesis Rabbah* (48:9): "The tent of Abraham opened at both sides," which is to say, "whether people came from the west or the east, [Abraham] would welcome them into his home to offer hospitality." The reference was brought to my attention by my friend, Rabbi Dr. David J. Zucker, whose commentary on the passage is quoted above from a letter to the author. He alerted me also to the following texts related to Abraham's hospitality: *b Shevuot 35b; Genesis Rabbah* 43.7; 52.1; *Leviticus Rabbah* 34.8; *Numbers Rabbah* 2.12; *Song of Songs Rabbah* 1.3.3; *Abot deR. Natan* (A)7; see also the sources cited in James L. Kugel, *The Bible As It Was* (Cambridge, MA: The Belknap Press, 1997), pp. 189-91. On the later Midrash compilations cited above, see Jacob Neusner, *The Classics of Judaism: A Textbook and Reader* (Louisville: Westminster John Knox Press, 1995).

20. See the discussion in David A. DeSilva, *Perseverance in Gratitude: A Socio-Rhetorical Commentary on the Epistle "to the Hebrews"* (Grand Rapids: Eerdmans, 2000), pp. 487-88. Cf. also the author of James, who, reflecting on the care of a brother or sister who is naked and hungry, refers to the stories of Abraham and Rahab (2:14-26), although only the latter story speaks specifically of her hospitality, "when she welcomed (ὑποδέχομαι) the messengers and sent them out by another road" (2:25; cf. Heb. 11:31). Note also that the major theme of 2 and 3 John relates to the proper practice of hospitality, although there are no

age liberality toward strangers and the poor. Ambrose, the fourth-century Bishop of Milan, wrote, "Hospitality should not fail at our table . . . this especially was Abraham's praise, for he watched at the door of his tent, that no stranger by any chance might pass by. . . . Therefore as a reward for his hospitality, he received the gift of posterity."[21]

Abraham in John 8:31-59

According to ancient Jewish and early Christian texts then, Abraham and hospitality go together — he is the example *par excellence* of the virtue.[22] Returning to the Gospel then, a Gospel that turns at one level specifically on the theme of hospitality, it should be no surprise that Abraham makes an appearance in John. To be sure, his appearance is timely. Jesus' major discourse with "the Jews," which began in 7:14 at the feast of Tabernacles has, by 8:31-59, turned into a heated argument, complete with invective, innuendo, and finally an attempted mob-lynching. The argument centers on the Jewish rejection of Jesus, their lack of hospitality for him and his word.

For their part, these "Jews" allegedly "had believed" in Jesus, at least their faith is reported as such by the narrator in v. 31.[23] Such belief, how-

---

explicit or implicit allusions to Abraham in those letters. Cf. also the importance of this theme in *Didache* 4.8; 5.2; 11.1-6; 12.1-2; 13.1-7.

21. *Duties of the Clergy* 2.21 (NPNF, 2nd series, 10.59). Cf. his *On Belief in the Resurrection* 2.96 (NPNF, 2nd series, 10.189-90). See also Chrysostom, where the theme is particularly prominent: *The Acts of the Apostles,* Homily 45 (NPNF, 1st series, 11.276-77); *Letters to Olympias* 2.3 (NPNF, 1st series, 9.295); *Homilies on First Corinthians,* Homily 34.10 (NPNF, 1st series, 12.207); *Concerning the Statutes* Homily 2.15 (NPNF, 1st series, 9.349): "Abraham . . . looked around wherever there chanced to be a stranger, or a poor man, in order that he might succour poverty, and hospitably entertain the traveler." Of course, I would be remiss to neglect mentioning that the theme of hospitality figures prominently in Greco-Roman literature in antiquity too. On the topic generally, see L. J. Bolchazy, *Hospitality in Early Rome: Livy's Concept of Its Humanizing Force* (Chicago: Ares, 1977); and with respect to Christian studies in particular, see the fine study of Andrew Arterbury, *Entertaining Angels: Early Christian Hospitality in Its Mediterranean Setting,* NTM 8 (Sheffield: Sheffield Phoenix Press, 2005). Arterbury's earlier study, "Abraham's Hospitality," is a succinct and quite helpful review of the topic. Interestingly, in his discussion of the relevant New Testament texts, he nowhere refers to the Johannine literature, a significant omission for his study.

22. Lot figures oftentimes as an exemplar of hospitality in both of these traditions too; see further, T. D. Alexander, "Lot's Hospitality: A Clue to His Righteousness" *JBL* 104 (1985): 289-91.

23. On the nature of this faith, see below.

ever, is perhaps akin to the belief "the Jews" showed earlier in Jerusalem in ch. 2, when the narrator reported that Jesus nevertheless "would not entrust himself to them . . . for he himself knew what was in everyone" (2:24-25). The narration proceeds to make Nicodemus the poster-child of such insufficient faith, a faith that rests on signs alone, in ch. 3.[24] In one sense, history repeats itself here in ch. 8. As soon as Jesus challenges them, they challenge and question him in v. 33, and then implicitly challenge his relationship to Abraham (v. 39) and to God while simultaneously attempting to portray him as a child of fornication (v. 41). Then, responding to Jesus' *ad hominem* attack in v. 44, "the Jews" return the insult, characterizing Jesus pejoratively as a Samaritan and as demon-possessed in v. 48, repeating the latter point again in v. 52. After questioning Jesus dismissively in v. 53 and again sarcastically in v. 57, they attempt to kill him in v. 59. The Prologue describes the situation in our narrative well: "He came to what was his own and his own people did not accept him" (1:11).

For his part, several times in the discourse, Jesus refers to their rejection of him and his word. The wholesale appropriation of the theme of hospitality, or in this case, the lack thereof becomes clear particularly in this narrative. Jesus drives the discourse forward here with his explicit and implicit condemnations of Jewish inhospitality. So, to highlight their inhospitality, Jesus says:

8:31: "If you continue in my word you are truly my disciples. . . ."
8:34: "Very truly I tell you, everyone who commits sin is a slave to sin."[25]
8:37: "I know that you are descendants of Abraham; yet you look for an opportunity to kill me, because there is no place in you for my word."
8:40: ". . . but now you are trying to kill me, a man who has told you the truth that I heard from God."
8:42: "If God were your Father, you would love me, for I came from God . . . he sent me."

24. See my "Nicodemus, Lazarus and the Fear of 'the Jews' in the Fourth Gospel," in *Repetitions and Variations in the Fourth Gospel: Style, Text, Interpretation*, ed. G. Van Belle, M. Labahn, and P. Maritz, Bibliotheca Ephemeridum Theologicarum Lovaniensium 223 (Leuven: Peeters Press, 2009), pp. 199-212.

25. In the context of John, rejecting Jesus and his word is the sin to which Jesus refers. This is clearly a departure from the Pauline understanding of slavery to sin (cf. Rom. 6:15-23).

8:43: "Why do you not understand what I say? It is because you cannot accept my word."

8:44: "You are from your father the devil, and you choose to do your father's desires. He was a murderer from the begin-ning."

8:45: "But because I tell the truth, you do not believe me."

8:46: "If I tell the truth, why do you not believe me?"

8:47: "The reason you do not hear [my words] is that you are not from God."

8:49: "I honor my Father, and you dishonor me."

8:51: "Whoever keeps my word will never see death"

8:55: ". . . if I would say that I do not know [God], I would be a liar like you."

In the midst of all of this discord, Jesus said, "If you were Abraham's children, you would be doing what Abraham did" (8:39b). Their actions are manifestly unlike their father's.

But what exactly did Abraham do? And when did he do it? Can we even attempt an answer to these questions? First off, we must be clear: Jesus refers in 8:39 to "the works" (τὰ ἔργα) that Abraham did. Presumably because of this plural, Rudolf Bultmann writes: "Jn. 8.39 scarcely has special works [of Abraham] in view."[26] In other words, it is not any *one work* in particular that Abraham did, but rather the works of a life devoted to obeying the voice of God. Indeed, the LORD said to Isaac after Abraham's death, "Abraham obeyed my voice and kept my charge, my command-ments, my statutes, and my laws" (Gen. 26:5; cf. 12:4; 22:15-18). Many schol-ars follow Bultmann's lead and do not even raise the questions we have raised above.[27] They simply assume the widest possible referent: Abraham was obedient to the voice of God; "the Jews" are therefore unlike their fa-

26. *The Gospel of John* (ET Oxford: Blackwell, 1971), p. 442, n. 6.
27. Cf. the major commentaries on the Fourth Gospel by R. E. Brown *(John)*, C. K. Barrett *(The Gospel According to St. John,* 2nd ed. [Philadelphia: Westminster Press, 1978]), F. F. Bruce *(The Gospel of John* [Grand Rapids: Eerdmans, 1983]), D. M. Smith *(John,* Abingdon New Testament Commentaries [Nashville: Abingdon Press, 1999]), E. Haenchen *(John,* 2 vols., Hermeneia [ET Philadelphia: Fortress Press, 1984]), D. A. Carson *(The Gospel According to John* [Grand Rapids: Eerdmans, 1991]), T. Brodie *(The Gospel According to John: A Literary and Theological Commentary* [Oxford: Oxford University Press, 1993]), R. Schnackenburg *(The Gospel According to St. John,* 3 vols. [ET vols. 1-2 New York: Seabury, 1980; vol. 3 New York: Crossroad, 1982]), L. Morris *(John)*.

ther when they reject the word of Jesus. Beasley-Murray, for example, notes that their attempt to kill Jesus in 8:59 "is totally opposed to everything known about Abraham, whose life was marked by faith in and obedience to God's word."[28]

Others see in Jesus' statement in v. 39 simply an allusion to Abraham's reception of the LORD in Genesis 18:1-33. These scholars suggest that Jesus was only challenging "the Jews" to receive him in the way Abraham received the LORD. E. C. Hoskyns, for example, writes when commenting on this text, "it was the distinction of Abraham to have received the emissaries of God with faith and with obedience. . . . His physical descendants, however, reject Him whom God has sent, and plan his murder."[29] Likewise, A. T. Lincoln writes of John 8:39, "Presumably in view here is Abraham's reception of and hospitality to God's messengers in Gen. 18:1-8."[30]But can more be said on the subject? In view of how this specific narrative develops and concludes in 8:56-59, and in keeping with the Gospel's emphasis on the deity and pre-existence of Jesus, we will argue for a more concrete understanding. In order to make our case, we must not miss the unvarying prominence of Abraham and particular details related to his story in our narrative. Truly, Abraham's story is *the* crucial background to the story of John 8:31-59. Readers should note at least the following details:

First, Abraham undergirds the entire narrative, beginning to end, being mentioned explicitly eleven times in the passage.[31] He never drops from sight. The repetition of his name and the spacing with which it occurs throughout, especially with its prominence at the beginning and the end of the narrative, demonstrates his importance for the story. Of course, this point comes into sharper relief when one notices Abraham's conspicuous absence in the rest of the Gospel. Abraham figures only here in John's Gospel, nowhere else.

Second, "the Jews" invoke Abraham as their father repeatedly in this section (vv. 33, 39, 53), a point that Jesus appears to concede at the beginning of the narrative (v. 37) and at the end (v. 56) even if he seemingly withdraws it in the middle (vv. 39-41) when he proceeds to declare that they are from their "father the devil" (v. 44). The point, of course, turns on the distinction between the σπέρμα of Abraham and the τέκνα of Abra-

28. *John,* Word Biblical Commentary (Dallas: Word, 1987), p. 134.
29. Hoskyns, *Fourth Gospel,* p. 342.
30. Lincoln, *John,* p. 271.
31. 8:33, 37, 39 (3x), 40, 52, 53, 56, 57, 58; see also Brown, *John,* 1:361.

93

ham. Jesus will allow them the former term, that is, they are physically descendants of Abraham, but in their reaction to Jesus they show that they are not his true children.[32]

Third, our narrative is preceded by the notice that "as he was saying these things many believed (ἐπίστευσαν) in him" (v. 30). Then our narrative begins when Jesus addresses himself to "the Jews who had believed (πεπιστευκότας) in him" (v. 31). A number of scholars have suggested that the group in v. 30 should be distinguished from the group in v. 31. Whereas the former are likely legitimate followers of Jesus, the latter had believed at one time and evidently do so no longer.[33] Hence Jesus' comments midway through our narrative: he asserts that they do not believe (πιστεύετε) in 8:45 and then asks why they do not believe (πιστεύετε) in 8:46.

The verb used in each of these texts is precisely the verb in the LXX of Genesis 15:6: "And [Abraham] believed (ἐπίστευσεν) the LORD, and the LORD reckoned it to him as righteousness."[34] The importance of this verse in Genesis for early Christian writers need not detain us here. While the verb used here is common enough for this Gospel,[35] its use in the context of a narrative entirely devoted to the story of Abraham is hardly coincidental. To put the matter more properly would require our recognition that its prominence in this Gospel overall is related to its us-

32. So also John A. Dennis, *Jesus' Death and the Gathering of True Israel*, WUNT 217 (Tübingen: Mohr Siebeck, 2006), p. 129. Thomas B. Dozeman's study *"Sperma Abraam* in John 8," *CBQ* 42 (1980): 342-58, accepts the two-level drama hypothesis for the Gospel and argues on that basis that the σπέρμα Ἀβραάμ in this passage represents "Christian Jews who advocate a law-observing mission. This law-observing mission comes into conflict with the law-free Christians in the Johannine community, resulting in a controversy similar to ones reflected in the Pauline corpus" (p. 343). Thus this story is not really about Jesus and "the Jews" in the temple but about a later controversy involving the Johannine community and other early Christian groups. Cf. also C. H. Dodd's essay, "Behind a Johannine Dialogue," in *More New Testament Studies* (Grand Rapids: Eerdmans, 1968), pp. 41-57.

33. Of course, such a reading is hotly contested. It is likely that the narrator's use of the perfect participle πεπιστευκότας in 8:31 intends a pluperfect meaning: this group had believed in Jesus but does so no longer. See Terry Griffith's helpful discussion in "'The Jews Who Had Believed in Him' (John 8:31) and the Motif of Apostasy in the Gospel of John," in *The Gospel of John and Christian Theology*, ed. Richard Bauckham and Carl Mosser (Grand Rapids: Eerdmans, 2008), pp. 183-92. See also the short note of James Swetnam, "The Meaning of πεπιστευκότας in John 8,31," *Biblica* 61 (1980): 106-9.

34. Interestingly, the verb is used only here in the Abraham story in Genesis.

35. Various forms of the verb occur 98 times in John. By contrast, the verb occurs only 34 times in the entire Synoptic tradition.

age in early Christian circles, and its usage there is directly related to the text of Genesis 15:6.

Fourth, Abraham "rejoiced" and was "glad" when he saw Jesus' day in v. 56. The notion of "seeing" God, so important to this Gospel since the Prologue (1:18), has important connections to the story of Abraham too (cf. Gen. 12:7; 17:1; 18:1-2).[36]

Fifth, in v. 57, "the Jews" mock Jesus' claim in the previous verse, sarcastically questioning if Jesus has seen Abraham (8:57). The narrator's use of the statements and questions of Jesus' opponents is quite instructive in the Gospel, oftentimes revealing truth lost on those making the comment or asking the question.

Sixth and most important, Abraham creates the point of contrast in the conclusion in v. 58. Jesus' statement, "Very truly, I tell you, before Abraham was, I am" is so dramatic, indeed to Jewish sensibilities it is so blasphemous, that they "picked up stones to throw at him" right in the Temple complex (v. 59). The import of vv. 56-58 for our argument will be discussed in what follows.

Finally, there is also a clear allusion to the story of Abraham's sons, Isaac and Ishmael, in John 8:35: "The slave does not have a permanent place in the household; the son has a place there forever."[37] Significantly, in the next clause Jesus implicitly links himself with Isaac: "So if the Son sets you free, you will be free indeed" (8:36). Jesus' connection to Isaac will be important later on in the narrative, as we anticipate how Abraham saw Jesus' day and rejoiced (8:56).[38]

---

36. On the theme generally in Biblical Studies, see the outstanding work of Richard Elliot Friedman, *The Hidden Face of God* (San Francisco: HarperCollins, 1995).

37. Cf. Gen. 21:8-14; so also Dozeman, *"Sperma Abraam,"* p. 355.

38. In addition, there are a number of interesting correspondences of vocabulary between the LXX of Genesis 18 and the Gospel of John. I have not explored them and some of them may be attributed to nothing more than coincidence; in view of the Fourth Gospel's thorough steeping in, and often playful use of, Old Testament texts, however, there may be more here than meets the eye. Consider the following examples: the twice-repeated verb τρέχω is used in Gen. 18:2, 7 to describe Abraham's running, and the same twice-repeated verb is used to describe Mary's and the two disciples' running in John 20:2, 4; the verb νίπτω is used in both Gen. 18:4 and John 13:5 (here an infinitive) to refer to the washing of feet; Abraham invites the visitors to rest "under the tree" (18:4) and then stands "under the tree" himself (Gen. 18:8), whereas Jesus repeats twice that he saw Nathanael "under the fig tree" (1:48, 50); the noun σκηνή ("tent") figures prominently in Gen. 18:1, 2, 6, 9, 10, whereas the verbal form σκηνόω ("tented") is hugely important in John 1:14; the twice-repeated promise to return in "due season" (Gen. 18:10, 14) includes the noun ὥρα ("hour"), a critical noun in

John 8:39-40: The Works of Abraham

Recognizing Abraham as the *crux interpretum* for our narrative,[39] how might we argue for a more concrete understanding of the text, an understanding that is commensurate with the importance of Jesus' deity and pre-existence in this Gospel?

Paul Miller notes that for the author of John "Scripture is the enduring record of those who saw the activity of the divine Logos prior to its appearance in Jesus and then testified to what they had seen."[40] If Miller is right, and he surely is, then scholars should be seeing more in the twice repeated reference to the works of Abraham in 8:39-40.

First, the reference to the "works of Abraham" in these verses, far from being merely a generic reference to his obedience to the command of God, specifically refers in this context to Abraham's encounter with the LORD in Genesis 18. Since in both Jewish and Christian traditions Abraham is the exemplar of hospitality, the context of Genesis 18, the text behind his exemplary behavior, is very much at home in our narrative. Showing hospitality to the one sent from God, speaking the word of God, figures prominently in the text at hand, as we have seen. Therefore, if we give the major motif of Jesus' deity and pre-existence in the Gospel its due weight here, the necessary conclusion is that "the works" of Abraham in

---

Jesus' understanding of his mission in John (see, e.g., 2:4; 4:21, 23; 5:25, 28; 7:30; 8:20; 12:23, *passim*); the twice-repeated use of the noun υἱός ("son") is found in both Gen. 18:10, 14 and John 8:35-36; the verb φοβέω ("afraid") is used to describe both Sarah (Gen. 18:15) and Jesus' disciples (John 6:20); Genesis uses the verb κρύπτω ("hide") in reference to the LORD's plan to speak with Abraham about his intention to judge Sodom (Gen. 18:17), whereas in John the same verb is used to describe Jesus' hiding from "the Jews" after they attempt to kill him (8:59); Abraham's "becoming" (γίνομαι) is important in both texts (Gen. 18:18; John 8:58); both texts employ the verb φύλασσω ("keep") similarly: Gen. 18:19 refers to keeping the "way of the LORD" and John 12:47 to keeping "the words" of Jesus; the combination of "righteousness and justice" (δικαιοσύνη καὶ κρίσις) is found in both texts (Gen. 18:19; John 16:8); cf. also Abraham's ἐγὼ δέ εἰμι in Gen. 18:27 with Jesus' ἐγὼ εἰμί in John 8:58; finally, both texts make use of the word πεντήκοντα ("fifty"; Gen. 18:24, 26, 28; John 8:57).

39. *Contra* Barnabas Linders, "Discourse and Tradition: The Use of the Sayings of Jesus in the Discourse of the Fourth Gospel," *JSNT* 13 (1981): 83-101, who maintains that Abraham's role is only "ancillary to the main argument" (p. 90).

40. "They Saw His Glory and Spoke of Him," in *Hearing the Old Testament in the New Testament*, ed. Stanley Porter (Grand Rapids: Eerdmans, 2006), p. 134. Miller's discussion of Johannine hermeneutics is very well conceived, drawing particular attention to the witness Abraham, Moses, Isaiah, and John the Baptist provided on Jesus' behalf.

8:39-40 relate to his reception of the LORD in Genesis 18, which, in the Johannine theological landscape, was really his reception of an earlier manifestation of the Word, who is now Jesus. Jesus is saying in effect, "If you were Abraham's children, you would be showing the hospitality that Abraham showed when he welcomed me and received my word. In trying to kill me, you are doing the opposite of what Abraham did." In a Gospel dominated at every turn by Jesus' deity and pre-existence, the burden of proof should reside with those who would seek to argue against this simple understanding.

Remember, Jesus' rejection by "the Jews" is stated precisely in terms of hospitality in the Prologue: "He came to what was his own, and his own people did not accept him" (1:11). Importantly, his reception is described in the next verse of the Prologue through this lens too, adding only the virtually synonymous idea of belief to the equation: "But to all who *received* (ἔλαβον) him, *who believed* (τοῖς πιστεύουσιν) in his name, he gave power to become children of God" (1:12). On another occasion, when Jesus was arguing with "the Jews" in the synagogue of Capernaum, they asked, "what must we do to perform the *works* of God?" (6:28). Jesus responded, describing "the *work* of God" as singular: "that you *believe* (πιστεύητε) in him whom he has sent" (6:29). This is precisely what Abraham did in Genesis 15:6. As in the Prologue, in John 8 we see how the two themes, hospitality and belief, come together so clearly. Hospitality for Jesus is simply another way of referring to belief in him, belief that continues in his word and does not rely on signs alone.[41] The two themes merge seamlessly throughout the Gospel. The works of Abraham therefore refer at once to his warm welcome of an earlier manifestation of the Word as in Genesis 18 and to his belief in the LORD as in Genesis 15 when "the word (ῥῆμα) of the LORD came to him" (Gen. 15:4).[42]

---

41. On the difficult relationship between signs and faith and their rather "ambiguous function" in the Gospel of John, see Craig S. Keener, *The Gospel of John: A Commentary*, 2 vols. (Peabody, MA: Hendrickson, 2003), 1:275-79.

42. Is it possible, in the context of John 8:31-59, that "the works" of Abraham (both times specifically in the plural in 8:39-40) also anticipate Jesus' point in 8:56? Jesus says to "the Jews," "Your ancestor Abraham *rejoiced* that he would see my day; he saw it and was *glad*." Abraham's rejoicing and gladness at the sight of Jesus' day serves to flesh out further his "works" in 8:39-40. His reaction to the ministry of Jesus therefore is in stark contrast to that of "the Jews."

John 8:56: When Abraham Saw Jesus

At least since the time of Irenaeus's comments on the passage in the late second century, John 8:56 has proven a difficult text.[43] Indeed, Linders refers to the argument in these final verses as "tortuous."[44]

Understood from purely a Jewish background, Abraham saw the future. Consider, for example, the author of the late first- to mid-second-century c.e. *Apocalypse of Abraham,* who spends the majority of the text (chs. 9–32) relating the visions of Abraham. In 9:6, God says to Abraham, "I will announce to you guarded things and you will see great things which you have not seen, because you desired to search for me, and I called you my beloved" (9:6). Another Jewish text, 4 Ezra, dated to approximately the same time, makes a similar claim about Abraham's visions. Ezra says to God, "You loved [Abraham] and to him only you revealed the end of the times" (3:14). Rabbi Akiba, who died in the *Bar Kokhba* rebellion against Rome in 135 c.e., also bears witness to this understanding of Abraham's vision of the future. Basing their midrashic claims on the "deep sleep" and the "terrifying darkness" that fell upon Abraham in Genesis 15:12-16, when God revealed to him that his descendants would go into slavery and be oppressed for four hundred years, these authors all understand Abraham to have seen the future.[45] That three unrelated texts from roughly the same period make reference to the way God granted visions to Abraham demonstrates that the concept of his visionary experiences pre-dates the second century and conceivably therefore goes back well into the first century if not earlier still. Doubtless, it is this background that forces Schnackenburg to conclude that "Jewish speculations definitely form the context" of John 8:56.[46]

---

43. See his *Against Heresies,* 4.5-7 (ANF 1.466-70). Irenaeus takes a remarkably similar approach to the text as the one presented here. See also the inauthentic longer recension of Ignatius of Antioch's letter to the *Magnesians* 9 (ANF 1.62), which also makes reference to this text. If this latter text were authentic, this would be the earliest reference to John 8:56 in Christian literature. On the subject of the letters of Ignatius and their authenticity, see especially the dated yet very helpful discussion in ANF 1.45-48.

44. Linders, "Discourse and Tradition," p. 96.

45. See other later Jewish sources that make similar claims in Kugel, *The Bible As It Was,* pp. 168-70.

46. Schnackenburg, *John,* 2:222. A. T. Hanson, *The Prophetic Gospel: A Study of John and the Old Testament* (Edinburgh: T&T Clark, 1991), p. 130, notes that in his study of this verse "all other commentators whom I have consulted adopt either the view that Abraham was shown a pre-vision of Christ, or that he had (as the Logos) encountered Abraham in paradise."

But can we say more on the subject? Some early Christians understood the reference to Abraham's vision of Jesus' day in 8:56 quite differently. Indeed, why would they have understood this text simply in the light
of Genesis 15:12, which speaks of Abraham's "terrifying darkness" (φόβος
σκοτεινὸς μέγας) during the vision,[47] when John 8:56 refers to an Abraham
who "rejoiced" (ἀγαλλιάομαι) and was "glad" (χαίρω) when he saw Jesus'
day?

Nearer to our context of rejoicing and gladness, and in keeping with
early Christian understandings of this text, are the various references to
the laughter that accompanies both the promise and the birth of Isaac. At
first, in Genesis 17:17, Abraham himself laughs incredulously at the idea
that he will have a son. In Genesis 18:12-15, Sarah laughs at the prospect too,
and the narrative emphasizes that fact when the LORD questions Abraham
about it and then Sarah in what follows. Laughter follows Isaac's birth too.
Sarah said, "God has brought laughter for me; everyone who hears will
laugh with me" (v. 6). Besides the Hebrew play on the name Isaac, which
means "he laughs," note the climactic and altogether fitting poetry that begins the story of Isaac's birth:

> The LORD dealt with Sarah as he had said,
> and the LORD did for Sarah as he had promised. (21:1)

Note also the feast Abraham made when Isaac was weaned (21:8).
Thus, while the laughter in Genesis that precedes Isaac's birth comes off as
incredulity, the laughter that follows seems joyfully sincere. More important, Jewish tradition related to the birth of Isaac speaks of Abraham's
great rejoicing at the birth of his son. The second-century B.C.E. Jewish
text Jubilees refers explicitly and repeatedly to Abraham's rejoicing at both
the prospect (14:21-22) and the birth (16:19-20, 25-27, 31; 17:1-4) of Isaac.[48]

It is the connection our text makes between Jesus and Isaac that begins to tie this all together. As we have seen, Jesus and Isaac are linked early
on in John 8:35-36: Jesus says, referring to Isaac, "the son has a place [in the
household] forever" and then immediately says of himself, "So if the Son
makes you free, you will be free indeed."[49]

---

47. Note how the second-century B.C.E. text Jubilees amplifies the fear of Abraham
when it relates the story of Genesis 15: "And it came to pass when the sun set that a terror fell
upon Abram. And behold a great dark horror fell upon him" (14:13).

48. Cf. Philo, *De Mutatione Nominum*, 154-69.

49. See the similar connection that Paul makes of these ideas in Gal. 3:16; 4:1-7.

Holding this connection in mind, consider then the *Akedah*. While nothing in the text of Genesis would suggest that Abraham rejoiced at the so-called "binding of Isaac" (although see Jubilees 18:17-19 in this regard), still, Abraham's statement to Isaac that "God himself will provide the lamb" (Gen. 22:8) becomes critical to the theological presentation of Jesus in John. Only in this Gospel do we read, in a twice-repeated confession of John the Baptist, that "Jesus is the lamb of God" (1:29, 35).[50] This clear allusion to the *Akedah* in John 1 comes to its proper conclusion as the theme merges with the Gospel's important Passover motif. These come together most obviously when Jesus is crucified at "about noon" on the "day of Preparation for the Passover" (19:14), around the time that the Passover lambs are beginning to be slaughtered in the Temple for the festival that began later that evening.[51] Likewise, when the guards approached Jesus in order to expedite his death by breaking his legs, they found Jesus dead already. The narrator records that they did not break them, "so that the Scripture might be fulfilled, 'None of his bones shall be broken'" (19:31-36). The quotation modifies the text of Exodus 12:46 (cf. Num. 9:12), which gives instructions about the Passover lamb. In John, therefore, Jesus is God's lamb, "who takes away the sin of the world" (1:29).

For our purposes, one major question remains in Genesis 22: How did Abraham know that God would provide the lamb? The answer according to our narrator is this: Abraham saw Jesus' day. We need not rely solely on the Jewish traditions that relate to Abraham's visionary experiences, however, to make sense of this information. Several features of the text of the LXX of Genesis 22 support this connection between these two texts.[52] Three times the text of Genesis emphasizes that the place that Abraham was to sacrifice his son was a place that God "told" him about (22:2, 3, 9).[53] But in Genesis 22:4, the text goes out of its way to indicate that Abraham "looked up" with

50. On Jesus as "lamb" in this Gospel, particularly as paschal lamb, see the helpful presentation of Brown, *John*, 1:58-63.

51. On the theological significance of the timing, see the very helpful comments in Keener, *John*, 2:1129-31.

52. Unfortunately, I received a copy of David Moessner's forthcoming essay, "'Abraham Saw My Day': Making Greater Sense of John 8:48-59 from the LXX Version than the MT of Genesis 22," only a couple of days before my essay went to press. I was unable therefore to interact with it on any significant level in this essay. Still, I am struck by the similarity of his argument to mine in what follows.

53. Both the Hebrew as well as the LXX in these verses refer to God's "saying" the place, not "showing" as in the NRSV. The RSV and the NIV render the expression more literally; the TNIV follows the NRSV in v. 2 and the NIV in vv. 3 and 9!

"his eyes"[54] and "saw the place far away." Not only does the text of John repeat the notion of Abraham's "seeing" twice (i.e., "Abraham rejoiced that he would *see* my day; he *saw* it and was glad"), but the verb "saw" in Genesis 22:4 is precisely the verb used of Abraham's "seeing" in John 8:56.[55]

That the place for sacrifice was "far away" (μακρόθεν) in Genesis might have been understood by our narrator to highlight the distance between Abraham and Jesus, the very point "the Jews" will make when they respond in 8:57. Note also that the event in Genesis takes place "on the third day" (τῇ ἡμέρᾳ τῇ τρίτῃ), an expression paralleled exactly in the Greek of John 2:1. The language there, when Jesus was in Cana, foreshadows Jesus' own cryptic reference to his resurrection on the third day when he is in Jerusalem in John 2:19. That the narrator finds the language important is obvious: "the Jews" repeat it again in 2:20 (although they misunderstand) and the narrator explains Jesus' point in 2:21-22.

To bring our discussion of this verse to a conclusion, Jesus' statement in 8:56, that Abraham saw his day and was glad, does not refer to Abraham's reception of an earlier manifestation of the Word, but to his vision of Jesus' "day," or, more commonly in this Gospel, "his hour."[56] While the theme of Jesus' pre-existence is not to the fore in 8:56, in 8:57 the theme surfaces again, when the narrator redirects, employing Jesus' interlocutors to make the theological point clear. To 8:57 we now turn.

John 8:57: When Jesus saw Abraham

This background with reference to the *Akedah* in the LXX of Genesis 22 helps to explain the unexpected question "the Jews" ask next: "Have you seen Abraham?" The question is most telling. Note first that it is preceded by their comment that Jesus is not yet fifty years old. While the reference to his age can be nuanced in various ways,[57] the purpose of their dismissive

---

54. The NRSV does not refer to "his eyes," but both the Hebrew and LXX do.

55. Consider also the repeated reference to Abraham's "seeing" the visitors in Gen. 18:2: "He *looked up* and *saw* three men standing near him. When he *saw* them. . . ."

56. Thematically, the text relates to Jesus' earlier comment that "[Moses] wrote about me" (5:46) and the narrator's later comment that "[Isaiah] saw his glory and spoke about him" (12:41).

57. See the discussion in Schnackenburg, *John*, 2:223. Interestingly, Irenaeus uses this text to support his view that Jesus was older than forty years at this point in his ministry (*Against Heresies*, 1.22.6 [ANF 1.392]).

comment in relation to their sarcastic question that follows is simply to say, as so many scholars have noted, that compared to Jesus' young age, under fifty, he could not possibly have seen Abraham who lived so long ago.[58] While scholars have rightly handled the text-critical issue related to their question,[59] they have not fully reckoned with its import.

Before we can address that, however, we need to take a short digression into the narrative art of the Gospel. Generally, people in the Gospel of John do one of two things in response to Jesus' statements — they either take him too literally, thereby showing their complete lack of understanding,[60] or they speak truths unwittingly, thereby creating irony in the text.[61] Both are prominent techniques in the Gospel. As examples of the former tendency one need look no further than the story of Nicodemus. When Jesus says to Nicodemus that "no one can see the kingdom of God without being born from above" (3:3; cf. 3:7), Nicodemus misunderstands and questions whether one can enter a mother's womb a second time to be reborn (3:4). Nicodemus simply misses the point.

Consider also the Samaritan woman in John 4. When Jesus challenges the woman to drink the water that he will give her so that she will never be thirsty again (4:13-14), she responds by saying: "Sir, give me this water, so that I may never be thirsty or have to keep coming here to draw water" (4:15). The woman misses Jesus' symbolic reference to the Spirit's ability to give life and thinks only on the literal level of physical thirst. The woman therefore, like Nicodemus, misses the point.

But the Gospel does not just employ misunderstanding alone to show that Jesus' statements convey meanings that move well beyond the merely physical and literal: it also uses irony. Consider among the many examples in the Gospel the obvious irony in the statements of Caiaphas in

58. So, e.g., Barrett, *John*, p. 352: "Probably . . . no more is intended than to point to the contrast between a short life-time and the great interval separating Jesus and Abraham."

59. The reading, ἔχεις καὶ Αβραὰμ ἑώρακας ("Have you seen Abraham?") is supported by the majority of scholars primarily because it is more broadly attested in the ms. tradition. See the discussion in Bruce Metzger, *A Texual Commentary on the Greek New Testament* (Stuttgart: United Bible Society, 1975), pp. 226-27. The variant, ἔχεις καὶ Αβραὰμ ἑώρακέν σε ("Has Abraham seen you?") is almost universally dismissed owing to the fact that it appears to be an assimilation to Jesus' statement in v. 56: i.e., "Abraham saw my day" so "the Jews" respond, "Has Abraham seen you?"

60. See on the concept of misunderstanding in the Gospel R. Alan Culpepper, *Anatomy of the Fourth Gospel* (Philadelphia: Fortress Press, 1983), pp. 152-65.

61. See the outstanding study of irony in John by Paul D. Duke, *Irony in the Fourth Gospel* (Atlanta: John Knox Press, 1985); cf. also Culpepper, *Anatomy*, pp. 165-80.

ch. 11 or Pilate in ch. 18. Both are used to great effect by the narrator. First, in 11:49-53, it is Caiaphas's statement to the council that "it is better for you to have one man die for the people than to have the whole nation destroyed" that provokes the council finally to put Jesus to death.[62] The use of irony could not be more obvious. Jesus, according to John's Gospel, will die for the people.[63] The narrator's commentary on Caiaphas's statement substantiates this understanding. Caiaphas's unwitting claim is clearly ironic.[64]

So also is Pilate's declaration in John 19:14. When Pilate announces Jesus as "the king of the Jews," he is obviously not making a statement about Jesus with which he agrees; he is simply using the title to procure an oath of fidelity to the Roman emperor from "the Jews." It is only after they have said "we have no king but the emperor" that Pilate releases Jesus to be crucified (v. 16). Likewise, when Pilate has an inscription written in Hebrew, Latin, and Greek and put on the cross proclaiming Jesus the "king of the Jews" (19:19-20), he is not proclaiming his own view of Jesus; he is rather mocking those who would set themselves up as such and warning potential claimants to the title that such aspirations will not be tolerated or go unpunished. But Pilate's power is not only undone by Jesus (19:11); it is also undone by the narrator, who uses Pilate's own words against him. In the world of the narrator and his audience, Pilate is the unwitting fool whose speech and actions are profoundly ironic. The narrator has been employing the motif of kingship and messiahship related to Jesus in many ways since early on in the story.[65] Indeed, Nathanael proclaims him the "King of Israel" as early as 1:49. It is a testimony Jesus does not reject, even if he will redefine it in his own way later on in the story (18:36-37).

To sum up, people responding to Jesus in the Gospel either take him

---

62. On other plans or attempts to take Jesus' life in the Gospel, see 5:18; 7:1, 19, 25; 8:37, 40, 59; 10:31-33; 11:8; 12:10. This scene in ch. 11 is presented as more decisive, as it is a definitive ruling on the part of the council.

63. The narrator's use of the preposition ὑπὲρ ("for") here and in other texts related to the death of Jesus is almost formulaic. So, for example, the bread Jesus will give "for the life of the world" is his flesh (6:51); Jesus, as the good shepherd, will lay down his life "for the sheep" (10:11, 15); Jesus' love command is fulfilled most decisively in laying down one's life "for one's friends" (15:13). On ὑπέρ in John, see Dennis, *Jesus' Death,* pp. 13-24.

64. The narrator repeats the claim for emphasis just before the crucifixion too, in order to make the connection even clearer (18:14).

65. See Larry Hurtado, *Lord Jesus Christ: Devotion to Jesus in Earliest Christianity* (Grand Rapids: Eerdmans, 2003), pp. 358-64.

too literally, thereby demonstrating their lack of understanding, or they speak truths unwittingly, truths with which they would surely disagree, thereby creating irony in the text.

Returning to our issue in 8:57, when "the Jews" ask Jesus "have you seen Abraham?" how is the narrator using their question? Are they simply misunderstanding him, or should readers be attentive to the possible truth inherent in their question? The majority of scholars understand this as another classic example of misunderstanding in the Gospel, thereby missing entirely the question's ironic force.[66] But viewed as irony, "the Jews'" incredulous and sarcastic question becomes in the hands of a skillful narrator a moment of Christological truth, a truth understood only within the broader framework of Jesus' deity and pre-existence in the Gospel. So while "the Jews" clearly assume a negative answer to the question, the narrator intends for readers to answer in the affirmative. Yes, Jesus did see Abraham. The question, then, is "when?"[67]

As we have seen, Jesus already explicitly referred to his visit with Abraham in Genesis 18, when the patriarch received the pre-existent Word so graciously. Still, references in Genesis to the LORD's "seeing" are wholly absent in that text. And while there are a number of texts that make clear that the LORD "appeared" to Abraham (Gen. 12:7; 17:1; 18:1[68]), employing the aorist middle/passive of ὁράω, none of these places specifically talks about the LORD seeing Abraham, even though the idea is implicit in his appearance.

---

66. So, e.g., Smith, *John*, p. 188, writes of 8:57, "in effect ['the Jews'] misunderstood in a typically Johannine way, seeing Jesus only as a man less than fifty years old"; so also Lincoln, *John*, p. 276, who speaks of "the Jews" as "totally misunderstanding Jesus by remaining on the earthly level." Lincoln goes on to say, however, that "their incomprehension provides the foil for Jesus' climactic statement about himself." Cf. also Bruce, *John*, p. 205; Carson, *John*, pp. 357-58; Morris, *John*, p. 419. Brodie, *John*, p. 336, on the other hand, explicitly refers to the irony in their question.

67. Other questions in the Gospel are clearly used ironically too. Consider the obvious irony when the Pharisees ask the temple police, "Has anyone of the authorities or of the Pharisees believed in him?" (7:48). Of course, the Pharisees expect a negative answer. Our narrator not only brings Nicodemus into the discussion precisely at this point (7:50-52), but makes clear later in the narrative that "many, even of the authorities, believed in him" (12:42). Or consider the question Pilate put to Jesus at his trial: "What is truth?" (19:38). Pilate (anticipating post-modernism?) evidently cannot even fathom an answer. Duke (*Irony*, p. 130) notes, however, that the profound irony in the question "lies in our knowledge that the one to whom the question about truth is asked is himself the Truth (14:6)."

68. Cf. the related ideas in texts such as Gen. 16:13-14; 17:22; 18:22, 33.

The story of the *Akedah* in the LXX, however, plays on this theme of "seeing" in important and remarkable ways. In Genesis 22:8, for example, when Isaac asked about the sacrifice itself, Abraham declared that the LORD "will see (ὄψεται),"[69] which in the context explicitly refers to the lamb. Hence our translations: "God himself *will provide* the lamb."

After Abraham attempted to sacrifice his son, however, the same verb switches to an aorist form, when Abraham calls the place of sacrifice simply "the LORD saw (Κύριος εἶδεν)." Note, importantly, that he does not explicitly mention the ram in 22:14. Modern translations assume the text here refers again to the LORD's provision of the ram — hence the NRSV's "The LORD will provide." Such a translation, however, misses the double entendre in the text. To be sure, in the simple phrase "the LORD saw" readers are to understand that the LORD provided the ram, but they are also to see this in light of the climactic pronouncement just two verses earlier in 22:12 after Abraham attempted to sacrifice his son. There, the angel of the LORD said, "Do not lay your hand on the boy or do anything to him; for now I know that you fear God, since you have not withheld your son, your only son, from me." The pronouncement in v. 12 explains why reference to the ram does not figure into v. 14. Verse 14, following on this tightly written narrative, suggests then that God provided the lamb to be sure, but more important, that God saw what Abraham was willing to do in obedience to his word (22:1-2). Our translations should not obscure this more nuanced understanding of the passage.

Finally, note also how the narrator in Genesis begins to conclude the story according to the NRSV: "On the mount of the LORD, it shall be provided." But the word translated here "it shall be provided" is, in Greek, the aorist middle or passive, ὤφθη, the very word used almost exclusively elsewhere in Genesis to say that the LORD appeared to Abraham, or Isaac, or Jacob. A better translation, in keeping with the narrator's use of the verb elsewhere, would be, "on the mount of the LORD, he appeared." Our translations obscure the author's playful use of the word "see," a word used with three different nuances in this narrative.[70] But what is missed in our English versions may very well have been noticed by the author of John, an author steeped in Old Testament traditions, who not only uses the *Akedah*

69. The root of the Hebrew verb here is ראה, a verb used metaphorically in various ways. See the discussion in BDB, p. 906; TWOT, 2:823.

70. Cf. Gerhard von Rad, *Genesis,* The Old Testament Library (Philadelphia: Westminster Press, 1972), p. 242. For a similar type of playfulness with the concept of "seeing" in the Abraham stories, see the conclusion to the Hagar narrative in Gen. 16:13-14.

powerfully in the Passover motif of the Gospel but implicitly refers to Isaac precisely in our narrative in 8:35. The ironic truth behind "the Jews'" question is that an earlier manifestation of the Word saw Abraham, and he saw him precisely at the moment when their ancestor demonstrated his obedience to the command of God most profoundly. Understood in this fashion, their ironic question reinforces Jesus' claim that while "the Jews" may be Abraham's physical descendants, they are certainly not his children.

One more detail remains: when "the Jews" confront Jesus, they ask, "have you seen Abraham?" The verb translated "have you seen" is ἑώρακας, a perfect tense verb. One of the discourse functions of the perfect tense form in narratives is, according to Stanley Porter, to "frontground" action over against the aorist and even the present tense forms.[71] The use of that tense here to frontground the action vis-à-vis the background aorist verbs of v. 56 should not be missed. A verbal aspectual analysis would suggest therefore that the narrator intends to emphasize not what Abraham saw in v. 56 (as important as that is) but what Jesus saw in v. 57. Clearly, the narrator's deliberate switch to the perfect tense lends some credibility to the entire line of argument taken here. In keeping with our suggestion that the narrator uses John 8:31-59 to advance his claims about the deity and pre-existence of Jesus, the frontgrounded focus on pre-existence comes to the fore again in v. 57, having dropped from sight momentarily in v. 56.

In sum, the truth that Jesus' opponents proclaim unwittingly in this narrative is that Jesus has seen Abraham. When the twin themes of Jesus' deity and pre-existence are given their due, and when the swirl of texts related to Abraham in Genesis 15, 18, and 22 is seen as the primary background for this passage, the text comes alive as yet another vehicle for the evangelist's Christology. If we somehow miss the emphasis on Jesus' deity and pre-existence in these verses, and therefore on Abraham's reception of Jesus and his word, the narrator forces the reader to such a conclusion in v. 58, when Jesus announces solemnly: "Very truly I tell you, before Abraham was, I am."

John 8:58: The I AM and Abraham

That our reading of the material heretofore presented is on track is seen most clearly in the final proclamation of Jesus in this discourse. I do not intend to get into a thorough discussion of the "I am" statements in

71. Stanley Porter, *Idioms of the Greek New Testament* (Sheffield: Sheffield Academic Press, 1995), p. 23.

John.[72] Suffice it to say that Jesus' proclamation is about more than simply his pre-existence. That is, Jesus did not say, "Before Abraham was, I was."[73] He could have said that, had he wished only to make a point about his pre-existence. Instead, he said, "Before Abraham was, I am." The statement obviously alludes to Exodus 3:13-18, and the implications are clear. Keener puts the matter succinctly: "Here Jesus plainly identifies himself with the God of Scripture."[74] We would hasten to add that here Jesus identifies himself with the one who "appeared to Abraham." While pre-existence is implicit in Jesus' statement, more important is the appropriation of the divine name. But it is precisely his use of that title here that shows that our reading of Jesus' pre-existence in this narrative is in keeping with the narrator's intentions. Early on in the story of Abraham in Genesis we read,

> Then the LORD appeared to Abram, and said, "To your offspring I will give this land." So he built there an altar to the LORD, who had appeared to him. From there he moved on to the hill country on the east of Bethel, and pitched his tent . . . ; and there he built an altar to the LORD and invoked the name of LORD. (Gen. 12:7-8)

That the LORD appeared to Abraham and Abraham invoked his name is *prima facie* evidence that our author, who stresses Jesus' deity and pre-existence so prominently, intended readers to understand Jesus' references to Abraham's encounter with the LORD as concrete examples of Jesus' pre-existence, as concrete examples of an earlier manifestation of the Word made flesh. A. T. Hanson concludes his discussion of this passage similarly:

72. See Philip B. Harner, *The "I Am" of the Fourth Gospel: A Study in Johannine Usage and Thought* (Philadelphia: Fortress, 1970); David M. Ball, *"I Am" in John's Gospel: Literary Function, Background, and Theological Implications*, JSNTSup 124 (Sheffield: Sheffield Academic Press, 1996).

73. Augustine capitalized on this nuance as well in his *On the Gospel of John* 43.17 (NPNF, 1st series, 7.244).

74. Keener, *John*, 1:768; so also Hurtado, *Lord Jesus Christ*, pp. 371-72: "In the Old Testament passages the Greek expression [ἐγὼ εἰμί], and the Hebrew expressions it translates, appear to function almost like the name of God . . . this absolute use of 'I am' in the Gospels amounts to nothing less than designating Jesus with the same special referential formula that is used in the Greek Old Testament for God's own self-declaration. That is, the 'I am' expression as used in GJohn reflects the belief that Jesus is in some direct way *associated with God*" (emphasis original). See also the important discussion of this text as well as the implications of Jesus' departing the Temple in v. 59, in W. D. Davies, *The Gospel and the Land: Early Christianity and the Jewish Territorial Doctrine*, The Biblical Seminar 25 (Sheffield: Sheffield Academic Press, 1994), pp. 290-96.

The hidden implication behind all this slightly ambiguous language is that Abraham has met the pre-existent Word, not in paradise, as some commentators have desperately suggested, but in the course of Abraham's life. This must mean that John identified one of the three men who visited Abraham as described in Genesis 18 with the pre-existent Word. Abraham prostrates himself before them and calls one of them "Lord." That was no doubt the pre-existent logos in John's view.[75]

Conclusion

The deity and pre-existence of the Word in the Prologue controls our reading of the story of Jesus in John. The vocabulary of the Gospel highlights these themes, emphasizing them repeatedly and in any number of ways. The themes are so ubiquitous that, when one turns to John 8:31-59 and Jesus speaks of the works that Abraham did, readers should assume that the narrator has something more in mind than a simple allusion to Abraham's obedience to the word of God. Indeed, as we have argued, the burden of proof should remain with those who would see nothing more in this narrative than a simple analogy, as opposed to a more concrete example of the pre-existence of Jesus, when, as the Word who was with God and was God in the beginning, he appeared to Abraham.

To reiterate, Genesis emphasizes that the LORD appeared to Abraham on several occasions. It stresses Abraham's belief in the word of the LORD (Gen. 15:6). It underscores Abraham's hospitality for the LORD when he visited and announced that he would soon have a son (18:1-15). It plays with the notion both that Abraham *saw* and that the LORD *saw* during the binding of Isaac (22:4, 8, 14). Finally, it asserts that Abraham invoked the name of the LORD in his worship as well (12:8). This entire collection of ideas comes to a head in John 8. Our narrative emphasizes Abraham's works of hospitality and his belief in the word, while simultaneously accentuating his opponents' refusal to accept Jesus and believe his word (esp. 8:45-46). It insists that Abraham rejoiced when he saw Jesus' day, and maintains that Jesus saw Abraham too. Finally, it ends with the climactic

---

75. Hanson, *The Prophetic Gospel*, p. 126. Hanson traces this interpretation of the text in the modern period (through H. J. Holtzmann) to the nineteenth-century German scholar W. Baldensperger. He cites A. Loisy (1903) and H. Odeberg (1929) as others who hold a similar view (p. 130).

claim that Jesus existed before Abraham as the "I am," a name that the Pentateuch implicitly links to the name that Abraham invoked as early as Genesis 12:8.

Some may object to this understanding, claiming that Jesus distinguishes himself from his Father in the Gospel and that he understands his Father to be the God of the Old Testament, and therefore the one Abraham encountered. But this is merely a trivial objection.[76] Modern readers, especially Christians, tend to read this text through the lens of various creedal statements such as the Nicene Creed. They therefore complicate a rather simple concept. Jesus is God, but he is distinct from God as well. So proclaims the first verse of this Gospel. The types of theological difficulties raised by our reading are therefore no more substantial than the inherent difficulties of John 1:1, a text full of paradoxical tension.

Before such creedal statements, however, Irenaeus of Lyon presented his own view on the matter at hand as it relates to John 8 in the late second century C.E. And so, we give the last word to him:

> Christ Himself, therefore, together with the Father, is the God of the living, who spake to Moses, and who was also manifested to the fathers. And teaching this very thing, [Jesus] said to the Jews: "Your father Abraham rejoiced that he should see my day; and he saw it, and was glad." . . . The Lord [Jesus], therefore, was not unknown to Abraham, whose day he desired to see. . . . For not alone upon Abraham's account did [Jesus] say these things, but also that He might point out how all who have known God from the beginning, and have foretold the advent of Christ, have received the revelation from the Son Himself; who also in the last times was made visible and passable, and spake with the human race.[77]

---

76. Hanson notes those who, arguing for the historicity of the narrative in John, would object simply "to disembarrass themselves of the conclusion that the historical Jesus claimed to have met Abraham" (*The Prophetic Gospel*, p. 131).

77. Irenaeus, *Against Heresies* 4.5-7 (ANF 1.467-70); Chrysostom understood the issue similarly; he writes, "Abraham received the strangers in the place where he abode himself; his wife stood in the place of a servant, the guests in the place of masters. He knew not that he was receiving Christ." *The Acts of the Apostles,* Homily 45 (NPNF, 1st series, 11.277); see too his *Homilies on St. John,* 8.1 (NPNF, 1st series, 14.30); cf. also Ambrose, *On Belief in the Resurrection* 2.96 (NPNF, 2nd series, 10.189-90), *On the Christian Faith* 1.80 (NPNF, 2nd series, 10.214-15); of course, not all early Christians viewed the text this way: see, e.g., Augustine, *The City of God,* 16.29 (NPNF, 1st series, 2.327-28); *On the Trinity,* 2.19-20 (NPNF, 1st series, 3.46-47); Ephraim Syrus, *Hymns on the Nativity* 1 (NPNF, 2nd series, 13.225).

"The Tomb That Abraham Had Purchased" (Acts 7:16)

ELAINE PHILLIPS

Introduction

A careful reading of the details in Stephen's speech in Acts 7 compared with the record in Genesis unearths some intriguing differences. Acts 7:16 is the most notable: "They [the bones of Jacob's sons] were brought back to Shechem and placed in the tomb that Abraham had purchased from the sons of Hamor at Shechem." A brief tour through the salient passages in Genesis produces the following data. When Sarah died at Kiryat Arba (that is, Hebron), Abraham went to mourn for her. He then purchased from Ephron the Hittite the field in Machpelah near Mamre that included the cave in which Sarah and subsequent matriarchs and patriarchs were buried. The field and the cave were deeded to Abraham as a burial site (Gen. 23:17-19). It was Jacob who purchased a plot of ground from the sons of Hamor, the father of Shechem, for one hundred pieces of silver. There he pitched his tent and set up an altar (Gen. 33:18-20).[1] After the debacle with

---

1. Jacob was following the pattern of Abram who, when the Lord appeared to him in Shechem, built an altar there (Gen. 12:7) and subsequently pitched his tent between Bethel and Ai where he also built an altar (Gen. 12:8).

It is with deep gratitude that I offer this paper in honor of Dr. Marvin Wilson's 75th birthday. From my very first days at Gordon College, Marv has been an excellent colleague, consistently offering encouragement at every turn, and serving as a source of wisdom on issues both practical and erudite. He is a peerless teacher, having raised up multiple generations of students (Avot 1:1).

110

Dinah at Shechem (Gen. 34), Jacob moved south with a brief stop at Bethel. He came home to Isaac in Mamre near Hebron, and when Isaac died his sons buried him (Gen. 35:27-29). Likewise, when Jacob died, he told his twelve sons, then in Egypt, to bury him with his fathers "in the cave in the field of Ephron the Hittite, the cave in the field of Machpelah, near Mamre in Canaan, which Abraham bought as a burial place from Ephron the Hittite, along with the field" (Gen. 49:30). The sons of Jacob did as their father commanded; they took him to Canaan and buried him "in the cave in the field of Machpelah, near Mamre, which Abraham had bought as a burial place from Ephron the Hittite, along with the field" (Gen. 50:13). Joseph's bones, on the other hand, were buried at Shechem in the land that Jacob had purchased from the sons of Hamor (Josh. 24:32). The distance between Hebron and Shechem is approximately 60 miles.

While the Hebrew Bible is silent about the burial place(s) of the rest of Jacob's sons, Josephus asserted (*Ant* 2.199; *Wars* 4.532), most likely following Jubilees 46:8-10 and each of the Testaments of the Twelve Patriarchs, that the sons of Jacob were buried at Hebron in the double cave at Machpelah. In addition, rabbinic midrash on Genesis 50:25-26 states: "'You shall carry up my bones away hence with you' (Exod. 13:19), which means, when you go up. And how do we know that the bones of the tribal ancestors too were taken up with him? Because it says, 'with you' [a plural form]" (Gen. Rab. 100:11).

The Issues: Sources, Influences, Motives, and the Claim for Inerrancy

This single verse (Acts 7:16) raises a number of questions, some of them shaped by developments and discussion within evangelical circles, particularly over the last quarter century. Stephen's speech as a whole figured rather prominently in the vigorous inerrancy debates of the 1970s and beyond.[2] When that meta-question has guided the inquiry, a common re-

---

2. See Rex A. Koivisto, "Stephen's Speech: A Case Study in Rhetoric and Biblical Inerrancy," *Journal of the Evangelical Theological Society* 20 (1977): 353-64. Koivisto's unpublished Th.D. dissertation, "Stephen's Speech and Inerrancy: An Investigation of the Divergences from Old Testament History in Acts 7" (Dallas Theological Seminary, 1982), cites the literature on the issue. Going back several centuries, Calvin declared that the text was wrong in its reference to Abraham and should be amended (John Calvin, *Commentary on the Acts of the Apostles* [repr. Grand Rapids: Baker Book House, 1993], p. 265).

sponse has been to distinguish between what Stephen said and what Luke recorded. Luke's mandate as a historian was faithfully to record Stephen's speech to the Sanhedrin, rather than correcting it to fit the account in Genesis. Stephen could be in error; Luke was not. In other words, recorded rhetoric is not inerrant, divinely approved revelation but an inerrant record of that speech.[3] A related question addresses the relationship between recorded rhetoric and theology.[4] Of equal interest is the internal unity and consistency of the speech; a major thread of scholarship finds no recognizable connection between verses 2-16 and the rest of the chapter.[5]

Even for those not particularly caught up in the inerrancy debate, there continue to be significant avenues for investigation. These range from socio-religious contexts to authorial intentions. There is considerable question as to the primary focus of the accusations against Stephen and whether his response was, in fact, an answer to those charges.[6] Did his opponents accuse him before the Sanhedrin primarily because of what he ostensibly had said about the Temple? The false witnesses who were brought forward certainly made this seem like the case and Stephen did respond forcefully to that issue. Initially, however, they seemed to be more vexed at the implications of his preaching for the status of Moses and for the Torah. For his part, a steady drum-beat throughout Stephen's speech indicted the people for their own disobedience.[7]

3. Albert Barnes, *Notes on Acts*, rev. ed. (New York: Harper, 1879), p. 138; Clark Pinnock, *Biblical Revelation* (Chicago: Moody, 1971), pp. 78-79; E. F. Harrison, *Acts: The Expanding Church* (Chicago: Moody, 1975), p. 115, are representative examples. Koivisto, "Stephen's Speech," p. 353, criticized the position that separates Stephen from Luke, claiming that categorizing the speech as secondarily authoritative has consequences for how it may be used in developing historical and theological understanding of Scripture. Instead, Luke's presentation of an extensive and positive character description of Stephen gives authorial sanction to the speech (Koivisto, "Stephen's Speech and Inerrancy," pp. 4-9). Nevertheless, even though the speech appears to have Luke's approval, it is still necessary to address Stephen's errors and/or Luke's ignorance.

4. The issues here are who (Stephen or Luke) chose to include "errors" and what function these errors might have performed in the context of the speech. See in this regard, John J. Kilgallen, *The Stephen Speech: A Literary and Redactional Study of Acts 7:2-53* (Rome: Biblical Institute Press, 1976), pp. 58-59; and Koivisto, "Stephen's Speech and Inerrancy," pp. 188-89.

5. Kilgallen, *The Stephen Speech*, pp. 10-14, summarized the positions on both sides of the issue.

6. Kilgallen, *The Stephen Speech*, pp. 6-10.

7. Darrell L. Bock, *Acts*, Baker Exegetical Commentary on the New Testament (Grand Rapids: Baker, 2007), pp. 276-77, suggested that Stephen never finished the speech;

The spotlight has initially been turned on Stephen himself. Why, if he indeed gave this speech, did he pose the historical details as he did? This is not the only altered datum in his recital of covenant history.[8] Perhaps it was simply a matter of Stephen's response to the pressure of that particular situation. Clearly, Stephen summarized vast reaches of Scripture through the course of this speech.[9] Arguing for his life before the high court might cause him to compress[10] or alter details and, like many figures under stress, possibly not really respond to the question![11] Nevertheless, a reasonable

---

his comments about the disobedience of the people caused the mob to "lynch" him. Israel had rejected its messengers as well as proper worship. See also James P. Sweeney, "Stephen's Speech (Acts 7:2-53): Is It as 'Anti-Temple' as Is Frequently Alleged?" *Trinity Journal* 23.2 (2002): 208-10.

8. Stephen indicated that Abraham's call was initially articulated in Mesopotamia which he distinguished from Haran (Acts 7:2, but see Gen. 12:1). F. F. Bruce (*Commentary on the Book of Acts,* New International Commentary on the Old Testament [Grand Rapids: Eerdmans, 1974], p. 146) noted that the author of Stephen's speech had the Old Testament fully in his mind, quoting Gen. 12:1 with reference to Neh. 9:7 to the effect that God also called Abraham from Ur, not only Haran. Stephen also declared that Terah died before Abraham left for Canaan (Acts 7:4), but that raises some complexity with Terah's age at death in conjunction with Abraham's age when he arrived in Canaan. Genesis 11:26 states that Terah became the father of Abram, Nahor, and Haran after he had lived 70 years; Gen. 11:32 indicates that Terah lived 205 years and died in Haran. Genesis 12:4 has Abram setting out from Haran at the age of 75. One way of addressing the matter without amending the text is to note that, although Abram is listed first, that is because he was the most significant, not necessarily the firstborn. Additional alterations in the text include Stephen's declaration that Jacob's whole family included seventy-five persons in all (Acts 7:14). This is what the LXX and DSS have in Exodus 1:5; the MT has seventy (see Gen. 46:27). Stephen embellished Moses' abilities, indicating that he was "powerful in speech and action" (Acts 7:22), in contrast with Exodus 4:10. Finally, angels have a distinct place in Stephen's rendition of the Moses narratives (Acts 7:30, 35, 38, 53).

9. Cf. C. K. Barrett, *A Critical and Exegetical Commentary on the Acts of the Apostles,* 2 vols., International Critical Commentary (Edinburgh: T&T Clark, 1994, 1998), 1:350.

10. Thus, these two purchases were telescoped just as the two calls of Abraham were put together in the first part of the chapter (Bruce, *Acts,* p. 149, n. 39). This is the position advocated in Peter H. Davids, F. F. Bruce, Manfred T. Brauch, and Walter C. Kaiser Jr., *Hard Sayings of the Bible* (Downers Grove: InterVarsity Press, 1996), p. 522; and I. Howard Marshall, "Acts," in *Commentary on the New Testament Use of the Old Testament,* ed. G. K. Beale and D. A. Carson (Grand Rapids: Baker, 2007), p. 560. Historical accuracy was not the point of Stephen's speech; rather, this was a summary, combining two accounts.

11. Richard N. Longenecker, *The Acts of the Apostles,* Expositor's Bible Commentary, rev. ed. (Grand Rapids: Zondervan, 2007), pp. 818-19, views the conflations and imprecision as reflecting both Stephen's speaking "under intense emotion" and general popular piety. To expect him to be entirely free from error in this recital of Israel's history is putting too heavy

counter-question is: Given the emphasis in the narrative on the presence of the Holy Spirit (Acts 6:3, 5, 10; 7:55), can we presume that Stephen succumbed to fear?

One avenue for reconciling the conflicting data presumes that Abraham had indeed purchased a plot of land from the "sons of Hamor," a dynastic label, after he arrived at Shechem and received a confirming vision from the Lord. On that ground, he built an altar. The altar Abraham built at Shechem gave the location lasting significance. An actual purchase was not recorded in Scripture but survived in reliable oral tradition to which Stephen had access. Because the legal right lapsed due to Abraham's nomadic life, Jacob renegotiated it in the same manner that Isaac renegotiated for the wells in the Negev (Gen. 21:25-30; 26:25-32).[12] While this is ingenious, it does not account for a number of details in the text. Stephen specifies a "tomb," but Abraham's hypothetical first purchase was not designated for such usage. Other than Joseph, there are no known traditions of patriarchal burial in Shechem.[13] In addition, in his response, Stephen indicated that Abraham did not inherit a "foot of ground" (Acts 7:5).

---

a demand on the humanity of Stephen. On the other hand, it does not seem likely that Stephen would inadvertently err in regard to such major figures as Abraham and Jacob, especially when the rest of his speech is brimming with historical detail (R. J. Coggins, "The Samaritans and Acts," *New Testament Studies* 28.3 [1982]: 425). In fact, since covenant history is the framework for his speech, an error at this point would have engendered a "storm of protest" (W. Harold Mare, "Acts 7: Jewish or Samaritan in Character?" *Westminster Theological Journal* 34 [1971]: 20).

12. Gleason L. Archer, *New International Encyclopedia of Bible Difficulties* (Grand Rapids: Zondervan, 1982), pp. 379-81; and William J. Larkin, *Acts*, InterVarsity Press New Testament Commentary Series, vol. 5 (Downers Grove: InterVarsity, 1995), pp. 110-11. According to Koivisto ("Stephen's Speech and Inerrancy," pp. 184-89), however, to suggest that it was necessary to purchase land for the altar is a large presumption. Abraham did not purchase land in every place that he built an altar. This runs counter to the fact that he was a sojourner and only acquired a tract of land when he buried Sarah. See also Heb. 11:8-10. Further, the altar built at Shechem is an implicit declaration of his *faith* that he would inherit, even though he did not own the land.

13. On the possibility of a local tradition that the twelve sons of Jacob were buried at Shechem, see Barrett, *Acts,* p. 351; and I. Howard Marshall, *Acts,* Tyndale New Testament Commentary (Grand Rapids: Eerdmans, 1980), pp. 138-39. The question is whether Stephen expanded the statement of Josh. 24:32 to cover Joseph's brothers or was dependent on some local Shechemite tradition. Jerome, *Epistles* 108.13, asserted that when Paula came by Shechem, she saw there the burial places of the twelve patriarchs. Barrett doubts that the Samaritan tradition was strong enough to "inhibit the rise and spread of the alternative Hebron tradition."

Considerable attention has been given to the possibility that Stephen's responses were the result of his background and exposure to Samaritan traditions and ideas. Some parts of the speech could imply a reading of the Samaritan Pentateuch (SP) rather than the MT.[14] There was a degree of fluidity in Hebrew text tradition in the first century C.E.,[15] and the Samaritan sectarians made some intentional changes to emphasize the primacy of Gerizim and Shechem over Jerusalem. If, perchance, Stephen's mission involved proclamation of the gospel in a Samaritan context, the Jerusalem Temple was an obstacle, and he may have tried to downplay it.[16] It is difficult, however, to envision that Stephen (and Luke) would have given credibility to a textual tradition falsifying the Pentateuch to the effect that the Gerizim temple was of heavenly construction whereas Solomon's was not.[17]

14. Coggins, "Samaritans and Acts," pp. 423-34, suggested that Stephen was from a Palestinian sectarian group that had little use for the Temple and also had some connections with Samaritans. Abram Spiro detailed the influences from the Samaritan Pentateuch (SP), including linguistic data, emphases on certain persons, institutions, and places, and textual correspondences. First, in Gen. 11:32, the SP reads 145 years for Terah's age at death instead of 205. This could reflect a Greek text no longer extant (see Bruce, *Acts,* pp. 146-47, n. 31). Second, in Acts 7:37, Stephen discussed Moses' leadership role in the Exodus, the Sinai experience, and the wilderness wanderings, drawing on Deut. 18:15. The SP has an interpolation after Exod. 20:17 (the giving of Torah), which contains passages from Deuteronomy. Third, Haran is very significant in Samaritan tradition because the sanctity of Gerizim and the Samaritan Pentateuch were authorized there; Stephen mentioned Haran twice. Fourth, the term "place" (Acts 7:7) was standard Samaritan parlance for the shrine at Gerizim (see John 4:20; Acts 6:14). Fifth, Solomon's Temple was not only in the wrong "place" but was made by human hands. Because Acts 6:1 refers to "Hebrews," and the Samaritans for centuries called themselves "Hebrews" while Jews did not, Luke was drawing on Samaritan Christian sources (Spiro, "Stephen's Samaritan Background," Appendix V, revised by W. F. Albright and C. S. Mann, in Johannes Munck, *The Acts of the Apostles,* Anchor Bible 31 [New York: Doubleday, 1967], pp. 285-300). Martin H. Scharlemann modified Spiro's position somewhat, viewing Stephen as someone influenced by Samaritan ideas and convinced that the Temple was a divine institution (*Stephen: A Singular Saint,* Analecta Biblica 34 (Rome: Pontifical Biblical Institute, 1968], pp. 10-20, 53-56).

15. F. M. Cross, *The Ancient Library of Qumran,* 3rd ed. (Sheffield: Sheffield Academic Press, 1995), pp. 124-42. See also Earl Richard, "Acts: An Investigation of the Samaritan Evidence," *Catholic Biblical Quarterly* 39.2 (1977): 190-208; and Koivisto, "Stephen's Speech and Inerrancy," pp. 171-73.

16. Scharlemann, *Stephen: A Singular Saint,* p. 121. It is noteworthy that Stephen mentioned nothing of Abraham's greatest trial, the binding of Isaac on Mt. Moriah, which was the location of the Solomonic Temple (2 Chron. 3:1).

17. The alleged connections with the SP were summarized and thoroughly critiqued by Mare, who concluded that none of these claims can be substantiated. He demolished

Equally possible, the Shechem allusion may have been part of a pointed theological polemic directed to Stephen's audience. The Jewish Sanhedrin would not be particularly sanguine about a heightened spiritual profile for Shechem, the location of the Samaritan temple on Mt. Gerizim until its destruction by John Hyrcanus just about 150 years prior.[18] Perhaps this was an intentional modification designed to vex his already hostile audience.

Acknowledging the thread of theological conflict woven into this narrative inevitably redirects the reader to Luke and the matter of *his* possible sources and intentions. Views range from Luke's access to the entire speech as Stephen gave it to his having created it to fit his own theological agenda.[19] Those who affirm that this was an authentic representation of

---

Spiro's hypothesis that Acts 7 was "Stephen's missionary tract" and was never a defense delivered to the Sanhedrin. In fact, most of the material in Stephen's speech is close to the LXX. Where details differ, it is not necessary to posit a Samaritan viewpoint or doctrine. Instead, the speech represents a Jewish-Hellenistic background that is in keeping with the first part of Acts (Mare, "Acts 7: Jewish or Samaritan," pp. 1-21). Koivisto, "Stephen's Speech and Inerrancy," pp. 171-83, addresses each of the points raised by both Spiro and Scharlemann as well as the refutation by Mare and concluded that most of the arguments for Samaritan influence are weak. Richard's assessment of the issue, while somewhat critical of Mare's methodology, reached the same conclusion regarding the weakness of the Samaritan connection ("Acts: An Investigation of the Samaritan Evidence," pp. 207-8).

18. Josephus, *Ant.* 13.9.1; *War* 1.2.6. Harrison, *Acts,* pp. 115-16, declared that Stephen's reference to Shechem was a deliberate move to call attention to Samaria in a context that would rather forget the patriarchal contacts with that despised entity. See also Bruce, *Acts,* p. 149.

19. See Bock, *Acts,* p. 277. Martin H. Scharlemann, "Stephen's Speech: A Lucan Creation?" *Concordia Journal* 4.2 (1978): 56-57, concluded that Luke followed the pattern of Thucydides, keeping both the general sense of the speech and even Stephen's phrases. In Stephen's speech there are twenty-three words that occur nowhere else in Acts or the New Testament. Typical Lucan expressions are absent, suggesting that this speech was not created by Luke but was Stephen's. Furthermore, interpreters who do not think this was Stephen's speech are hard-pressed to explain its unusual use of the Old Testament (Scharlemann, *Stephen: A Singular Saint,* pp. 28-29). Stephen directly quoted fifteen Old Testament passages, thirteen from the Pentateuch and two from the prophets. This is not characteristic of Luke (Simon Kistemaker, "The Speeches in Acts," *Criswell Theological Review* 5.1 [1990]: 34-35). On the other hand, J. A. Fitzmyer, *The Acts of the Apostles,* Anchor Bible (Garden City: Doubleday, 1998), pp. 365-68, said the speech draws on Hellenistic Christian tradition but was ultimately composed by Luke. See also Luke Timothy Johnson, *The Acts of the Apostles,* Sacra Pagina Series, vol. 5 (Collegeville: Liturgical Press, 1992), pp. 119-20, who concluded that Luke wrote as a classic Hellenistic historian, having Stephen give a history lesson at this point. F. J. Foakes-Jackson likewise claimed that Luke "took some old prophecy denouncing

Stephen's words to the Sanhedrin presume that Luke acquired his information from a member of the Sanhedrin, perhaps Paul, who would have been present as Stephen's defense unfolded.[20] While no one thinks of this as a "stenographer's account,"[21] Luke claimed that he investigated his subject carefully (Luke 1:1-4) and no doubt sought reliable sources. At the same time, to what extent did Luke shape the details of Stephen's speech in order to prepare the reading audience for the dramatic move into Samaria in the very next chapter of Acts, developing the "itinerary" in Acts 1:8 that included Samaria in the expansion of the gospel?

Kilgallen summarized the options for addressing the issues of sources and intentions as follows: (1) Stephen erred, whether knowingly or otherwise; (2) Stephen reworked the Genesis traditions for his own purpose as he was arguing before the Sanhedrin; (3) Stephen knew of a tradition that we no longer have in which Abraham did indeed buy a tomb. For his part, Luke (1) may have simply accepted Stephen's speech not knowing that it was not factually accurate; (2) Luke may have realized the error but kept Stephen's words to represent Stephen faithfully; (3) Luke wanted to preserve Stephen's insights even though they were based on the error; (4) Luke did not correct the data because he had his own agenda, different from Stephen's, that he wanted to communicate. (5) Finally, Luke may have known of the lost tradition and felt justified in quoting Stephen in this fashion.[22]

---

the sins of Israel and put it into the mouth of Stephen" ("Stephen's Speech in Acts," *Journal of Biblical Literature* 49 [1930]: 286). Likewise, Martin Dibelius, *The Book of Acts: Form, Style, and Theology,* ed. K. C. Hanson (Minneapolis: Fortress, 2004), p. 70, averred that Luke had the martyrdom of Stephen tradition and inserted this largely "irrelevant" speech into that story. See also Ward W. Gasque, "The Speeches of Acts: Dibelius Reconsidered," in *New Dimensions in New Testament Studies,* ed. R. N. Longenecker and M. C. Tenney (Grand Rapids: Zondervan, 1974).

20. Witherington suggested that Saul of Tarsus had heard the speech, either in the Synagogue of the Freedmen or as a member of the Sanhedrin, realized its critical nature in the relationship between Christian and non-Christian Jews in Jerusalem, and related it to Luke when the latter was researching (Ben Witherington III, *The Acts of the Apostles: A Socio-Rhetorical Commentary* [Grand Rapids: Eerdmans, 1998], p. 265).

21. Scharlemann, *Stephen: A Singular Saint,* p. 23.

22. Kilgallen, *The Stephen Speech,* pp. 58-59; also summarized in Koivisto, "Stephen's Speech and Inerrancy," pp. 188-89. See also John Kilgallen, "The Speech of Stephen, Acts 7:2-53," *Expository Times* 115 (2004): 293-97.

The Charges against Stephen

Opposition against Stephen arose specifically among those who were members of the Synagogue of the Freedmen, all of them from locations outside the Land including Cyrene, Alexandria, Cilicia, and Asia.[23] Stephen performed miraculous signs among them, prompting antagonism that might have blossomed from envy. Worse yet, when they attempted to argue with him, they were no match for the Holy Spirit! The charge they therefore planted initially was, "We have heard Stephen speak words of blasphemy against Moses and against God" (Acts 6:11).[24] By the time they got him in front of the Sanhedrin, that charge, borne by false witnesses, had grown explicitly to include "speaking against the holy place and against the law" (Acts 6:13). This last was a twist of Jesus' own words. "Destroy this place . . ." (John 2:19) was turned into "Jesus of Nazareth will destroy this place and change the customs Moses handed down" (Acts 6:14). It is evident that Stephen envisioned changed roles for both the Temple and the Torah in the face of Jesus' death and resurrection. Thus, to a certain extent, the charges were true: Stephen's acknowledgment of Jesus as Messiah was an offense against the Temple, the Torah of Moses, and God.

Stephen's Responses to the Charges

The entire speech falls neatly into three parts. Initially, Stephen identified with his audience, referring to "our fathers"[25] and emphasizing Abraham and Joseph, both of whom received revelation from God outside the Land (vv. 2-16). This section serves as an introduction to the history of God's covenant people, a necessary matrix for his defense.[26] It does not directly

23. Acts 6:9; Longenecker, *Acts*, p. 813, suggested that the Hellenistic Jews represented in the Synagogue of the Freedmen would have been particularly zealous about keeping deviant views out of their membership because they were already pegged as being liberal.

24. Spiro, "Stephen's Samaritan Background," pp. 297-98, addressed the puzzling nature of the blasphemy charges and concluded that Stephen was not tried before the Sanhedrin; rather this speech was simply his missionary tract. He was lynched by an angry mob that rejected his Samaritan propaganda! Speaking against the law might have garnered a charge of blasphemy against Moses although that was not the verdict in the cases of Paul and Jesus himself. Perhaps declaring that Jesus would destroy the Temple was construed as blasphemy against God.

25. Bock, *Acts*, p. 279.

26. Witherington's rhetorical analysis of the speech emphasized the importance of its

address any of the accusations although highlighting Mesopotamia and Egypt does draw attention away from the Land and Temple as the primary loci of God's revealed presence.[27] The second and longest section of the narrative deals with Moses and the giving of Torah, also outside the Land (vv. 17-43). Here the emphasis is on the *Israelites'* rejection of both Moses' leadership and the commands of God. Stephen had the temerity to bring up the painful subject of the golden calf, reminding his audience that idolatry was the affront that made God turn away from them and eventually send them into exile.[28] In the third part, the Tabernacle and the Temple are favorably mentioned but with the immediate qualification that God's presence transcends spatial and temporal boundaries.[29] Clearly, this addressed the charge that Jesus and his followers were advocating a destruction of the Temple. God's prophetic Word itself (Isa. 66:1-2) declared that houses made with hands were only a small reflection of God's heavenly dwelling.[30] Stephen concluded by repeating the charge against *them* of

---

length and appeal to Israelite history in the face of Stephen's hostile audience (*The Acts of the Apostles*, pp. 260-61). F. F. Bruce deemed it a sample of early Hellenistic Christianity's critique of Judaism's departure from what God intended for his people ("Stephen's Apologia," in *Scripture: Meaning and Method*, ed. Barry P. Thompson [Hull, England: Hull University Press, 1987], pp. 30-40).

27. In addition, verses 6-7 broadly address themes that are more fully developed as the speech unfolds, notably the enslavement in Egypt and returning to worship (Marion Soards, *Speeches in Acts: Their Content, Context, and Concerns* [Louisville: Westminster John Knox, 1994], p. 62).

28. Of all issues in the anti-Jewish polemic that developed in subsequent centuries, this was the most painful one, and Christian apologists exploited it for all it was worth. See, as early examples, Justin Martyr, *Dialogue with Trypho* 20; Tertullian, *An Answer to the Jews* 1; and John Chrysostom, *Homilies Against the Jews* V.4.4; VI.2.6; VI.4.5. See also L. Smolar and M. Aberbach, "The Golden Calf Episode in Postbiblical Literature," *Hebrew Union College Annual* 39 (1968): 91-116, for a summary of the patristic and rabbinic literature.

29. The first dwelling place, the Tabernacle, was a movable tent that may have been viewed with more favor by Stephen. See F. F. Bruce, *The Acts of the Apostles: Greek Text with Introduction and Commentary*, 3rd ed. (Grand Rapids: Eerdmans, 1990), pp. 22-23. See also Sharlemann, *Stephen: A Singular Saint*, p. 119, on the implication that the Tabernacle was better because the *presence* of God moved with it while the stationary Temple distorted the nature of God.

30. See Marshall, *Acts*, p. 146. Based on use of the word "made with human hands," he suggested that the Temple itself had become an idol. Sharlemann, *Stephen: A Singular Saint*, p. 119, noted the possible parallel of that idolatry with the formation of the golden calf. Nevertheless, the Tabernacle was also made by human hands, and both were constructed in accordance with God's directions. The Isaiah quote is basically a restatement of what Solomon acknowledged in his prayer of dedication of the Temple (Sweeney, "Ste-

murderous opposition to the messengers of God culminating in the crucifixion of Jesus. In the end, they were *outside* the covenant, being
uncircumcised in heart (Acts 7:51). Each section of the speech highlights
the Israelites' opposition to the persons whom God had chosen as their
leaders, closing with Jesus.[31]

A Proposal: Looking through Rabbinic Lenses

Re-Presentation as Revelation

Stephen's choice to ground his response in covenant history affirmed his
stance within his Jewish tradition.[32] History was God's arena for interacting with his people, demonstrating that his word was effective. Even in
this initial portion of Stephen's speech (vv. 1-16), it is evident that he engaged in a compelling re-presentation of the patriarchal narratives, selecting the persons and events that would best introduce the broad sweep of
his response. Clearly, he was steeped in the traditions of his people as numerous allusions to biblical stories along with frequent use of Old Testament words and phrases are interwoven in his narrative.[33] It does not
seem likely that the embellishments that stray from the Genesis text were
accidental on his part. Likewise, it is difficult to imagine that he would lob
a few cheap shots in the midst of this masterpiece simply aimed to vex his
opponents in regard to the Samaritan issue. After all, his life was in the
balance.

Instead, drawing on a deeply embedded heritage, Stephen presented
a dynamically intertextual reading of the Scripture, a process that was evi-

phen's Speech," pp. 199-200). Witherington did not see the speech as a criticism of the Temple (*The Acts of the Apostles*, pp. 262-63).

31. Witherington, *The Acts of the Apostles*, p. 267.

32. The pattern is evident throughout the Hebrew Bible. Deuteronomy 1–3 and Josh.
24:2-13 provide the paradigm.

33. Soards, *Speeches in Acts*, p. 60. Two examples from Exodus and Deuteronomy figure more prominently into this discussion: Stephen's declaration that God did not give
Abraham even so much as a foot step of ground as the inheritance (Acts 7:5), reflecting Deut.
2:5; and the statement that, after their enslavement in Egypt, Israel would worship God in
"this place," perhaps drawing on Exod. 3:2 and its reference to Mt. Sinai. Neither of these
passages is directly tied with Abraham. Abraham preceded the Sinai revelation, and yet that
promise was so deeply planted in the redemptive Exodus experience that Stephen included
it as part of the promise articulated to Abraham.

dent already in the Hebrew Bible[34] and was developed extensively in subsequent centuries of rabbinic study. As the rabbis created their interpretations, they interwove a rich fabric of biblical references, filling in gaps in narratives, deriving conclusions based on analogous elements among texts, employing anachronism when it suited their objectives, and demonstrating remarkable command of every aspect of the language and the text. Within the framework of their affirmation that God was the source of the Torah and that Torah shaped their world, they engaged in a good deal of freedom with the text.[35] This was possible because God's revelation at Sinai was not a singular moment nor did it have one singular meaning; it was a universal, ongoing revelation, always adaptable. Jews from all times and places merged into one group, standing before Sinai.[36]

Revelation and Worship: Inside or Outside the Land

In the minds of Stephen's audience, the covenant promises as given to Abraham were intrinsically tied to land, people, and the prospect of worshiping God.[37] These views had too easily become calcified. For his part, Stephen chose to review covenant history with a specific focus on the times that God's revelation transcended the confines of the Land; the Abraham section introduces this emphasis and Joseph, like Abraham, re-

34. Michael Fishbane, "Inner Biblical Exegesis: Types and Strategies of Interpretation in Ancient Israel," in *Midrash and Literature,* ed. Geoffrey H. Hartman and Sanford Budick (New Haven: Yale University Press, 1986), pp. 19-37, spoke of the complex interdependence of revelation and interpretive tradition. Notably, in the biblical prophetic tradition, interpretation transformed the text of Torah and itself became revelation for succeeding generations and cultural matrices.

35. Judah Goldin, "Freedom and Restraint of Aggadah," in *Midrash and Literature,* pp. 63-64.

36. Michael A. Singer, "How the Bible Has Been Interpreted in Jewish Tradition," in *The New Interpreter's Bible,* vol. 1, ed. Leander E. Keck (Nashville: Abingdon, 1994), pp. 65-82; James Kugel, "Two Introductions to Midrash," in *Midrash and Literature,* pp. 77-103. The precedent for this was set in that corporate experience of all Israel standing at Sinai as recorded in Deut. 29:2-15. Rashi's comment on Deut. 29:14b expresses this existential communion: "'and with whoever is not here' — even with future generations who are to come." See also Exodus Rabbah 28:6: "All souls, even those which were still to be created, were present at the revelation on Mt. Sinai."

37. Stephen directly took on the three pillars of popular Judaism (Land, Torah, and Temple) in his response, starting with the dangerous tendency to venerate the Land (Longenecker, *Acts,* p. 815).

ceived God's revelation outside the Land.[38] No doubt, Stephen's encounters with members of the Synagogue of the Freedmen, whose origins were outside the Land (Acts 6:9), made this a more significant issue. While they may have been more sympathetic to this opening gambit, Stephen's immediate audience at this point was the Sanhedrin and the dual mention of Shechem would have been jarring in that context.

Stephen's speech also created a separation between the promises of God's covenant presence and the standing Temple.[39] Stephen addressed primarily God's promises to Abraham, and he did not include Abraham's worship practices in his recital, but they included altars to the LORD at Shechem, between Bethel and Ai, and at Hebron (Gen. 12:6-8; 13:18). In fact, Abraham's most dramatic encounters with God occurred at Hebron (Gen. 15) and Mount Moriah (Gen. 22). Notwithstanding, Stephen mentioned none of these, and the passing reference to worship "in this place" (Acts 7:7) seemed to pale next to the importance of a burial location — in Shechem.

Burial and Inheritance

"They [the fathers] were brought back to Shechem and laid in the tomb" (Acts 7:16a).[40] Why single out burial of the twelve sons of Jacob as such a critical event? After all, Abraham had already purchased the cave of Machpelah near Hebron, buried Sarah there, and was, along with Isaac and Jacob, interred in that location. And why bind that purchase together with one by Jacob at Shechem? Jacob had made Joseph swear that they would take him back to rest with his fathers in the Land (Gen. 47:29-31); Joseph in turn did the same (Gen. 50:24-25). Both oaths were kept (Gen. 50:13; Exod. 13:19; Josh. 24:32).

Stephen affirmed the promises that God gave Abraham; he along with his descendants would possess the Land (Acts 7:5). In the interval,

---

38. Harrison, *Acts*, pp. 114-15; Rex Koivisto, "Stephen's Speech: A Theology of Errors?" *Grace Theological Journal* 8.1 (1987): 106. Essentially skipping Isaac and Jacob continued the "outside the Land" focus as it moved directly to Joseph. Stephen had also spoken of the covenant declaration that Abraham's descendants would be enslaved and mistreated in a foreign land. Joseph was the means of getting them there.

39. Notably, the portable Tabernacle that Stephen addressed later in the speech was made outside the Land.

40. It is important that the text says "they" and not "their bodies" or "their bones."

there would be an Egyptian sojourn. It may be that the land purchase is viewed in the context of this "delay" in Egypt. Abraham's original purchase for Sarah's tomb near Hebron took place before the tribes went to Egypt, but Stephen wanted to make the point that the *inheritance* came after their redemption from Egypt; that redemption was intrinsically tied with Joseph.[41] Thus, he focused on the Shechem burial of Joseph's bones and reconnected it all with Abraham to whom the promise had been made. The final resting place for the patriarchs, whether in Hebron or Shechem, insured inheritance of the land God promised.[42] Stephen's reference to Abraham in verse 16 serves a literary inclusio for this section; the promise first came to him and it was fulfilled with the burial of all the patriarchs who were brought back because of what Joseph did.

Land was as important in the context of physical death as it was in life; being with the ancestors in death meant they were bound together approaching the eschatological inheritance, the fullness of the Kingdom or the world to come.[43] It was important from that perspective that these twelve ancestors all be "in the same place," affirming the indivisibility of the children of Israel. The covenant and the promised redemption were for the whole people, the twelve tribes.

Porous Boundaries: Times and Places

Transcending chronological boundaries is evident early in Stephen's speech. God "did not give to him an inheritance (κληρονομία) in [the land], not even a foot's length, but promised to give it to him as his possession (κατάσχεσις) and to his descendants after him, even though he had no child" (Acts 7:5).[44] In that one verse, Stephen declared that Abraham would

41. Soards (*The Speeches in Acts*, pp. 62-63) noted that this is the only mention of Joseph in the book of Acts and it is presented with a clear emphasis on the sovereignty of God in preparing Joseph for his position.

42. That Jacob and his sons were buried in the Land indicates that the promise of God was fulfilled. Even if they died in Egypt, their bodies were brought back in faith (Bruce, *Acts*, pp. 148-49).

43. In its fullest sense, κληρονομία (inheritance) refers to lasting possession in an eschatological sense. Inheriting the earth is a foretaste of inheriting eternal life; that is part of the hope and expectation. In the New Testament, the inheritance is God's kingdom (Werner Foerster, κλῆρος, in *Theological Dictionary of the New Testament*, vol. 3, ed. Gerhard Kittel [Grand Rapids: Eerdmans, 1965], pp. 778-79).

44. Κληρονομία frequently translates נחלה in the LXX with reference to the Land as it

participate in the inheritance across the barrier of his own death. We are to understand κληρονομία in this context as the apportionment of the Land by lot. That would not be Abraham's; his purchase at Machpelah was but a small parcel. When, however, his promised descendents were united in burial, he and they had a lasting hold (κατάσχεσις), even as *their* living descendents apportioned the conquered land. Abraham's participation in the purchase reinforces that sense of organic unity, the indivisible nature of this people across time and space, that infused rabbinic Judaism. Categories of time and distinctions between past, present, and future were set aside.[45]

And what possible warrant is there for this interpretation? Even within the New Testament, we have a possible parallel, albeit in reverse. Just as Levi is said to have participated in the tithe that Abraham gave to Melchizedek because he was "in Abraham's loins" (Heb. 7:9-10), so here Abraham was a party to Jacob's purchase because he was still alive, as it were.[46] Stephen's declaration becomes a subtle allusion to resurrection; Abraham would indeed inherit the "land" as God promised. One of numerous rabbinic arguments affirming resurrection of the dead also demonstrates the same time warping method. As the Sages understood it, the biblical injunction ". . . and you shall set aside [from the tithes] the *t'rumah* of the Lord to Aaron the priest" (Num. 18:28b) meant paying tithes to Aaron when they would be in the Land, a proof for his resurrection, even though he was long dead, physically speaking (Sanh 90b).[47] In sum, the ac-

---

was apportioned to Israel (Foerster, κλῆρος, pp. 758-69). The "foot of ground" is an allusion to Deut. 2:5, the only place it appears. In that context, God declared that he would not give Israel so much as a foot step of Edom's territory. Even so, Stephen went on to say that God "promised to give it (the Land) to him and to his seed with him εἰς κατάσχεσις." The latter expression appears solely in the LXX as a translation of אחזה, something that is held firmly. In Gen. 17:8 and 48:4 the expression refers to the land as a "possession forever." See Barrett, *Acts*, 1:343-44.

45. See Jacob Neusner, "Theology of Genesis Rabbah," in *Encyclopaedia of Midrash: Biblical Interpretation in Formative Judaism*, 2 vols., ed. Jacob Neusner and Alan J. Avery-Peck (Leiden: Brill, 2005), pp. 105-8. See also Jacob Neusner, ed., *Genesis Rabbah: The Judaic Commentary to the Book of Genesis, A New American Translation*, vol. 3, Brown Judaic Studies 106 (Atlanta: Scholars Press, 1985).

46. Mare ("Acts 7: Jewish or Samaritan," p. 20) affirmed that Abraham was "included with Jacob in his later purchase [since] . . . , in the pattern similar to Hebrew 7:9 . . . Levi is said to have participated in Abraham's earlier tithes."

47. When Jesus declared that the God of Abraham, Isaac, and Jacob is God of the living and not the dead (Matt. 22:32; Mark 12:27; Luke 20:38), he was firmly within the sphere of Pharisaic and subsequent rabbinic thinking.

tivities of key patriarchal figures (and others as well) transcended the chronological boundaries established during their physical presence on earth.[48]

In Closing

What might we learn from Stephen's references to "our father Abraham"? Stephen's recital of history teaches that God's promises are sure and his sovereign interventions bring his will for Abraham's descendents to fruition. To our unending benefit as those grafted in, his promises and presence transcend temporal and national boundaries.

In regard to the questions surrounding the nature of Scripture, Stephen's preaching and Luke's record of it illustrate the rich tapestry that emerged as he wove together biblical narratives to convey profound truths about God's inviolable promises of participating in everlasting inheritance, even as he acknowledged the physical deaths of the patriarchs and in the face of his own impending death. These theological truths expanded the meanings of the original texts in the Torah. For Stephen, the Scriptures were "living and active" (Heb. 4:12); he apprehended the power of the dynamic, ever-effective word of God and preached it toward that end.

48. This is likely related to the last of the "Thirty-two Rules" for rabbinic interpretation ascribed to Rabbi Yose ben Eleazar in the second century: "there is no early and late in the Torah" (Günter Stemberger, *Introduction to the Talmud and Midrash*, 2nd ed., trans. Markus Bockmuehl [Edinburgh: T&T Clark, 1996], pp. 22-30).

Who Are Abraham's True Children?
The Role of Abraham in Pauline Argumentation

GORDON D. FEE

The purpose of this study, as the subtitle indicates, is to investigate the role of Abraham in Pauline argumentation. And it is probably fair to say at the outset that Abraham would have played almost no role at all had it not been for the "agitators"[1] who had tried to disrupt Paul's churches in Galatia by insisting on the circumcision of Gentile believers.[2] The result is that Abraham plays a major role at the beginning of Paul's first argument from Scripture in Galatians 3:6-29, a matter to which Paul then returns briefly at the beginning of his second scriptural argument in 4:21-23. Abraham is then brought in, but with a bit less passion, at a similar point in the argument of Romans (4:1-25). However, Abraham plays a considerably different role in this later letter, so one of the concerns of this study is to ask whether our understanding of Paul's use of Abraham would be different if

---

1. For this language, see my *Galatians* (Blandford Forum, Dorset, UK: Deo Publishing, 2007), p. 6; it is what Paul actually calls them in 5:11. Since it is very difficult for a person to write twice on the same material without repeating what has been said elsewhere, I offer the necessary apologies for this in advance, and trust that the reworking of that material for this paper with its singular focus will be deemed acceptable in this case.

2. Abraham's appearance in Romans, then, is due simply to the fact that Galatians serves as a basic template for this later letter.

I am delighted to offer these musings in honor of a friend of many years. Maudine and I lived two houses from Marv and Polly on Martel Road during the twelve years I taught at Gordon-Conwell (1974-86), and he was at that time already teaching Old Testament at Gordon College. Perhaps this contribution will make some amends for the forgotten dinner invitation many years ago!

we possessed only one of these two letters. The only other mention of Abraham in the Pauline corpus appears in one of those passing moments when Paul is justifying his own Jewishness in 2 Corinthians 11:22 and in a lesser way in Romans 11:1. We begin this study with the latter two passages, not because they are the more significant, but because they reveal something of the nature of the contentions with which Paul had to deal.

I. Paul as a "Son" of Abraham

The *ad hominem* nature of the argumentation in 2 Corinthians 11:22 suggests that those who have circulated in some of the Pauline churches, urging the Gentiles to come to "completion" by submitting to circumcision, have been on Paul's case for some time.[3] In the redundancy of his rhetoric against his opponents, he bursts out with the threefold affirmation: "Are they Hebrews? So am I! Are they Israelites? So am I! Are they Abraham's offspring? So am I!" While the first two of these rhetorical questions set the stage for ethnicity, the last one focuses on the real issue between Paul and these agitators, namely, "who constitute the genuine children of Abraham?" Paul's point in this case seems to be the earliest moment in his letters where he feels compelled to assert his own genuine Jewishness. And since, by his own confession, he lived as a Gentile when among Gentiles,[4] his true birthright as a Jew was the fact that he "was circumcised on the eighth day."[5]

Similarly, in Romans 11:1 Paul again offers himself as primary evidence that by including the Gentiles in the newly formed people of God, God had not thereby cast off his ancient people. "I myself am an Israelite," he reminds them, which is then further legitimated by his being also "of

3. This point would be strengthened, of course, if we argued that Galatians was Paul's earliest letter, but it almost certainly was not. See my *Galatians*, pp. 4-5. Speculating on whether or not the same opponents stand behind these letters is not helpful, since we can never know for sure. Still, since we find similar types of arguments in these letters, I will assume here that Paul is responding at least to similar situations.

4. See especially his argumentation in 1 Cor. 9:19-23 for the "right" to do this. This assertion probably had to do with association in general and food in particular.

5. Phil. 3:5. Nor did it hurt that he could trace his ancestry as a Benjaminite, the one tribe that stayed faithful to Judah and was carried off into exile with them. According to Ezra/Nehemiah, they were therefore one of the two tribes that returned to their native land. Although Paul's own family was a part of the Diaspora, these references make clear that he was well instructed in the significance of his kinship.

the seed of Abraham," where the language "seed" picks up the important point of the dialogue between Abraham and Yahweh in Genesis 15:1-5. Thus in both of these passages Paul's concern is to establish or assert his own legitimacy as a *Jewish* follower of Christ, a need brought about by his special calling to bring the gospel to the Gentiles — without at the same time demanding that they "go through Jewish hoops," as it were, in order to have integrity as part of God's newly formed people. If these intruders, as seems most likely, have actually appealed to their own legitimacy as Jews, then Paul is prepared to go "toe to toe" with them on this crucial point. He too is a true "child of Abraham."[6]

II. The Role of Abraham in Galatians 3:6-29

Although one must use due caution in mirror-reading any text, the very uniqueness of the argument of Galatians 3 leads one here to ask the "so what's going on in Galatia?" question as a matter of course; and in this case Paul's own rhetoric arguably gives us the needed clues. Thus, after the opening series of *ad hominem* rhetorical questions appealing to their own past (vv. 2-4) and present (v. 5) experience of the Spirit, Paul moves directly into an argument from Scripture itself, where Abraham plays the leading role. Indeed, as the TNIV has tried to show, perhaps a bit awkwardly, our verse 6 is not a stand-alone sentence, but is in fact the final clause of the rhetorical question posed in verse 5. Thus, "Does God give you his Spirit and work miracles among you by your observing the law, or by your believing what you heard, just as Abraham 'believed God, and it was credited to him as righteousness'?"[7] The very uniqueness of this argumentation would seem to justify a kind of mirror-reading that sees Paul here as taking on the basic argument of the "agitators" themselves. Their point would have been made on the basis of Genesis 17, where Abraham sealed the covenant with Yahweh by having himself and all the males in his household circumcised. Thus circumcision was deemed a necessary sign for the Gentiles of their inclusion

6. It is perhaps of further interest that in a similar appeal to his Jewish credentials in Phil. 3:4-6, Paul does not mention Abraham, but simply affirms his *tribal* identity. Cf. also Col. 4:11.

7. The TNIV, in keeping with the earlier NIV policy of offering shorter sentences for the sake of second-language readers, punctuates with the question mark at the traditional place at the end of v. 5; but the translators, by their paragraphing, have at least made it clear that v. 6 belongs to that question.

in "the people of God," just as had been practiced for some centuries on any Gentiles who chose to convert to Judaism.

Paul's own rejection of this point of view is based on his and his churches' experience of the Spirit, whereby God gave evidence that these Gentiles were also in fact included in his people by grace alone, hence the nature of the rhetoric that begins in Galatians 3:1. Their response to this grace was "faith," which for Paul meant total trust in God to be as good as his word. Crucial for Paul was the historical fact that the declaration of Abraham's "righteousness" preceded, and was therefore independent of, the Mosaic Law that came 430 years later.[8] The Mosaic Law, indeed circumcision too, were for Paul external signs of covenant loyalty and thus of identification. For Paul, therefore, Abraham became the key to all Gentile acceptance with God — on the basis of their trusting God, not on the basis of "doing the law," just as was the case with Abraham.

Two matters would seem to be at work that brought Paul, himself a rigorous Pharisee and thus "keeper of the Law," to this conviction on behalf of his Gentile converts. First of all would be Paul's own experience of grace on the Damascus Road. Whatever else Paul needed to "sort out" in Arabia (Gal. 1:17) in terms of what had happened to him, he ultimately came from that experience deeply convinced that God accepted people by grace alone, and that all his prior "Jewish privileges," including his passionate adherence to the Law, counted for nothing in terms of one's own relationship to God (1:13-14). After all, even though Paul never put it quite this way, Abraham himself was uncircumcised (and thus the same as a Gentile) when he was called.

Second, and what serves as Paul's greatest coup in all of this argumentation, is the fact that the narrative of Abraham's acceptance with Yahweh in Genesis 15, the "believing" of which was counted to him as "righteousness," *preceded* the narrative in Genesis 17 of his also accepting the identifying marker of circumcision. Furthermore, and equally significant for him, the *pisteuō* (= believe = have faith = trust) word group does not occur at all in this latter narrative. Thus even though, as his opponents would most likely have argued, Abraham had in fact been circumcised as a way of "sealing" the covenant, nonetheless for Paul the key to the Genesis narrative lay with the affirmation (in 15:6), "Abraham *believed* Yahweh, and Yahweh credited it to him as righteousness." It is probably fair to argue that this ordering of the Genesis narrative, and its language regarding Abra-

8. Cf. the similar historical argument in Rom. 4.

ham's relationship to Yahweh, was not simply a *convenience* for Paul, but a matter of deep theological *conviction*. How else, one might well ask, apart from Paul's own experience of God's sovereign grace on the Damascus Road, could he have carried such deep conviction as to God's acceptance of Gentiles by their trusting Christ Jesus alone, quite apart from their relationship to the Torah in any shape or form?

This crucial role played by Abraham in Paul's argument is confirmed by the way the complementary paragraph (our 3:10-14) concludes, so that the two paragraphs are held together as two sides of a single argument by their chiastic structure. The first paragraph (vv. 7-9) begins with Abraham and concludes that "those who rely *on faith* are blessed along with Abraham, the man of faith" (TNIV), while the second paragraph (vv. 10-14) begins with the antithesis "those who rely on observing the law are under a curse" and concludes that those who have experienced redemption through Christ have thus entered into "the blessing given to Abraham." Moreover, despite centuries of misunderstanding among Protestant interpreters of this second paragraph, the option Paul presents is not *inability* to keep the law, which is not so much as hinted at,[9] but the *necessity* of doing so, in terms of keeping the *whole* law. This in turn thus automatically cut one off from putting one's trust in Christ. Paul's point seems clear: it is "either-or," not "both-and," regarding trusting Christ or doing the law. Partial obedience to the law is simply not an option of any kind.[10]

In this argument, therefore, Abraham serves as the prime example of one who trusted God and whose trust was thereby credited to him as righteousness. So Paul concludes this portion of the argument (in 3:14) by referring to "the blessing of Abraham" to which these Gentile believers are heirs — heirs not by way of the same circumcision that Abraham had, but by having the same *faith* that he had, a trust in God that was reckoned to him as "righteousness."

Then in 3:23-29, the first of his two conclusions to this argument

9. This seems to be one of those places where one's theological proclivities have gotten in the way of a good reading of the text, since there is not a hint of any kind in Paul's sentence that people are unable to keep the law. At issue, as is pointed out, is whether partial obedience is viable.

10. This seems also to be reflected in the fact that the three "boundary markers" that gave Diaspora Judaism its identity (circumcision, food laws, and Sabbath observance [including the rest of the Jewish calendar]) are all spoken to in some way in Galatians (circumcision throughout; food laws in 2:11-14; Sabbath observance incidentally in 4:10).

from Scripture,[11] Paul picks up the issue of "who are *Abraham's true heirs*" by affirming at the end, "if you belong to Christ, then you are Abraham's seed, and heirs according to the promise."[12] And the whole of this argumentation is best understood as both response and correction to the assertions of the agitators and their insistence on *circumcision* as the proper evidence of being Abraham's heirs. Abraham's true heirs are those who have like "faith" with Abraham, since that alone was attributed to him as "righteousness" regarding his own relationship with Yahweh.

III. The Role of Abraham in Galatians 4:21-31

When Paul returns to Abraham at the beginning of his second argument from Scripture,[13] his primary concern is not directly with Torah obedience as such, but with the related issue of "freedom and slavery" — *freedom from* the law and for Christ vis-à-vis *slavery to* the law and thus alienation from Christ. Although Paul's primary concern in this new section is to show once more that the true children of Abraham are not under confinement to Torah — and thus are "free" — he now returns to these matters by way of the theme of slavery that emerged in 4:1-7. This theme, however, is not elaborated by way of the sons, but of their mothers; and it is made possible for Paul through Hagar, who in the Septuagint is regularly called "the slave woman" (6 times in Gen. 16:1-8). This then is how Abraham himself comes into the argument, by way of the statement, "Abraham had two sons" (v. 22). The issue, therefore, remains the same: "enslavement to the law," with perhaps a hint of their being "enslaved" by the agitators. The theme of "freedom," however, is now picked up through Sarah and her son Isaac, who, Paul asserts, was "born according to the Spirit." Paul then concludes the argument by making the same point he made in 3:29 and 4:1-7, that "we are children of freedom (= Christ), not of slavery (= the law)."

11. The second one, of course, is 4:1-7.

12. The second conclusion (4:1-7) then asserts that "those in Christ are *God's true 'sons.'*" At issue, then, is who constitutes Abraham's true heirs (i.e., children of the promise), because such people are at the same time the true "heirs of God" (4:7).

13. The first argument from Scripture in 3:1–4:7 is concerned about "who are Abraham's true children," the answer to which is, "those who have faith similar to that of Abraham." This second argument from Scripture deals with "who are the children of Abraham's true wife, Sarah?" the answer to which, put negatively, is "those who are not born of the slave woman."

Near the end (4:29), he clearly refers to the agitators again, as "sons according to the flesh," who are persecuting those born "according to the Spirit" and who, like Hagar and Ishmael, must be "thrown out."

It should be noted here, therefore, that the mention of Abraham, though a pickup of the discussion about him in 3:6-27, is incidental rather than significant. Furthermore, despite the "thesis sentence" about Abraham's having two sons, the focus is altogether on his two wives, one called "the slave woman" and the other consistently called "the free woman" in the section (4:22, 23, 26, 30, 31).

The question of interest, of course, is why Paul even spoke of the two sons, since the focus is altogether on the mothers. The answer to this seems to be that the language of "sonship/heirship" tends to dominate the preceding argument from Scripture. Since Paul had asserted, but not elaborated, that "the promises were spoken to Abraham and to *his seed*" (3:16), at issue in the analogy is "which seed? Isaac or Ishmael? the child of the 'free' woman or the child of the 'slave' woman?" Thus Paul begins by focusing on the twofold "seed," but his interest is altogether on the two mothers, because of the language in the Septuagint regarding Hagar, that she was "the slave woman" (Gen. 16:1-8). For Paul, by way of analogy, those who choose to "keep the law" are the heirs not of Sarah, but of Hagar, the slave woman, and thus they are "born to slavery," as over against being born into the freedom that Christ alone can give. As before, Paul almost certainly takes the analogy from the Abraham narrative because this was the Scripture used by his opponents to urge circumcision on Gentile believers in Christ — as the way of legitimizing their conversion. But Paul will have none of it.

IV. The Role of Abraham in Romans 4

Although the essential points Paul had made earlier in Galatians are reiterated in the argument of Romans 4, in fact Abraham functions in a considerably different way here, not in contrast to Galatians but as a reflective elaboration. Thus several further points are made by way of Abraham and his "faith." Here is also a place where the "chapter and verse numbers" get in the way of good reading, since in effect the whole of this argument is responding to the three basic questions posed in 3:27-31: (a) "Where, then, is boasting?" [v. 27]; (b) "Is God the God of Jews only? Is he not the God of Gentiles too?" [v. 29]; and (c) "Do we then nullify the law by this faith?" [v. 31]. Paul now proceeds to use Abraham to justify everything he has argued up to this point in chapters 1:16–3:26, and thereby aims to demonstrate that "faith establishes Torah," in the sense expressed in 3:21, as "bearing witness to it."

The entire passage (Rom. 4:1-25), it should be noted, apart from the momentary addition of David as supporting Paul's own theological viewpoint, is basically a midrashic exposition of Genesis 15:6. What is being demonstrated by Abraham's having been "justified by faith" is threefold. First, Paul's emphasis in verses 4-8 and 12 lies with the fact that it is especially true for "the Jew" that "faith alone" is the means by which one is justified before God. Indeed, Abraham's importance lies with the fact that he is the "father" of the covenant people themselves, and yet he himself was "justified" on the basis of his faith, not by his circumcision. Second, in verses 9-11 Paul argues that at the same time, because Abraham was thus "justified by faith" *before* he received the covenant of circumcision, he is thus by way of analogy the "father" of Gentiles who similarly have faith. After all, Abraham himself was in effect a "Gentile" when he was "reckoned" to be justified by faith. Finally, third, in verses 13-25 Paul notes that the *promise* made to Abraham (Gen. 18:18-19), that he would be the "father of many" nations and that his "heirs" would inherit the world, was based altogether on "the righteousness of faith" (v. 13), and *not* on Torah observance. Thus "through his faith" Abraham became the father of both Jew and Gentile who have faith comparable to Abraham's.

The *issue* in this passage, it should be noted, is not simply the "doctrine" of "justification by faith" *per se,* as the Protestant tradition historically has wished to put it. Rather, the issue Paul addresses is that "justification by faith" is for *Jews and Gentiles alike,*[14] as the conclusion to the first part of the argument in verses 11 and 12 make certain. It is for Jews, because the *possession* of Torah in itself gave the Jew no advantage over the Gentile; only *adherence* to it counted for anything. It is for Gentiles, because by Abraham's faith he became "the father of *many* nations" (v. 17). Such a view of things seems to be supported both by the structure of the argument and by its many details as well. The argument itself is in two major sections (vv. 1-12 and 13-25), with two subsections each (vv. 1-8/9-12 and vv. 13-15/16-25), and Abraham plays the major role throughout.

14. This, after all, is where the whole argument of the letter is heading, which its ringing conclusion in 15:5-12 makes certain. Christ became "a servant to the Jews . . . so that the Gentiles might glorify God for his mercy," the affirmation of which is then supported by four texts whose common denominator is the word *ethnē.*

Romans 4:1-12. In this first section Paul argues that Abraham serves as the demonstration from Torah itself that righteousness is by faith, and not by works of Torah. Thus he begins by way of rhetorical questions that conclude with a citation of Genesis 15:6: "Abraham *believed* God and it was *reckoned* to him for *righteousness.*" One can hardly miss how the three emphasized words are picked up in a variety of ways throughout this section. Included, of course, is the emphatic counter-declaration, that righteousness for Abraham was *not* reckoned on the basis of "works of Torah" (v. 2; supported by David in v. 6). So this becomes the first way that "faith upholds Torah," by the fact that it *precedes* Torah, and therefore Abraham's own "righteousness" was totally unrelated to it.

It should be noted here that Paul's concern is not simply that Abraham serves as Exhibit A for justification by faith alone, but that Abraham's own faith-before-circumcision eliminates all possibility of "boasting" on the part of the Jew (Jewish believers in Christ, in this case), which is quite the point of verse 2. "Boasting" of course in Paul does not have to do with *pride* as such, but with putting one's confidence in something ahead of God, and thus something other than God's own gracious acceptance of sinners. We know from elsewhere (esp. 1 Cor. 1:26-31) that Paul's use of "boasting" language stems from Jeremiah 9:23-24, where Israel was told that the only legitimate "boasting" is in God alone. Thus Abraham's "faith," his trust in Yahweh and his faithfulness, was alone reckoned to him as "righteousness."

The basic argument in verses 1-3 is then rehearsed in verses 9-12 in terms of the one crucial "work of Torah" — circumcision — since this was the covenantal "boundary marker." Here Paul makes two points regarding Abraham. First, he points out that the statement in Genesis 15:6, that Abraham's *faith* was reckoned to him as righteousness, was made while Abraham himself was "an uncircumcised Gentile," as it were; and thus circumcision was to be understood as "God's seal" regarding his faith. Second, and equally important to the argument, Paul urges that by this means (his faith, followed later by circumcision) Abraham became the father of both the circumcised Jews and the uncircumcised Gentiles — and both of them on the basis of faith, not of circumcision. All of this is concluded in verse 12 with a sentence having this remarkable word order: "the while-in-uncircumcision faith of our father Abraham." Although this word order cannot be carried over into English translation, one can scarcely miss the fact that the essential thing Paul wants to say here about Abraham is found in his enclosed prepositional phrase ("the while-in-uncircumcision faith") and its concluding genitive ("of our father Abraham"). One should also note the "our" in this final phrase, which by way of the preceding argumentation now means not simply "Abraham the father of the Jews," but "Abraham the father of all who believe in the way he did."

Paul's point, it should therefore be noted, is not simply the theological one — that salvation is by faith and not by doing the law — as though anyone were actually trying to do the latter. Rather, his point is that Abraham, the "father" of the Jews, was justified by faith while still an "uncircumcised Gentile," as it were; and thereby he is the father of Jew and Gentile alike, on the same grounds — by faith alone.

Romans 4:13-25. If Abraham's "justification" was by faith alone, however, equally important for Paul in this argument is that the *promise* made to Abraham is also based on faith, not on his obedience regarding circumcision; and this is the concern of the rest of the argument in Romans 4. Thus the whole of verses 13-21 is dominated by the concept of "promise"; but the "promise" takes two forms, resulting from Paul's concerns in the argument. Abraham now takes center stage throughout, until the crucial theological point regarding Abraham is made in verse 22. At that point the argument segues into an application that allows Paul thus to pick up the thread of the argument which he had momentarily dropped at the end of chapter 3. This is not to say that chapter 4 is not crucial to Paul's argument — it is indeed. But it is to say that it serves as a necessary adjunct so that he can establish the crucial point of the argument throughout the letter, that "justification by faith" is the necessary basis for the fulfilling of the Abrahamic covenant. Only in this way can both Jew and Gentile be included in the newly formed people of God on the same grounds.

This second part of the argument likewise has two (in this case, unequal) components, verses 13-22 and 23-25. Although the first part of this argument gets a bit convoluted, two essential points are made. First, the promise made to Abraham regarding "inheritance" was based on faith, not on the basis of "works," probably intending "works of Torah." Second, this promise was made to *all* his seed, which for Paul is understood to imply that there would indeed be such "seed," namely those mentioned in verses 11b-12, those both of circumcision and of uncircumcision. In making this point, yet another text from Genesis is brought forth, now from 17:5, that "I [Yahweh] have made you [Abraham] the father of *many* nations," cited by Paul in verse 17.

What is of interest is that, given that the primary point Paul wanted to make with this text seems self-explanatory in context, he *concludes* the argument in verses 17b-25 with an unexpected twist regarding Abraham's faith. Since the birth of Isaac was the result first of all of Yahweh's own faithfulness to Abraham, the nature of Abraham's faith in this regard is thus given an especially Christian interpretation. And although this has sometimes been perceived as evidence of Abraham's "great faith," Paul's concern in the immediate context is not with its "quantitative" nature, but with its special character. Indeed, what Abraham becomes for Paul at this point is the forerunner of all who have particularly "Christian faith," since the nature of Abraham's faith was that he believed in the one who gives life to the dead.

It seems fair to suggest that Paul himself may not have thought through how this argument would get to where it had to go, for the sake of the overall concern of the letter. But it does seem clear enough in terms of how he actually got to the affirmations of verses 24b-25, that God's crediting Abraham with righteousness was altogether on the grounds of his believing/trusting Yahweh. In effect, Paul says, Abraham's faith that God would keep his word, that the barren (and now "dead") womb of Sarah would bear a child, served as the precursor for believers in Christ — both Jew and Gentile — whose faith in God also rests on his bringing life from death. Thus God's assurance to Abraham that his "faith was credited to him as righteousness" has now reached its fulfillment in the resurrection of Christ from the dead. And having made that point, Paul cannot but conclude on the strongest kind of confessional note: "He (Jesus our Lord) was delivered over to death for our sins and was raised to life for our justification."

Thus in this way Abraham becomes "the father of us all," both Jew and Gentile, because ultimately his true "seed" was given up for us all so that we too might be raised to life through him.

V. Conclusion

At the beginning the question was posed as to whether our understanding of the role of Abraham in Pauline argumentation would have been different if we possessed only one of these letters. The answer seems to be a kind of "yes and no": "yes" because Romans fills out the picture in many ways; but "no" in that the essential understanding of Abraham's role in Paul's thinking seems to be very much on the same track. Perhaps the most striking observation that can be made from this brief overview is that in reading Paul's letters one must not let "quantity" get in the way of "quality" when it comes to setting forth a genuinely Pauline view of what God has done in Christ. In fact, it seems altogether likely that had it not been for the troublesome "agitators" who were invading his churches, Paul may not have mentioned Abraham in any significant way at all. But because of their encroachments into the churches he had founded, we get a more detailed understanding of Pauline theology in general and of his understanding of the role of Abraham as "the father of us all" (Rom 4:16) in particular. Abraham's ultimate significance for Paul was the simple fact that because he had received God's promise and had thus put his trust in Yahweh *before* he was circumcised (and thus was for all practical purposes himself a Gentile before his divine election), he could thereby — and here Paul maintained his integrity as a Jew — be understood as the "father" of all who have similarly trusted Yahweh and have had that trust credited to them as "righteousness" = "right-standing" with God.

The Law and the Promise:
God's Covenant with Abraham
in Pauline Perspective

William B. Barcley

It is a joy and an honor for me to contribute to this collection of essays dedicated to my former professor, mentor, and colleague, Marv Wilson. I owe so much to Marv and Polly. As a student at Gordon College, uncertain of my course of study, it was Marv's Old Testament survey course during my freshman year that got me excited about Biblical Studies and led me to become a Biblical and Theological Studies major. Marv gave me the opportunity to be his teacher's assistant in New Testament Greek and occasionally to teach while he was out of town, whetting my appetite for more classroom teaching. During one summer of study in Israel, Marv and Polly even kept my car for me. They looked after me while at college as second parents. Their impact has stamped my life.

Marv was instrumental in launching my teaching career, recommending me for a Greek Teaching Fellowship at Gordon-Conwell Theological Seminary, later inviting me to teach Greek for several years at Gordon College when they were in need of a part-time instructor and finally supporting me as I came on at Gordon as a full-time professor in New Testament. No one has had as big an influence on my professional career as Marv has. Frankly, I'm not sure where I'd be if it were not for Marv. And even now, as I have moved out of academia and into full-time pastoral ministry, I can still feel Marv's influence on my life. Marv's love for Christ, his dedication to the Word of God, and his commitment to his students have been a model that I have tried to emulate. I'm not sure Marv has quite gotten over the turn that I took theologically (!); still, I am indebted to him beyond what I can express.

As a scholar, I am indebted to Marv for two things in particular. The first is the grounding that he gave me in the Old Testament, impressing upon me that one cannot fully understand the New Testament without grasping the Old. I am also indebted to Marv for giving me a clear picture of Judaism. Long before I had heard of the so-called "New Perspective on Paul," I learned from Marv that Judaism was not a religion of crass legalism in which one's merits were measured against demerits. God chose Israel, redeemed them from slavery, entered into a covenant with them, and became their God. They became God's people. There was nothing to commend Israel to God, yet God chose them — simply because he loved them (Deut. 7:6-8). This is a clear indication of God's grace.

It is this gracious nature of God's dealings with Israel that I will use as a jumping off point for a study of Galatians 3. It is my purpose in this paper to demonstrate the unity, the continuity, and the gracious nature of God's covenants with his people in Scripture. Galatians 3 is a wonderful place to examine this because scholars have so often used this passage as proof of the contrast and discontinuity in the covenants. In particular, many have seen here a stark law/gospel contrast, or, to put it differently, a strong disconnect between the Abrahamic and Mosaic covenants.

This understanding often stems from a misreading specifically of Galatians 3:15-22, the focus of this paper. In this passage, Paul discusses the relationship between the promise(s)[1] given to Abraham and the law, which came 430 years later. A typical interpretation of this passage is that Paul is engaged in a bit of one-upmanship, attempting to show the superiority of the Abrahamic covenant to the Mosaic. The law, it is argued, is inferior because it was given later, was put in place through angels and required a human mediator, Moses. The promise to Abraham, on the other hand, came first and was given directly by God to Abraham. No mediator was required.

An initial problem with this reading is that it flies in the face of biblical and especially Pauline teaching elsewhere. If the earlier and unmediated covenant is always better, then the Abrahamic covenant is also superior to the new covenant, which was last of all and also required a mediator (cf. 1 Tim. 2:5). But the biblical picture is clearly that the new covenant is the climactic covenant, the greatest of all God's covenants with his people (cf. Jer. 31:31-34; 2 Cor. 3).

A key to understanding this passage, often missed by interpreters, is

---

1. Paul uses the plural in vv. 16 and 21, the singular in vv. 17, 18, 19, and 22. The singular is also used just prior to our passage, in v. 14, where Paul refers to "the promise of the Spirit."

that twice Paul says that the promise was made to Christ (vv. 16 and 19). It is the Christocentric nature of this passage that enables us to unpack not only the relationships between the covenants, but also to understand the many difficult statements in this passage.

Without a doubt, Galatians 3:15-22 contains some of the most difficult verses in Paul's letters. For example, does διαθήκην in v. 15 mean covenant, reflecting its Septuagintal meaning, or does it mean testament or will, as in Paul's Greco-Roman culture? Does Paul misuse Scripture when he capitalizes on the singular "seed," as referring to Christ (v. 16), when he knew that the word most commonly had a collective sense (cf. 3:29)? What is the meaning of the cryptic description of the law as added "because of transgressions" (v. 19)? And how are we to understand the equally cryptic v. 20: ὁ δὲ μεσίτης ἑνὸς οὐκ ἔστιν, ὁ δὲ Θεὸς εἷς ἐστιν. The verse is easy enough to translate. But what is the point in the present context? We will not have time in this brief essay to unpack all of the difficulties. But understanding the Christocentric nature of this passage will help to bring some initial clarity, will shed light on a few problematic verses, and will at least point us in the right direction on the others.

We need to begin our examination of this passage with a brief discussion of the context. For several hundred years, since the time of the Reformation, there has been a general consensus among Protestants, and for that matter even many Roman Catholics,[2] as to the problem that Paul was addressing in Galatians. A group of Jewish Christians had come to the Galatian churches and begun to teach the Gentile believers that if they wanted to be true Christians, they needed to be circumcised and keep the law of Moses. For Paul, this was tantamount to adding works to faith. So he opposed this teaching as a false, legalistic gospel in which human beings are saved not by God's grace through faith in Christ, but by human works.

This consensus has been shattered recently, especially with the rise of the so-called New Perspective(s) on Paul. This movement was spearheaded by the work of E. P. Sanders who argued that first-century Judaism was not a religion of legalistic works-righteousness.[3] If that is the case, then Paul in Galatians could not be defending his gospel against legalism. Instead, the New Perspective argues, the problem that Paul is refuting is not Jewish le-

---

2. See the discussion of Moisés Silva, "Faith Versus Works of Law in Galatians," in *Justification and Variegated Nomism*, vol. 2: *The Paradoxes of Paul*, ed. D. A. Carson, Peter T. O'Brien, and Mark A. Seifrid (Grand Rapids: Baker, 2004), p. 244.

3. E. P. Sanders, *Paul and Palestinian Judaism* (Philadelphia: Fortress, 1977).

galism, but a narrow Jewish nationalism in which Gentiles, as Gentiles, are being excluded. The "works of the law" in Galatians do not refer to legalistic attempts to win the favor of God and earn salvation. Rather, they are specific Jewish boundary markers, like circumcision, Sabbath, and food laws, that separate Jews from Gentiles. Gentiles were being excluded from full participation in the community until they converted to Judaism.

Thus, the New Perspective argues, the key issue in Galatians is not soteriology — how is one saved? how does a sinner become right with God? — but ecclesiology — how can Jews and Gentiles coexist in the church? This reading also seems to fit nicely with Paul's mission and call. This "Hebrew of Hebrews" and zealous former Pharisee was dramatically set apart and called by God to be the "apostle to the Gentiles." Indeed, a key element of Paul's work, in addition to preaching the gospel to the Gentiles, was the collection of an offering from the Gentiles to give to the Jewish Christians in Jerusalem. On the one hand, Paul desired to help those Jewish Christians who were suffering financial hardship because of their commitment to Christ. On the other hand, this collection was clearly also a symbolic gift to help unify the church along ethnic lines. (Marv, notice my use of the "Tevye construction" in the last two sentences!)

In this reading, then, the predominant issue in Galatians is the inclusion of the Gentiles in the people of God. T. David Gordon summarizes the interpretation of many in the New Perspective when he says that the "exclusion [of Gentiles] from full fellowship [in the church] is Paul's overriding concern."[4]

The problem with this reading, it seems to me, is an obvious one. It comes down to the question, To whom is Galatians addressed? If Galatians were specifically addressed to Paul's opponents, then it would leave open the possibility that Paul is calling them no longer to exclude the Gentile Christians. But Galatians is addressed to the Galatian Christians themselves, who seem to have been predominantly Gentiles. And as Paul addresses these "foolish Galatians," he does not ask them, "How does it feel to be excluded from fellowship with Jewish believers?" Nor does he tell them, "Fight for your rights to be included!"

Rather, he asks them, "How did you receive the Spirit?" And he warns them that if they seek to be justified by the law, they will be severed from Christ himself (5:4)! Clearly, Paul's primary concern is their relationship to God and their not being cut off from fellowship with Christ. The

---

4. T. David Gordon, "The Problem at Galatia," *Interpretation* 41 (1987): 41.

issues of fellowship and unity in the church are clearly important, as the later ethical injunctions indicate (Gal. 5:6–6:10). The exclusion of the Gentiles from fellowship almost certainly was an important concern for Paul. But soteriology, not ecclesiology, is what dominates Paul's discussion in this letter.

The assumption seems to be that because the tensions in Galatia involved ethnic division therefore the key issue is ethnic division. The opponents *may* have been preaching their gospel due to nationalism and a sense of ethnic superiority. But it is just as likely that their gospel came from confusion over the place of the law in the Christian life and their zeal for the commandments of God. Didn't Jesus say,

> Do not think that I have come to abolish the Law or the Prophets; I have not come to abolish them but to fulfill them. For truly, I say to you, until heaven and earth pass away, not an iota, not a dot, will pass from the Law until all is accomplished. Therefore whoever relaxes one of the least of these commandments and teaches others to do the same will be called least in the kingdom of heaven, but whoever does them and teaches them will be called great in the kingdom of heaven (Matthew 5:17-19)?

Does that not indicate that all the laws of God need to be obeyed (or so the opponents may have reasoned)?

The New Perspective on Paul has been helpful in many ways. It has pointed out some of the ethnic dimension that was missing in many former interpreters of Paul. In addition, it has highlighted the "covenantal" structure of the Bible and helped to demonstrate the gracious nature of God's covenants, even/especially the Mosaic covenant. The New Perspective has also warned us against reading first-century Judaism as a graceless religion of Pelagian works-righteousness in which one is saved by pulling himself up by his own bootstraps.[5] It also has shown clearly that salvation for most Jews was not a matter of crass legalism, the weighing of merits and demerits.

But the New Perspective has erred in seeing these as the only possible forms of legalism. Most importantly, in my view, the New Perspective, by imposing its own understanding of what Paul must have been battling against, has significantly mis-read the apostle to the Gentiles. This is true

---

5. This is the language of N. T. Wright, *What Saint Paul Really Said: Was Paul of Tarsus the Real Founder of Christianity?* (Grand Rapids: Eerdmans, 1997). Cf., e.g., pp. 18-20, 32.

even in the interpretations of Galatians 3:15-22 by two of the New Perspective's leading proponents, James Dunn and N. T. Wright. They will serve as conversation partners as we work our way through this text, though this will be kept largely to footnotes.

Galatians 3:15-22 comes in the midst of Paul's theological "proof" section, chapters 3–4.[6] Here Paul lays out his critical biblical and theological arguments as he seeks to convince the Galatian believers of the truth of his gospel. The Abraham story is central to his discussion. After some initial questions aimed at the Galatians and their experience (3:1-5), Paul moves on to Abraham's faith and God's promise to Abraham. But he also returns to the Abraham story at the end of chapter 4, contrasting Sarah and Hagar (4:21-31). So the Abraham story serves as an inclusio, Paul's central teaching tool in this all-important central section of the letter.

We can divide Galatians 3:15-22 into two sections — vv. 15-18 contrast the promises given to Abraham with the law, showing that the promised inheritance does not come through the law; vv. 19-22 ask the logical follow-up question, why then did God give the law? We will begin with the first section, focusing first on the promise.

The Promise (3:15-18)

We will approach this first section by asking two questions whose answers may seem surprising. First, to whom was the promise given? Second, what are the nature and the content of the promise? It is my contention that these two questions are the most commonly overlooked by scholars, and yet the most critical for understanding Paul's overall argument in this section.[7]

The first question, to whom was the promise given, has a three-part answer. The first part is no surprise — God's promise was given to Abraham, of course. But Paul does not stop there.

He goes on to say that the promise was also given to Abraham's "offspring" or "seed" (σπέρμα) whom, he says, are not Abraham's many descendants, but one descendant only, Christ (3:16). Paul repeats this in v. 19,

6. Betz, using the language and categories of ancient rhetoric, calls this the *probatio.* See H. D. Betz, *Galatians: A Commentary on Paul's Letter to the Churches in Galatia* (Philadelphia: Fortress, 1979), pp. 14-25.

7. This was pointed out by Sam Williams in his article, "Promise in Galatians: A Reading of Paul's Reading of Scripture," *Journal of Biblical Literature* 107.4 (1988): 709-20.

"until the offspring should come to whom the promise had been made."[8] God gave his promise to the Son whom he would later send into the world (4:4-5). Paul knew the word σπέρμα was used most often as a collective noun. In fact, he uses it that way in v. 29. Much ink has been spilt both vilifying Paul's sloppy exegesis and defending his methodology. I don't intend to enter the debate about the propriety of Paul's method, though we will see later why the reference to Christ is so important for Paul. For the time being, however, what matters is that for Paul God gave the promise to Christ.

Now, there is an important corollary to this, often overlooked by interpreters of Galatians. The presence of a "promise" assumes the presence of a covenant.[9] In other words, if God gave the promise to Christ, it means that God made an agreement or a covenant with his Son.[10] No reader of Genesis 15 would contest the fact that the promise to Abraham's descendants meant that God was establishing a covenant, not only with Abraham, but also with his seed. The same also holds true for Christ. The implications of this for our passage are vast. We will return to this below.

The third recipients of the promise are those who believe (v. 22). In context, those who believe are those who have faith in Christ.

8. Biblical quotations are from the English Standard Version.

9. Herman Witsius made this point a few hundred years ago. "But lest any should think, that Christ is, here only considered as the *executor* of the *testament*, bequeathed to us by God, the apostle twice repeats, that Christ was not promised to us, or that salvation was not promised to us through Christ, though that be also true; but that the promises were made to Christ himself, v. 16. That Christ was that seed . . . to which he had promised, or to which the promise was made; namely, concerning the inheritance of the world, and the kingdom of grace and glory. It is evident therefore, that the word διαθήκη does here denote some covenant or testament, by which something is promised by God to Christ. Nor do I see what can be objected to this, unless by Christ we should understand *the head*, together with *the mystical body*, which with Christ is that one seed to which the promises are made. This indeed we shall not refuse, if it also be admitted, that Christ, who is the head, and eminently the seed of Abraham, be on no account excluded from these promises, especially as the promises made to his mystical body ought to be considered as made to himself; since he also himself hath received gifts for men, Psal. lxviii. 19." *The Economy of the Covenants Between God and Man* (Kingsburg, CA: den Dulk Christian Foundation, 1990 [orig. pub. 1677]), p. 167.

10. On this, see S. M. Baugh, "Galatians 3:20 and the Covenant of Redemption," *Westminster Theological Journal* 66 (2004): 49-77. Baugh argues that Galatians 3 gives evidence of a *pactum salutis*, an eternal covenant of redemption between God the Father and God the Son. Baugh's claim may or may not be true. What is relevant for our purposes is that some sort of agreement between Father and Son is implied in our passage.

This leads to the second question, namely, what is the nature of the promise? Answers to this question vary in the commentaries, if the question is even asked at all. In one sense, it is true that for Paul simply the idea of God giving a promise is significant, regardless of its content, because a promise implies something believed and received, not earned. When a promise is given, the one to whom the promise is given simply accepts it by faith, trusting the one who gave the promise to keep the promise made. This fits Paul's argument in Galatians for the priority of faith.

At the same time, Paul gives some clues as to the content of the promise. Certainly the book of Genesis indicates that God's promises to Abraham had specific content. Commentators on Galatians describe the content of the promise in a variety of ways, including righteousness, life, offspring, the inheritance, and the blessing of the nations (cf. 3:8). But the first time the word "promise" is used in Galatians is in v. 14, immediately preceding our passage. There Paul refers to "the promise of the Spirit" (τὴν ἐπαγγελίαν τοῦ πνεύματος). Contextually, then, the Spirit is the promise that Paul refers to in the verses that follow.

This would be surprising to those readers who only have access to the book of Genesis. In Genesis 12 and 15, God's promises to Abraham include many descendants, the land, and all the nations being blessed in him. There is no mention of the Holy Spirit in these chapters. But as Sam Williams has shown, all of these promises to Abraham are fulfilled in Christ through the Spirit.[11]

Before looking at this we need to ask what to make of the relationship between the singular, "promise," and the plural, "promises," in vv. 14-22. Twice, in 3:16 and 21, Paul refers to "promises," plural. Does this mean that the Spirit is one promise among many? Williams responds by pointing out that the majority of references in this section are in the singular (vv. 14, 17, 18 [twice], 22). He states, "If Paul were thinking of several different promises (promises with different 'content'), the singular noun . . . would be inexplicable."[12] It is best then to think of one fundamental promise, with a variety of "versions." To put it differently, the promises to Abraham are fulfilled in the one promise, the Spirit.

How this is so becomes clear in chapter 4. For Paul, it is the Spirit that makes people children of God and children of Abraham. In 4:6, "God has sent the Spirit of his Son" into the hearts of his children. It is

---

11. In what follows, I will be closely following Williams, "Promise."
12. Williams, "Promise," p. 712.

by the Spirit that God's children cry out, "Abba, Father" — the Aramaic and Greek terms indicating that both Jews and Gentiles become true children only by the Spirit. It is in this way that the nations are blessed. Only the Spirit can transform Gentiles, formerly tied up in idolatry and enslaved to the elementary principles of the world (4:8-9), into the children of God.

Paul makes this point again when he returns to the Abraham story at the end of chapter 4. Even Isaac, Abraham's physical son, was born "according to the Spirit" (4:28). The miraculous nature of Isaac's birth indicates that it could only be brought about by the Spirit. But the same is true for all who are miraculously brought out of sin and idolatry into the family of God. The Spirit must bring about a "new creation" (6:15).

What then happens to the promise of the land? In Paul's scheme, it is transformed. Indeed, the blessing of the nations and the creation of children from every nation on earth means that Abraham's inheritance is not the land of Palestine, but the world. This is precisely what Paul says in Romans 4, "For the promise to Abraham and his offspring that he would be heir of the world did not come through the law but through the righteousness of faith" (v. 13).

As Williams puts it, at this point "the promise of numerous descendants and the promise of the world converge."[13] They are essentially identical. Both are God's promise of the Spirit. The Spirit's task is to empower mission (cf. Acts 1:8) and to create children, ultimately fulfilling Jesus' Great Commission. As the apostle to the Gentiles, Paul saw himself with a vital role to play in this.

For Paul, then, God's promise to Abraham must be seen simultaneously as a promise to Christ. Only in Christ can this promise be fulfilled. Furthermore, since the promise is the promise of the Spirit, it is an eschatological promise. Thus, Paul can say that God sent the Son "when the fullness of time had come" (4:4). He makes this point even more explicitly to the Corinthians when he asserts that "the end of the ages has come" upon us (1 Cor. 10:11).

The Christocentric nature of this passage is no leap in logic for Paul. For him, it is essential to a proper understanding of God's covenant with Abraham. The granting of descendants to Abraham is the work of the Spirit (4:29). The blessing of the nations is eschatological. Thus, the coming of the Messiah is integrally related to God's covenant with Abraham.

---

13. Williams, "Promise," p. 719. See his discussion of this, pp. 716-20.

The covenant with Abraham does not point forward to Christ. It presupposes God's covenant with his Son.

So far we have argued that God gave the promise, not only to Abraham, but also to his Son. The implication is that God entered into an agreement, or a covenant, with his Son. Furthermore, the promise specifically is the promise of the Spirit. But can the idea of this agreement be sustained biblically and in what way does God give the Spirit to the Son? A brief foray into the Gospel of John will help us to answer these questions.

John makes clear that there is a sort of agreement between the Father and the Son. Jesus did not come on his own authority. He came in the Father's name (5:43), to do the Father's will (5:30; 6:38). His work is the Father's work (4:34); his words are the Father's words (8:28; 15:15). He does only what the Father commands him (14:31). As he says in his final prayer, "I have glorified you on earth, having accomplished the work that you gave me to do" (17:4).

The Father, in turn, glorifies the Son (8:54; 13:32; 17:1). The Father gives the Son authority both to judge (5:27) and to give life (5:26). But Jesus does not just give life to anyone. Rather, Jesus says to the Father, "You have given [the Son] authority over all flesh, to give eternal life to all whom you have given him" (17:2). Those who come to Christ for salvation do so only because the Father has given them to him: "I have manifested your name to the people whom you gave me out of the world. Yours they were, and you gave them to me, and they have kept your word. Now they know that everything that you have given me is from you" (John 17:6-7). The Father, in other words, gives to the Son a spiritual seed, "sons of light" (12:36).

But the Father also gives the Spirit. In John, we are actually confronted by differing statements about the Spirit. On the one hand, Jesus says that the Father gives the Spirit: "And I will ask the Father, and he will give you another Helper, to be with you forever, even the Spirit of truth" (14:16-17). "But the Helper, the Holy Spirit, whom the Father will send in my name, he will teach you all things and bring to your remembrance all that I have said to you" (14:26). On the other hand, Jesus himself sends the Spirit: "Nevertheless, I tell you the truth: it is to your advantage that I go away, for if I do not go away, the Helper will not come to you. But if I go, I will send him to you" (16:7). And finally, 15:26: "But when the Helper comes, whom I will send to you from the Father, the Spirit of truth, who proceeds from the Father, he will bear witness about me." This last statement probably best summarizes John's teaching on the Spirit. The Spirit proceeds from the Father, but is given by Christ himself.

Thus, as the Son completed the work given him by the Father, the Father gives (the promised) Spirit to the Son, not for himself, but to bestow to his followers.

A large part of the Spirit's task, furthermore, is mission. The Spirit will come to convict the world concerning sin, righteousness, and judgment (16:8). At the end of John, Jesus gives the Spirit to his disciples, telling them to "receive the Holy Spirit" (John 20:22). The context of this passage is Jesus' commissioning them for mission, "sending" them (20:21) into the world and giving them judicial authority to grant or withhold forgiveness based on the response to their message (20:23). To use an earlier metaphor of Jesus, the Spirit's task is to bring in the other (Gentile) sheep, who are not of the Jewish fold, with the result that there will be one flock with one Shepherd (10:16).

Thus we see elsewhere in the New Testament similar themes to what Paul expounds in Galatians 3. An agreement (or covenant) exists between Father and Son. That agreement entails the promise of the Spirit whose ultimate goal is to transform sinners into the children of God and in so doing to make the world Christ's inheritance. Peter's speech on the Day of Pentecost also confirms this as a basic understanding in the early church: "Being therefore exalted at the right hand of God, and *having received from the Father the promise of the Holy Spirit,* he [Christ] has poured out this that you yourselves are seeing and hearing" (Acts 2:33).

Paul elsewhere makes clear that the reward of Christ's obedience is his lordship over the nations: "Therefore [as a result of Christ's obedience] God has highly exalted him and bestowed on him the name that is above every name, so that at the name of Jesus every knee should bow, in heaven and on earth and under the earth, and every tongue confess that Jesus Christ is Lord, to the glory of God the Father" (Phil. 2:9-11).

The Son is given a promise by the Father, the promise of the Spirit, guaranteeing that he, like Abraham, but in a far greater way, will be heir of the world. At the same time, God's covenant with Abraham presupposes and necessitates a covenant between God the Father and God the Son. Without that covenant, the promise to Abraham could never be fulfilled.

The Law (3:19-22)

In response to the nomistic agitators in Galatians, Paul asserts that the inheritance does not come by the law, but by the promise (v. 18). This leads to the logical question, "Why then the law?" (v. 19). We will look more closely below at the purpose of the law. Before we do, I want to focus our attention on perhaps the most vexing of all the problematic texts in Galatians 3:15-22, namely, v. 20.

In Galatians 3:20, Paul states, "Now an intermediary implies more than one, but God is one." Almost all translations insert extra words into this verse. The Greek simply says, ὁ δὲ μεσίτης ἑνὸς οὐκ ἔστιν, ὁ δὲ Θεὸς εἷς ἐστιν. To translate word for word without an attempt to give the sense, "But the mediator is not of one, but God is one."

In context, the mediator most likely refers to Moses. Paul has just said in v. 19 that the law was put in place through angels by a mediator. The most common interpretation is that Paul here is trying to show the superiority of the Abrahamic covenant over the Mosaic. God gave the law to Israel through angels by the mediator Moses. But he gave the promise directly to Abraham.

However, the most direct reference leading into v. 20 is not the promise to Abraham, but the promise to "the seed," Christ: "until the seed should come to whom the promise had been made" (v. 19).

Furthermore, the typical interpretation of v. 20a is essentially in line with the ESV quoted above. A mediator implies more than one party, God and Israel. Moses is the mediator between these parties. But the contrast that Paul draws here is not whether there is a mediator or not. The contrast is between one and more than one.

To be sure, the language is compact and difficult. But the point does not seem to be a contrast between the Mosaic covenant, which had a mediator, and the Abrahamic covenant, which did not. The point is that the Mosaic covenant was made between two parties, whereas God is one.

In light of what we have seen earlier, the best way to interpret this statement is not that Paul is making a point about the superiority of the Abrahamic covenant (which was also between two parties). Rather, Paul's statement that God is one refers to the covenant between God the Father and the God the Son, tying v. 20 to the more immediate reference to the promise made to the Son in v. 19.[14]

---

14. N. T. Wright has pointed out many of the problems of the typical interpretation of this passage, especially v. 20. See his "The Seed and the Mediator: Galatians 3:15-20," in *The Climax of the Covenant: Christ and the Law in Pauline Theology* (Minneapolis: Fortress, 1992), pp. 157-74. Wright's interpretation capitalizes on the theme of unity at the end of Galatians 3, as well as the collective use of "seed" in v. 29. Wright attempts to rescue Paul from the perception of a semantic trick in v. 16 by arguing that "Christ" should be understood in a representative or corporate sense. The singular "seed, who is Christ," refers not to

Paul's point, then, as Steven Baugh argues, is that Paul is not trying to show the superiority of the Abrahamic covenant over the Mosaic. It is, rather, to show that the Mosaic covenant cannot mediate the promised inheritance because there can be no mediation between God the Father and God the Son.[15] Furthermore, because the promise was given directly by Father to Son, it does not depend on anything that human beings can do.

This is a shrewd use of the Shema in Deuteronomy 6:4. The careful reader of Galatians will recognize Paul's claims for the deity of Christ. He is Lord (1:3). He is "sent forth" from the Father (4:4), a statement that assumes his preexistence. So when we read the statement "God is one" in 3:20, we are forced to think of the relationship between God the Father and God the Son. Paul is compelling his readers to reflect on this intra-Trinitarian relationship, and therefore also on the promise given from Father to Son.

The law, then, far from being inferior, actually has an important part to play in the history of redemption, even though it clearly is not the channel for receiving the promise. Receiving the promised inheritance, the Spirit, is rooted in the work of the Son and therefore can only be received by faith. It is not something human beings attain by their effort (3:2, 5). If

---

an individual person, but to the singularity of one family created in Christ and finding its identity in him. According to Wright, God promised a single family to Abraham. That promised family is brought into being in and through Christ alone. In this reading, the problem with the law is that it creates at least two families by separating Jews from Gentiles. Moses, therefore, is not the mediator of one family only (v. 20a). But since "God is one" God desires only one family (v. 20b).

This interpretation is ingenious, but is filled with problems. The biggest problem is that Wright is forced to understand Χριστός in an unnatural sense. According to Wright, Χριστός is "flexible . . . capable of different levels of meaning" (p. 166). It is certainly true that Paul uses phrases like "in Christ" in a corporate sense. But Wright gives no examples from Paul's writings where "Christ," without a preposition or other qualifiers, refers to anything other than Christ himself. It is impossible to imagine the first-century Galatians, hearing this letter read from beginning to end, understanding "Christ" in v. 16 as anything other than the person of Jesus Christ. Furthermore, Wright's reading puts an undue strain on v. 19, which, in light of the larger context, seems fairly clearly to refer to the coming of Christ himself (cf. especially 4:4). Paul's use of the collective "seed" in 3:29 comes only on the heels of his statement that "you are all one *in Christ Jesus.*" It is improper to read the carefully contextualized collective back into v. 16.

Wright's interpretation is characteristic of the New Perspective's tendency to read Paul's letters backwards, seeing the unity that is the result of the proclamation of the true gospel as the main point of Paul's letters. We would do well to heed C. S. Lewis's admonition to keep "first things first."

15. Baugh, "Galatians 3:20," p. 52.

the law is not the channel for receiving the promise, why did God give it? That is the primary question of vv. 19-22.

Paul gives us the answer right away, even though it is initially unclear: the law "was added because of transgressions" (v. 19). It is not until v. 22 that Paul makes this statement clear: "But the Scripture imprisoned everything under sin, so that the promise by faith in Jesus Christ might be given to those who believe." In other words, "because of transgressions" is directly related to being "imprisoned . . . under sin."

Some commentators take the phrase "added because of transgressions" in a positive sense. Dunn, for instance, in an attempt to highlight the grace of the law, takes the phrase to mean that God gave the law to deal with sin by providing atonement in the sacrificial system. This attempted positive spin is usually coupled with an appeal to understand παιδαγωγός in vv. 24-25 in a good light. That is, the παιδαγωγός, typically a slave put in charge of a child, cared for the child and protected the child.

But there are many problems with a positive spin on v. 19. First, the idea of imprisonment under sin (v. 22) decidedly points to a negative function. Second, Paul's use of language in vv. 19 and 22 is instructive. For Paul, "transgression" is typically used to refer to breaking a direct command from God. "Sin" is used in a broader way. Sin does not become transgression until there is law. Dunn's reading, that God gave the law to deal effectively with transgression, is essentially anachronistic, since transgression, technically, did not exist until the law was given. Dunn's reading would require v. 19 to say "it was added because of sin." Third, although the *paidagogos* in the ancient world was sometimes depicted in a positive way, more often he was depicted negatively, as a cruel disciplinarian.

A better reading of Galatians 3:19-22, then, is that God added the law (taking προσετέθη as a divine passive) to highlight the problem of human sin. Sin shows itself to be most egregious when committed against a known command of God, that is, when it becomes "transgression." The problem, however, is not with the law, which Paul says elsewhere is "holy and righteous and good" (Rom. 7:12). The problem is the sin that works in the human heart.

We can add to this two other aspects of the law that come out in Paul's discussion in Galatians. The law highlights God's requirement for perfect obedience. Those who would be justified by it must do all of it (cf. 3:10; 5:3).[16]

---

16. This point is rejected by the New Perspective. But this seems to be the clear implication of 3:10 and 5:3.

If the law imprisons all under sin, clearly that is impossible. In addition, the law highlights the legal demand that those who break God's commandments deserve punishment. The law carries a curse for disobedience (3:13).

Does this mean that the Mosaic covenant is not gracious? To quote Paul, "Certainly not!" To begin with, Paul makes clear that the law is not "contrary to the promises" (v. 21). The grace of the law can be seen especially in its continuity with the covenant with the Son and the way in which it anticipates fulfillment in the Son's coming. Verse 19 indicates that the law anticipates and looks forward to the coming of the Son. But it also was given in line with the promise made to the Son. The law "was added . . . until the seed should come to whom the promise had been made." The perfect tense verb, ἐπήγγελται, indicates a past event with results existing afterward.[17] The law was given to serve the promise already made.

The law ultimately finds fulfillment in the coming of the Son, who was "born under the law" (4:4) and bore the curse of the law (3:13). Although he fully kept the law of God, Christ took on himself the punishment of the law for the sake of his heirs, that they might inherit the promise of God. "For our sake [God] made him to be sin who knew no sin, so that in him we might become the righteousness of God" (2 Cor. 5:21).

Of course, the grace of law comes as no surprise to those who carefully read the Old Testament. The work of God that culminates in the covenant at Sinai began when God heard the groaning of his people under bondage in Egypt and "remembered his covenant with Abraham, with Isaac, and with Jacob" (Exod. 2:24). The Mosaic covenant is in clear continuity with the Abrahamic. Furthermore, the giving of the law itself is prefaced by the reminder of God's gracious redemption of his people: "I am the LORD your God, who brought you out of the land of Egypt, out of the house of slavery" (Exod. 20:2).

But it is particularly the covenant between God the Father and God the Son that binds all of the covenants together. The Mosaic covenant was not an interruption or parenthesis. It served the greater covenant, playing an important role in redemptive history until God's covenant with the Son was fulfilled by God's sending his Son into the world "in the fullness of time."

17. See Daniel B. Wallace, *Greek Grammar Beyond the Basics* (Grand Rapids: Zondervan, 1996), pp. 572-73. See Wallace's critique of the recent works of Stanley Porter and others, who argue that Greek tenses deal with aspect, not time (pp. 504-12).

Abraham and Empire in Galatians

Roy E. Ciampa

When New Testament scholars discuss Abraham, they tend to focus on debates regarding justification and the place of faith versus works in biblical teachings on salvation. Attention has also been given to biblical and early Jewish traditions associating Abraham with the covenant of circumcision and with the rejection of idolatry in favor of a monotheistic faith,[1] and to

1. In Second Temple Jewish literature Abraham is depicted in a variety of ways, including as the archetypal proselyte and/or rejecter of idolatry, a "proclaimer of the One God," "the first monotheistic leader," or "a hellenistic philosopher" (Nancy Calvert-Koyzis, *Paul, Monotheism and the People of God: The Significance of Abraham Traditions for Early Judaism and Christianity*, JSNTSS 273 [London: T&T Clark International, 2004], pp. vii-viii). Calvert-Koyzis points out that "Abraham functioned as a key to how the Jewish people perceived their identity" and "portrayals of Abraham . . . often reveal how the Jews of the time were to relate to members of nations other than their own" (p. 4). It has also been pointed out that "in Jewish literature Abraham is portrayed in the context of covenantal nomism," with some texts emphasizing the priority of the covenant relationship and others stressing the law itself (G. Walter Hansen, *Abraham in Galatians: Epistolary and Rhetorical Contexts*, JSNTSS 29 [Sheffield: JSOT Press, 1989], p. 199). References to Abraham in Second Temple literature are too frequent to be considered here. The theme of hospitality (φιλοξενία) in Recension A of the *Testament of Abraham* (see 1:1-2, 5; 4:6; 17:7; 20:15) may be understood as being in contrast to an oppressive or dominating attitude. It is said that Abraham "welcomed everyone — rich and poor, kings and rulers, the crippled and the helpless, friends and strangers, neighbors and passersby — (all) on equal terms did the pious, entirely holy, righteous, and hospitable Abraham welcome" (1:2; translation of E. P. Sanders in *OTP* 1:882).

As one of Marvin Wilson's former students, I consider it a joy and a privilege to offer this study as part of a celebration of his fruitful career and his 75th birthday.

153

Paul's inclusion of Gentile believers in the Abrahamic family on the basis of their (Abraham-like) faith in Christ. In more recent years attention has also been given to the way in which debates about Abraham were used to disinherit Jews in general or significant groups of Jews or others who considered themselves sons of Abraham.[2]

Without denying the important insights and points made about Abraham in the studies referenced above or suggesting that the issue being explored here is somehow more central to Paul's thinking, this essay intends to explore Paul's use of Abrahamic material in his letter to the Galatians in light of Old Testament and other early Christian indications that Abraham tended to be associated with liberation or freedom from various types of oppression.[3] First, some of the evidence from the Hebrew Bible and other parts of the New Testament that support this association between Abraham and liberation from oppression will be surveyed;[4] then more focused attention will be given to Paul's letter to the Galatians and how the use of Abrahamic material in that letter might relate to the same theme.

---

2. See Jeffrey S. Siker, *Disinheriting the Jews: Abraham in Early Christian Controversy* (Louisville: Westminster John Knox, 1991).

3. In his important work, *Our Father Abraham: Jewish Roots of the Christian Faith* (Grand Rapids: Eerdmans, 1989), Marv Wilson points out that in the Hebraic concept of salvation, "the main idea is 'to liberate,' 'to deliver from evil,' or 'to free from oppression'" (p. 179). This study will seek to show how Paul's interpretation of Abraham relates to precisely those ideas. Recent studies of Paul employing post-colonial criticism or paying special attention to issues of empire have shed some new light and opened up some new interpretive possibilities previously unnoticed, but they have not tended to pay much attention to the role of Abraham in Paul's argument and how it might relate to the issues that interest them. A partial exception would be the treatment of Gal. 4:21–5:1 in Davina C. Lopez, *Apostle to the Conquered: Reimagining Paul's Mission,* Paul in Critical Contexts (Minneapolis: Fortress, 2008), pp. 153-63. She offers an ideologically critical and more specifically "gender critical" reading of Paul. Neil Elliott's *Liberating Paul: The Justice of God and the Politics of the Apostle* (Minneapolis: Fortress, 2006) examines the role of traditional interpretations of Paul in supporting oppressive right-wing dictatorships and defends a more socially liberating reading of Paul. Both of these volumes are important contributions to reading Paul with greater sensitivity to social concerns and implications, although they both do so from within particular hermeneutical, political, and critical frameworks that I do not happen to share. See also Mark Forman, "The Politics of Promise: Echoes of Isaiah 54 in Romans 4.19-21," *JSNT* 31 (2009): 301-24.

4. Abraham is primarily associated with liberation from socio-political oppression in the Old Testament and liberation from other types of oppression (understood as extensions of the former) in the New Testament.

Abraham and Empire in the Hebrew Bible

Abraham is depicted as an imperial or dominant figure (with some heirs implicated in the abuses of dominion) in a variety of ways in the Hebrew Bible (as well as in the New Testament). This is perhaps most clear in Genesis 12:1-3. It has been pointed out that "[b]ehind the fourfold promise of nationhood, a great name, divine protection, and mediatorship of blessing, E. Ruprecht . . . has plausibly detected echoes of royal ideology. What Abram is here promised was the hope of many an oriental monarch."[5] It also anticipates God's promise to David in 2 Samuel 7:9. His military power is also demonstrated in his defeat of Chedorlaomer and the kings allied with him and his rescue of Lot (Gen. 14). His name change (to "father of many nations") and the associated promises in Genesis 17:1-6 link him with domination and/or dynasty again. He is destined to hold great influence over many nations.

There are a variety of ways, however, in which Abraham is depicted as an anti-imperial figure, and one who experiences the abuses of political power and brings liberty to others who have experienced it as well.[6] The great name promised to Abram comes on the heels of the failed attempt of the powerful city-state described as Babel to make a great name for itself through the construction of its tower. Those who grasp at that power do not achieve it, but Abram, who never grasped for it, receives it as a promise. And while the episode in Genesis 11 points to the power of a single dominant language and material culture, the narrative in Genesis 12 reflects no special interest in the establishment of one particular ruling culture, but rather in a blessing that would extend to "all the families of the earth" (Gen. 12:3).[7]

Abram's immigration to the promised land seems to entail his own departure from influential city-states — Ur of the Chaldeans and Haran (Gen. 11:29-31). Genesis narrates Abraham's own challenging experiences with powerful kings in the parallel experiences with the Egyptian Pharaoh in Genesis 12:10-18 and with King Abimelech of Gerar in Genesis 20.

---

5. Gordon J. Wenham, *Genesis 1–15*, Word Biblical Commentary (Waco: Word, 1987), p. 275, citing E. Ruprecht, "Der traditionsgeschichtliche Hintergrund der einzelnen Elemente von Gen 12:2-3," *VT* 29 (1979): 445-64.

6. For interesting reflections on Genesis and "Alienating Earth and the Curse of Empires," see Mark G. Brett, *Decolonizing God: The Bible in the Tides of Empire* (Sheffield: Sheffield Phoenix, 2008), pp. 32-43. Unfortunately he pays little attention to the texts we mention in the next few paragraphs.

7. Unless otherwise noted, all translations are from the NRSV.

While Abram's military power is seen in his defeat of Chedorlaomer, his behavior following his victory demonstrates an attitude that contrasts with Chedorlaomer's approach to dominating those he subdues. Abram does not keep any of the people or their goods; he does not require any ransom or submission of the peoples whose kings he defeated in his rescue operation (Genesis 14). His open-handed response to his victory reminds the reader of the same open-handed attitude he demonstrated when he allowed Lot to choose the land he preferred back in Genesis 13:8-12.

In Genesis 15 the LORD establishes a covenant with Abram and tells him his offspring "shall be aliens [גֵּר/πάροικος] in a land that is not theirs, and shall be slaves [וַעֲבָדוּם] there, and they shall be oppressed for four hundred years" (v. 13) before being delivered (v. 14). Abraham, then, is depicted as a man who knows something about being on the receiving end of political or imperial oppression and who refuses to exercise it himself.

Outside the Pentateuch Abraham tends to be mentioned in relation to the promises of land and posterity that come to be associated with the hope of redemption and liberation from oppressive powers. A look at the references to Abraham in the Psalms and prophets will show how often he is mentioned in conjunction with expressions of hope for redemption (often hope for redemption from oppressive foreign nations).[8]

Abraham and Liberation in the New Testament

This section will offer only brief comments on some of the passages where there is a clear or potential relationship between Abraham and liberation themes in the New Testament.

The first three references to Abraham in the Gospel of Matthew are found at the beginning and end of the opening pericope of the book (1:1, 2, 17). The genealogy is somewhat artificially divided up into groups of fourteen, with the deportation to Babylon being the only reference point other than the names and identities of those listed in the genealogy. Abraham is listed with three other key turning points in the history of Israel: the reign of King David, the Babylonian exile, and the coming of Jesus Christ. The point is that Jesus Christ will bring about the fulfillment of God's promises to both Abraham and David as well as bringing to an end Israel's experi-

---

8. See Pss. 47:9; 105:6-9, 42; Isa. 29:22; 41:8; 51:2; 63:16; Jer. 33:26; Ezek. 33:24; Micah 7:20.

ence of exile (or political oppression), stretching back to the original deportation to Babylon.

Here Abraham is tied both to hopes for Israel's own dominance, as associated especially with the anticipation of a universal Davidic and Messianic reign, and to the hope of liberation from political and cultural oppression by a dominant power. That hope had long been associated with God's promise to give Abram and his people their own land in which they would experience blessing. Matthew 3:7-9 and 8:5-13 (par. Luke 13:25-30) raise questions about who will actually enjoy the blessings associated with Abraham. Remarkably, Jesus indicates that people from all over the world (presumably including the Roman centurion whose need he has just met) will enjoy the Abrahamic blessings of the kingdom, while some Jews/Judeans will not. It becomes clear that the liberation that is associated with the promises to Abraham and David, and that would bring an end to the political oppression initiated and still symbolized by Babylon, would not work out the way many had anticipated.[9]

The first reference to Abraham in the Gospel of Luke comes in the *Magnificat:* Luke 1:46-55. Mary, like Hannah in 1 Samuel 2:1-10, interprets God's goodness to her as an example of his tendency to bring relief and redemption to the poor and lowly[10] at the expense of the rich and powerful. Although Abraham is not mentioned in 1 Samuel, in the *Magnificat* the undoing of the powerful and the rescue of the oppressed are understood to reflect a fulfillment of God's promise to Abraham. It is done "according to the promise he made to our ancestors, to Abraham and to his descendants

9. The last reference to Abraham in the Gospel of Matthew happens to be in the parallel text to the only reference to Abraham in the Gospel of Mark (Matt. 22:29-33; Mark 12:23-26). Here Jesus takes the statement in Exodus 3:6 where the LORD identifies himself as "the God of Abraham, the God of Isaac, and the God of Jacob" as evidence for life after death (in context, an argument in favor of the resurrection of the dead), since he "is God not of the dead, but of the living" (Matt. 22:32//Mark 12:26//Luke 20:37-38). It is unclear whether this should be taken as an indication that, for Jesus, Abraham is to be associated with liberation from the power of death.

10. In Jas. 2:21-3 Abraham is mentioned in the argument about being justified by works and not merely by faith. In context, the works James has in mind are those related to caring for the poor (2:5-16). The particular act of Abraham that is mentioned as an example of being justified by works (with faith being active along with his works, and faith being brought to completion by the works, v. 22), does not relate to mercy or care for the poor, but it seems from the broader context that Abraham's justifying actions are being expounded by James in such a way as to reinforce the importance of showing mercy and kindness to the poor and marginalized.

forever" (v. 55). The theme of liberation from the oppression of enemies is even clearer in Zechariah's *Benedictus* (Luke 1:67-79), which also cites God's promise to Abraham:

> Blessed be the Lord God of Israel, for he has looked favorably on his people and redeemed them. He has raised up a mighty savior for us in the house of his servant David, as he spoke through the mouth of his holy prophets from of old, that we would be saved from our enemies and from the hand of all who hate us. Thus he has shown the mercy promised to our ancestors, and has remembered his holy covenant, the oath that he swore to our ancestor Abraham, to grant us that we, being rescued from the hands of our enemies, might serve him without fear, in holiness and righteousness before him all our days. (vv. 68-75)

In Luke 13:11-16 Jesus brings deliverance to "a woman with a spirit that had crippled her for eighteen years" (v. 11). Jesus defends his sabbath-day act of deliverance by asking, If people think it acceptable to lead their donkeys to water on the sabbath, "ought not this woman, a daughter of Abraham whom Satan bound for eighteen long years, be set free from this bondage on the sabbath day?" He invokes Abraham's name in support of a woman's liberation from a satanic bondage that entailed physical crippling. This suggests that the theme of Abrahamic liberation has been extended or broadened beyond its original contours to address other basic human concerns and needs.[11]

Abraham is mentioned in only one passage in the Gospel of John (John 8:31-59), and the early part of the conversation reported there revolves around the relationship between Abraham and freedom or slavery. Jesus tells "the Jews who had believed in him" (v. 31) that by holding to his teaching they would find that "the truth will make you free" (v. 32). They react strongly (v. 33): "We are descendants of Abraham and have never been slaves to anyone. What do you mean by saying, 'You will be made free'?" They consider their status as free people rather than slaves to be based on their relationship with Abraham. As Jesus advances his argument he affirms that they are "descendants of Abraham" (v. 37), but denies that they are children of Abraham (vv. 39-41), thus reinforcing the idea we have found else-

---

11. In Luke 16:18-25 Abraham is associated with the inversion of the rich and the poor in the afterlife, while in Luke 19:8-10 Zacchaeus's experience with Jesus transforms him from a man marked by greed and abuse of power to one marked by integrity and generosity to the poor, and Jesus indicates that this makes him a true son of Abraham (v. 9).

where that to have Abraham as one's "father" requires either something more than or something different from being a descendant of Abraham. He also changes or broadens the conception of the liberty or freedom with which Abraham is to be associated when he asserts that "everyone who commits sin is a slave to sin. The slave does not have a permanent place in the household; the son has a place there forever. So if the Son makes you free, you will be free indeed" (vv. 34-36). Evidently the children of Abraham are to experience (among other things) freedom from the power of sin, a development or expansion of the older theme of political deliverance.[12]

Abraham and Empire/Liberation in Galatians

Given the association between Abraham and themes of freedom/liberation from domination (empire or other oppressive forces) found in the Hebrew Bible and other New Testament writings, it seems wise to pay attention to ways in which Paul's references to Abraham might also contribute to those themes. As it turns out, Paul's discussion of Abraham and his offspring in Galatians is tied to the theme of freedom in various ways. Exploration of the ways that theme is illuminated by Paul's exposition should prove fruitful.

The themes of freedom and slavery are introduced in Galatians 2:4 and are present in 3:38–4:7 and in 4:21–5:1, with terms for freedom and slavery appearing together at several points (see 2:4; 3:28; 5:1, 13). Paul's primary concern with respect to freedom and slavery in these texts is with the freedom experienced by Gentile believers in Christ, which entails, among other things, a freedom from any need to be circumcised or to adopt other elements of a traditional Jewish lifestyle (2:3, 14; 5:6). As we shall see, the roots of Paul's teaching suggest that this is but a specific application of the theme of Abrahamic liberty. Although that theme originally focused on freedom from political and cultural domination, we have already seen that it had come to be understood to have much broader applications in other New Testament texts.

While Abraham is not mentioned until Galatians 3:6, the issue of circumcision is raised in 2:3. It seems likely that the other teachers in Galatia would have tied the issue of circumcision to the figure of Abraham, since it

---

12. In Rom. 5–6 Paul describes the dominions of death (Rom. 5:14, 17; 6:9) and of sin (Rom. 5:21; 6:12-14) as though they were foreign imperial powers reigning over their captive slaves.

was the sign of the Abrahamic covenant, and Galatians 3:7 is probably to be understood in contradiction to the view that those who are circumcised are sons of Abraham.[13] The language that Paul uses in Galatians 2:3 raises questions about issues of domination and imperialistic behavior. Paul says that "even Titus, who was with me, was not compelled to be circumcised, though he was a Greek." Paul's expression "was compelled to be circumcised" (ἠναγκάθη περιτμηθῆναι) is interesting in that, although Paul may have in mind non-life-threatening social pressure to accept circumcision, we know that John Hyrcanus I in the second century B.C.E., "in the course of his successful wars of expansion among the Idumaeans, put into effect a policy of mass circumcision and compulsory Judaising."[14] Furthermore, "[t]he subjection of the Ituraeans in Northern Palestine by Aristobulus I (104-103 B.C.E.) followed a similar pattern, and though there is no direct attestation it seems highly probable that when Jewish law was imposed with the Jewish conquests of Alexander Jannaeus (103-76 B.C.E.) compulsory circumcision was included."[15]

In the case of Aristobulus I, Josephus's description of the event uses the same two verbs we have highlighted from Galatians 2:3: he "compelled the inhabitants . . . to be circumcised, and to live according to the Jewish laws."[16] Later Josephus recounts another case when Jews wanted to compel Gentiles to be circumcised[17] if they would live among them, but were persuaded by Josephus (who was serving as their military leader) not to follow through on their plan (*Life*, 113). The occasional Jewish compulsion of Gentiles to be circumcised under the Hasmoneans may be understood as a reaction to the Seleucid compulsion of Jews to reject their ancestral traditions, a reaction which in some ways mimicked[18] the Greek approach to

---

13. Cf. F. F. Bruce, *The Epistle to the Galatians: A Commentary on the Greek Text*, New International Greek Testament Commentary (Grand Rapids: Eerdmans, 1982), p. 155; Richard N. Longenecker, *Galatians*, Word Biblical Commentary (Dallas: Word, 1990), pp. 114-15.

14. R. Meyer, "περιτέμνω κτλ," in *TDNT*, 6:78 (referencing Josephus, *Ant.* 13:257).

15. R. Meyer, "περιτέμνω κτλ," in *TDNT*, 6:78. See also Shaye J. D. Cohen, *From the Maccabees to the Mishnah*, Library of Early Christianity (Philadelphia: Westminster, 1987), pp. 52-53.

16. *Ant.* 13:318 (Whiston's translation; Gk. ἀναγκάσας τε τοὺ ἐνοικοῦντας . . . περιτέμνεσθαι).

17. Gk. τούτους περιτέμνεσθαι τῶν Ἰουδαίων ἀναγκαζόντων.

18. On "mimicry" as a concept in post-colonial studies, see Bill Ashcroft, Gareth Griffiths, and Helen Tiffin, *Post-Colonial Studies: The Key Concepts*, Routledge Key Guides (London: Routledge, 2000), pp. 139-42. The mimicry to which I refer was unlikely to have been perceived as such by most Romans or Jews who observed it

cultural and religious totalitarianism and intolerance.[19] Some Jews seem to have adopted — or rather, adapted — the Greek approach to imposing cultural and religious hegemony once they were able to escape it themselves and were in a position to impose it on others.

The militaristic background to the idea of compelling Gentiles to be circumcised is reflected in the language Paul uses in Galatians. Betz has pointed out, in commenting on Galatians 2:4, that Paul "uses the language of political demagoguery, that is, military language turned into political metaphors. . . . These agitators are 'secretly smuggled in' (παρεισάκτοι), like undercover agents and conspirators. Their activity is the 'infiltration' (παρεισέρχεσθαι) and 'spying out' (κατασκοπεῖν) of what Paul calls 'our freedom which we have in Christ Jesus' (τὴν ἐλευθερίαν ἣν ἔχομεν ἐν Χριστῷ 'Ιησοῦ)."[20] The suggestion that the spying was being done with a view to enslaving those being spied upon (Gal. 2:4: "so that they might enslave us") fits with a common usage of the same verb (καταδουλόω) elsewhere. In 1 Maccabees 8:10 it was used of the Romans' enslavement (through imperial conquest) of the Greeks, while in 1 Maccabees 8:18 it was used of a similar enslavement of Jews by the Greeks (for similar usages see *Sib. Or.* 2:175; *T. Jud.* 21:7; LXX Jer. 15:14; Ezek. 34:27; Josephus, *Ant.* 13:1). In *Moses*, 1:142, Philo explicitly suggests an association with the treatment of prisoners of war, speaking of the Egyptians as people who "enslaved [καταδουλωσάμενοι] foreigners and suppliants, as if they had been prisoners taken in war" (Yonge's translation).

In Galatians 2:4 the relationship between the infiltration, spying, and enslavement clearly points to military conquest as the background to Paul's metaphorical language.[21] While slavery was associated with Egyp-

19. Cf. John M. G. Barclay, *Jews in the Mediterranean Diaspora: From Alexander to Trajan (323 BCE–117 CE)* (Edinburgh: T&T Clark, 1996), pp. 246-47.

20. Hans Dieter Betz, *Galatians: A Commentary on Paul's Letter to the Churches in Galatia,* Hermeneia (Philadelphia: Fortress, 1979), pp. 90-91.

21. In my previous work I have been guilty of improperly separating Paul's discussion of spiritual freedom and slavery from its military background, suggesting that the presence of Exodus traditions and themes served as evidence against the association of freedom and slavery with military themes (see Ciampa, *The Presence and Function of Scripture in Galatians 1 and 2,* WUNT 2/102 [Tübingen: Mohr Siebeck, 1998], p. 246). That is a false dichotomy, and recently scholars have been giving greater attention to the ways in which various intertextual relationships, including combinations of biblical, Jewish, and Greco-Roman intertexts, are reflected within New Testament texts. In fact, associations with imperial oppression experienced throughout Israel's history, and not only in the exodus, includ-

tian oppression at the time of the exodus, it was also associated with imperial subjection in the post-exilic period, and Paul's language will echo this other usage in chapter 4 when he expounds on the difference between Sarah and Hagar.

The flow of Paul's argument in Galatians suggests that a particular view of justification may result in oppressive behavior, not unlike that which was experienced by Jews and Gentiles under imperialistic domination. That is, the slavery he has in mind would be analogous to the oppression felt by a people that had been conquered by some foreign political power.[22]

Paul returns to the use of military language in Galatians 2:11 when he says that he opposed Peter to his face. As I have pointed out elsewhere, the language of "opposing someone to [their] face" is an idiom in the LXX relating to the successful or unsuccessful defense against a military invasion. "Κατὰ πρόσωπον modifies ἀνθίστημι eight times in the LXX: Deut. 7:24; 9:2; 11:25; 31:21; Judg. 2:14; 2 Chr. 13:7-8; Jdt. 6:4. Each example of the idiom communicates the idea of making a successful resistance to an opposing power or force. Ἀνθιστάναι κατὰ πρόσωπον is to succeed in resisting the opposing power (Deut. 9:2; 31:21; Judg. 2:14; 2 Chr. 13:8). Οὐκ ἀνθιστάναι κατὰ πρόσωπον is not to be able to offer successful resistance to the opposing power (Deut. 7:24; 11:25; 2 Chr. 13:7; Jdt. 6:4)."[23] In this way Paul represents his conflict with Peter as one in which Peter was implicated in an act associated with a militarily enforced compulsion of Gentiles to be circumcised, while he himself served as the defending power, preserving the freedom of those who would otherwise have experienced the equivalent of slavery under a dominating foreign power.

Paul's discussion of Abraham takes place in a context where the upholding of the justification of Gentiles on the basis of faith, apart from any

---

ing the more recent Jewish experience under Greek and Roman domination, are likely to give Paul's language whatever emotional power it had.

22. See the discussion of the relative power and influence of Jewish communities in Asia in Barclay, *Jews in the Mediterranean Diaspora*, pp. 259-81. On the extent of Jewish colonizing in the Diaspora, see Philo, *Embassy* 281-84.

23. Ciampa, *The Presence and Function of Scripture in Galatians 1 and 2*, pp. 157-58. The fact that in Judith 6:4 the idiom is found on the lips of Holofernes, the commander of the Assyrian army, raises the possibility that the idiom is not distinctly scriptural, but reflective of a broader cultural background, but a search of the TLG indicates that there are no pre-Pauline examples of this idiom outside the LXX. Examples post-dating Paul usually consist of quotations from Gal. 2:11 in the church fathers.

requirement to accept circumcision and enter into the Mosaic covenant, is expressed in terms of a defense of their freedom in the face of those who would enslave them. The language of freedom and slavery does not explicitly appear again until 3:38, at which point it becomes dominant through 5:1 (with the exception of 4:12-20). Paul's primary argument about Abraham has to do with the basis upon which one is eligible to claim Abrahamic (and thus divine) sonship and participates in the present and future manifestations of the blessings pertaining to the children of Abraham.

Along the way, the nature of those blessings is described in a variety of ways that unpack their significance. Paul reminds his readers that the blessing promised to Abraham was that "All the Gentiles [or nations] shall be blessed in you" (Gal. 3:8, citing Gen. 12:3). That blessing entails (among other things) justification (Gal. 3:6-8) and the promise of the Spirit (3:14; possibly also redemption from the curse of the law, 3:13). It has to do with an inheritance (ἡ κληρονομία) granted to Abraham through a promise (3:18).[24]

On a very fundamental level, Paul's argument in Galatians suggests that the promise to Abraham has to do with the liberation of all things from their imprisonment under the power of sin (ὑπὸ ἁμαρτίαν; 3:22). In this world Jews and Gentiles together are "children of God" (3:26), being "clothed with Christ" (3:27), being "one in Christ Jesus" such that in some sense the Jew/Greek, slave/free, and male/female dichotomies are overcome (3:28). This is all part of what it means to be "Abraham's offspring, heirs according to the promise" (3:29).

---

24. In biblical tradition the inheritance associated with Abraham was first and foremost the land that had been promised (Gen. 15:7-8). But Second Temple Jews (including Jesus and the early Christians) had come to understand that the promise should not be understood to be limited to the confines of the original territory promised to Abraham, but, rather, that just as the blessing of Abraham was to extend to all the families and nations of the earth, the territory that the sons of Abraham would inherit was also limitlessly expanded. While the inheritance was still frequently associated with the land of Israel (e.g., *T. Dan.* 7:3; *Pss. Sol.* 9:1), the language of inheritance came to be used more expansively of inheriting life (or eternal life; e.g., *Sib. Or.* 23:47; *Pss. Sol.* 14:10; Matt. 19:29; Mark 10:17; Luke 10:25; 18:18), the kingdom (or kingdom of God [e.g., Matt. 25:34; 1 Cor. 6:9-10; 15:50; Gal. 5:21; Eph. 5:5; Jas. 2:5]), or the earth (a simple widening of the referent of the word "land," or γῆ; e.g., *1 En.* 3:6-8; *Apoc. Sedr.* 6:2; Matt. 5:5). Paul clearly reflects such a development in the understanding of the inheritance not only in 1 Cor. 6:9-10; 15:50; Gal. 5:21; Eph. 5:5, but most explicitly and remarkably in Rom. 4:13, where he refers to "the promise that [Abraham] would inherit the world" (ἡ ἐπαγγελία τῷ Ἀβραὰμ ἢ τῷ σπέρματι αὐτοῦ, τὸ κληρονόμον αὐτὸν εἶναι κόσμου). For a recent discussion of the biblical background to the inheritance theme and Paul's development of it, see Forman, "The Politics of Promise," pp. 309-16.

We will need to pay more attention to Galatians 3:26-28 for at least two reasons. First, vv. 26 and 28 emphasize that "all" believers are "sons of God" and "one in Christ Jesus" (cf. Rom. 4:16), regardless of their national, ethnic, or cultural background. This is a significant development from prophetic descriptions of the post-exilic blessing in which it was understood that Israel, God's sons, would no longer be the tail, but would become the head. That is, they would be the dominant power rather than the dominated people. There would be a great inversion by which God would exalt them over all the other nations.[25] But what happens when all the other nations are adopted into the family so that they are also sons of God and heirs of the promises given to Abraham? If Jews and Gentiles, persons from every people, nation, and language, are all equally "Abraham's offspring, heirs according to the promise" (v. 29), then who will dominate whom when the promises are fulfilled? Rather than passing the baton of imperial domination from the pagan nations to Israel (so that Israel might do unto others as had been done unto them), the stage is set, it seems, for an end to the pattern of imperial oppression.[26]

Second, v. 28 highlights two of the relationships that are clearly understood in terms of real or potentially oppressive relationships. The slave-free relationship is intuitively understood that way, and clearly intended to be understood that way since Galatians 2:4 and in the light of the repeated contrast between the two in Galatians 4. The Jew-Gentile (or, here, Jew-Greek) relationship has been seen to have a history in which people on both sides have found themselves oppressed by the other.

It is remarkable that Paul mentions the male-female relationship here as well since it is not developed elsewhere in this letter, but was clearly susceptible to expressing oppressive dynamics, as other Pauline, New Testament, and other ancient (not to mention modern) texts make clear. This

25. For a discussion of Isa. 54:1-3 as background to Rom. 4, see Forman, "The Politics of Promise," pp. 319-20.

26. Lopez's comments on the "Jerusalem above" in Gal. 4:26 have little basis in what is said there, but have much in common with what is being argued here. She suggests that the "Jerusalem above" represents "the transformed, reconfigured Jews and nations in the new creation. . . . The new creation represents the reconciliation of all the nations into Jerusalem above through their service to the God of Israel" (*Apostle to the Conquered*, p. 160). "In Paul's imagination the free woman is the reconstituted Jerusalem who is the light to the nations, where all peoples should gather in peace, reconciliation, and self-determination according to First Testament prophetic rhetoric. The people of this city are called out of exile, and the peoples from the ends of the earth — all the nations, all those defeated — are called to enter her gates" (p. 162).

verse suggests that the blessing of Abraham could be understood (as we have seen throughout this essay) to point to liberation or freedom from a broad variety of oppressive relationships or circumstances. Paul's understanding of the blessing of Abraham, therefore, does not substitute physical land promises with a limited set of spiritual promises of one kind or another. Rather, he understands the blessing(s) in a much more expansive way, so that the blessing may be applied to an almost limitless range of relationships or situations in which people come to need and hope for freedom from oppression of one type or another.

In Galatians 4:1-7 Paul continues his discussion relating to what it means to be an heir. He does not mention Abraham in this passage, but it is understood that what is being discussed is what it means to be an heir to the promises given to Abraham. The discussion of heirs being no better than slaves until they enter into their inheritance (4:1-2) reflects a twist on a well-known narrative. The standard narrative alluded to elsewhere in various early Jewish and Christian writings is that God's people, heirs of the promise, were suffering as slaves under the thumb of the great foreign powers. In the fullness of time, however, God would redeem Israel from their oppressive situation by sending his Messiah, pouring out his Spirit, and bringing Israel into a time of eschatological salvation and restoration.[27] The twist in Paul's version of the narrative is that he never explicitly refers to the Roman empire or any foreign political powers, but rather speaks of being enslaved under τὰ στοιχεῖα τοῦ κόσμου (Gal. 4:3, literally, "the elements of the world") and of the redemption of those who were "under the law" (v. 5; ὑπὸ νόμον). And this redemption is understood to have been experienced by Jews and Gentiles alike (vv. 6-7), despite the fact that Israel's socio-political situation does not seem to have changed.

This brings us back to Galatians 3:22-23, where the fulfillment of the promise was related to the liberation of those who were imprisoned under the power of sin, as well as being guarded and imprisoned under the law. Like Jesus (and other Jews) before him, Paul understood that Israel's real problem was not the Romans or other oppressive political powers. In its early phase the Zealot movement seems to have understood, in its own distorted way, that Israel's problem was Israel, and that God would take care

---

27. Cf. Roy E. Ciampa, "The History of Redemption," in *Central Themes in Biblical Theology: Mapping Unity in Diversity,* ed. Scott Hafemann and Paul House (Grand Rapids: Baker & Leicester, England: InterVarsity, 2007), pp. 254-308.

of the Romans if Israel could put its own house in order.[28] Jesus demonstrated his messianic power not by casting the Romans out of Israel's land, but by casting demons out of spiritually oppressed people and addressing the physical, social, and spiritual needs of the people. This should not be taken as a full spiritualizing of the Abrahamic promise, but as a recognition of the broader and deeper set of challenges and needs that needed to be addressed in any ultimate divine plan to bring blessing and restoration not only to Jews but to all the nations of the earth. Paul and the rest of the New Testament do not reflect the substitution of one reductionistic view of what eschatological redemption might entail with a different but similarly reductionistic view.

The issue of slavery and freedom is explored via an allegorical comparison of Sarah and Hagar based on the Genesis narrative and related biblical traditions. In this comparison one is identified by her status as a slave woman and the other by her status as a free woman. Paul says Hagar is "from Mount Sinai, bearing children for slavery" (v. 24) and "is Mount Sinai in Arabia and corresponds to the present Jerusalem, for she is in slavery with her children" (v. 25). These statements about Jerusalem being "in slavery with her children" echo biblical statements made in prayer while standing in post-exilic Jerusalem. Ezra 9:8-9 speaks of the situation as one in which God has shown his people a ray of light "in the midst of our slavery [בעבדתנו/ἐν τῇ δουλείᾳ ἡμῶν]. For we are slaves [כי־עבדים אנחנו/ὅτι δοῦλοί ἐσμεν]." Nehemiah 9:36 is similar: "Here we are, slaves to this day [הנה אנחנו היום עבדים/ἰδού ἐσμεν σήμερον δοῦλοι]." These self-descriptions come in the context of penitential prayers in which the nation's failure to keep God's law is forthrightly confessed and understood to be the cause of their on-going experience of slavery. This biblical background to Jerusalem's slavery points to her experience of imperial domination (Ezra 9:7; Neh. 9:37), even as Paul reemploys and reapplies it to describe not merely Jewish experience of domination by foreign political powers, but (in light of what Paul has said in Gal. 3:10-13, 22-24; 4:3-5) human subjugation to the power of sin and (a reflection of that same subjugation) of the law.[29]

---

28. See Martin Hengel, *The Zealots: Investigations into the Jewish Freedom Movement in the Period from Herod I until 70 A.D.*, trans. David Smith (Edinburgh: T&T Clark, 1989), pp. 146-49.

29. Lopez, *Apostle to the Conquered*, p. 158, intriguingly suggests: "The allegorical Hagar who generates a son according to the flesh could be any nation for Rome: Judea, Gallia, Armenia, Britannia, Germania, Hispania, Africa. She is defined by the patriarchal dy-

The "other woman," on the other hand, "corresponds to the Jerusalem above; she is free, and she is our mother" (v. 26). The free woman, we are told, has undergone a wonderful and redemptive transformation. Paul quotes from Isaiah 54:1, which reflects the inversion motif we have mentioned above. Israel had been childless and desolate, but now her children "are more numerous than the children of the one who is married" (Gal. 4:27, citing Isa. 54:1).[30] But while Galatians 4:21–5:1 describes one of the women as free and the other as a slave (and although we know from Gen. 16:3 that Hagar was Sarah's slave-girl [παιδίσκη]), there is nothing in this passage about the slave woman being enslaved to the free woman, and no suggestion that the children of the slave woman were to be slaves of the children of the free woman.[31] Rather, the context leading up to this passage (especially 3:22–4:7) has suggested that those who remain enslaved are enslaved not to those who are free, but to other, outside forces.

The slave woman is the one who has borne children who persecute the children of the free woman, suggesting that people who mimic the behaviors of oppressive imperial powers have no legitimate claim to true Abrahamic sonship and the blessings that Abraham's children are destined to enjoy.

Like many of the texts that associate Abraham (or David, or Christ) with imperial types of power, Paul's paraphrase of Genesis 21:10 in Galatians 4:30, "But what does the scripture say? 'Drive out the slave and her child; for the child of the slave will not share the inheritance with the child of the free woman,'" certainly had great potential to be used in oppressive ways. And it is unfortunate that that potential came to be realized, especially once Christianity came to enjoy considerable political power in the world. It should have been remembered that Paul had already pointed

---

namics of submission and co-optation, generating children for imperial production." Furthermore, "she is not figuratively enslaved to Torah, but rather stands for imperial co-optation and resultant distortion of that same Torah. . . . Hagar in Galatians represents Jewish adherence to Roman world order" (p. 159).

30. On Paul's use of the Old Testament in Gal. 4:21-31 and especially his use of Isa. 54:1, see Karen H. Jobes, "Jerusalem Our Mother: Metalepsis and Intertextuality in Galatians 4:21-31," *WTJ* 55 (1993): 299-320.

31. It should be kept in mind that (as Paul himself would have understood) Isa. 54:1 does not exactly reflect the situation described in Gen. 21, and Paul avoids drawing out more than some minimal contrasts between the two women. See Jobes, "Jerusalem Our Mother," pp. 302, 316-17; Dietrich-Alex Koch, *Die Schrift als Zeuge des Evangeliums: Untersuchungen zur Verwendung und zum Verständnis der Schrift bei Paulus,* BHT 69 (Tübingen: J. C. B. Mohr [Paul Siebeck]), pp. 205-6.

out (see again 3:22–4:7) that all Jews and Gentiles had experienced the slavery to which he refers, and that Paul was actually attempting to free his readers from what he considered an erroneous and oppressive teaching rather than attempting to exert oppressive power over others (cf. Gal. 5:6; 1 Cor. 10:32–11:1).[32]

In Galatians 5:1, 13 Paul puts the finishing touches on his arguments about freedom and slavery in which Abraham has played such an important role. Christ has set them free, and they must not turn back from their new-found freedom (v. 1). Galatians 5:13 brings in a dramatic and ironic twist: his Galatians readers "were called to freedom," but the true nature of their freedom was to be demonstrated in their selfless choice to "become slaves to one another" through love (διὰ τῆς ἀγάπης δουλεύετε ἀλλήλοις). Like Abraham and Jesus himself, followers of Jesus Christ are not to be people who grasp after power or who use their freedom and resources for their own advantage, but people who use the resources God has given them in the loving service of others.[33] There can hardly be clearer evidence that the reign of sin and of self has been overcome.

This survey of Paul's use of the Abrahamic theme in Galatians has suggested that Paul, like other New Testament authors and Second Temple Jews, associates Abraham not only with justification or purely spiritual and abstract concepts, but also with a very broad range of oppressive realities. That association goes back to the very source — sin — and implicitly including all of its manifestations, including sin's attempt to turn even the good and righteous law into something oppressive, and to turn a community committed to righteousness into one that mimics the very imperialistic domination from which it longs to be rescued. May God help all those who consider themselves children of Abraham learn to walk in his footsteps by promoting freedom and liberty wherever slavery or oppression of any kind may be found.

---

32. Paul marks the conclusion to his argument in Gal. 4:31 with "so then, friends" (διό, ἀδελφοί). The conclusion was not that some action should be taken against others, but the defensive assertion that he and his readers "are children, not of the slave but of the free."

33. Abraham Joshua Heschel has suggested (*The Insecurity of Freedom: Essays on Human Existence* [New York: Farrar, Straus & Giroux, 1966], p. 15): "Freedom is the liberation from the tyranny of the self-centered ego. . . . Freedom presupposes the capacity for sacrifice. Although all men are potentially free, it is our sacred duty to safeguard all those political, social, and intellectual conditions which will enable every man to bring about the concrete actualization of freedom which is the essential prerequisite of creative achievement."

Abraham, the Father of Many Nations in the Book of Revelation

DAVID MATHEWSON

One of the persistent themes in the book of Revelation is the conversion of the nations from idolatry to worship of the one true God.[1] In his articulation of this theme, the author consistently grounds his vision of the destiny of the nations in allusions to Old Testament texts that anticipate the inclusion of the nations in eschatological salvation.[2] In the spirit of this collection of essays dedicated to Marv Wilson, who has devoted much of his academic career to the significance of the Old Testament figure of Abraham for religious thought,[3] I want to suggest that the Abrahamic covenant forms an important scriptural matrix for the theme of the inclusion of the nations in eschatological salvation in Revelation.[4] That is, the nations are redeemed to worship the true God and become the true children

---

1. For a detailed explication of this theme, see R. J. Bauckham, *The Climax of Prophecy* (Edinburgh: T&T Clark, 1993), ch. 9; R. Herms, *An Apocalypse for the Church and the World: The Narrative Function of Universal Language in the Book of Revelation*, BZNW 143 (Berlin: de Gruyter, 2006). Cf. also D. Mathewson, "The Destiny of the Nations in Revelation 21:1–22:5: A Reconsideration," *TynB* 53 (2002): 121-42.

2. Bauckham, *Climax*, p. 238; D. Mathewson, *A New Heaven and a New Earth: The Meaning and Function of the Old Testament in Revelation 21.1–22.5*, JSNTSS 238 (London: Sheffield Academic Press, 2003), ch. 6.

3. *Our Father Abraham: Jewish Roots of the Christian Faith* (Grand Rapids: Eerdmans, 1989).

4. As will become clear in the rest of this study, I am not claiming that the Abrahamic promise plays the dominant role or the most important role, but only that, as it does in the Old Testament, it plays an important and foundational role in establishing the thematic of the salvation and inheritance of the nations.

of Abraham and recipients of the promised land given to Abraham and his descendents. Abraham is the father of the many nations in Revelation. This influence emerges in the text of Revelation at least at two levels. First, the conversion of the nations in Revelation is a broad thematic extension of the promise made to Abraham that "in you all the families of the earth shall be blessed" (Gen. 12:3c) as well as the promise of the land, both integral parts of the Abrahamic promise. Second, Revelation appears to evoke the patriarchal promise through specific allusion to references to the Abrahamic covenant from Genesis and other Old Testament texts that resonate with the Abrahamic covenant theme. I am not aware of any study devoted specifically to the influence of the Abrahamic covenant on Revelation. The ensuing discussion is a contribution toward filling that void.

Echoes of the Promise to Abraham in Revelation

Two important elements of the promise made to Abraham in Genesis are the theme of blessing for all nations and the theme of inheritance of the land (Gen. 12:3). Both of these elements are reflected at a broad thematic level in Revelation. The notion of the conversion of the nations in Revelation thematically reflects the Abrahamic promise from Genesis 12:3 and elsewhere in the Old Testament. That is, the inclusion of the nations in salvific blessing is a fulfillment of the promise to Abraham that as the father of many nations (Gen. 17:4, 5) all the families/nations of the earth would be blessed in him (12:3c; 22:18). Though Abraham's name appears nowhere in Revelation, the inclusion of the nations in eschatological salvation is certainly, in part, to be seen as the final fulfillment of the blessing mediated to the nations through Abraham. In the original promise to Abraham in Genesis, the patriarch is to be the father of a multitude of nations (LXX ἐθνῶν) in 17:4, 5 and a blessing to all the nations of the earth in 22:18 (LXX πάντα τὰ ἔθνη τῆς γῆς, repeating 12:3c πᾶσαι αἱ φυλαὶ τῆς γῆς). The thematic of blessing or salvation for the nations is picked up elsewhere in the Old Testament, especially in Isaiah (Isa. 2:2-6; 9:1-2; 60), a book that forms an intertextual matrix for much of Revelation.[5] In Revelation, the

---

5. See Jan Fekkes, *Isaiah and Prophetic Traditions in the Book of Revelation: Visionary Antecedents and Their Development*, JSNTS 93 (Sheffield: JSOT Press, 1994). That the promise to Abraham is in mind in Isaiah's conception of restoration can be seen in Isa. 51:1-2, where Isaiah's anticipated restoration is explicitly linked with the promise to Abraham. See M. Fishbane, *Biblical Interpretation in Ancient Israel* (Oxford: Clarendon, 1985), pp. 375-76.

term ἔθνη occurs numerous times (e.g., 2:26; 11:2, 18; 16:19; 19:15; 20:3, 8; 21:24, 26; 22:2) as well as the phrase πάντα τὰ ἔθνη (e.g., 12:5; 14:8; 15:4; 18:3, 23; cf. Gen. 22:18). These expressions occur with reference to the deception of the nations by the dragon and the beast and their complicity with Babylon. But the nations are those who turn to worship God (15:4; 21:24, 26: 22:2), attesting to the universal scope of John's vision of eschatological salvation. So according to Revelation 15:5, the song of Moses sung by the redeemed anticipates a time when "all the nations shall come and worship before you." The term ἔθνη occurs seven more times, in varying order, in the fourfold formula "every tribe, language, people, and nation (ἔθνη)" (5:9; cf. 7:9; 10:11; 11:9; 13:7; 14:6; 17:16). In Revelation 21–22 the nations (21:24, 26; 22:2) enter the new creation, with the New Jerusalem at its center. John's usage of this term and his inclusion of the nations in eschatological salvation clearly stand in the stream that has its origin in the promise made to Abraham.

Furthermore, the Abrahamic promise is reflected in the inheritance of the land motif, a key component in the climactic vision of Revelation 21:1–22:5. An integral feature of the Abrahamic covenant was the possession of the land that would be given to Abraham's descendents (cf. Gen. 12:1, 7; 15:7-8; 17:8; 22:17). Abraham's offspring would "inherit" (LXX κληρονομέω) the land that God promised as an everlasting possession (Gen. 15:7-8; 22:17; cf. Heb. 11:8). "In Gn. and throughout the Bible there is constant reference to this promise. On it rests the belief of [Old Testament] Israel that possession of Palestine by Israel is based on the promise to Abraham."[6] Based on this promise of land to Abraham, many prophetic texts anticipate a return from exile at which time Israel will possess the land that was promised to Abraham (cf. Ezek. 33:24; 36:24; 37:25; cf. 40–48; Isa. 60:21 [LXX κληρονομήσουσιν]). Ezekiel's vision of restoration, which provides an important model for John's own vision (Rev. 21–22), promises the exiles that "You shall live in the land that I gave to your ancestors" (Ezek. 36:28; cf. 37:25), clearly connecting restoration in the land with the promise of land made to Abraham. In Revelation 21:1-8 the "overcomer" is promised an inheritance (21:7, κληρονομῆσαι), a notion that ultimately reflects the promised inheritance of the land to Abraham and his offspring (Gen. 15:7-

---

6. W. Foerster and J. Herrmann, "κληρονόμος," in *TDNT*, 3:769. Cf. H. Seebass, "Ἀβραάμ," in *NIDNTT*, 1:76. Cf. Deut. 1:8; 6:10; 9:5, 27; 29:13; 30:20; 34:4; Pss. 37:18; 105:9-11; Isa. 60:21; Ezek. 20:5, 6, 42; 28:25; 3:24; 37:25. For a treatment of the development of the land theme throughout the Bible, see C. H. Scobie, *The Ways of Our God: An Approach to Biblical Theology* (Grand Rapids: Eerdmans, 2003), pp. 541-66.

8; 22:17; Heb. 11:8). The object of κληρονομῆσαι in Revelation 21:7 is ταῦτα, which anaphorically refers to the whole previous section of vv. 1-6.[7] Included in this inheritance is the new heavens and *new earth* (21:1, 4; cf. Isa. 65:17), which provides the literary framework for the other eschatological blessings. Clearly, then, John sees the gift of the land, which is an integral part of the Abrahamic covenant, as fulfilled in the new creation that is now inherited by God's people. Thus, the promise of the possession of the land to Abraham and his offspring reaches its eschatological climax in the *new earth* of Revelation 21:1–22:5.

Therefore, Revelation's depiction of the ultimate destiny of the nations and the inheritance of the land (new heavens and *earth*) broadly finds its basis in and stands as the ultimate fulfillment of the promises to Abraham that he would bring blessing to all nations and that his offspring would inherit the land.[8] Yet these themes are sufficiently broad to warn against too hastily concluding that John had the Abrahamic promise specifically in mind. However, what makes it likely that John had the Abrahamic promise specifically in mind in the Apocalypse is the presence of specific allusions to the Abrahamic covenant from Genesis and elsewhere at key points in Revelation.

Allusions to Specific Old Testament Texts

Throughout his vision, the author of Revelation alludes both to the Abrahamic promise from Genesis and to Old Testament prophetic texts that have been influenced by the Abrahamic promise. The following texts are the most significant.

---

7. R. H. Charles, *A Critical and Exegetical Commentary on the Book of Revelation*, vol. 2, ICC (Edinburgh: T&T Clark, 1920), p. 215; cf. U. B. Müller, *Die Offenbarung des Johannes*, ÖTKNT 19 (Gütersloh: Gerd Mohn, 1984), p. 353.

8. Another possible point of connection with the Abrahamic promise is the Exodus motif, a motif that provides an important model for Revelation's articulation of eschatological salvation (cf. J. S. Casey, "Exodus Typology in the Book of Revelation [unpublished Ph.D. dissertation, Southern Baptist Theological Seminary, 1981]). As Fishbane has shown, Abraham was used typologically in connection with the Exodus, demonstrated by (1) Abraham's migration to Egypt, and (2) the plagues that come upon Pharaoh and his household. Fishbane, *Biblical Interpretation*, p. 376.

Revelation 1:7

At the very beginning of his book the author signals his evocation of the Abrahamic promise through a modification of a combination of Old Testament texts. Revelation 1:7 combines allusions to both Daniel 7:13 and Zechariah 12:10 (a combination also found in Matt. 24:30). While John's Ἰδοὺ ἔρχεται μετὰ τῶν νεφελῶν (v. 7a) draws on Daniel 7:13, the second part of this citation in v. 7b comes from Zechariah 12:10.

> καὶ ὄψεται αὐτὸν πᾶς ὀφθαλμὸς
> καὶ οἵτινες αὐτὸν ἐξεκέντησαν
> καὶ κόψονται ἐπ' αὐτὸν πᾶσαι αἱ φυλαὶ τῆς γῆς (Rev. 1:7b-d)[9]

The latter part of the quotation, πᾶσαι αἱ φυλαὶ τῆς γῆς, is a significant modification to the Zechariah text. The phrase may reflect the הארץ משפחות משפחות/LXX ἡ γῆ κατὰ φυλὰς φυλάς in Zechariah 12:12, but as Bauckham argues it is more than just an interpretive rendering of this text.[10] Rather, it constitutes an allusion to the patriarchal promise in Genesis 12:3.

> Gen. 12:3: LXX πᾶσαι αἱ φυλαὶ τῆς γῆς (cf. 28:14)
> Rev. 1:7: πᾶσαι αἱ φυλαὶ τῆς γῆς

The language of the patriarchal promise from Genesis 12:3 (כל משפחת הארץ) would have been linked lexically to the similar language in Zechariah 12:12 (הארץ משפחות).[11] Though this addition to Zechariah 12:10 was already part of the traditional form of the quotation (see its inclusion in Matt. 24:30) upon which John drew, John would have likely recognized its significance as an allusion to the Abrahamic promise in Genesis 12:3. Therefore, at the very outset of his work the author ties in his conception of eschatological salvation of all peoples that he will develop in the rest of his work with the promise made to Abraham. This initial appeal to the promise to Abraham leads the reader to find other references to the promise made to Abraham. John intends the reader to see the conversion of the nations as a fulfillment of the Abrahamic promise. This conclusion also supports those who would

---

9. That Rev. 1:7 is not dependent on Matt. 24:30, but draws on a common tradition of combining these two texts, can be seen from the fact that Rev. 1:7 quotes from more of Zech. 12:10 than is found in Matt. 24:30.

10. See Bauckham, *Climax*, pp. 319-21.

11. Bauckham, *Climax*, p. 321.

interpret the mourning of the tribes of the earth in Revelation 1:7 in terms of their repentance rather than mourning because of judgment.[12]

Revelation 7:9

Revelation 7:1-17 consists of a vision comprised of two parts. The first (vv. 1-8) revolves around John "hearing" the number of those sealed from each of the twelve tribes of Israel, twelve thousand from each tribe, followed by a section (vv. 9-17) where John now "sees" a great multitude. The latter group is probably to be seen as identical to the former.[13] So while John "heard" (ἤκουσα) the number 144,000 from the tribes of Israel, what he "saw" (εἶδον) in v. 9 is a "great crowd, which no one was able to number, from every nation and tribe and people and language" (ὄχλος πολύς, ὃν ἀριθμῆσαι αὐτὸν οὐδεὶς ἐδύνατο, ἐκ παντὸς ἔθνους καὶ φυλῶν καὶ λαῶν καὶ γλωσσῶν). This phrase reflects the Abrahamic promise from the Genesis narrative in two respects. First, a clear allusion to the patriarchal promise in this section emerges in the description of the multitude that John sees in v. 9 as that "which no one was able to number" (ὃν ἀριθμῆσαι αὐτὸν οὐδεὶς ἐδύνατο). This phrase draws on the repeated reference in Genesis to Abraham's innumerable descendents (Gen. 13:16; 15:5; 22:17; 32:12; cf. Hos. 1:10; Heb. 11:12), an allusion recognized by several commentaries.[14] The following comparison demonstrates the verbal correspondences with the most important texts.

---

12. Bauckham, *Climax*, p. 322; G. K. Beale, *The Book of Revelation*, NIGTC (Grand Rapids: Eerdmans, 1999), p. 197; G. R. Osborne, *Revelation*, BECNT (Grand Rapids: Baker, 2002), p. 68. *Contra* R. H. Mounce, *The Book of Revelation*, NICNT (Grand Rapids: Eerdmans, 1977), p. 73.

13. "Die 144,000 und die große Schar sind . . . identisch" (H. Giesen, *Die Offenbarung des Johannes*, RNT [Regensburg: Friedrich Pustet, 1997], p. 197). Cf. Bauckham, *Climax*, pp. 215-16. See further J. L. Resseguie, *Revelation Unsealed: A Narrative Critical Approach to John's Apocalypse*, Biblical Interpretation Series 32 (Leiden: Brill, 1998), pp. 33-37, on the "heard"/"saw" dialectic more generally.

14. J. P. M. Sweet, *Revelation* (London: SCM, 1979), p. 150; P. Prigent, *L'Apocalypse de Saint Jean* (Paris: Delachaux et Niestlé, 1981), p. 123; Mounce, *Revelation*, p. 171; Bauckham, *Climax*, p. 223; Beale, *Revelation*, p. 426; D. E. Aune, *Revelation 6–16*, WBC 52b (Nashville: Thomas Nelson, 1998), p. 466; S. Pattemore, *The People of God in the Apocalypse: Discourse, Structure and Exegesis*, SNTSMS 128 (Cambridge: Cambridge University Press, 2004), p. 142; S. S. Smalley, *The Revelation to John: A Commentary on the Greek Text of the Apocalypse* (Downers Grove: IVP, 2005), p. 190; Osborne, *Revelation*, p. 318; M. Reddish, *Revelation*, Smyth & Helwys Bible Commentary (Macon: Smyth & Helwys, 2001), p. 148.

Rev. 7:9: ὃν ἀριθμῆσαι αὐτὸν οὐδεὶς ἐδύνατο

Gen. 13:16: LXX εἰ δύναταί τις ἐξαριθμῆσαι

Gen. 15:5: LXX εἰ δυνήσῃ ἐξαριθμῆσαι αὐτούς

Gen. 32:13: LXX οὐκ ἀριθμηθήσεται ἀπὸ τοῦ πλήθους[15]

As Aune has suggested, the promise made to Abraham consists of two distinct aspects: (1) the promise of innumerable descendents (cf. Gen. 13:16; 15:5; 22:17; 32:12 (LXX 32:13), and (2) the promise that Abraham would be the father of many nations (cf. Gen. 17:4-6, 16).[16] What is remarkable is that Revelation 7:9a draws upon the first of these two aspects: the promise of innumerable descendents, which in the Genesis narrative applies to the physical seed of Abraham. So John has taken a reference to the physical descendents of Abraham and has now applied it to those "from every nation and tribe and people and language" in v. 9. As Aune observes, "[t]his passage implies that the promise of Abraham has been fulfilled, though not through physical descent through Abraham."[17] Rather, all nations now become the true Israel, the true spiritual descendents of Abraham, and heirs to the promise made to him.

Second, as Bauckham has convincingly argued, the παντὸς ἔθνους is probably also exegetically significant here.[18] Grammatically it sits awkwardly in this context due to the fact that unlike the other four occurrences in Revelation of πᾶς with this fourfold formula (cf. 5:9; 13:7; 14:6), παντὸς ἔθνους is the only singular member of the fourfold grouping here in 7:9 (tribes, peoples, and tongues being plural). Furthermore, only in 7:9 and 14:6 does ἔθνη come first in the fourfold listing.

5:9: πάσης φυλῆς καὶ γλώσσης καὶ λαοῦ καὶ ἔθνους

7:9: *παντὸς ἔθνους καὶ φυλῶν καὶ λαῶν καὶ γλωσσῶν*

13:7: πᾶσαν φυλὴν καὶ λαὸν καὶ γλῶσσαν καὶ ἔθνος

14:6: πᾶν ἔθνος καὶ φυλὴν καὶ γλῶσσαν καὶ λαὸν

---

15. I have not included Gen. 16:10 (LXX καὶ οὐκ ἀριθμηθήσεται ἀπὸ τοῦ πλήθους) for comparison since it refers to the offspring of Hagar and not to the covenant seed of Abraham.

16. Aune, *Revelation 6–16*, p. 466.

17. Aune, *Revelation 6–16*, p. 466. Cf. Beale, *Revelation*, p. 427: "Therefore, the multitudes in Rev. 7:9 are the consummate fulfillment of the Abrahamic promise and appear to be another of the manifold ways in which John refers to Christians as Israel." Cf. Reddish, *Revelation*, p. 148.

18. Bauckham, *Climax*, p. 225.

This placing of ἔθνους first, as well as the grammatical awkwardness that sets it apart from the other three, can be explained, according to Bauckham, through an allusion to the patriarchal promise.[19] According to Bauckham, John's vision of an ὄχλος πολύς . . . ἐκ παντὸς ἔθνους alludes to the promise to Abraham (Gen. 17:4: LXX πατὴρ πλήθους ἐθνῶν).[20] While this is plausible, Beale argues that a more appropriate intertext is Genesis 22:17-18, since there (1) the nations are clearly recipients of *salvific blessing*, and (2) the blessing of the nations is coupled with the mention of innumerable seed. One textual tradition in the LXX includes the reading "which cannot be counted because of their number" in Genesis 22:18.[21] Both notions also come together in Revelation 7:9, making it possible that John had this text explicitly in mind.

Thus, the author is drawing on several texts from the Genesis narrative that evoke the blessing to all nations and the innumerability of Abraham's seed. John seems to be aware of both strands in the Abrahamic promise alluded to in Revelation 7:9. In Genesis it is with the physical seed of Abraham that the covenant is made (17:7-8; 22:17). Through the establishment of the physical seed, then, blessings will be mediated to the multitude of nations (22:18; cf. 21:3), of which Abraham is the spiritual father (17:4-6).[22] However, in Revelation both strands of the promise, the blessings to the multitudes *and* the establishment of the seed, are now provocatively applied to the nations. Thus, the blessing of all nations through

19. Bauckham, *Climax*, p. 225.

20. Beale also recognizes the possibility of this allusion based on the grammatical incongruity (*Revelation*, pp. 429, 431). For grammatical awkwardness in Revelation as a possible signal of Old Testament allusions, see G. K. Beale, "Solecisms in the Apocalypse as Signals for the Presence of Old Testament Allusions: A Selective Analysis of Revelation 1–22," in *Early Christian Interpretation of the Scriptures of Israel*, ed. C. A. Evans and J. A. Sanders, JSNTS 148 (Sheffield: Sheffield Academic Press, 1997), pp. 421-46. G. Osborne thinks that this is only secondary, and that the emphasis is on "every nation" and that it focuses on the universal mission to all nations found elsewhere in Revelation and the pilgrimage of the nations motif from the Old Testament (*Revelation*, p. 319). However, I would argue that the universal mission to all nations and the Old Testament pilgrimage of the nations motif have their roots in and are an outworking of the promise to Abraham, which may be what John is suggesting based on his allusion to the patriarchal promise here.

21. Beale, *Revelation*, p. 430. ητις ουκ (εξ)αριθμηθησεται απο του πληθος: Tht I 196 661. For this reading, see J. W. Wevers, ed., *Septuaginta Vetus Testamentum Graecum, I, Genesis* (Göttingen: Vandenhoeck & Ruprecht, 1974), p. 217.

22. See P. R. Williamson, *Abraham, Israel and the Nations: The Patriarchal Promise and Its Covenantal Development in Genesis*, JSOTSS 315 (Sheffield: Sheffield Academic Press, 2000), p. 255.

Abraham's seed is fulfilled in the salvation of all nations. However, the promise of an innumerable seed is also applied to all the nations in Revelation, not just to Abraham's physical lineage. It is *by becoming the innumerable seed* that *all the nations are blessed!* In Revelation 7:9, then, both notions come together, and John sees "a great crowd which *no one was able to number,* from *every nation. . . .*"

Revelation 21:11-21

Revelation 21:1–22:5 plays a key role in the author's conception of eschatological salvation, because it is here that the theme of the conversion of the nations receives its "eschatological ultimacy."[23] At first glance there appears to be little reason to include Revelation 21:11-21 in a discussion of the influence of Abraham in the book of Revelation, since there are no clear thematic or lexical connections to the Abrahamic promise from the Genesis narrative. However, the intertextual relationship between a text and its prior text should be understood as a broad interplay between the two texts that goes beyond what is explicitly cited. According to R. Hays, "Allusive echo functions to suggest to the reader that text B should be understood in light of a broad interplay with text A, encompassing aspects of A beyond those explicitly echoed."[24] Such an understanding of allusive echo provides a more sophisticated way of examining the broader context of Old Testament texts to which New Testament authors allude. Though in Revelation 21:11-21 the author weaves a visionary mosaic consisting of a number of Old Testament texts, Isaiah 54:11-12 plays a key role. The conception of the precious jewels that adorn the New Jerusalem in Revelation 21 stems primarily from its *Vorbild,* Isaiah 54:11-12, which John metaphorically interprets as founding members of the eschatological community.[25]

23. R. J. Bauckham, *The Theology of the Book of Revelation* (Cambridge: Cambridge University Press, 1993), p. 103.

24. R. B. Hays, *Echoes of Scripture in the Letters of Paul* (New Haven: Yale University Press, 1989), p. 20. For this approach applied to the book of Revelation, see S. Moyise, *The Old Testament in the Book of Revelation,* JSNTS 115 (Sheffield: Sheffield Academic Press, 1995).

25. Cf. J. Comblin, "La liturgie de la Nouvelle Jérusalem (Apoc xxi-xxii5)," *ETL* 29 (1953): 14; J. A. Draper, "The Twelve Apostles as Foundation Stones of the Heavenly Jerusalem and the Foundation of the Qumran Community," *Neot* 22 (1988): 41-61. See 4QpIsa[d].

Isa. 54:11-12	Rev. 21:11-21
foundations (11)	foundations (14, 19)
battlements (12)	—
gates (12)	gates (12-13, 21)
walls (12)	wall (12, 14, 17-18)

In its Old Testament context, the oracle of Isaiah 54:11-12 referred to the glorious reversal that would take place when God restored the presently afflicted (v. 11a) Jerusalem and its people.[26] Yet when one examines the broader context of this oracle beyond that which is explicitly cited in Revelation 21 for further possible resonances, the city is also compared to a barren woman who never bore a child in Isaiah 54:1, but who now gives birth to numerous children. Though this notion of a barren woman who now gives birth may be a general metaphor applied to the situation of the Israelites in exile and their promise of national restoration, it probably more specifically reflects the patriarchal narrative from Genesis.[27] In Genesis 11:30 Sarah is described as barren and without child (LXX: καὶ ἦν Σαρα στεῖρα καὶ οὐκ ἐτεκνοποίει; cf. Gen. 16:1). Thus, in LXX Isaiah 54:1 we read στεῖρα ἡ οὐ τίκτουσα. In other words, "Isaiah reminds Israel that just as Yahweh intervened to transform Sarah from a barren woman as good as dead to a fruitful mother of many children, so he will transform a Jerusalem destroyed by sin into a city with a thriving population of righteous seed."[28] That Isaiah 54:1 should be understood as a reference to the patriarchal narrative is confirmed by its clear use in this manner in Galatians 4:27 in connection with the Sarah-Hagar "allegory."[29] But more than just an analogy between the situation of the reversal of Sarah's barrenness and the plight of Israel, the restoration of Israel from exile is seen as a *fulfillment* of the promise made to Abraham of the multiplication of his descendents, which would come through the reversal of Sarah's barrenness (Gen. 17:15, 16). Thus the restoration of Jerusalem and the return of the nation of Israel to the restored city find their basis in the patriarchal promises.

26. On Isaiah 54, see R. Marin-Achard, "Esaïe liv et la nouvelle Jérusalem," *Congress Volume Vienna 1980*, VTSup 32 (Leiden: E. J. Brill, 1982), pp. 238-62.

27. Cf. W. A. M. Beuken, "Isaiah LIV: The Multiple Identity of the Person Addressed," *OTS* 19 (1974): 29-70. *Contra* B. Childs, *Isaiah*, OTL (Louisville: Westminster John Knox Press, 2001), p. 428.

28. K. H. Jobes, "Jerusalem Our Mother: Metalipsis and Intertextuality in Galatians 4.21-31," *WTJ* 55 (1993): 311.

29. For a compelling treatment of Isa. 54:1 in Gal. 4:21-31 and how it affects the interpretation of this latter text, see Jobes, "Jerusalem Our Mother."

When we turn to Revelation 21:11-21, John's appeal to Isaiah 54:11-12 should be seen as invoking the entire context of the Isaianic oracle. As Hays suggests, "the figurative effect of the echo can lie in the unstated or suppressed (transumed) points of resonance between the two texts."[30] By alluding to Isaiah 54:11-12, then, John's visionary piece (Rev. 21:11-21) resonates with the tones of that prior text. John's visionary finale of eschatological salvation and restoration ultimately is to be seen as the fulfillment of the Abrahamic promise so that the people from all nations (21:26; 22:2), the innumerable multitude (7:9), now enter upon their inheritance (21:7) of the new creation (21:1), with a restored Jerusalem at its center (21:2). They are true seed of Abraham, the true children of Sarah, in covenant relationship with their God (21:3, see below).

Other Possible Allusions/Echoes

Revelation 12

Revelation 12:1-2 opens with a vision of a woman decked out with the constellations (the sun, moon, and stars), and preparing to give birth to a son. It appears that a number of Old Testament texts provide the intertextual background for John's portrayal of the woman. The figure of a woman or wife to metaphorically represent the people of God was stock Old Testament imagery, especially in the prophetic expectations of restoration (Isa. 54:1-3; 60:19-20; 61:10; 62:1-5; 66:7-13). And Israel in distress is often compared to a woman suffering the pangs of birth (Isa. 26:17-18; 37:3; Jer. 4:31; 6:24; 13:21; 22:23; 30:6; Mic. 4:9; cf. also *1QH* 3:7-12). Furthermore, in Isaiah 60:19-20 the restored Israel is associated with the sun and moon, and in 62:3-5 she is likened to a crown.[31] More specifically, both Isaiah 26:17-18 and 66:7 (cf. 7:14) provide a number of close verbal parallels to Revelation 12:1-5, depicting a woman who is in pain and about to give birth to a child. Furthermore, the main elements of Revelation 12 (woman, pain in childbirth, dragon, conflict) also resonate with and can be seen as an expansion of Genesis 3:15.[32]

30. Hays, *Echoes of Scripture,* p. 20.

31. Cf. Prigent, *L'Apocalypse,* p. 186.

32. See Beale, *Revelation,* pp. 679-80, 688. Cf. also M. Koch, *Drachenkampf und Sonnenfrau: Zur Funktion des Mythischen in der Johannesapokalypse am Beispiel von Apk 12,*

However, it is also possible that this section resonates with themes from the patriarchal promise. As can be seen, John is fond of juggling more than one Old Testament precursor at the same time in his own visionary depictions, and often Revelation's allusion to the Old Testament is multi-layered. As Beale has suggested, the constellations mentioned in Revelation 12:1 (sun, moon, stars) were associated with the patriarchal family.[33] Genesis 37:9, which formed the basis for later developments, portrays Jacob, his wife Rachel, and the eleven tribes of Israel as the sun, moon, and eleven stars in Joseph's dream. Moreover, in *Testament of Abraham* B 7:4-16 Abraham, Sarah, and their children are depicted as the sun, moon, and stars (cf. *Midr. Rab.* Num. 2:13). Therefore, the woman who is decked out in the constellations is to be understood as the Messianic community in continuity with and in fulfillment of the patriarchal family and the promise given to Abraham and his offspring. Furthermore, given the pervasive influence of the Isaianic texts as seen above, it is likely that John also had in mind two other texts that clearly resonate with the Abrahamic promise. Isaiah 54:1-3 depicts a woman who is in labor and about to give birth. Lexically this text provides the following parallels with Revelation 12:1-2:

Isa. 54:1-2:   Sing, O barren one, who never *gave birth* (LXX τίκτουσα); burst into song, shout for joy, you who were never *in labor* (LXX ὠδίνουσα).

Rev. 12:2:   She was pregnant and cried out in *pain* (ὠδίνουσα), as she was about to *give birth* (τεκεῖν).

In addition, in Isaiah 51:2 both Abraham and Sarah are designated in this text as "the source of the nation's true identity."[34] Sarah in particular is described as the one "who gave birth to you in pain" (LXX ὠδίνουσαν).

If John has these texts in mind along with the other Isaiah texts mentioned above, then the woman who gives birth to the Messiah (as well as apparently producing other offspring, see 12:17 below) is clearly linked to the patriarchal promise. That Christ would be depicted as born from Sarah here would be close to the Pauline notion that Christ is the true seed of

WUNT 184 (Tübingen: Mohr Siebeck, 2004), pp. 134-35. See especially the clear allusion in Rev. 12:9.

33. Beale, *Revelation*, p. 625.
34. Childs, *Isaiah*, p. 402.

Abraham (Gal. 3:16).[35] Yet there may be one further resonance in this context: the mention of the woman's seed (σπέρμα) in Revelation 12:17: "Then the dragon was enraged at the woman and went off to make war with the rest of her offspring (σπέρμα)." While this most clearly reflects the "seed" of the woman from Genesis 3:15 (LXX σπέρματος), this may also echo the repeated reference to the offspring, or seed, of Abraham and Sarah (LXX Gen. 12:7 [σπέρματι]; 13:16 [σπέρμα]; 26:4 [σπέρμα, σπέρματι]; 28:14 [σπέρμα, σπέρματι]). More specifically, due to the influence of Isaianic texts, John may also have in mind Isaiah 54:3, which refers to the barren woman's (Sarah's) children as "seed" (LXX σπέρμα). Thus, the Messianic community in Revelation 12 constitutes the offspring (σπέρμα) of Abraham and his wife, Sarah. Therefore, along with the story of creation and the story of restoration from exile and new exodus, Revelation 12 also resonates with the patriarchal story — Abraham's progeny, the reversal of Sarah's barrenness through the birth of the promised son (the Messiah), and the multiplication of her offspring.

Revelation 21:3

In Revelation's climactic vision (21:1–22:5), the audition in 21:3 repeats the Old Testament covenant formula (Lev. 26:11-12; Ezek. 37:26-28): "Now the dwelling of God is with humanity, and he will live with them. They will be his people, and God himself will be with them and be their God." In addition, John may have in mind a number of other Old Testament texts that include the covenant formula in the context of the restoration of Israel (Jer. 31:33; Ezek. 36:28; Zech. 8:3, 8).[36] But there might also be a faint echo of Genesis 17:7-8 in the covenant formula in Revelation 21:3. In this section of Genesis God makes a covenant with Abraham (Gen. 17:4) that Abraham would be the father of many nations. This covenant would be an *everlasting covenant* with Abraham and *his descendents* (v. 7). This included possession of the land of Canaan as an *everlasting possession* (v. 8). In the midst of the section the author invokes the language of the covenant formula:

---

35. Cf. Matt. 1:1. Christ is the "son of Abraham."

36. For other texts, see Mathewson, *New Heaven and New Earth*, p. 53; Beale, *Revelation*, p. 1048.

> I will establish my covenant . . . to be *your God* (LXX σου θεός), and the God of your descendents after you. (Gen. 17:7)

> . . . and I will be their God (LXX ἔσομαι αὐτοῖς θεός). (v. 8)

Along with other Old Testament texts, Genesis 17:17-8 provides a number of parallels with Revelation 21:1-3. Consequently, in Revelation 21:3 the covenant formula promises that God "will be their God" (αὐτὸς ὁ θεὸς μετ' αὐτῶν ἔσται αὐτῶν θεός).[37] This occurs in the context of the inheritance of the land, the *new creation* (21:1). Once again, John's allusive appeal to the Old Testament texts may reflect multilayered intertextuality, and his inclusion of the covenant formula is part of a stream that goes back to the everlasting covenant that God made with Abraham and his descendents, which included possession of the land. Thus along with Leviticus 26:11-2 and Ezekiel 37:36-38, if an echo of the Abrahamic covenant is heard in Revelation 21:3, the eschatological people of God made up of all peoples (cf. τῶν ἀνθρώπων in v. 3)[38] as the true children of Abraham now possess the land (the new creation, v. 1) in fulfillment of the covenant God made with Abraham and with his descendents, a covenant fleshed out in subsequent covenant formulas in the Old Testament.

Conclusion

Central to John's vision of eschatological salvation are the twin themes of the inclusion of the nations and inheritance of eschatological salvation in the new creation. Yet lurking behind Revelation's conception of the salvation of the nations and their inheritance of eschatological salvation, anchored as they are in Israel's Scriptures, is the patriarchal promise of blessing to all nations and inheritance of the land. John's conception of the inclusion of the nations in salvation stands at the climax of a long thematic stream concerning the inclusion of the nations in eschatological salvation and the inheritance of the land developed in the Old Testament, which

37. The transposition from first person to third person in Rev. 21:3 is necessary since the covenant formula in 21:3 is uttered by the voice from the throne. For acceptance of the reading that includes θεὸς αὐτῶν, see D. E. Aune, *Revelation 17–21*, WBC 52c (Nashville: Thomas Nelson, 1998), p. 1111.

38. For John's adaptation of the covenant formula in Rev. 21:3, see Mathewson, *New Heaven and New Earth,* pp. 50-57.

have their roots in the promise made to Abraham. Further, Revelation draws on two features of the Abrahamic promise: the blessing to all nations and the multiplication of Abraham's physical descendents. But John applies both of them, including the promise to Abraham's ethnic seed from Genesis, to the transcultural people of God consisting of people from every tribe, nation, language, and people. Therefore, the transcultural people of God, the new Israel, fulfills not just the promise of blessings to all nations, but the promise of multiplied seed for Abraham, an interpretive move reflected elsewhere in the New Testament.[39]

There is no need to make the promise to Abraham the dominant theme in Revelation, nor to deny it since there are clear references to other prophetic texts (Daniel, Isaiah, Ezekiel). And not all will find all of the proposed allusions/echoes above convincing. As suggested, at times John's allusive appeal to the Old Testament may be multilayered, with later texts building on earlier ones. And like an orchestra that provides a rich texture of instruments that complement each other at various levels, so John appeals to numerous texts that all contribute to the rich mosaic of his visionary piece. One of those instruments that sounds its note throughout John's vision of eschatological salvation, and a foundational note at that, is the promise made to Abraham. The intention of God to make Abraham's seed innumerable and to bless all the nations and give them their inheritance in covenant relationship with them reaches its eschatological finale in the vision of Revelation where God's people is made up of those from every nation. Indeed, "our father Abraham" is the father of many nations in Revelation.

---

39. Gal. 3:6-7; Rom. 4:9-17. Cf. J. Jeremias, "Ἀβραάμ," in *TDNT,* 1:9.

Abraham and Interdisciplinary Studies:
The Dialogue Continues

"They Are Loved on Account of the Patriarchs": Zekhut Avot *and the Covenant with Abraham*

Elaine Phillips

Introduction

In Judaism, there is a concept of imputed righteousness for corporate Israel in which the meritorious actions of the ancestors are efficacious for their offspring.[1] "Merit of the fathers" *(zekhut avot)* is a complex, multi-faceted concept that has links with the most compelling theological issues within Judaism and Christianity. It rests squarely in the "nest" of God's justice and mercy, surrounded by the concepts of measure-for-measure reward and punishment and the necessity for balanced justice.[2] In the context of the covenant with Abraham, merit of the fathers intersects with faithfulness of both Abraham and God. It also connects with self-sacrifice on behalf of God's people and obedience to Torah. Because God's justice focuses not only on individuals but also on corporate Israel, *zekhut avot* transcends time constraints. It is based on the boundless goodness of God "which cannot be limited to the short space of a lifetime."[3]

Clearly, setting parameters for this investigation is necessary at the outset. Because I have dealt elsewhere with the concepts of measure-for-

1. Solomon Schechter, *Some Aspects of Rabbinic Theology* (London: Adam and Charles Black, 1909), pp. 170-71.

2. Max Kadushin, *The Rabbinic Mind* (New York: Blaisdell, 1965), p. 15, addresses justice as one of four foundational "value-concepts." The others are God's love, Torah, and Israel.

3. Solomon Schechter, "The Doctrine of Divine Retribution in the Rabbinical Literature," *Jewish Quarterly Review,* Old Series 3 (1891): 39.

measure justice[4] and self-sacrifice[5] in rabbinic Judaism, I will address those only as they directly intersect with key passages in this study. Furthermore, even though the title has a tantalizing allusion to Paul, I do not intend to venture far into the tumultuous sea of Pauline studies; that would be another tome altogether. Instead, these next pages probe selected rabbinic perceptions of the nature of *zekhut avot*, perhaps cracking open a bit further a window on the socio-religious contexts of the first centuries of the Common Era.[6] It appears that some of the Sages wrestled with the implications of the covenant and particularly merit of the fathers as they addressed the ebb and flow of stress for the Jews in the wider Roman empire.

Definitions

The rabbis coined the phrase *zekhut avot* "to designate a sort of fund on which Israel could draw provided they followed in the footsteps of the Patriarchs."[7] The verbal root *zakhah*, used in biblical Hebrew, means to be pure, clear, right.[8] The basic meaning of *zekhut* has to do with acquittal,

---

4. Elaine Phillips, "The Tilted Balance: Early Rabbinic Perceptions of God's Justice," *Bulletin for Biblical Research* 14.2 (2004): 223-40.

5. Elaine Phillips, "*Natan Naphsho:* Paradigms of Self-Sacrifice in Early Judaism and Christianity," *Bulletin for Biblical Research* 9 (1999): 215-32. Self-sacrifice and the suffering of the righteous accrue merit for succeeding generations as well as contemporaries and thus bring the concept of atonement into the discussion as well. In fact, the narrative of Abraham's binding Isaac on the altar became in later legend a narrative of Isaac's atonement. See Ephraim Urbach, *The Sages: Their Concepts and Beliefs,* vol. 1, trans. Israel Abrahams (Jerusalem: Magnes Press, 1979), pp. 501-4. To suffer for and with Israel was an ideal already set by Moses; this conduct is expected from every Jew (Schechter, "Doctrine of Divine Retribution," pp. 43-44).

6. While even the earliest rabbinic texts were compiled some centuries after the New Testament, they reflect long traditions. Nevertheless, I take seriously Neusner's warning that direct comparisons between New Testament and rabbinic materials may be seeking to make two very different communities "converse" with each other. To do so, each thought world needs to be presented with its own terms and in its own contexts ("The Use of Later Rabbinic Evidence for the Study of Paul," in *Approaches to Ancient Judaism*, vol. 2, ed. William Scott Green [Chico: Scholars Press, 1980], pp. 43-63). Here I attempt to lay out only one of those fields.

7. A. Melinek, "The Doctrine of Reward and Punishment in Biblical and Early Rabbinic Writings," in *Essays Presented to Chief Rabbi Israel Brodie on the Occasion of His Seventieth Birthday*, ed. H. J. Zimmels, J. Rabbinowitz, and I. Finestein (London: Soncino Press, 1967), p. 287.

8. HALOT, vol. 1, p. 269.

but its most prominent connotations involve the "protecting influences of good conduct," i.e., merit.[9] That God remembers and fulfills his covenant with Israel is due to merit accrued by the good deeds of the patriarchs. One strand of thought pursued the possibility that the self-sacrificial good deeds of some achieved no benefit for themselves but stored up merit for others in succeeding generations. At the same time, the Sages acknowledged that merit intersects with obedience of the righteous in every generation. "[T]he long series of Tanaaim who ascribed the miracles and salvations to the merit of Israel's deeds, and not to that of the Patriarchs, were afraid of too much reliance on this merit and the consequent weakening of the sense of duty and of the need to fulfill the commandments."[10] To make the matter even more complicated, some of the Sages taught that God's deliverances were the "result" of merit in the future; the crossing of the Sea occurred because of the Torah that was to be given or establishing the place of Jerusalem as the site of the Temple, centuries away.[11] For the rabbis, chronological succession was not nearly as important as the closely knit web of biblical texts, always expanding to include one more interpretation and thus enriching the whole fabric of the world of Torah.

Even though chronological concerns were not foremost, there were attempts to determine just how long ancestral merit was meritorious. Some even set dates and gave textual warrant for doing so; it ceased in the days of Jehoahaz (2 Kings 13:23), or it continued until the time of Hosea (Hos. 2:12) or Elijah (1 Kings 18:36) or Hezekiah (Isa. 9:6). Rabbi Aha's view happily prevailed: "The merit of the fathers endures forever" (citing Deut. 4:31), as long as study of Torah and obedience accompanied it (JT Sanh. 10:1 27d; Leviticus Rabbah 39:6; Shab. 55a).

Methodological Concerns

A Theology of Judaism?

Until the last forty years or so, scholarly work on rabbinic midrash was characterized by painstakingly detailed presentation of parallel occur-

---

9. Marcus Jastrow, *A Dictionary of the Targumim, the Talmud Babli and Yerushalmi, and the Midrashic Literature* (London: Shapiro, Vallentine & Co., 1926), p. 398.

10. Urbach, *The Sages*, p. 497.

11. Urbach, *The Sages*, pp. 498-507.

rences of given traditions or ideas, whether they be halakhic or aggadic, and by catalogs of names and terminology.[12] This comprehensive approach was deemed necessary because "rabbinic thought" was considered to be indivisible.[13] Thus, any given issue was addressed by ranging through the wide spectrum of texts without regard for the possible effects of changing social, political, and religious circumstances in Late Antiquity. The situation was no different in regard to studies of merit of the fathers as a concept related to justice. Urbach's magisterial work devoted a lengthy chapter to all the issues related to the concept of justice as they were illustrated by manifold incidents and homilies across the stretch of all genres of the literature.[14] The extensive sub-section on merit cites multiple examples of rabbis' opinions without particular concern for their specific locations in the vast rabbinic corpus.

Subsequently, comparative methods have gathered the materials pertinent to a subject, arranging them according to the assumed chronological development and then making observations regarding the development of the tradition.[15] Of increasing importance has been the emphasis, propelled by the voluminous corpus of Jacob Neusner's studies, on assessing individual rabbinic texts for what they can tell us about the most pressing social constructs for the rabbis who compiled those specific texts.[16]

12. See Peter Schäfer, "Research into Rabbinic Literature: An Attempt to Define the *Status Quaestiones," Journal of Jewish Studies* 37 (1986): 139-48, for an assessment of the various approaches to rabbinic literature. Louis Ginzberg's *Legends of the Jews* (vols. 1-7, trans. H. Szold [Philadelphia, 1909]) encompassed everything that was connected with the history of God's people as related in and to the Hebrew Bible. Urbach's *The Sages* explored individual theological themes as they occur in the literature. The shortcoming of this method is that it artificially imposes themes onto texts which themselves do not systematically consider them.

13. Even so, the matter of "rabbinic theology" was recognizably ambiguous. Schechter called it "a complicated arrangement of theological checks and balances," not a system (*Some Aspects,* p. 414).

14. Chapter 15, "Man's Accounting and the World's Accounting" (pp. 420-523), addresses such topics as sin and death, reward and punishment, the attribute of justice and the attribute of mercy, repentance, the righteous and the wicked. It is in conjunction with the last that the issue of merit arises.

15. See Renée Bloch, "Note méthodologique pour l'étude de la littérature rabbinique," *Recherches de Science Religieuse* 43 (1955): 194-227, trans. W. S. Green and W. J. Sullivan, "Methodological Note for the Study of Rabbinic Literature," in *Approaches to Ancient Judaism: Theory and Practice,* ed. W. S. Green, Brown University Judaica Studies 1 (Missoula, 1978), pp. 51-75; and Geza Vermes, *Scripture and Tradition in Judaism* (Leiden, 1961; reprint, 1973).

16. Presented early on in *Ancient Judaism and Modern Category-Formation* (Lanham:

Which Texts to Read

Recognizing that (a) the corpus is indeed vast and (b) there may be particular socio-cultural patterns that have shaped given presentations of the issue, I have chosen to explore *zekhut avot* on a much more limited scale. My
primary focus will be on the instances of merit in *Mekhilta deRabbi
Ishmael* (MRI), a tannaitic midrash that addresses the narrative of Israel's
redemption in the book of Exodus.[17] MRI contains consecutive commentary, starting at Exodus 12:1 and ending with 23:19, followed by the Sabbath
addenda addressing Exodus 31:12-17 and 35:1-3. The commentary includes
multiple interpretations, some quite long and involved, of numerous key
passages, especially in the narrative parts of the biblical text under discussion. The selection of both the biblical text and the extensive interpretive
offerings seemingly was conscious, guided by specific purpose(s) of the
authorship.[18] High profile is given to the commands and narratives indicating God's communication and presence with Israel and Israel's obliga-

University Press of America, 1986), Neusner's methodology has subsequently appeared in his
translation and treatment of a large number of rabbinic texts. Rivka Kern-Ulmer, "Theological Foundations of Rabbinic Exegesis," in *Encyclopaedia of Midrash: Biblical Interpretation in
Formative Judaism,* 2 vols., ed. Jacob Neusner and Alan J. Avery-Peck (Leiden: Brill, 2005), pp.
944-64, assessed the recent developments in the study of rabbinic hermeneutics, among them
the work of Neusner, indicating that understanding the hermeneutical rules that underlie
rabbinic exegesis gives the reader a window into the theological stance of given texts.

17. "Tanna'im" are those teachers from the first two centuries of the Common Era, up
to the point of the compilation of the Mishnah in 220 c.e. Thus, a tannaitic midrash reflects
materials attributed to that time period. Although there has been considerable discussion
regarding the date of this text, I would argue that it was composed in the second half of the
third century c.e. See Herman L. Strack and Günter Stemberger, *Einleitung in Talmud und
Midrasch* (Munich: Beck, 1982), trans. M. Bockmuehl, *Introduction to the Talmud and Midrash* (Edinburgh: T&T Clark, 1991; Minneapolis: Fortress, 1992), pp. 273, 278-79.

18. That MRI was an intentional composition is not by any means a uniformly held
opinion. Representative of a considerable portion of traditional scholarship, J. N. Epstein,
Mevo'ot leSifrut HaTannaim (Jerusalem, 1957), pp. 565, 572-84, viewed it as a collection of independent segments. Jacob Neusner characterized it as solely an "encyclopedia" serving as a
repository for the conventions of the faith. As such it was a compilation with no distinct
viewpoint (*Mekhilta According to Rabbi Ishmael: An Introduction to Judaism's First Scriptural
Encyclopedia* [Atlanta: Scholar's Press, 1988], pp. 118, 133-43). For both socio-historical and
literary reasons that are beyond the scope of this paper, I suggest that the authorship intended to address in a subtle manner the claims made by the Christian community that had
co-opted the most significant symbols in the text of Exodus. The Sages firmly reclaimed
them for Jews, lodging those claims in the extensive and intricate interweaving of Torah
texts.

tions in return. Key concepts are revelation, redemption, and relationship. Not surprisingly, merit of those fathers whose deeds are recorded in Genesis is viewed as efficacious toward all of these ends.

Because the covenant with Abraham is foundational to the development of rabbinic thinking on merit, the commentary in Bereshit (Genesis) Rabbah (BR) 39-58 addressing the Abraham narratives in Genesis 12–23 also provides insight. Bereshit Rabbah was likely composed in the fifth century,[19] and there were important factors in the wider environment in which it arose: the Roman empire had changed from pagan to Christian and the Sages were dealing with the implications of the triumph of ideological Christianity.[20]

Bereshit Rabbah commences its commentary with Genesis 1 and works steadily through the entirety of that book. It is both exegetical, in that it deals systematically with the text, and homiletical, exhorting its audience to think and act in keeping with their position as God's covenant people. After citing the given lemma from Genesis, an intersecting verse from the Ketuvim is characteristically brought in to shape the discussion.[21] In fact, it is the choice of that latter verse that is often instrumental in determining the ethical lesson(s) to be gleaned. The commentary is generally less expansive than MRI and is often primarily directed to the messages found in the intersection of the verses.[22]

19. Strack and Stemberger, *Introduction*, p. 279.

20. The rabbis' hopes for the salvation promised to God's chosen people are evident in BR as they re-presented the lives of the patriarchs pre-figuring the life of Israel. In their re-shaping of the narratives, Esau symbolized Christian Rome which was the chief foe of the Jews. See Jacob Neusner, "Genesis in Genesis Rabbah," in *Encyclopaedia of Midrash: Biblical Interpretation in Formative Judaism*, 2 vols., ed. Jacob Neusner and Alan J. Avery-Peck (Leiden: Brill, 2005), pp. 88-105.

21. See Moshe D. Herr, "Midrash," in *Encyclopaedia Judaica*, 2nd ed., vol. 14, pp. 182-85 (Jerusalem: Keter, 2007). Neusner, "The Documentary Form-History of Rabbinic Literature: The Aggadic Sector," in *Formative Judaism*, New Series, vol. 2 (Atlanta: Scholars Press, 1997), pp. 3-27, claimed that BR was the last of the conventional commentary-style midrashim and the first to use the intersecting-verse form that would predominate in rabbinic midrash from this point forward.

22. Exceptions do occur; there are parts of the Abraham narrative that garner more attention. The famine in the land (Gen. 12:10) prompts an excursus to the ten famines in the land. The Sages addressed the seemingly unthinkable nature of Abraham's treatment of Sarai when faced with the threats posed by Pharaoh and Abimelekh. The separation of Abraham and Lot is presented so as to prepare the reader to think of Lot as less than exemplary. The introduction to the war between the kings of Mesopotamia and Canaan (Gen. 14), "and it came to pass," touches off a long list of similarly introduced incidents and the debate

How to Present These Selected Texts

It is important to reiterate that BR is generally thought to be a later composition than MRI. For that reason, I initially address the major pericopae having to do with merit of the fathers as they are recorded in MRI, even though that is "out of order" from the biblical perspective.[23] As might be expected, the discussions in MRI draw on materials also included in BR, likely from common sources. From both texts, I have selected the portions that specifically mention merit of the fathers, of Israel, and of named individuals. In BR, the most prominent figures are Abraham, Isaac, and Sarah. That focus is significantly expanded in MRI as the Tanna'im explored the various implications of merit through the sweep of covenant history of God's people.

There are some methodological drawbacks to this approach. It creates artificial boundaries and omits numerous pericopae that do address cognate foundational themes of faithfulness, obedience, and justice. Further, limiting the study to two texts only captures fleeting moments in the whole array of rabbinic thought. Nevertheless, it does define a working core, much of which also surfaces elsewhere, attesting to its significance as representative of developing rabbinic thought.[24]

---

as to whether they were for good or for ill. A recurring thematic digression mentions the four nations from the visions in Daniel. This is not surprising given the focus on Israel's enemies that is embedded in both the biblical text and the contemporary context. What is of interest is that the Sodom and Gomorrah narrative, which, in other expansions, becomes part of a lengthy excursus on measure-for-measure punishment (see M. Sot. 1:7-9; Tos. Sot. 3-4; *MRI* Shirta 2), here is supplemented by only one added example, based on the suspected wife of Numbers 5.

23. This would not be surprising from a rabbinic perspective in which issues of time and chronology are less important than re-presenting the fabric of Torah. Because redemption and revelation are at the core of the Israelite and hence Jewish experience, MRI is a central and extraordinary midrashic composition.

24. This approach tends to follow those scholars who attempted to find developments in the traditions over time (cf. Bloch and Vermes). The ever-present question, of course, is how long and in what form all of these traditions were circulating prior to the two very distinct composition styles evident in MRI and BR.

Presentation of the Concept in MRI

Pisha 1 [I.42-113]²⁵ — "And the LORD spoke unto Moses and unto Aaron in the land of Egypt, saying" (Exod. 12:1).

That God would reveal himself "in the land of Egypt" needed explanation and the midrash poses a complicated one! It initially focuses on the conditions under which revelation generally occurred, notably in the Land, Jerusalem, and the Temple, and via the priesthood and the Davidic line.²⁶ That there were, however, exceptions to these restrictions is a major point of the chapter. These exceptions were the result of merit of the ancestors, who served to mediate the space between the human and divine. Their merit ensured continuity in God's communication via prophetic voices when the surrounding circumstances caused doubt. Thus, when Israel was in dire straits, God's word came to Moses and Aaron "in Egypt."

The identity and contributions of the initial meritorious individual at this point are unusual. Immediately after the mention of *zekhut avot* (the fathers), the midrash cites Jeremiah 31:14-16, *Rachel's* weeping for her children, as the proof text. Her cry as the mother of all Israel (see BR 71:2) moved God to speak through the prophets in the Exile, promising the return to the Land.²⁷ What is particularly compelling about this reference to Rachel's merit is the wider context of the biblical proof text. Rachel was weeping for *her* children (Joseph and Benjamin) who *"are no more"* (Jer. 31:15). The tribes associated with Joseph were long exiled by that point and the voice was heard "in Ramah," at the crossroads in the tribe of Benjamin, which itself was subject to terrible internal violence (Jer. 41). Nevertheless,

---

25. In order for the material to be as accessible as possible, I have used Jacob Lauterbach's translation (*Mekilta de-Rabbi Ishmael*, 3 vols. [Philadelphia: Jewish Publication Society, 1933]), which presents both Hebrew text and English translation. The bracketed references are to the volume and line numbers in that edition. Each tractate is indicated by its name; Pisha is the first tractate in the midrash.

26. All of these were key symbols, which were either gone or not maintaining their biblical characteristics and functions. In the post-70 world of the rabbis, reality needed to be reconciled with the ideal. One way of doing that was to demonstrate that God continued to communicate and that the gap between his Presence and the condition of Israel was bridgeable. See Susan Niditch, "Merits, Martyrs, and 'Your Life as Booty': An Exegesis of Mekilta Pisha 1," *Journal for the Study of Judaism* 13 (1982): 160-71.

27. See Lauterbach, *Mekilta*, vol. 1, p. 5, n. 5; and further comments and references in W. D. Davies, "Reflections on the Spirit in the Mekhilta: A Suggestion," in *Jewish and Pauline Studies* (Philadelphia, 1984), pp. 72-83.

the Lord says "your work will be rewarded" in that "they will return from the land of the enemy; there is hope for your future . . . your children will return to their own land" (Jer. 31:16-17). Her meritorious work was weeping, and the promised return is like a resurrection of sorts.

There is a seamless connection between this reference to the prophets, the issue of inside or outside the Land, and the matter of self-sacrifice. It is initiated by the suggestion that Jonah could indeed flee the Divine Presence by leaving Israel, a possibility disproved by a plethora of proofs and a schematic presentation of those prophets who did or did not honor God and Israel. As a result of Jonah's not honoring the Father, his prophecy was cut short but in the process, he "gave himself" (or "gave his life") in his request to be pitched into the sea; he would rather die than see Israel's mortal enemy spared. In like manner, continues the midrash, Moses and David also "gave themselves" for Israel, Moses when he asked God to blot out his life if God would not forgive Israel after the debacle with the golden calf (Exod. 32:32), and David when he asked that the Lord's hand be against him instead of the people after the sin of numbering the people (2 Sam. 24:17).

The section closes with "and thus in every place you find that the ancestors and the prophets gave their lives for Israel." Ancestors and prophets, significant mediating figures in the covenant relationship between God and Israel, now in effect saved Israel; for them to give their lives meant merit stored up for Israel. At the same time, it seems that the merit of Israel itself was necessary for God to speak through the prophets. In response to the use of "saying" at the end of the verse, the midrash claims that Israel's sin led to God's silence in the wilderness, i.e., outside the Land.[28] Because, however, that would be the time when they most needed the prophetic voice, the merits of the ancestors and vicarious suffering in whatever form were the means for continuing the communication.[29]

Pisha 7 [I. 78-82] — "and when I see the blood . . ." (Exod. 12:13b; repeated in chapter 11 in conjunction with Exod. 12:23).

28. Lauterbach, *Pisha* 1, lines 135-41. The use of the term שבזכותם (a form that includes the term *zekhut* in line 137) in regard to Israel is a bit challenging. It could mean "on account of the merit of Israel" or simply "for the sake of." In either case, R. Akiva declared that God was silent for the thirty-eight years in the wilderness because Israel's sin angered him.

29. Lauterbach, *Pisha* 1, lines 148-66. Niditch, "Merit, Martyrs, and 'Your Life as Booty,'" pp. 168-71.

While this pericope is compressed and does not specifically mention "merit of the fathers," it refers to the foundational incident in the lives of Abraham and Isaac that is inexorably linked to *zekhut avot* and returns repeatedly throughout the Mekhilta.[30] Here, as an immediate response to the biblical reference to the blood of the Passover lamb, the midrash reads:

> I am seeing the blood of the binding of Isaac as it is said, "And Abraham called the name of that place *The Lord will see* . . ." (Gen. 22:14).[31] Further on, it says, "In his destroying, the Lord saw and relented. . . ." (1 Chron. 21:15). What did he see? He saw the blood of the binding of Isaac as it is said, '. . . *God will see for Himself the lamb.* . . .'

The midrash establishes a parallel between the imminent destruction in Exodus and that wreaked by the destroying angel in conjunction with David's numbering the Israelites.[32] These were two occasions on which the meritorious blood of the binding of Isaac was efficacious, and God would have mercy.[33] To make the point even stronger, this pericope is immediately preceded by Rabbi Ishmael's claim that the significance of the words "and when I see the blood" is to link God's revelation of himself and his protection of his people.[34]

What is of particular interest is the source of the merit in this case — the *blood* of Isaac. The plain sense of Genesis indicates that Abraham was specifically prevented from harming Isaac and BR 56:7 emphasizes that, even though Abraham suggested drawing a drop of symbolic blood, the angel of the Lord would not allow it. Yet, contrary to the explicit biblical record, there was a persistent legend from at least the second century

---

30. Urbach, *The Sages,* pp. 502-5 (and see especially notes 82-88, pp. 912-13) gives an exhaustive treatment of the evidence. See also Shalom Spiegel, *The Last Trial: On the Legends and Lore of the Command to Abraham to Offer Isaac as a Sacrifice: The Akedah* (New York: Schocken, 1969).

31. The parallel develops solely on the multiple meanings for the verb ראה, which means "to see" but also "to provide." The visual aspect is significant. It was seen — and therefore provided.

32. The Hebrew verb for destroy in both contexts is a form of שחת.

33. The interpretation itself was repeated twice as well (see Pisha 11); it was obviously a critical issue.

34. The verb commonly translated "pass over" (פסח) in this context does not appear very frequently in the Hebrew Bible, but the midrash notes Isa. 31:5 where it clearly means protect.

that the blood of Isaac was shed,[35] that his ashes were on the altar.[36] And the biblical text does leave some room for this midrashic development. There is the matter of the wide-ranging meaning of תחת (Gen. 22:13). While it is customarily translated "instead of," it might also mean "under" or "after," implying a spatial or temporal relationship between an actual sacrifice of Isaac and the ram. Further, the second utterance from the heavens declared "because you have done this thing and have not withheld your son, your only son" (Gen. 22:16). That is followed by God's reiterated promise that Abraham's descendants would indeed be blessed — i.e., enjoy the merit of this deed of Abraham and Isaac. Finally, when Abraham returned to his servants, there is no mention of Isaac (Gen. 22:19) even though Abraham had promised that Isaac would return with him (Gen. 22:5).[37]

Pisha 16 [I.165-173] — "Today you are going out, in the month of Aviv" (Exod. 13:4).

> Rabbi Eleazar ben Azariah says: By the merit of Abraham our father the Omnipresent (המקום) brought Israel out of Egypt as it is said, "For He remembered His holy word to Abraham His servant" . . . and it says ". . . and He brought forth His people with joy . . ." (Ps. 105:42-43).[38] Rabbi Shimon bar Yohai says: By the merit of circumcision the Omnipresent brought Israel out from Egypt as it is said, ". . . and I passed by

35. This appears already in *Mekhilta of Rabbi Shimon bar Yohai,* a second, partial commentary on the book of Exodus: "Rabbi Yehoshua says: 'The Holy One Blessed Be He said to Moses, I am obligated to pay the reward of Isaac, son of Abraham, from whom a fourth of blood came out on the altar'" (*Mekhilta d'Rabbi Shim'on b. Yochai,* ed. J. N. Epstein and E. Z. Melamed [Jerusalem, 1955], p. 4).

36. The reference to ashes appears in an anonymous statement in *Sifra,* Behuqotai 8, responding to Lev. 26:42 — "then I will remember My covenant with Jacob, even My covenant with Isaac, and even My covenant with Abraham I will remember." And why was "remember" not included with regard to Isaac? Because "his ashes are regarded as though he were scooped up on the altar" (Jacob Neusner, trans., *The Components of Rabbinic Documents: From the Whole to the Parts,* vol. 1, part 3 [Atlanta: Scholars Press, 1997], pp. 266-67).

37. Spiegel, *The Last Trial,* pp. 17-27, noted the peculiar ambiguities in the biblical text that allow this development and traced the theme through centuries of Jewish literature. From a Christian perspective, Hebrews 11:19 might reflect this tradition (ἐν παραβολῇ) about Isaac. See further below in conjunction with BR.

38. The connection here is the use of the verb "to go out" in both Exodus and Psalm 105.

you and saw you wallowing in your blood[39] [and I said to you in your blood 'live!' and I said to you in your blood 'live!'"]

The repeated declaration in Ezekiel 16:6 to "live" was significant for the Sages. In the allegory, the first referred to the blood of circumcision and the sign of the covenant with Abraham; the second was presumed by the rabbis to be the blood of the Passover sacrifice and redemption. A final opinion, expressed by Rabbi (Judah the Prince), was that Israel went out by the strength of God, notably without any mention of individual or corporate merit. Instead, "with a mighty hand, the LORD brought us out of Egypt" (Exod. 13:16). What is interesting here is that these three positions addressed the critical concerns undergirding the ongoing discussion of the issue: Would Israel depend on merit previously stored away? Would their own obedience be necessary? Or was it all God's doing in His sovereign might and majesty?

Beshallah 1 [I.86-151] — "And Moses took the bones of Joseph with him because he had made the children of Israel swear saying, God will surely visit you and you must bring up my bones with you from here" (Exod. 13:19).

Relishing the chance to embellish the spare biblical text, the Sages first posed two narratives to address how Moses *found* those bones of Joseph. But then they moved along to the instruction which, in this case, involved an intricate interweaving of measure-for-measure justice and individual merit. Here, obtaining merit took on an active and very present sense. The words, *zekhut avot,* are not evident in the developing midrash but *zakhah* is. Miriam, Joseph, and Moses all acted meritoriously and were rewarded measure-for-measure in kind and to the excess in quan-

---

39. The Hebrew word for "blood" here is plural (possibly dual), prompting the Sages to indicate that there had to be multiple significant instances where blood was efficacious. Further, the portion of Ezekiel in brackets does not appear in the text of MRI but the listening/reading audience would know the wider context. While some Hebrew mss and the LXX leave out the repeated line, it was further grounds for the Sages' exegesis. A brief comment in Pisha 5 (I.3-14), addressing the need to keep the sacrificial lamb four days before its slaughter, reads as follows: "But as yet they had no *mizvot* to perform in order that He would redeem them. . . . The Holy One Blessed Be He gave them two *mizvot,* the duty of the Passover sacrifice and the duty of circumcision, which they should perform so as to be worthy of redemption." There the proof text from Ezek. 16:8 is accompanied by Zech. 9:11, referring to release for prisoners in the context of the blood of the covenant.

tity.[40] Even more, Joseph's obedience to the Torah, painstakingly demonstrated by pairing proof texts from the Joseph narratives in Genesis with the Ten Words plus several additional mizvot from Leviticus, meant that his coffin (ארון) was accompanied on the way to the Land by the ark (also ארון) of the Lord. Never mind that the Torah had not been given nor the ark constructed until well into the Sinai experience! The lesson of individual merit was the focus; obedience to Torah meant the intimate Presence of God.

Beshallah 1 [I.193-208] — "and the LORD went before them . . ." (Exod. 13:21).

Here was yet one more opportunity for the Sages to forge the link between meritorious action and measure-for-measure reward. Whatever would move the Lord to go before the children of Israel as they left Egypt? The answer again resided with Abraham. Because Abraham accompanied the angelic visitors as they set off for Sodom (Gen. 18:16), so the Lord accompanied his children forty years in the wilderness. The same verb form is used in each clause, prompting the equation. And that was not all; each detail of the Genesis narrative became a basis for God's accompanying his people through the wilderness and providing for them water, food, a place to rest, and protection. Just as Abraham provided those necessities for his visitors, so God provided them for Israel; every demonstration was explicitly founded on the pairing of biblical passages.[41] Thus, like the preceding material, although the term *zekhut* is not used here, the concept infuses the lesson which has to do with God's justice and the assurance of reward for meritorious actions.

Beshallah 4 [I.20-97] — "And the LORD said to Moses: Why are you crying out to Me? Speak to the children of Israel that they go forward" (Exod. 14:15).

The questions for the rabbis here were several fold. First, there is no previous indication in the biblical text that Moses cried out to the Lord. In

40. See Phillips, "The Tilted Balance," pp. 223-40, in regard to the patterns evident throughout such presentations of the measure-for-measure principle.
41. Here the controlling rubric is measure-for-measure. This same block of material, exquisitely expanded, appears in BR 48:10. See the discussion below.

fact, he had just encouraged the Israelites to take heart in the deliverance they would experience. Why did God raise *this* question? Second, on what basis should Moses have expected that the Israelites *could* go forward? At that point, the expanse of the sea still stood in front of them. This command to go forward preceded God's word to Moses that he lift up his rod, extend his hand, and part the waters so that the people could go through the sea on dry ground. The chronology occasioned a lengthy discussion among a number of named Sages regarding the basis for the Lord's rescue of Israel. It was evident to them that the implicit promise to divide the sea for Israel was wrapped up in prior events involving the forefathers.[42] The issue of merit takes center stage and in the discussion that unfolds, it proves to be a complicated matter:

> Rabbi Ba'anah says: By the merit of the *mizvah* which Abraham our father did, I will split for them the sea as it is said, "And he split the wood for the burnt offering . . ." (Gen. 22:3) and it says [here] "and the waters were split. . . ."[43] Shim'on the Temanite says: By the merit of circumcision, I will divide[44] for them the sea as it is said, "If I had not established my covenant for day and for night, the statutes of heaven and earth . . ." (Jer. 33:25). Go and see which covenant it is that is in effect both day and night. You will only find it is the covenant of circumcision.

There is an extensive digression at this point in which several rabbis explored the implications of long versus short prayers. And then they got back to the point:

> For the sake of His Name He did this for them as it is said, "For My own sake, for My own sake, I will do it . . ." (Isa. 48:11) and it is written, ". . . who divides the waters before them . . . " (Isa. 63:12). Why? "To

---

42. Each of these proof texts has a lexical connection with dividing the sea, even if the contexts do not always warrant a logical one!

43. The Hebrew verb in each of these passages is the same, בקע. It has the implications of forceful separation; "break open" and "breach" are two additional possible translations (Victor P. Hamilton, בקע, *New International Dictionary of Old Testament Theology and Exegesis [NIDOTTE]*, vol. 1, ed. Willem van Gemeren [Grand Rapids: Zondervan, 1997], pp. 702-4).

44. The Hebrew, קרע, is much less forceful, most frequently used to indicate tearing cloth (Cornelius van Dam, קרע, in *NIDOTTE*, vol. 3, p. 993). Whenever "divide" is used in the translation that follows, it is this Hebrew term.

make for Yourself a glorious Name" (Isa. 63:14).[45] Rabbi[46] says: Sufficient was the faith with which they believed in Me that I should divide for them the sea as it is said, ". . . and let them turn back and camp . . ." [which the Israelites, obeying the word of God, did even though the prospect was frightening]. Rabbi Eleazar ben Azariah says: By the merit of Abraham our father I will divide for them the sea as it is said, "For He remembered His sacred word to Abraham His servant . . . " (Ps. 105:42) and it is written, ". . . and He brought forth His people with joy . . . " (Ps. 105:43). Rabbi Eleazar ben Judah, from Kefar Tota, says: By the merit of the tribes I will divide for them the sea as it is said, "You have pierced the head of his warriors with his rod . . ." (Hab. 3:14-15).[47] . . . Shema'yah says: Sufficient was the faith with which Abraham their father believed in Me that I should divide for them the sea as it is said, "And he believed the LORD . . ." (Gen. 15:6). Avtalion says: Sufficient was the faith with which they believed in Me that I should divide for them the sea as it is said, "And the people believed . . ." (Exod. 4:31). Shim'on from Kitron says: By the merit of the bones of Joseph, I will divide for them the sea as it is said, "And he left his garment with her and fled . . ." (Gen. 39:12) and it says, "The sea saw and fled . . ." (Ps. 114:3).[48]

Following another foray back to Moses' crying out, the midrash set its course for the conclusion:

Rabbi Aha says: Why are you crying out to Me? For your sake, I will do it. The Holy One Blessed Be He said: Except for your outcry, I would already have destroyed them from the world as it is said, "And He said He would destroy them except that Moses His chosen one stood in the

45. The connections here are built around the use of "Name" in Isa. 48:9-11 and the fact that God would not give his glory to another. It is assured by the repetition of "For My own sake." Both "name" and "glory" appear in Isa. 63:12-14 in the context of dividing the sea at the Exodus event.

46. Whenever "Rabbi" is used alone, it refers to Rabbi Judah the Prince, the compiler of the Mishnah (220 C.E.).

47. This opinion operates on a more complicated level. First, the word in the verse that is translated "rod" may also mean "tribe" and on that basis R. Eleazar suggested that the enemy fell because of the tribes. Habakkuk 3 is a poem about God's deliverance with strong allusions to the Exodus experience; "God came from Teman, the Holy One from Mount Paran" echoes Deut. 33:2, and verse 15 talks about God's trampling the sea with His horses. The word translated "warriors" is only used here in the Hebrew Bible.

48. "Fleeing" is the lexical connection here; Joseph fled from the potential entrapment of Potiphar's wife and, on the basis of that merit, the sea fled.

breach before Him to turn aside His wrath from destroying" (Ps. 106:23). . . . Rabbi Eleazar of Modi'in says: "Why do you cry out to Me?" Do I need commands concerning My children? As it is said, "Concerning My children and concerning the work of My hands, will you command Me?" (Isa. 45:11). Are they not already prepared from the six days of creation to be before Me? As it is said, "If these statutes are removed from before Me," says the LORD, "so also the seed of Israel will cease from being a nation before Me all the days" (Jer. 31:35). Others say: Sufficient was the faith with which they believed in Me that I should divide for them the sea. . . . Rabbi Yosi the Galilean says: When Israel entered the sea, already the mountain of Moriah was uprooted from its place and the altar of Isaac that had been built on it and the arrangement of the wood on it and Isaac as if he was bound and set on the altar, and Abraham as if stretching out his hand and taking the knife to slaughter his son; the Omnipresent said to Moses, "Moses, My children are in distress; the sea is a barrier, the enemy is pursuing and you are standing and praying a long prayer?" Moses said: What should I do? And [God] said: "Lift up your staff. . ." (Exod. 14:16); you must be lifting up,[49] glorifying, praising, and singing songs of praise, and greatness, and glory, and thanksgiving and praise to the One whose is the battle."

The reasons for redeeming Israel were manifold, ranging from the meritorious *actions* of Abraham, Isaac, Joseph, and Israel, to the *faith* of Abraham and Israel, to God's sovereign design and concern for his own name and glory. Abraham's name recurs. Because of his readiness to sacrifice Isaac,[50] his fulfilling the obligation of circumcision, and the faith with which he believed in God, the sea split apart for the children of Israel. The chapter draws to a close with an arresting description of the binding of Isaac on Mount Moriah with Abraham ready to slaughter him. Although it is not explicit, Abraham's outstretched knife in hand represents the merit whereby Moses could lift up his staff and cause the sea to

49. The same verbal root as the command to lift the rod.

50. The *akedah* is mentioned in chapters 2 and 4 of Beshallah, both of which emphasize Abraham's uplifted hand ready to slay Isaac. Both the willingness of Abraham and the blood of Isaac are part of this picture. These emphases will return in BR. Reuven Kimelman, "Rabbi Yohanan and Origen on Song of Songs: A Third Century Jewish-Christian Disputation," *Harvard Theological Review* 73 (1980): 583-84, noted that the merit of Abraham was a central focus of Rabbi Yohanan to counter Christian claims about Jesus when both scholars resided in Caesarea.

part. The final lines draw the matter forward and speak of singing and giving praise to God.[51]

Beshallah 6 [I.28-71] — "and the children of Israel went into the midst of the sea on dry ground . . ." (Exod. 14:22).

In characteristic fashion, the midrash atomized the biblical text at this point in order to derive its lessons. The phrase "on dry ground" was left out of the picture for the moment. Instead, Rabbi Judah envisioned bickering among the tribes as to who would jump first into the tumultuous waters; because Amminadav, of the tribe of Judah, ventured in first, the Holy One, Blessed Be He, declared that he would make the tribe of Judah king over Israel. This is followed immediately by a folksy discussion between Rabbi Tarfon and the Elders at Yavneh on the general theme of merit of the righteous. They had been talking, while sitting in the shade of the dovecote in Yavneh, about the merit of Joseph that earned for him a journey to Egypt with a spice caravan instead of being overwhelmed by the odor of camels! In response to a further query from the elders as to the merit whereby Judah got the kingdom, Tarfon led them in a guessing game. To every suggestion regarding Judah's possible merit, he declared it was only sufficient for the specifics of that particular occasion. Stymied, they finally said: Rabbi, you teach us by what merit Judah merited the kingship. His response linked back to the Exodus context; his was the tribe going first into the sea.[52] Nevertheless, efficacious merit, in this discussion, was primarily confined to the generation of the given individual.

Beshallah 7 [I.130-164] — "and they believed in the LORD and in His servant, Moses" (Exod. 14:31c).

---

51. Almost every one of the opinions in this section is attributed to a named individual in the tannaitic period, indicating that this was a long-standing issue that had been discussed for considerable time. In fact, Shema'yah and Avtalion were among the famous pairs noted in M. Avot 1 and pre-date the Common Era. While Beshallah 1 is distinctly different in *Mekhilta of Rabbi Shim'on bar Yohai*, the two texts are almost identical in this chapter, indicating that it was a standard piece.

52. Each of the suggestions posed by the elders at Yavneh involved Judah's own actions: saving Joseph's life, confessing that Tamar was more righteous than he, and offering to stay in Egypt instead of Benjamin. According to Rabbi Tarfon, these did not transcend the time boundaries. Instead, it had to be on account of a member of the tribe of Judah present at the sea.

The chapter and tractate close with an encomium on the greatness of faith and faithfulness, declaring that God will reward persons according to their faith. As a result of Israel's faith, the Holy Spirit rested on them and they sang, preparation for the forthcoming song in Exodus 15. Abraham inherited this world and the world to come as a reward for his faith; Israel was redeemed from Egypt because of their faith; and Aaron and Hur held up the hands of Moses by faith.[53] God remembers the faith of the fathers, equivalent in this context to merit of the fathers. And so, faith also enters into the sphere of justice. All people of faith, both now and in the future, shall enter the gates of the Lord with singing. Both Israel's faith and God's faithfulness are established firmly throughout this pericope on a series of biblical quotations.

In the tractate at large, merit is a central issue. It seemed to be important to show, in a number of ways, that God is responsive to human faith and action. If those actions were meritorious, his response involved rewards; if they were evil, he measured out just punishment. In making the case for the merit of Israel, the demonstration of continuity was essential so as not to miss the point. All of the possible sources of merit mentioned in Beshallah 4 transcended the boundaries created by shattering events. The greatest of them all was faith in God and in Moses. The end of chapter 7 reaffirms this fact.

Vayassa 3 [II.1-18] — "behold, I shall cause to rain for you bread from heaven . . ." (Exod. 16:4b).

In a set of exchanges between Rabbis Joshua and Eleazar of Modi'im,[54] the latter highlighted two specific lexical issues in the verse in order to declare that the Lord gave the bread from heaven on account of the merit of the fathers, Abraham, Isaac, and Jacob.[55] On the other hand,

---

53. Each of these declarations is supported with at least one proof text.

54. These two teachers are the defining rabbinic figures in the tractates of Vayassa and Amalek, although their names are frequently joined by additional named Sages. Characteristically, Rabbi Joshua, always cited first, held to the plain meaning of the text often to the point of apparently not adding anything new. In some cases, his "simple" rendition of the text appears to be a foil for the increasingly figurative or symbolic interpretations that follow. It may have been presented as the appropriate method for dealing with biblical texts that might otherwise be subject to dangerous allegorizing, such as had happened under some of the early Christian interpretations. Eleazar of Modi'im frequently rendered opinions that alluded to merit of the forefathers and directed attention to divine intent.

55. "Behold," a word used frequently in the patriarchal narratives, expressed their

Rabbi Shim'on ben Gamliel stated that the Israelites themselves were so beloved that the natural order got reversed; bread came from heaven and dew went up from the earth (Exod. 16:14). In other words, the same tension evident in prior materials surfaces here again; did God bless Israel with the manna on account of *zekhut avot,* or was their own merit as God's beloved covenant people sufficient?

Vayassa 5 [ii.53-77] — "And Moses said: Eat that today . . ." (Exod. 16:25a).

While the noun "merit" *(zekhut)* does not appear in this pericope, Rabbis Joshua, Eleazar of Modi'im, and Eliezer speculated on the possibility of rewards if Israel were able (*zachah* is the verb) to keep the Sabbath. Merit was bound up in obedience to the Sabbath commandment and there were significant rewards in the broader scope of Israel's identity. With reference to the verse, they had stored up manna from the previous day and now Moses commanded them to enjoy it "today." What were the implications of that "storing up"? First, Rabbi Joshua suggested that the three major festivals to be instituted at Sinai would be the reward.[56] Rabbi Eleazar of Modi'im said keeping the Sabbath would result in God's giving Israel six good *middot* ("measures") — the Land, the world to come, the "new world," the kingdom of David, the priesthood, and the Levites.[57] Finally, Eliezer's focus was thoroughly eschatological: rescue from evil and judgment in the day of Gog, the pains of the Messiah, and the great day of judgment.

The Exodus narratives underlying this tractate have primarily to do with the tests that Israel endured in the wilderness. In that context, the symbols of manna and the Sabbath are both rich with potential. Not only were they gifts to Israel that mined the reservoir of merit; when treated properly, they would be the springboard for the full experience of Israel's inheritance as God's covenant people forever.

---

readiness to do God's will; "for you" is actually unnecessary in the verse and thus it may be reasoned that it was addressed to the patriarchs (Lauterbach, II. 102, nn. 1-2).

56. Each of the three was a seven-day festival, perhaps viewed as parallel to the Sabbath, and very soon to be part of the picture.

57. This is a comprehensive list, spanning from the covenant promise of the Land to eschatological expectations. The order is unusual. The Temple is obviously implied by the last two. The two eschatological events interrupt the more familiar sequence of Land, Kingdom, and Temple. On the difficulties in distinguishing between the world to come and the new world, see Urbach, *The Sages,* pp. 649-52.

Amalek 1 [II.94-98] — ". . . tomorrow I will stand on the top ('head') of the hill . . ." (Exod. 17:9b).

Continuing the pattern, Rabbi Joshua read the incident in strictly literal terms. "Rabbi Eleazar of Modi'im says: Tomorrow we shall decree a fast and we shall be dependent on the deeds of the fathers. 'Head' means the deeds of the fathers; 'hill' refers to the deeds of the mothers." According to Eleazar of Modi'im, what got Israel extricated from their self-induced predicament was the merit of the fathers and mothers and the Israelites' renewed belief as they could see Moses with his upraised hands. At the same time, the figure of Moses is not unduly exalted. In each of his actions that led to Israel's belief, the Sages were careful to point out that it was the work of the Holy One, Blessed Be He, as well as Israel's zeal for the words of Torah.

Amalek 1 [II.138-164] — "the hands of Moses were heavy . . . they took a stone and placed it under him and he sat on it . . . and his hands were steady until the sun went down" (Exod. 17:12).

According to Eleazar of Modi'im, when the sins of Israel weighed so heavily upon him that he could not bear it, Moses ". . . turned to the deeds of the fathers, as it is said, 'and they took a stone and placed it under him'; these are the deeds of the fathers. 'And he sat upon it'; these are the deeds of the mothers." Aaron and Hur on either side of him likewise affirm the deeds of each other's tribe. Merit from all quarters was necessary.

These two tractates (Vayassa and Amalek) that address Israel's journey toward Sinai have a decidedly different style from what has preceded. The commentary moves relatively swiftly through the narratives, just as a journey would, and a noticeably different set of named Sages tackle the problems.[58] The main focus lay ahead in the revelation at Sinai.

58. While these characteristics may suggest that MRI is merely a haphazard compilation of separate traditions, the underlying thread that ties all of MRI together is the steady focus on the events and symbols that were central to Israel's relationship with God. These particular events unfold in the very chapters of Exodus that the authorship chose to address, notably commencing with the Passover in Exodus 12 and continuing through Israel's deliverance at the Sea, God's provision of manna, water from the rock, the Sinai experience, and closing with the Sabbath instructions in Exod. 31:12-17 and 35:1-3. The authorship drew on the rich body of existing exegetical traditions. While many of these symbols had been adopted by the church, the Sages reclaimed them for Judaism, pointedly refraining from

Bahodesh 2 [II.7-9] — ". . . thus you shall say to the house of Jacob, and tell the children of Israel" (Exod. 19:3b).

It is a matter of course that one of the interpretations of this parallelism would be merit of both Jacob and Israel that effected God's communication.

Bahodesh 6 [II.125-143] — ". . . visiting the iniquity of the fathers upon the children to the third and the fourth generations of those who hate Me but doing *hesed* to thousands to those who love Me and keep My commandments" (Exod. 20:5b-6).

The most heinous offense against the covenant was idolatry and most of *Bahodesh* 6 addresses the nature of other gods, graven images, and the folly of idolatrous worship. The biblical passage is integral to understanding the workings of God's justice, from the imputation of merit for those who love God to all forms of measure-for-measure justice. Thus, although there is no explicit mention of *zekhut avot* in this context, it rides just below the surface as the warning against disobedience is sounded. It was the one of the passages that surfaced most often in the Sages' discussions about merit. Some rabbis felt that "doing *hesed* to thousands" referred to two thousand generations; others that it meant an infinite number of generations. In any case, God's mercy in rewarding the righteous far exceeds his wrath against sinners.[59]

Drawing together the themes of merit, love, obedience, and self-sacrifice, the second-century Rabbi Nathan responded to more general dicta about Abraham and the prophets loving God and keeping his commandments by applying each phrase of the verse to the palpable anguish of those times:

> "Of them that love Me" — this is Abraham our father and those like him. "Of those who keep My commandments" — these are the prophets and the elders. Rabbi Nathan says: "Of those who love Me and keep My commandments" — these are they who are living in the Land of Israel and giving their lives for the commandments. "Why are you going out to be killed?" "Because I circumcised my son to be an Israelite."

---

commentary on the plagues in Egypt, the Tabernacle's construction, or the incident with the golden calf.

59. Schechter, *Aspects of Rabbinic Theology,* pp. 181-82.

"Why are you going out to be burned?" "Because I read the Torah." "Why are you going out to be crucified?" "Because I ate the unleavened bread." "Why are you getting one hundred lashes?" "Because I took the Lulav." And it says: "[the wounds] with which I was smitten in the house of my friends . . ." (Zech. 13:6). These wounds cause me to be beloved of my Father in heaven.[60]

Now Rabbi Nathan's own contemporaries were joining Moses, David, and Abraham as meritorious. He named them "beloved of the Father in heaven," those who in the face of the persecutions in the second century, were giving their lives to keep the commandments. The punishable offenses were circumcision, study of Torah, and observance of Passover and Sukkot. The punishment matched with Passover was crucifixion, perhaps not a coincidence.

There are several final allusions to merit in MRI, although they are much more abbreviated. In response to ". . . they said to Moses: You speak with us and we will hear" (Exod. 20:19), the midrash explains this unusual request of the people essentially to replace God with Moses; they did not have the strength to receive more than the Ten Words. Nevertheless, their declaration that they would hear implied obedience and, as a result, they merited the prophetic institution sooner than originally "planned" (Bahodesh 9.62-69).

The rest of MRI is fundamentally halakhic midrash, dealing with the instructions in the Torah, and is therefore not fertile ground for comments about zekhut avot. There are, however, several exceptions. The warning not to oppress the stranger (Exod. 22:20) is based on the principle that strangers (gerim) are beloved. The midrash demonstrates from a number of perspectives that this is consonant with the biblical worldview. "Abraham our father was not circumcised until he was ninety-nine years old. If he had been circumcised at the age of twenty or thirty, then only those gerim under thirty could become proselytes. Thus, The Omnipresent bore with him until he was ninety-nine in order not to lock the door to the gerim" (Nezikin 18.36-41). And the Sabbath discussions demonstrated that the Sabbath was an enduring symbol. It exists from creation to the resurrection of the dead and its holiness is the thread connecting this world and the world to come (Shabta 1.38-41). The Sabbath adds holiness to Israel, serving in its own meritorious fashion (Shabta 1.45-46).

60. See Phillips, "Natan Naphsho," pp. 228-29.

Observations Regarding MRI

Not surprisingly, those tractates that are aggadic and embellish God's interventions on behalf of Israel frequently address the issues of merit, self-sacrifice, and faith. In Beshallah, the key feature is God's justice as evident in measure-for-measure punishment of enemies, represented by Egypt which figures so prominently in the biblical text. This theme is accompanied by evidences of God's responses to the faith and merit of individuals.

Once the nature of the biblical text turns primarily to instructions, the references to merit in MRI are both diffuse and abbreviated. Instead, the focus is on the interpretation of these regulations and Israel's own obedience. Put another way, the discussion develops from merit *for* Israel by predecessors to merit *of* Israel on account of their own faithfulness. The merit, faith, and action of Abraham, especially prominent in Pisha and Beshallah,[61] give way to exhortations in Bahodesh to faith and action on the part of Israel as the whole nation takes on the covenant. Measure-for-measure reward in regard to Abraham's activities gives way to justice practiced in Israel. For reasons that are deeply lodged in the covenant narratives of Genesis, Moses is not as significant as Abraham when it comes to the issue of merit. In Moses' case, what the midrash includes is primarily a product of following the text of Exodus and depicting his role as that of a present mediator. In the person of Abraham, on the other hand, the midrash transcends the biblical text.

61. Other figures such as Joseph and Judah appear sporadically, but Abraham is consistently mentioned. In this regard, see the conclusions of Norman J. Cohen, "Analysis of an Exegetic Tradition in the *Mekhilta de-Rabbi Ishmael:* The Meaning of *'Amanah* in the Second and Third Centuries," *Association for Jewish Studies Review* 9 (1984): 19-25, and Kimelman, "Rabbi Yohanan and Origen," pp. 583-84, to the effect that Abraham was a central focus of the rabbis in order to counter Christian claims about justification through faith in Jesus. Abraham demonstrated that active obedience and faith are inseparable; together they effect merit. Lloyd Gaston, *Paul and the Torah* (Vancouver: University of British Columbia Press, 1987), pp. 47-63, suggested that the righteousness of Gen. 15:6 is not that of Abraham but of God. Righteousness was promised to Abraham when he believed and was "counted to" him when God spared Isaac and when Israel crossed the sea. Because Paul most often speaks not of Abraham's faith but of his "seed," his "heirs," and the promise to Abraham, "[w]hat Abraham 'merited' for later generations is pure grace, as in the Rabbinic concept of the merits of the fathers. Paul certainly shared the concept of the merit of the fathers where Israel was concerned ('as regards election they are beloved for the sake of their forefathers' Rom 11:28); why should he not also use this same concept as a basis for speaking of God's gracious action toward the Gentiles?" (p. 62).

In sum, several conclusions might be offered at this point in regard to *zekhut avot* in MRI. It is woven inextricably into the wider fabric of understanding God's justice, including measure-for-measure reward and punishment. Second, there is a strong focus on faith along with action as meritorious. This will be an important consideration as our attention turns to BR.

Contributions from Bereshit Rabbah[62]

The relevant Abraham narratives span from Genesis 12 to 23. I have chosen generally to summarize the rabbinic expansions of Abraham's unfolding story instead of citing each specific mention of merit as a separate entity to be treated. What is of particular interest is the manner in which the most compelling incidents in Abraham's life, those which might be prime territory for a discussion on *zekhut*, are treated in the midrash. The consistent thread throughout is not merit itself, but the Sages' ability to weave the fabric of textual parallels that demonstrated a relationship between Abraham and his descendants. In fact, as the foundational figure for the covenant people, Abraham is presented in the contexts of those major events as one who often questioned! Some of those questions had to do with the future of his descendants, the very issue at which merit aimed.[63]

Parashah 39 of BR commences by posing the intersection of Genesis 12:1 and Psalm 45:11-12 which says, "hear, see, and incline your ear; forget your people and your father's house; the king desires your beauty for he is your Lord, and do homage to him." Although the psalm was addressed to a "daughter," never mind; the connection was the call to leave and forget. Abraham was told to "go, go" (their creative reading of לך לך) twice, first at this point and then in Genesis 22:1. Both instances of obedience are declared to be equally precious, the underlying assumption being that Abraham obeyed God's word in faith each time (BR 39.9.1). In fact, the pathos of the exchange between God and Abraham over the specific choice of

---

62. As with MRI, I have elected to use a translation of BR that is accessible. Thus, I cite from Neusner's translation (*Genesis Rabbah: The Judaic Commentary to the Book of Genesis: A New American Translation*, vol. 2, Brown Judaic Studies 105 [Atlanta: Scholars Press, 1985), following his system of dividing the text. I have, however, consulted the critical edition and notes in Yehuda Theodor and Chanoch Albeck, *Midrash Bereshit Rabba*, 3 vols. (Jerusalem: Wahrmann, 1965) for each pericope.

63. The one exception, as we have already seen, is the ultimate test in Gen. 22.

Isaac (see also BR 55.7.1) is imported into this context and is more arresting than the discussion of God's promise in Genesis 12 that Abraham would be a blessing. To be sure, those who interacted with Abraham, even on the most mundane of issues, were blessed. In fact, one example is rather humorous: "No one ever haggled with Abraham about the price of a cow without being blessed" and Rabbi Hanina said: "Even ships that sail on the ocean would be saved on account of the merit of Abraham" (BR 39.11.8). Perhaps of greatest import was the declaration that "rain and dew will come on account of your merit" (BR 39.12.3).

When Abraham built the altar between Bethel and Ai (Gen. 12:8), there were more grounds for far-ranging symbolism, particularly with regard to the Land (BR 39.16.1). "Said R. Eleazar: He built three altars, one on the occasion of receiving the good news of the coming gift of the Land of Israel, one to mark the right of possession of the Land, and one so that his descendants not fall at Ai [Josh. 7:6ff]." Of course, the descendants did fall there and, afterward, put dust on their heads "to call to mind the merit attained by our father, Abraham, who said, 'I am but dust and ashes'" (Gen. 18:27).

In response to Abraham's sojourn in Egypt (Gen. 12:10-20), Rabbi Phineas in the name of Rabbi Hoshaiah said: "The Holy One, Blessed Be He, said to our father, Abraham, 'Go, and prepare a way before your children'" (BR 40.6.1). That meant that each one of Abraham's activities was an adumbration of and preparation for Israel's subsequent experience. Rabbi Phineas noted, no doubt with great pleasure, eleven lexical parallels between the narrative in Genesis 12 and Israel's sojourn in Egypt.[64] Notably, however, this extended discussion of merit is linked with one of the less savory stories about Abraham, given his ambiguous instructions regarding Sarai.

After Melchizedek blessed Abraham, "he [Abraham] gave him [Melchizedek] a tenth from all things" (Gen. 14:20). As a result of that blessing, Abraham, Isaac, and Jacob, designated "the three great pegs on which the world depends," all gained sustenance, which is established by a proof text for each patriarch that also uses the word "all." For good measure, an additional benefit, the blessing of the priests, is said likewise to accrue to Israel because of Abraham, Isaac, and Jacob. On what basis? Of course, at the conceptual level, it was Melchizedek's identity as a priest that was foundational. But the lexical connection is foremost in the presentation: just as the priestly benediction is introduced in Numbers 6:23 with כה

---

64. Neusner observed that this was intended as a response to claims that there were new children of Abraham (*Genesis Rabbah*, p. 85).

so the same word appears in three separate key texts regarding the futures of Abraham, Isaac, and Jacob (BR 43.8.2-3).

Genesis 15, where God reiterated the promises and cut the covenant with Abraham, did not elicit extensive comments about the merits of faith; in fact, verse 6 was essentially bypassed. Instead, considerable attention was given to God's opening statement to Abraham: "Don't be afraid!" At one point, the midrash gives us a window into Abraham's questioning:

> Who had second thoughts? Abraham did. He said before the Holy One, Blessed Be He: LORD of the ages, you made a covenant with Noah that you would not wipe out his children. I went and acquired a treasure of religious deeds and good deeds greater than his, so the covenant made with me has set aside the covenant made with him. Now is it possible that someone else will come along and accumulate religious deeds and good deeds greater than mine and so set aside the covenant that was made with me on account of the covenant to be made with him?
>
> The Holy One, Blessed Be He, said: Out of Noah I did not raise up shields[65] for the righteous, but from you I shall raise up shields for the righteous. And not only so, but when your children will fall into sin and evil deeds, I shall see a single righteous man among them who can say to the attribute of justice, "Enough." I shall take him and make him an atonement for them all." (BR 44.5.2)

There are several remarkable statements here. First, the matter of Abraham's religious deeds, given to him by God as shields, would suffice for the righteous. The origin of any merit, even Abraham's, thus lands back in the sphere of God's grace. Even more fascinating, however, is the ambiguity of God's "assurance" to Abraham about the future. God did not declare outright that Abraham's merit would be nullified or the covenant set aside. At the same time, in the framework of Abraham's question, God implied in the vaguest possible way that God would recognize a single righteous one among Abraham's descendants who could satisfy justice and God would make that one an atonement for all of Abraham's children. In effect, there would no longer be need of Abraham's merit on behalf of his descendants.

And that is really the extent of this discussion regarding Abraham's belief and the righteousness accredited to him. What follows is a focus on Abraham's next question: How shall I know that I shall possess the land? (Gen. 15:8). Rabbi Hama bar Haninah: "It was not as though he was com-

---

65. Based on God's declaration that He would be Abraham's "shield" (Gen. 15:1).

plaining, but he said to him, 'On account of what merit?' And [God] said
to him, 'It is on account of the merit of the sacrifice of atonement that I
shall hand over to your descendants'" (BR 44.14.1). In the biblical text, the
ensuing terrifying ritual, attended by the manifestations of God's presence
and accompanied by prophetic statements, sufficed to convince Abraham.
In the midrash, that covenant-cutting ceremony is re-presented to take
into account the plethora of sacrifices that would eventually serve as
atonement (BR 44.14.2). In other words, the rituals of the cult, formally established in the covenant at Sinai, really originated with Abraham. That
would mean they are timeless, an important affirmation given the ongoing
absence of the Temple. What is paradoxical here is that atonement is both
the connection and the disjunction between this pericope and the preceding one because it would be accomplished in such very different ways.

The actual covenant ceremony and look into the future of Abraham's
descendants, again potential territory for a discussion about merit crossing
generations, prompted little of it. Instead, Abraham was given a choice between his children going down into Gehenna or subjugation to the four
nations, threats based on the thick darkness and the flaming torch. There is
only one passing allusion: ". . . and when birds of prey came down . . ."
(Gen. 15:11) referred to the nations of the world that would afflict Israel. In
that context, Rabbi Azariah said: "When our children become corpses,
lacking sinews and bones, your merit will sustain them" (BR 44.16.1). And
that is the end of it. The midrash moved on, perhaps intentionally avoiding a passage chock full of theological land mines.

God's commandment regarding circumcision likewise did not attract immediate mention of merit earned either by Abraham or by his
descendants. Instead, merit and Abraham oddly intersect in conjunction
with "then Abram fell on his face . . ." (Gen. 17:3-4).[66] The midrash presumed that falling on one's face was an act of disbelief.[67] Abraham's faith
was not the focus; rather the evidences of his wavering were.

> Rabbi Phineas says in the name of Rabbi Levi: Two times Abraham fell
> on his face, and for that reason, the merit of circumcision was taken

66. The same statements are repeated in BR 47.3.1 (Gen. 17:17), where Abraham again
fell on his face, this time accompanied by laughter.

67. If not disbelief, at least unwilling submission to what God had commanded. As a
result, Israel later would lapse in the command to be circumcised (Neusner, *Genesis Rabbah*,
p. 161; citing Freedman on p. 393, n. 2). The Hebrew (ויפל . . . צל־פניו) does not include the
word so clearly linked with "worship" (השתחוה — "to prostrate oneself").

away from his sons twice, once in the wilderness and once in Egypt. In Egypt, Moses came along and circumcised them and in the wilderness, Joshua came along and circumcised them. (BR 46.6.1)

Nevertheless, Abraham did take upon himself and his entire household the covenant obligation of circumcision. As a result, "and the LORD appeared to him . . ." (Gen. 18:1) and its intersecting passage from Psalm 18:36 are joined to emphasize God's condescension and special favor to Abraham.[68] Abraham's obedience in regard to circumcision merited God's Presence. Not only that; God remained standing, the posture of a servant, because Abraham was still incapacitated from the circumcision (BR 48.1.1 and 4.1). Abraham's presence at the "door of his tent" (Gen. 18:1) is grounds for the midrashic claim that, apart from Abraham, God would not have created heaven and earth, the orb of the sun, or the moon. Each of these is founded on the appearance of "tent" in a crucial proof text (BR 48.8.1). It is as if the audience was being prepared for an upsurge in attention to the true merit of Abraham!

They would not be disappointed. The forthcoming exegetical highlight is a literary masterpiece in every way. Details regarding Abraham's activities in Genesis 18 are presented as *comprehensively* meritorious for the Israelites.[69] These details include Abraham's providing water, washing for cleansing, rest in shade, bread, provision of meat, and standing by his angelic visitors. This exegetical enterprise was no small undertaking because the future recompense for Israel would occur not only in the wilderness. It would happen again in the Land and was also to be the case in the world to come; and there was a proof text for each detail in each time period. The overwhelming point was that every last one of Abraham's activities in this context when the Lord appeared to him would serve Israel for the rest of time (BR 48.10.2).[70] The clear emphasis in the text, at least with regard to merit, is on what Abraham *did,* not on what he believed or even on what

---

68. "You have given me your shield of salvation and your right hand has held me up; your stooping down has made me great." The shield connects back to Gen. 15:1, God's right hand assisted Abraham through the confrontation with the foreign kings, and this context is deemed ample evidence of God's stooping down.

69. This is considerably developed from the pericope in MRI Beshallah 1, where the focus was more on justice as it could be divined in the immediate context of Israel's experience in the wilderness.

70. The polemic would have been evident. No outsiders could claim to be Abraham's descendents in the face of this eternal relationship (Neusner, *Genesis Rabbah,* p. 186).

God had promised. Even Sarah's actions were meritorious; kneading and making cakes for the angelic visitors meant that manna would later be provided for Israel (BR 48.12.3).

Not only were Abraham's provisions for the visitors meritorious adumbrations; in the context of God's expressed intent to visit judgment on Sodom and Abraham's intercession, Abraham's declaration ". . . I who am but dust and ashes . . ." (Gen. 18:27) implied to the Sages that his descendants would have a means of atonement through ashes [of the red heifer] (Num. 19:9,17), a further allusion to the importance of worship and the sacrificial rituals. This is further demonstrated in the ashes ritual that was part of a declared fast (M. Ta'anit 2:1). Citing this verse, Rabbi Yudan bar Menasseh said it was on account of the merit obtained by Abraham. Rabbi Samuel bar Nahman said it was on account of the merit obtained by Isaac (BR 49.11.1-2). Implicit in the latter is the interpretation of Genesis 22 that Isaac's ashes were indeed upon the altar, a conclusion we have already encountered.

As a brief addendum to the Sodom incident, when Lot attempted to protect the angelic visitors from the townsmen on the rampage, he said: ". . . for they have come under the shelter of my roof" (Gen. 19:6). The Sages in BR had already set the stage for lack of righteousness on the part of Lot in their earlier discussions; here a simple dismissal was sufficient. "They did not come on account of the merit I have accrued, but on account of the merit attained by Abraham" (BR 50.6.2). Likewise, when they all finally left Sodom, it was the merit of Abraham that joined Raphael in bringing them out (BR 50.11.2).

Several brief references to merit appear before the climactic event of Genesis 22. "And the LORD remembered Sarah" (Gen. 21:1). A number of responses to this lemma affirm the trustworthy nature of God and His word as found in a wealth of intersecting verses. "Then R. Aha said: Sarah entrusted to the Holy One, Blessed Be He, the religious duties and good deeds that she had performed, and He returned to her the reward of doing religious duties and good deeds . . ." (BR 53.5.6). Further, when Abraham sent Hagar away, it was nevertheless his merit that was responsible for the Lord calling to her in the wilderness. Ishmael himself was not outside the realm of earning merit; ". . . the LORD has heard the voice of the boy where he is . . ." on account of Ishmael's own merits (Gen. 21:17; BR 53.14.2).

Turning to the final trial of Abraham (Gen. 22), the midrash begins a slow crescendo toward the peak of the drama. At the outset, both Abraham and Isaac were declared to be meritorious in their acceptance of the command. Isaac's role is equally prominent:

> Said the Holy One, Blessed Be He . . . if he [Abraham] were told to sacrifice his son to me, he would not hold him back. [Subsequently, Isaac and Ishmael were arguing as to which was more beloved in the context of the respective ages at which they were circumcised.] At that moment, Isaac said, "Would that the Holy One, Blessed Be He, appeared to me and told me to cut off one of my limbs. I would not object." Said the Holy One, Blessed Be He, to him, "If I should tell you to offer yourself up to me, you would not refuse." (BR 55.4.2)

When Abraham said, "Here I am" (Gen. 22:1), he declared himself ready for the priesthood and for the monarchy,[71] and he had the merit to attain to both (BR 55.6.2). This is followed immediately by the heart-wrenching exchanges between the Lord and Abraham as to just exactly which son was to be offered. "Why did He not tell him to begin with? It was so as to make Isaac still more precious in his view and so to give him a reward for each exchange" (BR 55.7.1). Further discussion ensued regarding the location to which they were to go. "And Abraham rose early in the morning, saddled the donkey . . ." (Gen. 22:3). This action of Abraham became paradigmatic for additional deeds, all of which were set in contradistinction to non-exemplary actions of evil persons, notably Balaam and Pharaoh, and which served effectively to counter those (BR 55.8.1-2). In addition, when Abraham cut the wood, it was merit that was held ready for when God would split the sea (BR 55.8.4).

The entirety of BR 56 is given over to the *Aqedah*, the binding of Isaac. In the context of this discussion, BR expands the notion of merit in two remarkable ways. First, responding to ". . . on the third day Abraham lifted up his eyes and saw the place afar off" (Gen. 22:4), it presents a typical enumeration list, this time of significant events that occurred on the third day. These include giving the Torah (Exod. 19:16), the prospect of resurrection from the dead (Hos. 6:2), Jonah (2:1), and Esther's approach to the king (Esth. 5:10), followed by the question: "On account of what sort of merit?" The Rabbis say: "On account of the third day of giving Torah.

---

71. The role of priest is presumed to be necessary here in order to carry out the sacrifice. Both roles are supported by biblical texts, the first by appealing to Ps. 110:4 and the second to Gen. 23:5 — "a prince among us." This is not the only place Ps. 110:4 is applied to Abraham; see BR 55.7.3.

Rabbi Levi said that it was on account of Abraham's merit" (BR 56.1.1). Second, Abraham's declaration to his servants that they would go, worship, and return (Gen. 22:5) meant, according to the Sages, that Abraham returned in peace only on account of the *zekhut* of worship. In fact, Israel was not redeemed, Torah was not given, Hannah was not visited, the exiles would not be regathered, the Temple was not built, and the dead would not be raised except for the merit of worship (BR 56.2.5). In subsequent rabbinic texts, the theme of resurrection in conjunction with Isaac grows increasingly emphatic.[72]

"So they went both of them together . . ." (Gen. 22:6): "This one to tie up and that one to be tied up; this one to slaughter and that one to be slaughtered," a repeated refrain (BR 56.3.3 and 56.4.1).[73] Both are presented as sharing equally in the task before them and thus in the merit. All the time that Abraham was binding Isaac, the Holy One, Blessed Be He, was binding the heavenly powers behind the nations (BR 56.5.2).

After the command from heaven not to touch Isaac and the sacrifice of the ram in Isaac's place, there are several significant discussions. The first has to do with the ram's serving as a substitute, its blood regarded as though it were the blood of Isaac, and its entrails as though they were Isaac's (BR 56.9.2). That is followed by a number of explanations of the name, "the LORD will provide." Unlike MRI, where the attention was directed to "seeing" the blood of Isaac, here the main point is to indicate that God would "see" Jerusalem and the building of the Temple, the place of sacrifice (BR 56.10.2-4). In fact, there is a strong thread woven through the commentary on the events of Abraham's life that sacrifice is still a vital component in the life of God's people.

"Because you have done this thing . . ." (Gen. 22:16), God reiterated the promises of covenant blessings. Somewhat incredulously, the midrash asks the question: Why does God refer to it as "this [one] thing"? There had been ten trials. The response: ". . . if he had not accepted this last trial, he would have lost the merit of all that he had already done."[74]

---

72. Spiegel, *The Last Trial*, pp. 28-50.

73. When Abraham put the wood for the burnt offering on Isaac (Gen. 22:6), the midrash adds: "It is like one who carries his own cross on his shoulder" (BR 56.3.1).

74. In this regard, note the title, aptly chosen, of the English translation of Shalom Spiegel's work, *The Last Trial*.

Comparisons and Contrasts: BR and MRI

It is quite clear that merit is much more emphatically linked with actions, especially those of Abraham, in BR than it is in MRI.[75] The most extensive discussions of merit appear in conjunction with the events in Egypt (Gen. 12), Abraham's care for the visitors (Gen. 18), and the "last trial" (Gen. 22). It would not be incorrect to suggest that most of the references to merit prior to the integral treatment of Genesis 22 are brief and almost idiosyncratic. This could simply be due to the fact that BR does indeed comment on consecutive verses of Genesis while MRI, in effect, looks back and reflects on all the possible reasons for Israel's meriting redemption in their current trying circumstances. Nevertheless, the fact that BR tends to avoid extensive discussion of merit and faith may mean that something further is afoot here. It might be that the Sages of that generation were loath to enter a "theological" debate regarding Abraham that was central to Christian doctrine.

For the compilers of BR, there is a clear connection between merit and worship. Sacrifice, atonement, and Jerusalem are high-profile topics, even though none of them would appear on the historical scene for Israel until centuries after the events of Genesis. Having said that, it seems there might be possibly a tantalizing "nod" to Christianity in the righteous person who would atone for Israel, apparently apart from the cult system. The midrash is not dismissive of this suggestion.

Some Concluding Reflections

Following the biblical prophetic tradition, the rabbis affirmed the inviolability of the covenant with Abraham and his descendants.[76] They reaffirmed the importance of both the deeds and the faith of the patriarchs and their descendants. The "blood of Isaac" was said to be meritorious in accomplishing the deliverance of Israel and his was a willing and humble sacrifice right along with Abraham's. There is an ongoing tension between expressing the assurance of *zekhut avot* and exhorting the current generations to obedience because the righteous of any given generation carried a

---

75. At the same time, Abraham is not set up as a paradigm of faith and belief but of doubt and questions.

76. See Jer. 33:25-26.

protective power for all of that generation.[77] Both were viewed as integral *parts* of the covenant which itself is a bigger concept. The Sages recognized that dependence on merit, whether of the ancestors or one's own good deeds, was incomplete. The covenant grace and compassion of God were the foundation of his response to either of those "merits."[78]

There is a historical dimension to the discussion as well. In the context of the second-century Hadrianic persecutions or fifth-century imperial Christianity, Jews could hope for deliverance obtained by an inseparable combination of merit and faith.[79] Given that the biblical concept of deliverance and salvation emphasizes its unfolding in this world, it is noteworthy that, by the time BR was compiled, there was a greater focus on the world to come, accompanied by a slender thread of references to resurrection from the dead.

And what of Paul's reference to "beloved on account of the patriarchs" (Rom. 11:28)? In Romans 9–11, Paul reflects some of the same tensions that shaped the discussions in the exegetical midrashim. The tangled web of God's covenant, Abraham's faithfulness within that covenant, and meritorious deeds in response to the covenant is all there. It is true that a distillation of Romans 9:30–10:2 might be that earning their own merit for the purpose of salvation was the wrong avenue for the Jews to pursue; many from the rabbinic communities might have said the same thing. That, however, was part of a much larger and complex argument, both for the Sages and for Paul.[80] In spite of the Jews' having been "broken off" the

---

77. Melinek, "The Doctrine of Reward and Punishment," p. 287. This reached its strongest expressions in those pericopae that emphasize measure-for-measure reward (and punishment) and the very contemporary response to Exodus 20:5-6: ". . . showing covenant love to thousands . . ." (MRI Bahodesh 6).

78. Urbach, *The Sages,* pp. 505-8.

79. Some pressure from the Christian apologists might be perceived in the emphasis on merit and faith. Cohen, "Analysis of an Exegetic Tradition," pp. 6-7, emphasized the indivisible nature of faith and obedience in the rabbinic conception. Faithfulness implied action, and there was reward for faithful observance of the commandments. This would be a necessary response to the claims of the early church that Abraham's faith was entirely separate from his actions of obedience.

80. While the amount of material written in this regard is staggering, of value for this paper are two recent works that explore the "enmity" of Israel in relationship to the covenant with the patriarchs in the context of contemporary Jewish-Christian dialogue: Michael J. Cook, "Paul's Argument in Romans 9-11," *Review and Expositor* 103 (2006): 91-111; and F. Scott Spencer, "Metaphor, Mystery and the Salvation of Israel in Romans 9–11: Paul's Appeal to Humility and Doxology," *Review and Expositor* 103 (2006): 113-38.

olive tree, being currently "enemies of God for your sake" through disobedience, they could and would be grafted back in again because "they are beloved on account of the patriarchs, for the gifts and the calling of God are irrevocable" (Rom. 11:28-29). The preceding verses make it evident that Israel's disobedience was solely for the sake of the wild olive branches, the Gentiles, being grafted into the root that remains vital and strong. Thus, even their enmity has, in God's sovereign design, a remarkable redemptive purpose. In fact, the possibility of a self-sacrificing role for Israel on behalf of the Gentiles may echo the redemptive role that Jesus performed in fulfillment of Isaiah 53.[81] And Paul's closure indicates that he fully expected God's mercy to be shown to Jews as well as Gentiles because of the covenant with the fathers.

As might be expected, the theme has been pervasive across centuries, geographical boundaries, and political circumstances. Wherever there have been Jewish communities, the question of the survival of God's people has been paramount. Thus, the assurance of God's unbreakable covenant with Abraham appeared in the context of the synagogue as well as the house of study. The central prayer to every synagogue service is the Amidah, also known as "The Eighteen Benedictions." Notably, the first one is the blessing regarding the Fathers.

> Blessed are You, O Lord our God and God of our fathers, the God of Abraham, the God of Isaac and the God of Jacob, the great, mighty and revered God, the Most High God who bestows lovingkindnesses, the Creator of all, who recalls the good deeds of the fathers and who brings a Redeemer to their children's children for his name's sake, in love. O king, helper, savior and shield. Blessed are You, O Lord, the shield of Abraham.

81. Spencer, "Metaphor, Mystery and the Salvation of Israel," pp. 120-27.

Sarah: The View of the Classical Rabbis

David J. Zucker

Introduction

Sarah is the Bible's first matriarch. More broadly, Sarah is the mother of the Jewish people.[1] Of the many literary and critical commentaries on the

1. In Jewish tradition, Abraham, Isaac, and Jacob are regarded as the patriarchs, as Sarah, Rebecca, Leah, and Rachel are deemed the matriarchs of Judaism (see Isa. 51:2). Often Sarah is referred to as "Sarah our mother." *Pesikta de-Rab Kahana: Rabbi Kahana's Compilation of Discourses for Sabbaths and Festal Days,* trans. William G. Braude and Israel J. Kapstein (Philadelphia: Jewish Publication Society, 1975), *Piska* 20.1.

I first met Marvin R. Wilson in the early 1990s at several National Workshops on Christian-Jewish Relations. I knew of Marvin. I had read his seminal volume *Our Father Abraham: Jewish Roots of the Christian Faith.* Throughout the years, we have kept in touch. Marvin very kindly agreed to review two of the books that I have written, *Israel's Prophets: An Introduction for Christians and Jews* (Paulist, 1994); and *The Torah: An Introduction for Christians and Jews* (Paulist 2005). Marvin made invaluable suggestions to the manuscripts. Further, he agreed to write a preface for each of these works. His kindness and friendship is something that I deeply value. When asked to contribute to this volume in his honor, I was delighted. I hope in some small measure to repay his goodness and generosity. May you, Marvin, know many years of health, happiness, productivity, and peace.

Special thanks to my friend and colleague, Rabbi Bonita E. Taylor, for reading this chapter in an earlier form and recommending that I both define and focus upon Sarah as a woman in her own right, and not simply as a woman in relationship to someone else. Likewise, I benefited from ideas offered by Rev. Jolain Graf and Rebecca Gates Brinton, as well as astute editorial suggestions by Professor Steve Hunt. Finally, I offer my appreciation to my son Ian Michael Zucker, for a close reading of the chapter, and for his cogent comments.

book of Genesis, a number of authors analyze Sarah and her life as portrayed in the Bible. Some consider her story within the biblical narrative, while others place her life within the context of ancient Near Eastern customs, laws, and mores.[2] Sarah and Sarah's world have been of special interest to women. More specifically, she is the focus of both women commentators and feminist commentators in particular.[3]

Alongside the biblical Sarah, there is the Sarah as portrayed and interpreted by the rabbis in classical Jewish texts such as the Talmud and various collections of midrash.[4] The rabbinic Sarah is a figure developed through the medium of midrash — sermonic interpretation — and is based upon the biblical text. "The Bible is a laconic, elliptical, and at times ambiguous text; thus it is open to a variety of interpretations of any one [word, phrase, or] verse."[5] By way of midrash, the rabbis use the brevity of the biblical text, as well as the actual words of the Bible, as an opportunity to develop further information about Sarah's life and times.

In the mind of the rabbis, there was a great deal more to a word or phrase than its simple surface meaning. Therefore they stated that each "biblical statement may carry many meanings."[6] This was true of the laws

2. E.g., Robert Alter, *Genesis* (New York: Norton, 1996); Paul Borgman, *Genesis: The Story We Haven't Heard* (Downers Grove: InterVarsity, 2001); David L. Lieber, ed., *Etz Hayim: Torah and Commentary* (New York: The Rabbinical Assembly, the United Synagogue of Conservative Judaism, 2001); W. Gunther Plaut, ed., *The Torah: A Modern Commentary* (New York: Union of American Hebrew Congregations, 1981); Nahum N. Sarna, *Genesis*, The JPS Torah Commentary (Philadelphia: Jewish Publication Society, 1989); *Understanding Genesis* (New York: Schocken, 1970); E. A. Speiser, *Genesis*, Anchor Bible (New York: Doubleday, 1964); Gerhard Von Rad, *Genesis: A Commentary*, rev. ed. (Philadelphia: Westminster, 1972).

3. E.g., Leilah Leah Bronner, *From Eve to Esther: Rabbinic Reconstructions of Biblical Women* (Louisville: Westminster John Knox, 1994); Tamara Cohn Eskenazi and Andrea L. Weiss, eds., *The Torah: A Women's Commentary* (New York: URJ Press and Women of Reform Judaism, 2008); Susan Niditch, "Genesis," in *The Women's Bible Commentary*, ed. Carol A. Newsom and Sharon H. Ringe (London: SPCK; Louisville: Westminster John Knox, 1992); Ilona N. Rashkow, *The Phallacy of Genesis: A Feminist-Psychoanalytic Approach* (Louisville: Westminster John Knox, 1993); Savina J. Teubal, *Sarah the Priestess: The First Matriarch of Genesis* (Athens: Swallow/Ohio University Press, 1984); Phyllis Trible, *Texts of Terror* (Philadelphia: Fortress, 1984); Aviva Gottlieb Zornberg, *Genesis: The Beginning of Desire* (Philadelphia: Jewish Publication Society, 1995).

4. The Talmud is the vast compendium of Jewish thought developed in the post-biblical world between c. 200 and 500 C.E. See Marvin R. Wilson, *Our Father Abraham: Jewish Roots of the Christian Faith* (Grand Rapids: Eerdmans, 1989), p. 31.

5. Bronner, *From Eve to Esther*, p. xv.

6. Babylonian Talmud *Sanhedrin* 34a.

and statutes; likewise, it applied to narrative sections, including the sacred stories of the matriarchs and the patriarchs. The actual words devoted to Sarah in the Bible itself were necessarily limited; what might be said about her was virtually limitless.

It is the rabbinic-enhanced Sarah that is the main focus of this chapter.[7] First, however, we will look briefly at the biblical Sarah.

The Sarah of the Bible

The Bible[8] presents Sarah's life in Genesis 11–23.[9] She is born Sarai. She holds this name for more than half of her life (cf. Gen. 17:15-16). She is barren. In midlife, along with her husband, Sarai leaves home and hearth and travels at God's invitation to a new, as yet undisclosed land. "Go from your country and your kindred . . . to the land that I will show you" (Gen. 12:1).[10] They eventually settle in the land of Canaan. Not long thereafter, due to measures beyond her control, the family and its entourage relocate to Egypt. The sojourn in Egypt is a temporary measure. Sarah and her husband have no plans to settle there; in fact, on the whole, the Egyptian encounter is quite unsettling.

7. Two important post-biblical Jewish writers of the ancient world mention Sarah. The first is the philosopher Philo Judaeus (Philo of Alexandria, c. 20 B.C.E.–50 C.E.). Because his concerns have little to do with the rabbinic corpus, Philo's writings are not presented in this chapter. The second writer is the historian Flavius Josephus (c. 37-100 C.E.). Though primarily a historian, at times Josephus offers his interpretation of events in a way that is midrash-like. Consequently, though not part of the rabbinic corpus, Josephus is briefly cited in the notes to this chapter.

8. In this chapter, the word "Bible" refers only to the Jewish Bible. The words "Jewish Bible," "Jewish Scriptures," "Hebrew Scriptures," and "Hebrew Bible" are used synonymously.

9. Sarah's life is depicted in Gen. 11–23. The other references to her in the Hebrew Bible are Gen. 24:36; 24:67; 25:10, 12; 49:31; and Isa. 51:2. Sarah is mentioned by name in the Christian Scriptures in the Epistles in several places: Rom. 4:19; 9:9; Heb. 11:11; 1 Pet. 3:6; and she is referred to, but not named, in Gal. 4:21-31. These references do not fall within the purview of this chapter.

10. Translations used for this chapter (unless specifically otherwise noted) come from The New Revised Standard Version (NRSV). This version was chosen because it presents both a modern translation and inclusive, gender-neutral language. Reference will be made to differences in verse numbering as reflected in the Masoretic (traditional Jewish) Text of the Hebrew Bible. The NRSV translation will be followed by the Hebrew verse in brackets and marked with an "H" for Hebrew (for example: Isa. 9:6 [9:5 H]).

In Egypt, Sarai's husband forces her to pretend to be what she is not — his sister, not his wife. He explains that he fears for his life, and that the Egyptians will kill him to get to her (Gen. 12:11-14).[11] On the face of it Sarai is regarded merely as her husband's property, to do with as he will. He asks her to take on this role, but this is a formality on his part. He assumes that she will give her consent. This is a "crass, male-centered . . . [account] where it is clear that Abram has more to gain as the brother of an unattached, protected woman than the husband of a 'used' one. . . . This is no woman-affirming tale. Sarai is an exchange item to be traded for wealth."[12]

Sarai is taken into Pharaoh's palace. God then afflicts Pharaoh, and so he releases her. In Egypt, her husband acquires "male and female slaves" for their household (Gen. 12:16). They leave Egypt, and then in time one of these women, Hagar, at Sarai's suggestion, becomes her husband's wife/concubine. Hagar's role is to function as a surrogate mother in place of Sarai. When Hagar conceives, tensions escalate between the two women. Hagar births a son who assures physical continuity for the Abraham-Sarah family line.

Over a dozen years pass by. Then God gives Sarai a new name, Sarah. With this new name comes an announcement of future blessings. God explains that Sarah "shall give rise to nations; kings of people shall come from her" (Gen. 17:16). Not long thereafter, in Genesis 18 some unexpected (and special) guests arrive at the family encampment. One of the strangers suddenly suggests that in about a year's time, when Sarah will be ninety, she will birth her own child. Sarah finds this incredible, for she is postmenopausal.[13]

In the meanwhile, Sarah and her husband temporarily move to the Philistine stronghold of Gerar. Once again, she is forced to pretend that she is her husband's sister, not his wife. The ruler invites the family to settle in Gerar, but eventually they leave and some months go by. To her surprise and delight, Sarah does conceive and then gives birth as predicted earlier.

11. Technically, Sarai is in fact Abram's sister. According to Gen. 20:12, they share a common father but not the same mother. As a note in the NRSV explains, "Marriage with a half-sister was permitted in ancient times (2 Sam 13.13) but later forbidden (Lev 18.9, 11; 20.17)."

12. Susan Niditch, "Genesis," in Newsom and Ringe, eds., *The Woman's Bible Commentary*, p. 18.

13. Often, when one halves the ages of people found in Genesis, the narrative makes greater sense. This means that Sarah was a "mere" forty-five and not nearly ninety as the Bible states, and Abraham was not one hundred, but fifty. This answer, however, does not explain how, with her being "after the manner of women" (Gen. 18:11), i.e., postmenopausal, she suddenly finds herself fertile. As shall be seen below, the rabbis offer their explanation for this remarkable phenomenon.

Their son is named Isaac (Gen. 21:2-3). When Isaac is about three, he is weaned.[14] Some time later, Sarah approaches her husband and demands that he expel Hagar and her son from the family encampment. Though upset by this turn of events, he capitulates when God tells the patriarch to defer to Sarah's wishes. At the end of a long life, Sarah dies at age 127. Her burial place is Kiryat Arba/Hebron (Gen. 23:1-2).

The biblical Sarah is a powerful figure in her own right. She speaks, and her husband not only listens but acquiesces to her suggestions. When Sarah offers the gift of Hagar as a surrogate womb, he assents (Gen. 16:2). When Sarah complains about Hagar, he defers to her judgment. He says to her, "Your slave-girl is in your power; do to her as you please" (Gen. 16:5). When, years later, Sarah demands that he send Hagar away, he consents. In that instance, she has divine support. God says to him, "Whatever Sarah says to you, do as she tells you" (Gen. 21:12).

Now that the biblical portrait of Sarah has been reviewed, we will next consider the rabbinic-enhanced Sarah.

Some Definitions

Rabbis

The classic rabbinic period is c. 200-500 C.E. in the lands of Israel and (Parthian and Neo-Persian) Babylon. The area of land between the Tigris and Euphrates rivers became a place of great cultural significance for the dispersed Jewish community in the third century C.E., some seven hundred years after the biblical Exile to ancient Babylonia.

The rabbis were teachers and expositors of Jewish tradition. "The term rabbi is derived from the Hebrew noun *rav*. It does not occur in the Bible as a word that refers to a teacher or communal leader, for the rabbinate is a post-Biblical institution. The term 'rabbi' means literally 'my master' and it initially referred to [the] Sages . . . [These Sages] were great scholars, teachers in the sense that they interpreted and expounded Jewish law."[15]

The rabbis often, but not always, based their teaching on the Jewish

---

14. Sarna, *JPS-Genesis*, p. 146.

15. David J. Zucker, *American Rabbis: Facts and Fiction* (Northvale, NJ: Jason Aronson; Lanham, MD: Rowman and Littlefield, 1998), p. xvii.

Scriptures. Whenever the Bible was not explicit or specific, or when conditions in the post-biblical world demanded new answers, the early interpreters of the post-biblical world (i.e., the sages of the rabbinic period, and their successors) sought to provide a new awareness and appreciation of matters. Consequently, alongside the Bible they developed an additional way to understand what God desires of humans, and more specifically, what it means to lead a Jewish life. The rabbis composed a supplement, a whole set of laws and commentaries on, and in addition to, the Jewish Scriptures. Broadly speaking, rabbinic literature is composed of the multi-volume Talmud and various collections of Midrash.

Midrash

The generic term for exegesis or interpretation of biblical texts is "midrash" (plural: "midrashim"). The Hebrew for sermon, "derasha," is based on the word "midrash."[16] Midrash is always grounded in the biblical text. "Midrash is a type of literature, oral or written, which has its starting point in a fixed canonical text, considered the revealed word of God by the midrashist and his audience, and in which this original verse is explicitly cited or clearly alluded to."[17]

Midrash allows the rabbis to fill in gaps in the Bible and offer new insights. Midrash involves many genres: tales and allegories, ethical reflections, epigrams and legends. Through midrash, the "sacred words became an inexhaustible mine . . . of religious and ethical teaching."[18] In the words of the rabbis, each word in the Torah has seventy possible interpretations.[19]

Through their midrashim, the rabbis teach about the values of their time such as the nature of God, opposition to idolatry, proper modesty, the importance of studying sacred texts, generosity, hard work, chastity, and loyalty, as well as discussing differences between the Jewish and non-Jewish communities.

16. Naomi M. Hyman, *Biblical Women in the Midrash: A Sourcebook* (Northvale, NJ: Jason Aronson; Lanham, MD: Rowman and Littlefield, 1998), pp. xxvii-xxxiii. See also the terms "Haggadah" and "Midrash" in Paul J. Achtemeier, gen. ed., *Harper's Bible Dictionary* (San Francisco: Harper & Row, 1985).

17. Gary G. Porton, "Midrash," in *The Anchor Bible Dictionary,* ed. David Noel Freedman (New York: Doubleday, 1992), 4:818.

18. A. Cohen, *Everyman's Talmud* (London: Dent; New York: Dutton, 1949), p. xviii.

19. *Shiv'im panim ba-Torah:* "The Torah has 70 faces." *Midrash Numbers Rabbah* 13.15.

Midrashic literature first appeared in spoken form, though later it was compiled by the rabbis. The rabbis often disagree amongst themselves. To say that something is *a* rabbinic view, or even *the* rabbinic view, does not mean that all rabbis support that position or that interpretation.[20]

Though redacted at later points, these rabbinic teachings both precede the time of the Christian Scriptures and continue for several centuries thereafter. The flowering of midrash as a unique genre begins around 200 c.e. It continued as late as the twelfth and thirteenth centuries c.e.[21]

The Sarah of the Rabbis

Genesis 11: Sarah linked to Zion

"Now Sarai was barren; she had no child" (Gen. 11:30; cf. 16:1). The sages link Sarah's delay in being able to bear a child to Zion. In this particular midrash, Zion is a metaphor for the people Israel. More specifically, Zion is a woman, and secondarily a country, which, while barren, will in due time give birth to a (reborn) fruitful people of Israel in their own land. "Zion is the seventh in the number of notable mothers in Israel who were barren a long time before God blessed them with children. Like the others, Zion's time will come: no longer barren, no longer uprooted from the Land, she will find peace."[22] "He gives the barren woman a home, making her the joyous mother of children" (Ps. 113:9). There were seven such barren women: Sarah, Rebecca, Rachel, Leah, Manoah's wife, Hannah, and Zion. Hence, the words "He gives the barren woman a home" apply, to begin with, to our mother Sarah: "Now Sarai was barren; she had no child" (Gen. 11:30); and the words "making her the joyous mother of children" also ap-

---

20. Not only are there differences of opinion among the rabbis, but there may be variations in some of the details of a given midrash in one midrash collection and another. Further, some midrash collections repeat a midrash that appeared earlier in that same volume. That I quote a specific midrash does not necessarily mean — or not mean — that there are variations to be found.

21. In this chapter, I cite many different midrashim. These come from midrash collections, as well as from midrashic *(aggadic)* materials from the Talmud and the Zohar. These documents were redacted at differing periods. A specific midrash may attribute a certain view to a given scholar. As with the Talmud, the certainty that such an attribution is absolutely accurate is doubtful.

22. *Pesikta de-Rab Kahana*, p. 330.

ply to our mother Sarah: "Sarah would nurse children. . . . I have borne him a child" (Gen. 21:7).[23]

Genesis 12

Sarah is exceedingly beautiful

Sarah at age sixty-five is still an extraordinarily beautiful woman. Her husband attests to this when he says to her, "I know well that you are a woman beautiful in appearance" (Gen. 12:11). Just how beautiful is she? The rabbis provide several answers. Eve was a beautiful woman. She transmitted her beauty to the reigning beauties of each generation. Yet Sarah was even more beautiful than Eve.[24]

Four women were surpassingly beautiful, and Sarah was one of these. The other three women were Rahab (the prostitute mentioned in Josh. 2:1), Abigail (one of David's wives, 1 Sam. 25:3), and Queen Esther (Est. 2:15).[25]

Sarah's journey from Canaan to Egypt is long and arduous. Despite hardships along the way, the midrash explains that Sarah maintains her beauty.[26]

When "the Egyptians saw that the woman was very beautiful . . . they praised her to Pharaoh. And the woman was taken into Pharaoh's house" (Gen. 12:14-15). The rabbis explain, metaphorically and poetically, that the light of Sarah's beauty filled all of Egypt.[27]

Sarah's dilemma

The Genesis text explains, "When [Abram/Abraham] was about to enter Egypt, he said to his wife [Sarai/Sarah], 'I know well that you are a woman beautiful in appearance; and when the Egyptians see you, they will say,

23. *Pesikta de-Rab Kahana, Piska* 20.1. The connection to Mother Zion is based on two verses in Isaiah: "Sing, O barren one . . ." (Isa. 54:1), and "Then you will say . . . 'Who has borne me these?'" (Isa. 49:21).

24. *Midrash Genesis Rabbah* 40.5.

25. Babylonian Talmud *Megillah* 15a.

26. *Midrash Genesis Rabbah* 40.4; *The Zohar*, trans. Harry Sperling and Maurice Simon (New York: Rebecca Bennet, n.d.), 1.81b. The *Zohar* is a mystical commentary on parts of the Bible. It dates from about the fourteenth century C.E. Technically not part of midrashic literature, nonetheless it contains midrash-like statements.

27. *Midrash Genesis Rabbah* 40.5.

"This is his wife"; then they will kill me and let you live. Say you are my sister, so that it may go well with me because of you, and that my life will be spared on your account'" (Gen. 12:11-13).

Abraham exploits his power over Sarah. He coerces her to agree and to submit to Pharaoh. She is forced to diminish her rightful status and is classified as merely part of Abraham's retinue. She acquiesces to this lesser status. Sarah does not claim that she is his lawful wife.[28] Her husband's focus is on his own well-being: "Say you are my sister, so that it may go well with me because of you." What was Sarah's reaction to this strange demand? Was she fearful? Was she resentful? Alternatively, did she have faith that somehow she would be protected? The biblical text does not address Sarah's feelings, nor is there any suggestion of what she replied.

A midrash offers Sarah's reaction. Interestingly, she does not attempt to dissuade her husband from this course of action. Rather, she turns directly to God and says in effect, I did not consent to this matter. I am an innocent party. I am here because Abraham trusted you. Implicit in her comments is the request that God save her.

> [Sarah] said: Sovereign of the World, Abraham came with you under a promise, since you had said to him (in Gen. 12:3): I WILL BLESS THOSE WHO BLESS YOU. Now I did not know anything except that, when he told me that you had said to him (in Gen. 12:1): GO, I believed your words. But now, <when> I have been left isolated from my father, my mother, and my husband, this wicked man [Pharaoh] has come to mistreat me. He (Abraham) had acted because of your great name and because of our trust in your words. The Holy One said to her: By your life, nothing evil shall harm you, as stated (in Prov. 12:21): NO HARM SHALL BEFALL THE RIGHTEOUS, BUT THE WICKED ARE FULL OF EVIL. So in regard to Pharaoh and his house, I will make an example of them. Thus it is written (in Gen. 12:17): THEN THE LORD AFFLICTED PHARAOH AND HIS HOUSE WITH GREAT PLAGUES AT THE WORD OF SARAI.[29]

28. This episode (and parallel episodes in Gen. 20 and 26) have been termed the "wife-sister" motif. While Speiser, *Genesis*, pp. 91-94, suggests connections with Nuzi documents, that view has been challenged. See Samuel Greengus, "Sisterhood Adoption at Nuzi and the 'Wife-Sister' in Genesis," *Hebrew Union College Annual* 46 (1975): 5-31. Abraham and Sarah *did* share the same father, but not the same mother (Gen. 20:12).

29. *Midrash Tanhuma, Genesis*, vol. 1. S. Buber Recension, trans. John T. Townsend (Hoboken, NJ: Ktav, 1989), *Lekh-Lekha*, 3.8 Genesis 14:1ff., Part III.

Sarah and Pharaoh

The biblical text explains that after Sarah (Sarai) "was taken into Pharaoh's house . . . the LORD afflicted Pharaoh and his house with great plagues because of Sarai, Abram's wife" (Gen. 12:15, 17). What happened? Did Pharaoh force Sarah into an adulterous relationship? Did Pharaoh rape Sarah? The Bible is unclear. Nahum Sarna comes close to suggesting that, at the very least, Pharaoh wanted to approach her. He explains that "there seems to be a word play behind the Hebrew expression . . . 'to afflict, plague,' as well as 'to come into physical contact with, to harass sexually.'" He also explains that there may be "a connection with Pharaoh's passion for Sarai . . . [and temporary] sexual impotence induced by some severe inflammation or acute infection of the genital area."[30]

Another modern commentator takes a different approach. "Abram's wife becomes another man's wife. Becoming a wife, in these narratives, always implies sexual relations."[31]

The rabbis however are unambiguous on this matter. They defend Sarah's virtue. Though he desired to do so, the Pharaoh was unable to touch her.

As in a previously quoted example, the midrash here focuses on the biblical words "the LORD afflicted Pharaoh" (Gen. 12:17). Sarah prays to God for deliverance. "Because [Pharaoh] dared to approach the shoe of that lady . . . the whole of that night Sarah lay prostrate on her face, crying, 'Sovereign of the Universe! Abraham went forth [from his land] on your assurance, and I went forth with faith; Abraham is without this prison, and I am within!' The Holy One said to her, 'Whatever I do, I will do for your sake, and all will say, "It is BECAUSE OF SARAI ABRAM'S WIFE."'"[32]

Another midrash collection surmises what happened at that fateful encounter between Sarah and Pharaoh.

> In that very hour an angel came down from the heavens with a rod in his hand. <When> Pharaoh came to take off her shoe, he smote him with his hand. <When> he came to touch her clothes, he would smite him. And the angel would consult with Sarah on each and every blow. If she said that he should be afflicted, he was afflicted. When she would say: Wait for him until he recovers himself, the angel would wait for

30. Sarna, *JPS-Genesis*, pp. 96-97.
31. Borgman, *Genesis*, p. 42.
32. *Midrash Genesis Rabbah* 41.2.

him, as it is stated (in Gen. 12:17): AT THE WORD OF SARAI. What is
the meaning of AT THE WORD OF SARAI? That <here> is not stated
"On the matter of," nor "over the cause of," nor "for the sake of," nor "in
consequence of," but AT THE WORD OF SARAI. Thus, if she said he
should be afflicted, he was afflicted; and if not, he was not afflicted.
R. [Rabbi] Judah b. [bar] Shallum the Levite said, The Holy One did
not allow a wicked man to occupy himself with a righteous woman.
Our masters have said: <When> he came to take off her shoe, leprosy
immediately overcame him, and his governors were also afflicted with
him — also the princes, also the servants, and also his family. And the
walls also were afflicted along with him, as stated (in Gen. 12:17): THEN
THE LORD AFFLICTED PHARAOH AND HIS HOUSE. Why? (Ibid.,
cont.:) AT THE WORD OF SARAI, ABRAM'S WIFE. . . ."[33]

Did Pharaoh not know Sarai's marital status? The biblical text
strongly suggests that Pharaoh was told that Sarai and Abram were merely
siblings, not husband and wife. A midrash then makes it clear why Pharaoh was punished so severely. Sarah unambiguously articulated her marital status to Pharaoh. "Because she told him [Pharaoh], 'I am a married
woman,' yet he would not leave her."[34]

A fair question is why did Abraham go to Egypt? Were there no other
alternatives? Why did he not turn back and go somewhere else? The *Zohar*
directly addresses this matter.

Rabbi Yesa said, "Abram knew that all the Egyptians were full of lewd-
ness. It may therefore seem surprising that he was not apprehensive for
his wife and that he did not turn back without entering the country.
But the truth is that he saw her with the Shekinah [*Shekhinah*, God's
feminine presence, sometimes associated with Wisdom],[35] and therefore was confident. THAT IT MAY BE WELL WITH ME FOR YOUR
SAKE: these words were addressed to the Shekinah, as if to say: 'that

33. *Midrash Tanhuma, Genesis, Lekh-Lekha*, 3.8 Genesis 14:1ff., Part III.

34. *Midrash Genesis Rabbah* 41.2. Josephus explains that "God put a stop to [Pha-
raoh's] inclinations by sending upon him a distemper, and a sedition against his government
. . . upon account of his inclinations to abuse the stranger's wife." Flavius Josephus, *Antiquities of the Jews*, trans. William Whiston (Boston: S. Walker, 1823), Book 1, ch. 8.

35. Abraham "saw with her [Sarah] the Shekinah. It was on this account that Abram
made bold to say subsequently, 'she is my sister', with a double meaning: one the literal, the
other figurative, as in the words 'say to Wisdom, thou art my sister' (Prov. VII, 4). SAY NOW
THOU ART MY SISTER" (*Zohar* 1.81b).

God may entreat me well for your sake'. AND THAT MY SOUL MAY LIVE BECAUSE OF YOU: because through this (the Shekinah) man ascends and becomes privileged to enter on the path of life."[36]

This explanation, that her husband saw Sarah with God's feminine presence, the Shekhinah, is high praise for Sarah. Nonetheless, he still puts Sarah in an untenable moral position.

Abram's request, which negatively compromises Sarai's status, does not go unnoticed. The medieval commentator, Ramban (Nahmanides), is scathing in his criticism. "Abraham committed a serious sin when he endangered Sarah's honor. Scripture does not record that Sarah agreed to this deception. When they arrived in Egypt, she was taken to Pharaoh's palace without questions being clarified as to her relationship with Abraham. (Abraham) only gave this information after the fact, after she was taken to the palace, and then only after Pharaoh blamed him when her identify became known."[37]

In the mind of the rabbis, there is a later benefit, which resulted from Sarah's chastity in Egypt. By her actions, she set an example for future generations. When Sarah "went down to Egypt, she took pains to hedge herself in against unchaste conduct of any kind; thereafter, all Israelite women, inspired by her example, also took pains to hedge themselves against unchaste conduct of any kind. According to Rabbi Hiyya bar Abba, such hedging in against unchastity was in itself of sufficient merit to bring about the redemption of Israel."[38]

The biblical text explains that, following the sojourn in Egypt, Abraham was quite wealthy, owning male and female slaves as well as silver and gold (Gen. 12:16; 13:2). A few chapters later, the narrative mentions that Sarah had a slave-girl, an Egyptian woman named Hagar (Gen. 16:1). These possessions were gifts from Pharaoh, explain the rabbis. "Rabbi Joshua ben Korchah said: Because of his love for her, (Pharaoh) wrote in his marriage document (giving her) all his wealth, whether in silver or gold, or in menservants, or land, and he wrote (giving) her the land of Goshen for a possession. . . . He (also) wrote (giving) her Hagar, his daughter . . . as her handmaid."[39] More specifically, "When Pharaoh saw what was done on Sa-

---

36. *Zohar* 1.81b-82a.

37. Ramban (Rabbi Mosheh ben Nahman, Nahmanides, Spanish, 1194-1270, commentator) on Gen. 12:13; cf. Borgman, *Genesis,* p. 43. See also Niditch's evaluation, n. 12 above.

38. *Pesikta de-Rab Kahana, Piska* 11.6.

39. *Pirke de Rabbi Eliezer,* trans. Gerald Friedlander (New York: Sepher-Hermon, 1981), ch. 26.

rah's behalf in his own house [the intervention of the angel, and the consequent plagues] he took his daughter and gave her to Sarah. He said, Better let my daughter be a handmaid in [Sarah's] house than a mistress in another house."[40]

After this introduction to Sarah in chapters 11–12, Sarah does not appear by name or reference in several of the next chapters (Gen. 13, 14, or 15). The next episode in the biblical account that focuses on Sarah is in Genesis 16, the surrogate motherhood, take-my-maid-to-impregnate-her (but do-not-become-too-attached-to-her) narrative.

Genesis 16: Sarah and Hagar, the early episodes

"Surrogate motherhood allowed a barren woman to regularize her status in a world in which children were a woman's status and in which childlessness was regarded as a virtual sign of divine disfavor (see [Gen.] 16:2; 30:1-2; . . . 38). Childless wives were humiliated and taunted by co-wives."[41]

The Sarah-Hagar relationship, at least initially, is an all-too-human dynamic reflecting many of the tensions that exist when the household contains stepparents and stepchildren.[42] Reading the biblical text, it appears that Hagar has no choice in this matter. She may — or may not — have had feelings about this new role for her; the Bible does not address this matter.

The rabbinic/midrashic tradition has mixed feelings about Hagar, and about Ishmael. Negative portrayals dominate, but there are positive comments as well.[43]

Sarah approaches Hagar. According to a midrash, Sarah "persuaded her with words, 'Happy are you to be united with such a holy man.'"[44]

40. *Midrash Genesis Rabbah* 45.1.

41. Niditch, "Genesis," p. 17. For the cultural context of this legalized surrogate motherhood, see Sarna, *JPS-Genesis*, p. 119, comment to verse 2; Speiser, *Genesis*, p. 120; Victor H. Matthews and Don C. Benjamin, *Old Testament Parallels*, fully revised and expanded 3rd ed. (New York/Mahwah: Paulist, 2006), pp. 48f., 110.

42. See David J. Zucker, "Blended Families: Sarah, Hagar, and All That . . . ," *Journal of Pastoral Care & Counseling* 57.1 (2003): 33-38.

43. As explained below in this chapter, Ishmael represented the "Other," the outsider, and therefore a probable threat to the family or community. See David J. Zucker, "Conflicting Conclusions: The Hatred of Isaac and Ishmael," *Judaism* 30.1 (1990): 37-46. For a fuller treatment of this subject, see the chapter "'The Other Woman': A Collaborative Jewish-Christian Study of Hagar" later in this volume.

44. *Midrash Genesis Rabbah* 45.3.

"Hagar . . . conceived; and when she saw that she had conceived, she looked with contempt on her mistress" (Gen. 16:4). When Hagar is with child, explain the rabbis, she speaks ill of Sarah. Hagar draws attention to the fact that while Sarah had been married for years, she was unable to conceive. Hagar suggests that Sarah deserves the punishment of being barren, because she is not a moral person. The unspoken message is clear. *I, Hagar, am a "moral" person, I conceived immediately.* A midrash explains that female visitors would come to visit and spend time with Sarah. Sarah would refer them to Hagar. "Hagar would tell them: 'My mistress Sarai is not inwardly what she is outwardly: she appears to be a righteous woman, but she is not . . . see how many years have passed without her conceiving, whereas I conceived in one night!' "[45]

Sarah is upset with Hagar. She blames her husband for this state of affairs. This is not how she imagined it would be. Sarah, "who wanted to be built up by way of having offspring, feels torn down."[46] "Then Sarai said to Abram, 'May the wrong done to me be on you! I gave my slave-girl to your embrace, and when she saw that she had conceived, she looked on me with contempt'" (Gen. 16:5). Her husband is unwilling to place himself in the midst of this dispute. He relinquishes his authority. He abdicates his responsibility to protect Hagar. He tells Sarah that it is up to her to solve the problem. In her anger, Sarah then mistreats Hagar. Sarah does everything she can to make life intolerable for Hagar, her husband's second wife.[47]

The Bible states that Sarah "dealt harshly" with Hagar (Gen. 16:6). Consequently, despite her pregnancy, Hagar ran off into the desert. There are no explanations as to what "dealt harshly" means. The rabbis come forward and offer suggestions. Sarah prevented Hagar and Abraham from sleeping together. She slapped Hagar's face with a slipper. Then, disregarding Hagar's newfound status as a second wife for Abraham, Sarah treated her as a slave, and forced Hagar to carry water buckets and towels to the bathing area.[48]

---

45. *Midrash Genesis Rabbah* 45.4; *Midrash ha Gadol,* ed. Mordecai Marguiles (Jerusalem: Mossad haRav Kook, 1947), Genesis 1.244.

46. Borgman, *Genesis,* p. 44.

47. Second wife, or concubine? Speiser and Sarna make the case that Hagar is a concubine, not a wife. Speiser, *Genesis,* p. 117; Sarna, *Genesis,* p. 119. The rabbis disagree. A midrash proclaims, "TO BE A WIFE, but not a concubine." *Midrash Genesis Rabbah* 45.3.

48. *Midrash Genesis Rabbah* 45.6.

Genesis 17

A change of name can bring a change of fortune

"Rabbi Hunya said in the name of Rabbi Joseph: A change of name or a change of conduct can . . . avert a harsh decree. A change of name, as is shown by the instance. . . . 'As for Sarai your wife, you shall not call her Sarai, but Sarah shall be her name' (Gen. 17:15). Sarah as Sarai could not bear children, but when renamed Sarah she could bear them."[49]

Sarah will give birth in her due time

In Proverbs it is said, "The crucible is for silver, and the furnace is for gold, so a person is tested by being praised" (Prov. 27:21). Like a refiner of metals such as gold and silver, so God refines the righteous according to their strength. Sarah was married for many years before she gave birth. "The Holy One . . . tried her according to HER strength."[50]

Genesis 18: Sarah and the visitors

Genesis 18 features the three visitors that come to the family encampment. They ask about Sarah's whereabouts. Then one of the visitors announces that "in due season . . . Sarah shall have a son" (Gen. 18:10). (Alternatively: "next year . . . Sarah will have a son!" — New Jewish Publication Society [NJPS/*TANAKH*] translation.) Sarah is incredulous. She is nearly ninety. She is postmenopausal. She laughs to herself, and notes that her husband (who now is ninety-nine) is old, as is she herself.[51] God challenges Sarah's response. "The LORD said to Abraham, 'Why did Sarah laugh? . . . Is anything too wonderful for the LORD?'" Sarah overhears this question and is embarrassed. She denies the fact that she

---

49. *Pesikta Rabbati (Discourses for Feasts, Fasts and Special Sabbaths)*, trans. William G. Braude (New Haven and London: Yale University Press, 1968), *Piska* 52.3.

50. *Pesikta Rabbati, Piska* 43.5.

51. Sarah seems to suggest not only that she is postmenopausal, but that Abraham is impotent: "and my husband is old" (Gen. 18:12). The rabbis note that when God reports Sarah's conversation to Abraham ("Why did Sarah laugh and say, 'Shall I indeed bear a child, now that I am old,'" Gen. 18:13) only Sarah's remarks about herself are mentioned. This was to preserve peace between husband and wife. *Midrash Genesis Rabbah* 48.18.

laughed, saying, "'I did not laugh'; for she was afraid. He said, 'Oh yes, you did laugh'" (Gen. 18:13-15).[52]

Sarah will laugh again, taking delight in the name of her son Isaac, which literally translates as *he will laugh.*

Genesis 20

Sarah and Abimelech

Some time after the special visitation, Sarah and Abraham travel to the stronghold of Gerar. There they encounter the ruler Abimelech. Once again, Sarah is presented as Abraham's sister, not his wife. "Abraham said of his wife Sarah, 'She is my sister.' And King Abimelech of Gerar sent and took Sarah" (Gen. 20:2). While this incident is similar to the encounter in Genesis 12, there are also significant differences. The rabbis were aware that Abimelech, through no fault of his own, was about to act in such a way that he could (unfairly) be accused of committing adultery. "God came to Abimelech . . . and said to him, 'You are about to die because of the woman whom you have taken; for she is a married woman'" (Gen. 20:3). In the biblical text, God acknowledges to Abimelech that the ruler is innocent of evil intent. "Then God said to him . . . 'Yes I know that you did this in the integrity of your heart'" (Gen. 20:6).

The rabbis embellish the biblical narrative. In the Bible, directly after Abraham claims that Sarah is his sister, the king sends for and takes Sarah. In the midrashic account, Abimelech explains to God that he made even further inquiries. He deliberately was misled. "Abimelech said: I asked Abraham, 'What is she — your wife?' He replied, 'She is my sister.' Then I asked Sarah, 'Are you his wife?' She replied, 'No, I am his sister.' Nevertheless, I went on to ask the people of his household, and they likewise said that she was his sister."[53]

According to the biblical text, "the LORD had closed fast all the wombs of the house of Abimelech because of Sarah, Abraham's wife" (Gen. 20:18). When God "closed fast," it was not merely a question of re-

---

52. This is a fine example of biblical humor; God is gently teasing Sarah. Ilona N. Rashkow, however, sees this as a criticism, and wonders "why Sarah is condemned for laughing?" Rashkow, *The Phallacy of Genesis*, p. 97.

53. *Pesikta Rabbati*, Piska 42.3.

production, explain the rabbis. God even closed up various parts of their bodies. This affected all in Abimelech's household, men, women, and children, as well as servants. All their bodily functions ceased to process normally. Their tear ducts were blocked; they could not weep. God closed their ears, and they could not hear. The plague affected Abimelech's flocks, herds, and cattle.[54] Another source suggests that the impact was more widespread. Abimelech became impotent. Further, even insects in Gerar became barren.[55]

Genesis 21

Mother Sarah

Genesis 21 celebrates the birth of Isaac. Sarah herself is astonished and delighted. She is filled with joyous laughter. "'God has brought laughter for me; everyone who hears will laugh with me.' And she said, 'Who would ever have said to Abraham that Sarah would nurse children? Yet I have borne him a son in his old age'" (Gen. 21:6-7).

For years, Sarah had to ignore the fact that many governors and governors' wives had jeered at her, calling her a "barren woman."[56] Then, in Genesis 18, the visitors had promised that in a year's time Sarah would give birth. Several months passed. The family had spent time in Gerar, and still she was not with child. The rabbis explain that in their frustration with God the angels took up Sarah's case. The angels actively advocate on her behalf. They entreat God that now is the time to act!

"The angels rose up, complaining: 'Master of the universe, all these years Sarah was barren and Abimelech's wife was barren [for a brief period]. . . . Now that Abraham has prayed [on behalf of Abimelech],'" the angels went on, "'Abimelech's wife was remembered; even his maidservants were. These were remembered, but Sarah remains barren. Justice demands that she also be remembered.' . . . Thereupon, says Scripture, And the Lord remembered Sarah." ["The Lord dealt with Sarah as he had said" (Gen. 21:1) and she gave birth to Isaac].[57]

54. *Pesikta Rabbati, Piska* 42.3, 6.
55. *Pirke de Rabbi Eliezer*, ch. 26.
56. *Pesikta Rabbati, Piska* 42.5.
57. *Pesikta Rabbati, Piska* 42.3.

When Sarah gave birth, she experienced no pain.[58] When Isaac was born, Sarah, Abraham, and their entourage celebrated. Not only that, the world celebrated. "All barren women everywhere in the world were remembered together with Sarah and were with child at the same time she was; and when she gave birth to a child, all of them gave birth to children at the same time she did. It was for this reason that Sarah said: God has given me occasion for laugher; every one that hears will laugh in joy with me (Gen. 21:6). . . . And not only this remembrance, but much more besides. When Sarah bore her child, every blind man in the world was given sight; every cripple was made straight; every mute was given speech; and every madman was healed of his madness." On the day that Isaac was born, God also intensified the light of the sun.[59]

Those were not the only miracles associated with Isaac's birth. People had heard that they had spent time in Gerar. There were those who suggested that Isaac was Abimelech's son, not Abraham's child. This was easy to disprove. Not only was Isaac born after a full nine-month pregnancy, but he looked just like Abraham.[60]

Others suggested that Sarah had never gotten pregnant, that the child was a foundling that the aged couple had found in the road.[61] Some alleged that the child was not hers, but her maidservant Hagar's. Sarah was only making believe when she said she was suckling him.[62] "And she said, 'Who would ever have said to Abraham that Sarah would nurse children? Yet I have borne him a son in his old age'" (Gen. 21:7). These allegations

---

58. *Midrash Tanhuma, Genesis, Wayyera,* 4.37 Genesis 21:1ff., Part VIII. The same was true of Jochebed, Moses' mother. *Midrash Exodus Rabbah* 1.20; Babylonian Talmud *Sotah* 12a.

59. *Pesikta Rabbati, Piska* 42.4. This midrash is a good example of fantasy and hyperbole. The rabbinic "sages utilized every sort of literary and rhetorical technique to make this material attractive and compelling to their audience," explains Joseph Heinemann. As he notes earlier in that chapter, they also used "wit and humor." Joseph Heinemann, "The Nature of the Aggadah," in *Midrash and Literature,* ed. Geoffrey H. Harman and Sanford Burdick (New Haven: Yale University Press, 1986), pp. 47, 42.

60. *Midrash Genesis Rabbah* 53.6. Some questioned Abraham's ability to father a child at his age. The midrash then explains that when this allegation was made, Isaac immediately took on Abraham's features. Some say that they looked so much alike that people confused them one for the other. The prooftext is "These are the descendants of Isaac, Abraham's son: Abraham" (Gen. 25:19), as if the text were saying "Abraham's son, Abraham." Babylonian Talmud *Baba Metzia* 87a.

61. Babylonian Talmud *Baba Metzia* 87a.

62. *Pesikta de-Rab Kahana, Piska* 22.1.

also were easy to disprove. In spite of her natural modesty and reluctance to nurse publicly, Sarah acceded to her husband's request. He "said to Sarah: 'Sarah, don't just stand there! This is not a time for modesty. For the hallowing of the Name [i.e., God] arise and uncover yourself! Sarah arose and uncovered herself, and her two nipples were pouring out milk like two jets of water."[63]

When the nations of the world heard about Sarah's miracle, noble-women brought their children to partake of Sarah's milk.[64] Her husband invited all the great men of the age to see this wonder, and Sarah invited the women. Sarah's super-abundance of milk clearly was well publicized. "Each [woman] brought her child with her, but not the wet nurse."[65] For those who came with sincere feelings, their children became proselytes to Judaism.[66] "The children who nursed from our mother Sarah, all of them became proselytes."[67]

The rabbis considered why it was that Sarah had taken so long to become pregnant. They had to reconcile an earlier biblical statement that she was barren (Gen. 11:30). She had been barren, they explained. She lacked ovaries, but then God fashioned them for her, and returned her youthfulness to her so she could become pregnant.[68]

Sarah and Hagar — the later episode

The Sarah narrative in Genesis 21 divides into two parts. The first seven verses describe Sarah's jubilation at Isaac's birth. The next seven verses demonstrate Sarah's protective stance regarding Isaac's welfare. The plain reading of Genesis 21:8-14 suggests that Sarah desires to banish Hagar and Ishmael, for they are a threat to the well-being of Isaac.[69] At this point Isaac is about three years old, and Ishmael about sixteen.

63. *Pesikta Rabbati, Piska* 43.4; Babylonian Talmud *Baba Metzia* 87a.

64. *Midrash Genesis Rabbah* 53.9.

65. Babylonian Talmud *Baba Metzia* 87a.

66. *Pesikta Rabbati, Piska* 43.4.

67. *Midrash Tanhuma, Genesis, Wayyera,* 4.38 Genesis 21:1ff., Part IX.

68. *Midrash Genesis Rabbah* 47.2; 53.5; 48.19. See also *Tanna Debe Eliyyahu: The Lore of the School of Elijah,* trans. William G. Braude and Israel J. Kapstein (Philadelphia: Jewish Publication Society, 1981), ch. (5) 6, p. 28. God also fashioned an ovary for Rebecca, *Midrash Genesis Rabbah* 63.5. Jochebed, Moses' mother, also is miraculously given ovaries. *Midrash Exodus Rabbah* 1.19.

69. If Sarah is actually casting Hagar out into the inhospitable wilderness, then this raises difficult ethical issues. "From a feminist perspective, the call for the expulsion of

The text states, "Sarah saw the son of Hagar the Egyptian, whom she had borne to Abraham, playing with her son Isaac" (Gen. 21:9). The final words of that sentence, "with her son Isaac," though part of many standard Christian translations of the Bible,[70] drawing on the Greek Septuagint, which includes that phrase "with her son Isaac," are not found in the traditional Hebrew (Masoretic) text, which ends with the word "playing."[71] Sarah then goes to Abraham and demands that he "Cast out this slave woman with her son; for the son of this slave woman shall not inherit along with my son Isaac" (Gen. 21:10).

Was Ishmael "playing with her son Isaac," or just "playing" (Gen. 21:9)? Further, what are the implications of the word "playing"? This has been the subject of much commentary and controversy. The word in Hebrew is *metzaheq*; it has multiple meanings.[72] Gerhard von Rad explains that whatever Ishmael did "need not be anything evil at all. The picture of the two boys playing with each other on an equal footing is quite sufficient to bring the jealous mother to a firm conclusion: Ishmael must go!"[73] E. A. Speiser writes that Ishmael's "'playing' with Isaac need mean no more than the older boy was trying to amuse his little brother. There is nothing in the

---

Hagar raises troubling questions. The story portrays the oppression of one woman by another." Eskenazi and Weiss, eds., *The Torah: A Women's Commentary*, p. 98. One interpretation of Sarah's act is that she "recapitulates in relation to the most vulnerable person in her household," namely Hagar, the "violence that is practiced by Abraham against Sarah," when "Abraham seeks to pass off his wife . . . as his sister in order to protect himself." "Thus, the cycle of abuse goes on." Judith Plaskow, "Contemporary Reflection," in Eskenazi and Weiss, eds., *The Torah: A Women's Commentary*, p. 107.

70. The NRSV, the New American Bible (Roman Catholic), and the Jerusalem Bible (Roman Catholic) include the words "with her son Isaac." The New English Bible features the words "laughing at him," which are ambiguous. Does this refer to Isaac, or to Abraham? The New International Version follows the traditional Hebrew (Masoretic) text.

71. The New Jewish Publication Society (NJPS) version reads, "Sarah saw the son whom Hagar the Egyptian had borne to Abraham playing" (*TANAKH: The Holy Scriptures* [Philadelphia: Jewish Publications Society, 1985]).

72. Depending on its context, *metzaheq (mem-tzadeh-het-quf)* can have such diverse meanings as "laugh," "play," "fondle," "revel idolatrously," "kill." See David J. Zucker, "What Sarah Saw: Envisioning Genesis 21:9-10," *Jewish Bible Quarterly* 36.1 (Jan.-March 2008): 54-62. For a different view, that the *metzaheq* issue centers on a religious/idolatry controversy related to circumcision as an Egyptian rite, see Teubal, *Sarah the Priestess*, pp. 37-41.

73. Von Rad, *Genesis*, p. 232. A note in the NRSV offers the suggestion that "The jealous mother [Sarah] could not stand seeing the two boys on the same level, even at play." *The New Oxford Annotated Bible with the Apocrypha (NRSV)*, ed. Bruce M. Metzger and Roland E. Murphy (New York: Oxford University Press, 1991), comments on Genesis 21:9-10, p. 26.

text to suggest that he was abusing him."[74] W. Gunther Plaut notes that some "commentators have suggested that it was sexual play that brought Sarah's strong reaction. There is nothing, however, to substantiate this."[75]

Or, it could be that the word *metzaheq*/playing is completely coincidental and without any negative connotations. Since in the traditional Hebrew text Isaac is not mentioned, it could be that Ishmael's playing had nothing to do with forming Sarah's opinion of him at all, but is simply a description of what Ishmael was doing while Sarah was making her case to Abraham.[76]

What was motivating Sarah's desire to force Hagar and Ishmael from the family encampment? There are many intriguing answers to that question. Sarah says explicitly that Ishmael "shall not inherit" along with Isaac (Gen. 21:10). This could mean that Sarah did not wish for Ishmael to inherit the property of Abraham along with Isaac. Yet it is likely that she means something else.

(1) Ishmael as "other"
Sarah thinks of Ishmael as "Other," and more specifically as Egyptian, the son of Hagar-the-Egyptian. Sarah has very bitter memories of Egypt where, to save her husband's life, she became part of Pharaoh's harem, and was subject to rape.

(2) Concerns for Isaac's physical safety
Sarah may be worried for the physical safety of Isaac. If Ishmael thinks that the presence of his younger (step-) brother by Abraham's "first wife" is a threat to his own (Ishmael's) primogeniture rights, he might harm Isaac.

(3) Too much of an influence
There is another possibility. As an older brother, Ishmael is a role model for Isaac. Sarah understands, as is often the case, that younger children

74. Speiser, *Genesis*, p. 155.

75. Plaut, *The Torah: A Modern Commentary*, p. 139. See Rashi (Rabbi Shlomo Yitzhaqi [French, 1040-1105], commentator) on Gen. 21:9 citing Exod. 32:6 and Gen. 39:17. On the other hand, in Ezkenazi and Weiss, eds., *The Torah: A Women's Commentary*, the note to Gen. 21:9 states that while *metzaheq* [*m'tzachek*] can be translated as "playing," it "can also mean 'mocking,' fooling around,' and toying with him sexually" (p. 98).

76. I am indebted to Rebecca Gates Brinton for this insight. In a letter to the author, Brinton notes that "the Hebrew verb form utilized, the *wayyiqtol* [*qal*] form, usually is used to express action that moves the plot of a story forward, not to indicate background or setting information."

idolize their older siblings. This is just what frightens her so much. Ishmael is not a threat to Isaac. Rather, the opposite is true. Ishmael is *too much of an influence* upon her son both psychologically and emotionally. Sarah is worried that Isaac will fall under undue influence from his older, teenage brother.[77]

(4) Religious/cultural concerns

Other reasons may influence Sarah's thinking. She and Abraham are considerably older than Hagar. Who knows how long the two of them will live? Sarah fears that Isaac will come under Hagar's religious influence. He will be "Egyptianized." She fears that Isaac will forget the cultural norms of his Mesopotamian-oriented parents. Sarah does not want the polytheistic religious ideas of Hagar-Ishmael in Isaac's life.[78] Sarah's intervention, sending away Hagar-Ishmael gives Isaac the opportunity to forge a relationship with God without any foreign influences in the family encampment.

Sarah's fear concerning the pagan religio-cultural influences of the "Other" is well founded. The Torah (Pentateuch), as well as later Israelite history, abounds with examples of how the Israelite community was seduced by alien cultures. In the next generation, Esau upsets his parents when he marries foreign wives (Gen. 26:34-35).[79]

(5) Concern with Ishmael's wicked behavior

The latter reasons for Sarah's seemingly precipitous actions notwithstanding, it is also possible that Sarah's apparent distaste for Ishmael may have had nothing to do with Ishmael's actions *toward or with Isaac,* but rather with Ishmael's actions in general, perhaps of a sexual nature, or immoral nature, or idolatrous nature. That is the position of many midrashim.

77. "Sarah fears that the danger of Ishmael corrupting his younger brother is greater than the prospect of Isaac being a good influence on Ishmael." Based on the teaching of the Hafetz Hayyim. David L. Lieber, ed., *Etz Hayim: Torah and Commentary,* comment on Gen. 21:9, p. 114. This idea and other factors in this section are considered in David J. Zucker, "What Sarah Saw."

78. "What the text implies is that Hagar was bringing up her son Ishmael in a traditional Egyptian way, and this was not the influence Sarah wanted around Isaac." Teubal, *Sarah the Priestess,* p. 40.

79. Consider Num. 25:1-9. At Shittim, Phineas acts quickly to curb foreign practices. Deuteronomy makes it clear that when the Israelites enter the Promised Land they are to eradicate idolatry, root and branch (Deut. 12:2-4). The Prophets frequently speak out against syncretistic religious practices. See also Ezra 10:2-5, 44.

Stated simply, in the mind of the rabbis Ishmael — and by extension Hagar — personified wicked behavior. The text reports that Ishmael was "playing." As noted earlier in this chapter, the Hebrew verb "to play" (*letzaheq,* and in its gerund form, "playing" — *metzaheq*) can have multiple meanings. The midrash explains,

> Now playing means nothing else but immorality, as in the verse "The Hebrew servant whom you have brought among us, came in to insult me" [*letzaheq*] (Gen. 39:17). [Alternatively, NJPS/*TANAKH* "to dally with me"; — or more clearly, given the context of this narrative, "to seduce me."] Thus this teaches [continues the midrash] that Sarah saw Ishmael ravish maidens, seduce married women and dishonor them.
>
> Rabbi Ishmael taught: This term *playing* refers to idolatry, as in the verse, [In front of the golden calf] "the people sat down to eat and drink, and rose up to revel" [*letzaheq*] (Exod. 32:6). This teaches you that Sarah saw Ishmael build altars, catch locusts and sacrifice them.
>
> Rabbi Eleazar said: The term *playing* refers to bloodshed, as in the verse "Let the young men come forward and have a contest before us" [*visahaqu* — from the root *sin-het-quf,* actually a close homonym of the root word *letzaheq* — and then a few verses on the text explains that the opponents killed each other with swords] (2 Sam. 2:14 [cf. 2:16]).
>
> Rabbi Azariah said in Rabbi Levi's name: Ishmael said to Isaac, "Let us go and see our portions in the field" and then Ishmael would take a bow and arrows and shoot them in Isaac's direction, while pretending to be playing. Thus it is written, "Like a maniac who shoots deadly firebrands and arrows, so is one who deceives his neighbor and says "I am only joking" (Prov. 26:18-19) [*mesaheq* — from the root *sin-het-quf,* again a close homonym of the root word *letzaheq* — "to play"]. But I say: This term *playing* refers to inheritance. For when our father Isaac was born all rejoiced, whereupon Ishmael said to them, "You are fools, for I am the firstborn and I shall receive a double portion."[80]

80. *Midrash Genesis Rabbah* 53.11. I have slightly modified the English from the Soncino translation, for example, which uses the term "sport" for playing. Cf. *Midrash Exodus Rabbah* 1.1; *Midrash Tanhuma-Yelammedenu, Genesis and Exodus,* trans. Samuel Berman (Hoboken, NJ: Ktav, 1996), Exodus 1.1, pp. 313-14; 347. Josephus has a different explanation. While "Sarah . . . at first loved Ismael [sic] . . . with an affection not inferior to that of a mother . . . when she herself had borne Isaac, she was not willing that Ismael should be brought up with him, as being too old for him, and able to do him injuries, when their father should be dead." Josephus, *Antiquities,* Book 1, ch. 12.

Casting Ishmael as a wicked person, and therefore deserving of punishment, would explain the basis for a midrash that suggests why Hagar was fearful that Ishmael was going to die when they lost their way in the wilderness (Gen. 21:14-17). According to this tradition, Sarah had put a curse on Ishmael, "whereupon he was seized with feverish pains."[81]

(6) A ruse to protect Isaac, Ishmael, Sarah, and Hagar

There is yet a different answer; one that is more benign. The surface meaning of the text may contain hidden messages. Many possibilities exist, possibilities in themselves that are both intriguing and full of intrigue. Biblical characters have multiple reasons for doing what they do, just as people today have varied reasons for their actions.

This explanation understands that the earlier tension between the two women had subsided. For thirteen years and more, both believed that Ishmael was the heir apparent. Sarah and Hagar, once rivals, learned to live with each other. Each was a significant figure in Ishmael's life. It was in their mutual interests to forge a working relationship;[82] they became co-mothers for him.[83]

Hagar realizes that Isaac's birth has changed the family dynamic. She worries that Abraham might send them away, for with this new heir Hagar and Ishmael are no longer "needed" in the same way.

The matter is exacerbated by Abraham's increasingly strange behaviors (Gen. 15: a covenant ritual involving walking between carcasses and then swooning; Gen. 17: adult circumcision; Gen. 18: entertaining angels/men/strangers; debating/bargaining with God), which impel Sarah and Hagar to take a proactive position to protect their young sons. Sarah consults and conspires with Hagar.

Abraham's God promised that both their sons will be great nations (Ishmael, Gen. 17:20ff.; Isaac, Gen. 17:15ff.). Therefore the time had come to take them away, to distance them from Abraham. Sarah and Hagar decide

---

81. *Midrash Genesis Rabbah* 53.13. See the chapter "'The Other Woman': A Collaborative Jewish-Christian Study of Hagar" later in this volume.

82. Savina J. Teubel, *Hagar the Egyptian* (New York: HarperSanFrancisco, 1990), p. 77.

83. The idea of co-mothers, with shared responsibilities, is repeated as a theme in Gen. 37:10. Joseph suggests that the sun and moon are to bow down to him. Jacob asks Joseph, "Are your mother and I to do this?" Yet Jacob's mother, Rachel, has been dead a long time. "Your mother" refers to Leah (or perhaps to Leah, Bilhah, and Zilpah, all of whom are Joseph's stepmothers) — the other mother figure(s) in Joseph's life. Thanks to Daniel M. Zucker for pointing out this parallel.

to seek out a safe place for themselves and their sons. This way each son will realize his own destiny.

By the time of the events portrayed at the weaning ceremony of Isaac in Genesis 21, Sarah and Hagar have colluded and concluded that Abraham is so God-intoxicated that who knows what he will do? It is physically and emotionally unsafe for the women and for their offspring.[84]

After due deliberation, they choose the natural oasis of Beer Lehai Ro-i.[85] Their arrangement is that initially Hagar and Ishmael will go to this oasis; and then, in due time, Sarah and Isaac will join them. Their plan nearly goes amiss when Hagar loses her way in the desert, but then an angel of God intervenes and sets them on the correct course.

Genesis 23

Sarah's death

The last time Sarah appears alive in Genesis is when she demands that Hagar and Ishmael be sent away (Gen. 21:9-10). Sarah is neither featured nor mentioned in Genesis 22, the fateful and faithful narrative of the "Binding of Isaac."[86] The next reference to Sarah is that she died at age 127 in Kiryat Arba/Hebron (Gen. 23:1-2).

Sarah's death at that advanced age[87] warrants serious questions; they

84. This alliance between Sarah and Hagar, Isaac and Ishmael is discussed in David J. Zucker, "The Mysterious Disappearance of Sarah," *Judaism* 55 (Fall/Winter 2006): 3-4, 30-39.

85. Genesis 16:14 refers to a well at Beer Lehai Ro-i. There, Hagar finds sustenance when she is in the desert. One can extrapolate that this well is an oasis, for, as mentioned below, Isaac also will live there (Gen. 24:62; 25:11). Beer Lehai Ro-i is mentioned only in Genesis, and the name itself means "the Well of the Living One who sees me." Though its locale is unknown today, it was somewhere in the Negev, perhaps twenty-five miles or so southwest of Beersheba, between Qadesh and Bered (Gen. 16:14). Bered is associated with the Nabatean ruins at Halutza (Elusa), some twelve miles southwest of Beersheba. *Encyclopedia Judaica* (Jerusalem: Keter, 1972), 6:690. Qadesh is probably some fifty miles southwest of Beersheba. Martin Noth, *Numbers: A Commentary* (Philadelphia: Westminster, 1968), p. 106.

86. Though it is not part of the classical rabbinic writings, in the *Testament of Abraham* (Recension A) Sarah overhears Abraham and Isaac crying in a loud voice because Isaac is going to be sacrificed. *Testament of Abraham* (Recension A), in James H. Charlesworth, ed., *The Old Testament Pseudepigrapha*, vol. 1 (New York: Doubleday, 1983), 5:11-14. The *Testament of Abraham* was written by an Egyptian Jew (or Christian?) around the second century c.e.

87. Sarah's age at her death "surpasses the ideal 120 with the sacred number of 7." Eskenazi and Weiss, eds., *The Torah: A Women's Commentary*, p. 113.

impact on Isaac's age at the Binding. If Genesis 23 follows directly on Genesis 22, then Isaac would be thirty-seven years old, for he was born when Sarah was ninety. If Genesis 22, however, follows reasonably soon after Genesis 21, then Isaac would still be a child. The figure of Isaac in Genesis 22, moreover, appears to be that of a young person. The Bible does not address this vital issue of Isaac's age at the Binding. Nor are there any statements as to where Sarah was living, much less what she was doing, between the time she was last seen about age ninety-three at Isaac's weaning and her death more than three decades later. The Bible simply does not address the matter of the intervening years. The classic rabbinic texts likewise do not mention it, though there are some comments as to whether or not Sarah and Abraham were living together when she died at Kiryat Arba/Hebron.[88]

The midrashic tradition, however, does offer some answers as to what precipitated Sarah's death at age 127. These sources would require Isaac to be thirty-seven years old at the time of the Binding/*Aqedah*, contrary to the sense of the biblical text, which pictures him as a child.[89]

One midrash suggests that, following the binding, Isaac himself returned home alone and reported the strange events of Mt. Moriah. "When Isaac returned to his mother, she asked him, 'Where have you been, my son?' He answered her, 'Father took me, led me up mountains and down valleys, took me up a certain mountain, built an altar, arranged the wood, bound me upon it, and took hold of a knife to slay me. If an angel had not come from heaven and said to him, "Abraham, Abraham, lay not your hand upon the lad," I would have been slain.' On his mother, Sarah, hearing this, she cried out, and before she had time to finish her cry her soul departed."[90]

There are several variations of this midrash. In one source, the evil angel Sammael (alternatively Satan) goes to Sarah and tells Sarah what her husband has done with Isaac. "'Your husband Abraham has taken your son Isaac and slain him and offered him as a burnt offering upon the altar.' She began to weep and cry aloud three times, corresponding to the three sustained notes [of the Shofar, the ram's horn sounded on the Jewish New Year], and (she gave forth) three howlings corresponding to the three disconnected short notes [of the Shofar] and her soul fled, and she

---

88. See the comments of Rashi and Ramban on Gen. 23:2. For a fuller discussion of what happened to Sarah, and where she might have been during those years, see David J. Zucker, "The Mysterious Disappearance of Sarah."

89. See David J. Zucker, "Isaac: Betrayed and Triumphant," *Jewish Bible Quarterly* 38.3 (July-September 2010).

90. *Midrash Ecclesiastes Rabbah* 9.7.1; *Pesikta de Rab Kahana, Piska* 26.3.

died."[91] In another source, Isaac brings her the news, and she utters the six cries and then she dies.[92]

There also is a tradition that Satan comes to tell Sarah about the incident on the mountain, and she answers him that Abraham is correct to follow God's will.[93]

Sarah's eulogy

The latter section of Proverbs 31 describes the "capable wife." She is responsible and industrious. She manages a well-to-do household. She increases the economic worth of the household. The woman deals with both wool and flax. She both considers and purchases property. She arranges the planting of vineyards. She assigns tasks for her servant girls. According to midrashic tradition, these words were Abraham's eulogy for Sarah.

> WHO CAN FIND A GALLANT WIFE? [Prov. 31:10]. About whom were the words spoken? <They were spoken about Sarah> since it is written (. . . in Gen. 23:2): AND ABRAHAM PROCEEDED TO MOURN FOR SARAH AND WEEP FOR HER, <i.e.,> he began to weep and eulogize. So he said: When shall I be able to get <another wife> like you? (Prov. 31:10) A GALLANT WIFE: This was Sarah, as stated (in Gen. 12:11): SEE HERE NOW, I KNOW THAT YOU ARE A BEAUTIFUL LOOKING WOMAN. (Prov. 31:10, cont.:) HER VALUE WAS FAR BEYOND THAT OF RUBIES, in that you came from afar. Thus it is stated (in Is. 46:11): SUMMONING A BIRD OF PREY FROM THE EAST, MY CONFIDANT FROM A FAR COUNTRY. (Prov. 31:11:) HER HUSBAND'S HEART HAD CONFIDENCE IN HER: This was Sarah, as stated (in Gen. 12:13): [PLEASE SAY YOU ARE MY SISTER] SO THAT IT MAY BE WELL WITH ME BECAUSE OF YOU. (Prov. 31:11, cont.:) AND HE HAS NO LACK OF PROFIT. This refers to our father Abraham, of whom it is stated (in Gen. 13:2): NOW ABRAHAM WAS VERY RICH. (Prov. 31:12) SHE DID GOOD FOR HIM AND NOT EVIL. This refers

91. *Pirke de Rabbi Eliezer,* ch. 32. In *Midrash ha Gadol* the messenger is Satan, not Sammael. Genesis 1.327.

92. *Midrash Leviticus Rabbah* 20.2.

93. When Sarah hears that Abraham has taken Isaac to sacrifice him, she faints. Then she rouses herself and says, "All that God told Abraham, may he do it unto life and peace." Louis Ginzberg, *The Legends of the Jews,* trans. Henrietta Szold (Philadelphia: Jewish Publication Society, 1909), 1:278.

to Sarah, since it is stated (in Gen. 12:16): AND BECAUSE OF HER, IT
WENT WELL WITH ABRAHAM.[94]

Sarah's burial place; her age at death

Sarah died and was buried at Kiriyat Arba/Hebron (Gen. 23:1-2). Abraham,
who is the only family member present, seeks to purchase land for a permanent sepulcher. That place, Kiriyat Arba, translates as City of Four. The
rabbis asked, Who were these four? Among the answers were four very special women, Eve, Sarah, Rebecca, and Leah, and four couples, Adam and
Eve, Abraham and Sarah, Isaac and Rebecca, Jacob and Leah.[95]

Sarah is also unique among biblical women, in that both her age at
her death and her burial place are noted.

Additional Comments about Sarah

As the first matriarch, Sarah is unique and merits special attention by the
rabbis.

Sarah's continuing influence

When Isaac finally marries Rebecca, he "brought her into his mother Sarah's tent . . . and she became his wife; and he loved her. So Isaac was comforted after his mother's death" (Gen. 24:67). As the first matriarch, Sarah
holds a special place in the minds of the rabbis. Taking Rebecca into Sarah's tent gives the rabbis a chance to compliment (and complement) both
Sarah and Rebecca. "As long as Sarah lived, a cloud [signifying the Divine
Presence] hung over her tent; when she died the cloud disappeared; but
when Rebecca came, it returned. As long as Sarah lived, her doors were
wide open; at her death that liberality disappeared; but when Rebecca
came, that openhandedness returned." This midrash then cites several
other special acts that were associated first with Sarah, and then latterly
with Rebecca.[96]

---

94. *Midrash Tanhuma, Genesis, Hayye Sarah,* 5.3 Genesis 24:1ff., Part III. *Midrash
Tanhuma-Yelammedenu,* Genesis 5.4, p. 157.

95. *Midrash Genesis Rabbah* 58.4; Babylonian Talmud *Eruvin* 53a; *Sotah* 13a.

96. *Midrash Genesis Rabbah* 60.16.

There is a tradition that, following her death, the image of Sarah appeared in her tent; Isaac drew comfort from this, as he looked upon it daily.[97]

Sarah is a princess, a prophet, and a provider

Sarah is a princess. The Hebrew word *sar* means "prince" (cf. Isa. 9:6 [9:5 H], *Sar shalom* — Prince of Peace). Sarah, the feminine version of *sar*, therefore translates as "princess." "Formerly she was a princess [Sarai] to her own people only, whereas now she is a princess [Sarah] to all humankind."[98]

Sarah is a prophet. The rabbis suggest that Sarah is the same person as Iscah, Haran's daughter (Gen. 11:29). "Rabbi Isaac observed, Iscah was Sarai, and why was she called Iscah? Because she foresaw [the future] by holy inspiration" (the Hebrew word Iscah is connected to the Aramaic root *sacah* [*sin-khaf-alef*], which means to gaze or to look).[99] Elsewhere Sarah is counted as one of seven female prophets (along with Miriam, Deborah, Hannah, Abigail, Huldah, and Esther).[100]

There is an additional understanding that Sarah was superior to Abraham in her prophecy; she was able to discern that Ishmael was wicked.[101] Aviva Gottlieb Zornberg explains that "Sarah who could tell Abraham . . . 'Cast out that slave woman and her son' . . . demonstrates not only inflexible will but an apparent lucid vision of reality that is hidden from the more entangled emotions of Abraham: 'The matter disturbed Abraham greatly, for it concerned a son of his ([Gen.] 21:10-11).'"[102]

Sarah is a provider. As noted above, in the section on Sarah's eulogy, she also was a provider for her family.

God spoke directly only to Sarah

God conversed with Sarah, teasing her for her lack of faith (Gen. 18:13-15). This is the one and only time, explain the rabbis, when God spoke directly to a woman. This greatly enhances Sarah's reputation. "Rabbi Judah bar

97. *Zohar*, 1.133b.
98. Babylonian Talmud *Berakhot* 13a; *Midrash Genesis Rabbah* 47.1.
99. Babylonian Talmud *Sanhedrin* 69b.
100. Babylonian Talmud *Megillah* 14a.
101. *Midrash Exodus Rabbah* 1.1; *Midrash Tanhuma-Yelammedenu*, Exodus 1.1, pp. 313-14.
102. Zornberg, *Genesis*, pp. 134-35. Cf. *Midrash Genesis Rabbah* 53.11.

Rabbi Simon, and Rabbi Johanan in the name of Rabbi Eleazar ben Rabbi Simon said: The Holy One . . . never condescended to hold converse with a woman save with that righteous one [viz. Sarah]."[103]

Sarah dominated Abraham

Sarah had a powerful influence over Abraham, surmise the rabbis. This was a backhanded compliment. "The Rabbis said: She is her husband's ruler. Usually, the husband gives orders, whereas here we read, 'In all that Sarah says to you, hearken unto her voice' (Gen. 21:12)."[104] On the other hand, the rabbis cite Abraham as an example of how someone profits by listening to his wife.[105]

Sarah and Abraham both were proselytes and actively proselytized

Sarah and Abraham were in themselves the first proselytes to the new faith.[106]

Sarah and Abraham brought people to the knowledge of the one God; Sarah converted the women, and Abraham the men. "Abram took his wife Sarai . . . and the persons whom they had acquired in Haran" (Gen. 12:5).[107]

---

103. *Midrash Genesis Rabbah* 45.10; 48.20 (cf. 53.5). *The Midrash on Psalms (Midrash Tehillim),* trans. William G. Braude (New Haven and London: Yale University Press, 1987), Psalm 9.7. The midrash goes on to say while God spoke directly to Sarah, in Genesis 16 God spoke to Hagar through the medium of an angel.

How does one explain this misogynistic comment? It is important to consider the rabbis in their own time and context. "The shapers and expositors of rabbinic Judaism were men, and the ideal human society that they imagined was decidedly oriented toward men. [The rabbis assumed that women had] lesser intellectual, spiritual, and moral capacities. . . . Rabbinic texts do not grant women a significant role in any aspect of rabbinic Judaism's communal life of leadership, study, and worship." Judith R. Baskin, "Women and Post-biblical Commentary," in Ezkenazi and Weiss, eds., *The Torah: A Women's Commentary,* pp. l-li. See also "Aggadic Attitudes toward Women," in Leilah Leah Bronner, *From Eve to Esther: Rabbinic Reconstructions of Biblical Women,* pp. 1-21. There she notes, "In talmudic life and literature, the proper role of women was restricted to that of wife and mother — enabling roles. Talmudic sources praise women for being supportive of their menfolk and for obeying their husbands and fathers," p. 3.

104. *Midrash Genesis Rabbah* 52.5; 47.1.

105. *Midrash Deuteronomy Rabbah* 4.5.

106. *Midrash Numbers Rabbah* 8.9.

107. *Midrash Genesis Rabbah* 39.14; *Midrash Song of Songs Rabbah* 1.3.3. Cf. *Midrash Numbers Rabbah* 14.11.

This understanding is based on reading the word "acquired" as a synonym for converted, not merely adding members to the household.

> *In the mind of the rabbis, Sarah and Abraham were a perfect couple*

Sarah was blameless in her generation, therefore a fitting mate for Abraham. They made a perfect couple.[108]

> *Sarah as a student*

Sarah was unique among biblical women; she studied Jewish texts, including the Torah, Mishna, and Talmud.[109] How can Sarah engage in writings written years after her death? This is not a problem for the midrashic tradition. According to the rabbis, there is no such thing as linear time when it comes to the Torah. Past, present, and future time merge. They are all part of one undivided continuum.[110]

Conclusion

Sarah is an important figure. Yet, compared to the material written about Abraham, she has a lesser role in the unfolding of the biblical drama. Nonetheless, she is the first matriarch and the mother of the Jewish people. Consequently, she was of great interest to the ancient rabbis of the Talmudic period.

108. *The Midrash on Proverbs,* trans. Burton L. Visotsky (New Haven and London: Yale University Press, 1992), Proverb 19; *Midrash Numbers Rabbah* 14.11; *Midrash Numbers Rabbah* 2.12.

109. *Midrash Ecclesiastes Rabbah* 7.28.1. In the Mishna, the first part of the Talmud, it states, "Whoever teaches his daughter Torah, it is as if he taught her frivolity [or: licentiousness/lasciviousness] (*Mishna Sotah* 3.4). "Rabbi Eliezer believed that women were unfit for Torah study . . . [*Babylonian Talmud Sotah* 21b]. His opinion expressed the dominant rabbinic attitude which limited women's access to traditional Jewish learning for centuries. The sage Ben Azai expressed the opposite point of view, 'A man is obligated to teach his daughter Torah' . . . [*Babylonian Talmud Sotah* 20a]; however, this remained a minority view." Ruth H. Sohn, "Post-biblical Interpretations," in Eskenazi and Weiss, eds., *The Torah: A Women's Commentary,* p. 539.

110. "*Ayn muqdam um'uhar baTorah* — There is neither later nor previous time in the Torah." Babylonian Talmud *Pesahim 6b.*

These rabbis sought to teach values that would enhance Jewish life and bring people closer to their religious traditions and to the presence of God. One way to do this was through legislation, by carefully worded interpretations of biblical laws. Alongside this legal material, they created a more fluid set of writings. Through midrash the rabbis teach their values. The tradition of midrash often takes biblical narratives and uses them as a springboard to develop additional materials about the lives of familiar ancient figures. It is through midrash that the rabbis created a whole other side of Sarah's persona. This is the Sarah as portrayed in classical Jewish texts, the Talmud and many collections of midrash.

The rabbis, for the most part, hold Sarah in great affection. She is the first matriarch, the mother of the Jewish people. They favor her and praise her, but they also recognize her faults. At times, they are critical of her. In their evaluations of Sarah, they necessarily reflect the values, standards, and mores of their own time. The rabbinic Sarah, among other roles, is a loyal wife; someone who supports her husband in his journeys; and a proud mother. She is a powerful figure in her own right. She is a princess, a prophet, and a provider. The rabbinic construction of Sarah is an important adjunct to the biblical Sarah. With their expanded portraits, the rabbis offered a broader and deeper picture: a person who was more complex, a figure who provided additional opportunities for people, and more specifically women, to relate, and engage with.

As modernists, we see Sarah, again, in a different light. Our understanding is a reflection of contemporary sensibilities. The actual words devoted to the biblical Sarah were necessarily limited; what might be said about her is virtually limitless.

"Go to the Root of Your Own Life": Some Contemporary Jewish Readings of the Abraham Saga

David Klatzker

I

Over the last twenty years or so, there has been an explosion of Jewish interest in the figure of Abraham.[1] Not only rabbis but also philosophers, psychologists, journalists, novelists, and artists have discovered or rediscovered the patriarch. To be sure, even Jews who seldom go to synagogue cannot avoid taking the biblical stories more seriously when they see that non-Jews have chosen to study them as well. But something more than Jewish pride is involved. The new readers find the story of Abraham so evocative that they wish to attach it to their own thoughts and life experiences. Moreover, they find themselves stimulated by the very experience of intensive reading — the excitement of filling gaps, finding analogies, and discovering new ideas and unexpected plots and complexities in the biblical texts.[2] The purpose of

1. David Lyle Jeffrey, "Genesis: Warts and All (What Christians Can Learn from Jews about the Bible's First Book)," *Christian Century* 116.13 (April 26, 1999): 77-81, is an intelligent survey of some recent readings. I will add some other interpreters to Jeffrey's list, focusing on how they treat Abraham.

2. The new interpreters often call this kind of intensive reading "midrash." However, despite the superficial similarity of postmodern literary theories to the classical midrashic enterprise, there are significant differences between the two, and the contemporary readers are usually closer to the new critics than to the old rabbis. See David Stern, *Midrash and Theory: Ancient Jewish Exegesis and Contemporary Literary Studies* (Evanston: Northwestern University Press, 1996); Robert Alter, "Old Rabbis, New Critics," *New Republic*, 5 January 1987, pp. 27-33.

this article is to introduce Christians to some contemporary Jewish inter-pretations of the Abraham saga that may have passed under their radar.[3]

The current crop of Jewish readers rarely cite critical academic stud-ies of the Bible, for they are not especially interested in the historical verac-ity or the original meaning of the texts. Instead, they focus on the emo-tional, aesthetic, and philosophical qualities of biblical literature. To these interpreters, the significance of Scripture is its significance to them per-sonally, so they often mix autobiography with their exegesis. Avivah Gottlieb Zornberg's citation of the Hasidic master, Rabbi Mordechai Yosef of Isbitza (nineteenth century C.E.) — that the meaning of *lech lecha* (Gen. 12:1) is "Go to the root of your own life" — may serve as an apt summary of the approach of these readers.[4] To them, the study of the Bible confers a depth of self that is not otherwise obtainable.

I will briefly chart three of the strongest currents flowing through these recent readings of the Abraham stories: (1) a psychologizing and moralizing approach that views Abraham as neither exemplary nor excep-tional, but "only human"; (2) a debate among religious Israelis about the meaning of the binding of Isaac, with special emphasis on the dialectic of submission and protest, and the themes of suffering and consolation; (3) an urgent search for a shared vision of Abraham around which Jews, Christians, and Muslims can unite, on the one hand, and, on the other, se-rious questions as to whether the term "Abrahamic" is likely to distort fun-damental differences among the religions.

II

Many of the new readers are exercised by the moral problematics and psychological dynamics of the "wife-sister" stories in which Abraham compromises Sarah (Gen. 12:10-20; 20:1-18). The first story of the dou-blet is of special interest to Burton Visotzky, the Conservative rabbi and seminary professor who inspired Bill Moyer's television roundtable on

---

3. Although I speak here of Christians of all varieties, I am especially impressed by the genuine interest in Judaism and the Jewish people shown by many Protestant evangelicals. Marvin Wilson has worked tirelessly to develop a Jewish-Evangelical dialogue on Boston's North Shore and nationally. I present this paper to him with gratitude for all that his work has meant to the Jewish community, and to me personally.

4. Avivah Gottlieb Zornberg, *Genesis: The Beginning of Desire* (Philadelphia: Jewish Publication Society, 1995), p. 87.

Genesis.[5] Visotzky provocatively declares that Abram "pimps" Sarai, not to save his skin (he knows that God will protect him), but to get rich (rendering *le-ma'an yitav li*, 12:13, as "that I may turn a profit," in contrast to NJPS, "that it may go well with me"). He depicts Abram as "a scoundrel, a trickster, an amoral profiteer," who takes advantage of the Egyptians' horror at the idea of taking another man's wife, since he is certain that they will pay hush money to avoid a scandal. Visotzky's focus is anthropocentric, so he does not ask why God continues to stand by the self-aggrandizing Abraham. To Visotzky, the very essence of morality is a questioning about morality. Thus, he insists that those who fail to confront the implications of Abram's actions "have a naïve view of religion" and are afraid to face the challenge of "rethink[ing] our accepted Judeo-Christian morality."[6] His remarks raised a firestorm of criticism from many of his rabbinic colleagues and others who found his approach ungenerous and irreverent.[7]

---

5. Rodger Kamenetz, "In the Beginning There Was a Bible Discussion Group, And Then PBS Came Calling," *New York Times*, 20 October 1996, sec 6, p. 64; David Van Biema, "Genesis Reconsidered," *Time*, 28 October 1996, pp. 66-75.

6. Burton Visotzky, *The Genesis of Ethics: How the Tormented Family of Genesis Leads Us to Moral Development* (New York: Crown Publishers, 1996), pp. 24-29. See also Visotzky, *Reading the Book: Making the Bible a Timeless Text* (New York: Schocken, 1991), pp. 59-63. Christian readers are likely to prefer Visotzky's 1991 book for its more extensive use of rabbinic midrash.

7. As one rabbi told other rabbis, "Even if I thought that there was any evidence that Abraham was a scam artist or pimp — and I don't — I would hope I'd think twice, three times or more before I would express that view in a public forum" (from Ravnet, the Conservative rabbis' internet discussion group, 4 November 1996). For some public criticisms, see Rabbi Benjamin Z. Kreitman, "Letter to the Editor," *New York Times*, 10 November 1996, sec. 6, p. 18; Jacob Neusner, "Do-It-Yourself Genesis," *National Review*, 9 December 1996, pp. 61-62.

The biblical scholar Jon Levenson later jumped into the fray, offering some sharp comments on Visotzky. Levenson argues that it is inappropriate to treat the wife-sister motif as a morality tale: "Abram acts *in extremis*, to preserve his life in a famine and in a land known for its sexual debauchery. . . . [Would Sarai] have been better off with him dead and her absorbed indefinitely into Pharaoh's harem[?]" He urges readers to consider the larger theological and ethno-political dimensions of the story, in the context of the entire Torah. Abraham, he writes, even if he does not always behave "at the highest level," is considered by Scripture to be "Abraham-our-father . . . not a figure in a work of fiction." Jon Levenson, "The Conversion of Abraham to Judaism, Christianity and Islam," in *The Idea of Biblical Interpretation: Essays in Honor of James L. Kugel*, ed. Nindy Najman and Judith Newman (Leiden and Boston: Brill, 2004), pp. 4-7. Also see Levenson's critique of Visotzky on the Akedah in his "Abusing Abraham: Traditions, Religious Histories, and Modern Misinterpretations," *Judaism* 47.3 (1998): 259-77.

Although he does not engage Visotsky directly, the *National Review*'s David Klinghoffer, author of *The Discovery of God: Abraham and the Birth of Monotheism,* clearly disagrees with him. Klinghoffer pays scant attention to ethical analysis of Abraham's dilemmas, choosing instead to look at the patriarch the old-fashioned way. He predicates that Abraham was a law-observing "Jew" before Sinai, fulfilling the commandments (or many of them), with circumcision as the preeminent *mitzvah.*[8] Klinghoffer approvingly cites rabbinic midrashim (stories that are explications of a text or meditations upon it) that find evidence of Abraham's zeal to convert pagans to the "gospel" of the One God, based on "the souls they made in Haran" (Gen. 12:5) and the understanding of Genesis 18:1 that Abraham sits at the door to his tent to spot travelers for him to welcome and proselytize. Traditional Judaism regards Abraham not only as the father of the Jewish nation but also as the archetype of a convert, and all converts to Judaism are considered "children of Abraham." It is surely relevant that Klinghoffer himself is a convert to Orthodox Judaism. However, he seems to vacillate somewhat between viewing Abraham as the figure enabling entry into Judaism and as the symbol of a common monotheism validating other religions outside of Judaism.[9]

Regarding the wife-sister motif, Klinghoffer says that it shows the wisdom of the rabbinic notion that "unless periods of separation are built into the relationship, sex between two people will grow stale." Abram and Sarai "offer a recipe for keeping married sex spicy." By ignoring such traditional understandings of the text, he says, modern scholarship supplies "interpretations so mundane that you wonder why anyone bothers reading the Bible."[10]

Nevertheless, the vast majority of the recent interpreters are embar-

8. David Klinghoffer, *The Discovery of God: Abraham and the Birth of Monotheism* (New York: Doubleday, 2003), pp. 145-52. To say that Abraham is "Torah-true" is a traditional Jewish understanding, grounded in an interpretation of Gen. 26:5. See Arthur Green, *Devotion and Commandment: The Faith of Abraham in the Hasidic Imagination* (Cincinnati: Hebrew Union College Press, 1989), especially pp. 24-50.

9. Klinghoffer, *The Discovery of God,* pp. 31-33.

10. Klinghoffer, *The Discovery of God,* p. 76. This is in response to E. A. Speiser's now discredited theory that the wife-sister motif reflects ancient Hurrian legal adoptions of wives as "sisters." On Speiser and more recent historical-critical studies, against the background of traditional Jewish commentaries, see Barry L. Eichler, "On Reading Genesis 12:10-20," in *Tehillah le-Moshe: Biblical and Judaic Studies in Honor of Moshe Greenberg,* ed. Mordechai Cogan, Barry L. Eichler, and Jeffrey H. Tigay (Winona Lake, IN: Eisenbrauns, 1997), pp. 23-38.

rassed by this sort of parochial or halakhic (legal/behavioral) reading of the Bible. Although many of them have an honest desire to discover texts that will anchor their Jewish identity, they feel no need to change their lifestyles. Their questions are more existential. Thus, the secular ethicist Leon Kass tries to reclaim Genesis for today's readers by representing it as "philosophy," by which he means reflections on human nature and guidance for ethical living, without reference to theology — although he acknowledges that the Bible is not strictly philosophical and might even be described as being deliberately "antiphilosophical" in its demand for the awe and reverence of God.[11] In line with his emphasis on the pursuit of human wisdom, he views all of Abraham's trials as related to lessons that the patriarch must learn about marriage or fatherhood. Once Abraham's education is complete, after the binding of Isaac, God does not speak to him again. This emphasis on Abraham's *paideia,* the cultivation of his rational morality, may seem more Aristotelian than biblical, but it leads to some fresh readings of the texts.

In the first wife-sister story, Kass argues that because Abram is not told, he does not understand that God is behind Sarai's deliverance from Pharaoh. Since Abram grows rich from his appalling behavior in Egypt, he has no reason to learn anything at all from the experience. After the subsequent incident in Gerar, when Abimelech impresses Abraham with his "delicate and noble" response to his falsehood, Abraham prays to God for the first and only time in Genesis. Rather than an act of empathy for Abimelech (the first prayer-for-others ever offered, as the rabbis interpreted it), Kass understands this prayer as a tacit acknowledgment of Abraham's guilt. Only then, when Abraham has learned to treat Sarah as an equal partner, do new possibilities arise, and she finally manages to get pregnant. "[The] promised great nation of innumerable descendants . . . depends upon man's proper regard for the status of wife and the meaning of marriage," Kass concludes.[12]

The English novelist Jenny Diski, a secularist who is fascinated by

11. Leon Kass, *The Beginning of Wisdom: Reading Genesis* (Chicago: University of Chicago Press, 2003), pp. 2-3. Kass is not a little surprised by his own newfound interest in Judaism (pp. xiv-xv). However, in line with his basic orientation, he refers more often to Aristotle and Plato than to traditional Jewish biblical commentaries. He also makes frequent use of Robert Alter, *Genesis: Translation and Commentary* (New York: W. W. Norton, 1997), to help him explain the literary features of the text, and Robert Sacks, *A Commentary on the Book of Genesis* (Lewiston, ME: Edwin Mellen Press, 1990), to explore its political implications.

12. Kass, *The Beginning of Wisdom,* pp. 287-88.

biblical storytelling and rabbinic midrash, also examines the complexity of Abram and Sarai's relationship. The title of her first biblical novel, *Only Human,* points to the vulnerability of the characters. When their father decides that they are to marry each other (at ages 23 and 13), Abram and Sarai must learn to think of each other as husband and wife rather than (half-) brother and sister.[13]

Driven by the logic of her imagination, Diski sees a contest between God and Sarai for Abram's affections. She has God say of Sarai, "She thought only that Abram betrayed her when he presented her on a plate to Pharaoh. But it was more profound than that. To betray his human love was one thing, but to betray his trust in me, in *I am,* who had chosen him out of all the world and all of time, that was betrayal indeed. She and I, though rivals for the affection of our chosen one, were more allied than she knew, or would admit to knowing. . . . But I saw something worse than a less than perfect faith. I saw resistance, the old willfulness, the desire to control his own destiny."[14] Nevertheless, God has fallen deeply in love with Abram, and cannot abandon him. Ultimately, God arranges everything to God's advantage. Thus Diski sticks (strangely enough) to the plot of Genesis, although she has vastly expanded the tale.

The most poignant and personal use of the Abram-Sarai stories is that of the classicist and travel writer Daniel Mendelsohn, whose book *The Lost: A Search for Six of Six Million* is an account of his journey around the world to discover the truth behind his family's tragic past in the Holocaust. Interspersed with his interviews and research are brief meditations on Genesis and the classic commentaries of Rashi (Rabbi Shlomo ben Yizhak, eleventh century c.e.). These reflections on the Bible conjure up the religious worldview of many of the murdered Jews and deepen the texture of Mendelsohn's narrative. Although he is an unrepentant secularist, he achieves a partial reconciliation with his Jewish heritage through these scattered explorations of the tradition.

Mendelsohn interprets Abram's abandonment of Sarai to Pharaoh as an example of what oppressed people need to do to survive: "the exploitation of a lie (there is no other word for it) for self-enrichment, the use of

13. Gen. 20:12 says that Sarah is the daughter of Terah but was not born to the same mother as Abraham.

14. Jenny Diski, *Only Human: A Divine Comedy* (New York: Picador, 2001), pp. 145-46. Her second biblical novel, *After These Things* (London: Virago Press, 2004), deals with the near-sacrifice of Isaac, which she sees as having severe repercussions, not only on Isaac and Sarah, but also on Jacob and Rebecca.

the wife to provide a kind of cover story for an escape that became, however improbably, a vehicle for self-enrichment, for the propagation of a successful new progeny in the new land."[15] Here he refers not only to Abram's goal of gaining the resources to establish his family in the promised land, but also to Rashi's comment that he was the forerunner of a greater biblical drama and was eager for his future descendants to leave Egypt similarly rewarded with gifts. Mendelsohn relates this not only to the few members of his family who survived the genocide but also to the Judenrat, the Jewish council in each town that (whether for power and prestige, or in the hope of saving lives) helped the Nazis carry out their plans.

To sum up, most of these interpreters think of Abram and Sarai as people we know, faces in the mirror, in a thoroughly modern and secular drama of relationships, ambitions, failures, and fulfillment. The differences between their approach, and the rabbinic notion that Abraham serves as a founder and moral exemplar, are striking.[16] Yet, no matter how far their degree of separation from Jewish tradition, the new readers find themselves unavoidably gripped by the patriarchal stories.

III

In the history of Jewish thought, the Akedah (binding of Isaac, Gen. 22:1-19) was frequently used to justify devotion. However, because of the centrality of morality to Jewish tradition, the rabbis stopped short of saying that the narrative endorsed "the teleological suspension of the ethical" (Kierkegaard's famous phrase). Many of them insisted that the Akedah was "non-normative" in the sense that it was a one-time event specifically targeting Abraham, and some made Isaac into the real hero of the story, in an effort to honor Jewish suffering and martyrdom.[17] Indeed, it was not until

15. Daniel Mendelsohn, *The Lost: A Search for Six of Six Million* (New York: Harper-Collins, 2006), p. 313.

16. For a discussion of the various techniques used by the medieval rabbis to lessen the moral problematics of the texts, in the context of the Jewish-Christian debate, see David Berger, "On the Morality of the Patriarchs in Jewish Polemic and Exegesis," in *Understanding Scripture,* ed. Clemens Thoma and Michael Wyschogrod (New York: Paulist Press, 1987), pp. 49-62.

17. Louis Jacobs, "The Problem of the Akedah in Jewish Thought," in *Kierkegaard's Fear and Trembling: Critical Approaches,* ed. Robert L. Perkins (Tuscaloosa: University of Al-

the twentieth-century "modern Orthodox" thinkers Yeshayahu Leibowitz and Joseph B. Soloveitchik that the model of Abraham at the Akedah became the very epitome of Jewish religiosity.

In Leibowitz's view, the Akedah serves to repair Abraham's earlier error in judgment, in the second wife-sister story, when he chided Abimelech for a lack of fear of God (Gen. 20:11). Leibowitz argues that Abraham's crucial mistake was his definition of the "fear of God." In truth, he had reduced God to "the supreme chief of police," little more than a symbol of the proper moral order. In the Akedah, he says, Abraham finally learns to think of God in a religiously appropriate way, as not subservient to human needs in the least.[18] This striking interpretation of the biblical story can be understood only in the context of Leibowitz's theological-political thought, which was grounded in a Maimonidean notion of God's radical otherness, and in Leibowitz's own conviction that Judaism in the State of Israel was being corrupted by being made into an instrument to boost nationalism (for example, he fiercely criticized the use of the Western Wall for military ceremonies and political gatherings).

Soloveitchik was known for his systematic unpacking of the conceptual world of Talmudic law. The rabbis emphasized the priests' thoughts during the performance of each step of the ancient Temple ritual, understanding the entire procedure as a kind of inner meditation. Thus, Soloveitchik's interpretation of the Akedah is based on the fine halakhic distinction between the sanctification of an offering and the actual performance of the sacrifice. He suggests that Abraham "gave up Isaac the very instant God addressed Himself to him and asked him to return his most precious possession to its legitimate master and owner. . . . There was no need for physical sacrifice, since experientially Abraham had fulfilled the command before he reached Mount Moriah."[19] In other words, God did

---

abama Press, 1981), pp. 1-9; Ronald M. Green, "Abraham, Isaac, and the Jewish Tradition: An Ethical Reappraisal," *Journal of Religious Ethics* 10 (1982): 1-21; Ze'ev Levy, "On the Aqedah in Modern Philosophy," *Journal of Jewish Thought and Philosophy* 15.1 (2007): 85-108.

18. Yeshayahu Leibowitz, *Judaism, Human Values, and the Jewish State* (Cambridge: Harvard University Press, 1992), pp. 42, 118-19; Jerome Gellman, *Abraham! Abraham! Kierkegaard and the Hasidim on the Binding of Isaac* (Burlington, VT: Ashgate Publishing, 2003), p. 106. I have also benefited from W. Z. Harvey, "Leibowitz on Abrahamic Man, Faith, and Nihilism" [Heb.], in *Avraham, Avi Ha-Ma'aminim*, ed. H. Kasher, M. Hallamish, and Y. Silman (Ramat Gan: Bar-Ilan University Press, 2002), pp. 347-52.

19. Joseph B. Soloveitchik, *Abraham's Journey: Reflections on the Life of the Founding Patriarch* (Jersey City, NJ: Ktav, 2008), pp. 10-12.

not actually reverse the command, since the true sacrifice had already been effected. Drawing on this understanding of the text, Soloveitchik maintains that in the daily prayer, the Amidah, the Jew offers a type of Akedah — he surrenders his "ontic pride" and gives himself up entirely to God.[20]

In many of his essays from the 1970s and 1980s, responding to Leibowitz (his friend) and Soloveitchik (his teacher), the American-born Israeli philosopher Rabbi David Hartman makes the case that the submission of the Akedah is balanced by the argumentativeness of Sodom. As covenant partners, Abraham tests God over the fate of Sodom (Gen. 18:23-25), and God tests Abraham over the fate of his son. The patriarch therefore knows both dignity and terror, autonomy and utter inadequacy.[21] Hartman is a vocal figure in Israeli intellectual life, and his aim is to provide a model for what halakhic Judaism might look like in the Jewish state. He hopes to show that the tension between Akedah-like acquiescence to the tradition (ultra-Orthodoxy, with its rejection of the secular world) and Sodom-like protest against it (secular Zionism, with its rejection of religion and Jewish law) can be resolved only by seeking a middle point between the two, or perhaps by a continual motion between one pole and the other.[22]

In his more recent work, Hartman has an even stronger negative response to the Akedah model, emphasizing Abraham's "integrity and consistency." He writes: "The words 'Here I venture to speak to my Lord, I who am but dust and ashes' [Gen. 18:27] are not those of a Promethean challenger to God but of a lover of God, a humble and reverent religious personality with a strong sense of moral autonomy . . . a religious consciousness that believes that the God you worship would never violate your fundamental moral intuitions of justice and of love."[23] In other words,

20. For some of his thoughts on sacrifice and prayer, see Soloveitchik, "The Lonely Man of Faith," *Tradition* 7.2 (Summer 1965): 5-67; Soloveitchik, *Worship of the Heart: Essays on Jewish Prayer* (Jersey City, NJ: Ktav, 2003).

21. David Hartman, *A Living Covenant: The Innovative Spirit in Traditional Judaism* (New York: Free Press, 1985), pp. 27-32, 81-84, 88, 268-69; Hartman, *Conflicting Visions: Spiritual Possibilities of Modern Israel* (New York: Schocken, 1990), pp. 101-2.

22. See Hartman, *A Living Covenant*, pp. 293-99; Hartman, *Conflicting Visions*, pp. 228, 263-65.

23. Hartman, *A Heart of Many Rooms: Celebrating the Many Voices within Judaism* (Woodstock, VT: Jewish Lights, 1999), pp. 12-14; Hartman, *Love and Terror in the God Encounter: The Theological Legacy of Rabbi Joseph B. Soloveitchik* (Woodstock, VT: Jewish Lights, 2001), pp. 182-87.

For an interesting critique, see Yehudah Gellman, "The Akedah in the Thought of David Hartman," in *Judaism and Modernity: The Religious Philosophy of David Hartman*, ed. Jon-

Abraham's premise is that he can appeal to God on God's own terms, the terms of justice. Hartman's growing criticism of the Israeli religious establishment helps to frame this interpretation. As he observes in an interview, "While [traditional Jews] may feel sympathy, for example, for an *aguna* [an abandoned woman, who is forbidden to remarry, since her husband did not give her a divorce], nevertheless they surrender their moral outrage to halakhic authority. Yet when halakhah violates essential principles of justice, moral outrage is a far more appropriate response."[24]

The Akedah never seems far from the mind of Avivah Gottlieb Zornberg, a traditional Jewish woman with a Ph.D. in English literature from Cambridge, who has emerged on the world scene as the primary contemporary teacher of Torah through postmodern literary and psychological analysis. Her published writings are reworkings of her *shiurim*, extended oral discourses on the weekly Torah portions, which she delivers in Jerusalem, mainly to groups of women, both modern Orthodox Jews and secular intellectuals. Because she prefers to speak in English, she is still a marginal figure in Israel, but she is receiving more attention there all the time.[25]

Zornberg's dazzling (and often dizzying) readings are based on the associations she makes between traditional midrash (in appreciation of the rabbis' sensitivity to the gaps in the biblical texts and their ability to hear echoes of distant passages in nearly any text), the insights of her favorite East European Hassidic commentators (who focus on the interiority of the reading experience), and contemporary philosophers and psychoanalysts (chiefly those who deal with the themes of separation and repair). Because she is careful not to imply that her readings represent the *peshat* (the simple meaning of Scripture, which of course is not so simple), she teaches that interpretations are never completely or uncomplicatedly equivalent to the biblical texts that they accompany. But she also shows how midrashic observations can then be read back into the origi-

---

athan A. Malino (Burlington, VT: Ashgate Publishing, 2004), pp. 171-86. The point of the Akedah, Gellman argues, is that "Abraham learns to transcend paradigmatic thinking altogether." In the end, after having thought it inconceivable that God would act against morality, Abraham accepts the possibility and "attentively listens to what God might say." In other words, he discovers that one's deepest selfhood cannot be identified in certitude with any single paradigm.

24. "Covenant and Moral Sensibility: An Interview with David Hartman," *Havruta: A Journal of Jewish Conversation* 1 (Spring 2008): 6.

25. See Tamar Rotem, "And God Created Woman" [Heb.], *Haaretz*, 3 August 2002.

nal texts, in a dynamic process that "loosen[s] the fixities" of preconceived readings.[26]

Zornberg imaginatively reinvents the text to explain why Abraham was willing to fulfill the awful command. In one of her lectures, she depicts God as a psychoanalyst who devises an extreme method to bring Abraham face-to-face with his deepest and most repressed memories, unlocking a heavy burden of emotional pain that goes back to his father Terah's attempt to kill him (based on a midrashic understanding of Gen. 11:28, "And Haran died in the presence of/because of his father Terah" — if it is "because of," did the idolator Terah then seek to murder Abram?). The rabbis probably tell this story to absolve Abraham from the sin of dishonoring his father by leaving him, but Zornberg deepens its meaning. According to her, by allowing him to relive the trauma of filicide, God brings Abraham from compulsive fear to a higher level of self-awareness. Thus the Akedah is not so much a test of faith as a prod to growth. When Abraham marries Keturah (Gen. 25:1), who is identified by the midrash as Hagar, he once again retrieves his past and fixes it.[27]

In another interpretation, Zornberg once again picks up hints from rabbinic literature that Abraham is weighed down by inner anxieties and is far from the man of perfect faith and action that many people still imagine him to be. Based on a Talmudic story that suggests that the Akedah was a punishment for his failure to offer sacrifices, she says that Abraham comes to question the symbolic idiom of his life, the table of hospitality, which is emphasized in the lush descriptions of the feast he serves the three "men" in Genesis 18 and the great banquet he makes to celebrate Isaac's weaning in Genesis 21. He questions whether his festive generosity to others, his giving of food (God's substance), has been anything more than self-indulgence. To help him clarify the meaning of his life, God demands the sacrifice of Isaac. In his obedience, Abraham earns the right to the metaphoric substitution of the ram for his beloved son. This interpretation deepens our appreciation of sacrifice as an attempt to satisfy one's spiritual longing for God, who becomes "a real Presence" in sharing the offering.[28]

In a third reading, Zornberg focuses on what might be called "the Akedah of the mother" (my phrase, not hers, for her approach is not explic-

26. Zornberg, *Genesis,* p. xii.

27. Zornberg, "Abraham Bound and Unbound," unpublished lecture, Pardes Institute, Jerusalem, 2003.

28. Zornberg, *Genesis,* pp. 97-122.

itly feminist). She cites Rashi's comment, itself based on an ancient midrash, that the death of Sarah is narrated immediately after the Akedah, "because, as a result of the tidings of the Akedah — that her son had been prepared for slaughter, and had been all but slaughtered — she gave up the ghost."[29] The binding precedes her death because it leads to her death. But why should the knowledge that Isaac is still alive be so traumatic as to kill her?

Zornberg suggests that Sarah "dies of the truth of *kime'at shelo nishhat* [Rashi's statement that 'he had been all but slaughtered'] — of that hair's breadth that separates death from life. This is what Sartre calls 'contingency,' the nothingness that 'lies coiled in the very core of being, like a worm.'" In other words, the news that Isaac survives changes nothing — it is not exactly shock but "vertigo," a condition of "radical doubt," that kills her.[30] She relates this to Sarah's characteristic "acuity, the laser beam that disentangles complexity and cuts to the quick, [which] makes her vulnerable when all structures and uncertainties are undermined."[31] As another example of Sarah's quality of *din*, strict judgment, Zornberg points to the matriarch's instantaneous understanding that Isaac and Ishmael cannot live together.

Although she never refers directly to current events, those who heard Zornberg deliver her lecture probably sensed that she was doing something more than simply describing Sarah's literary persona, or making a philosophical observation about the impossibility of full joy in the world. They most likely thought that she was communicating some of her own feelings (and theirs) about the experience of living in Jerusalem in a period when the fear of suicide bombers was omnipresent.[32]

---

29. Zornberg, *Genesis*, p. 123. For a transcript of her original Torah lesson that reflects the magic of her teaching, including her rapid-fire citations from her favorite interpreters, see Zornberg, "Cries and Whispers: The Death of Sarah," in *Beginning Anew: A Woman's Companion to the High Holy Days*, ed. Gail Twersky Reimer and Judith A. Kates (New York: Touchstone, 1997), pp. 174-200.

30. Zornberg, *Genesis*, pp. 128, 130, 134.

31. Zornberg, *Genesis*, p. 135.

32. I would suggest that Zornberg's near-obsession with the binding of Isaac reflects the pervasiveness of the Akedah motif in Israeli culture. On that theme, see Avi Sagi, "The Meaning of the Akedah in Israeli Culture and Jewish Tradition," *Israel Studies* 3.1 (1998): 45-60; Yael Feldman, "Isaac or Oedipus? Jewish Tradition and the Israeli Aqedah," in *Biblical Studies/Cultural Studies: The Third Sheffield Colloquium*, ed. J. C. Exum and S. Moore (Sheffield: Sheffield Academic Press, 1998), pp. 159-89; Anat Zanger, "Hole in the Moon or Zionism and the Binding (Ha-Akeda) Myth in Israeli Cinema," *Shofar* 22.1 (2003): 95-109; A. B. Yehoshua, "From Myth to History," *AJS Review* 28.1 (April 2004): 205-12.

Another noteworthy treatment of the Akedah is that of Rabbi Yoel Bin Nun.[33] As a young man, Bin Nun was a founder of the West Bank settlers' group that in the 1970s became Gush Emunim, or Bloc of the Faithful. Although he still lives on the West Bank and hopes that the majority of the Jewish settlements will survive in these uncertain times, he now accuses the more extreme settlers of condoning violence and splitting the Israeli public. Among the "national-religious" (that is, religious-Zionist) camp, the Gush Emunim were unusual in their appeal to the Bible for inspiration, since most Orthodox Jews focused more on Talmud than Bible and preferred the study of the semicanonical commentaries on Scripture to the writing of new ones.[34] Bin Nun took the Gush Emunim approach to the biblical texts and extended it. He is unusual among traditionalists in his willingness to cite historical-critical and archaeological studies (mainly to argue against those studies), but he always uses the traditional rabbinic commentaries as a springboard for his exegesis, because he shares the rabbis' respect for the holistic nature of the texts, and especially because he agrees with them that the biblical patriarchs not only teach lessons but also imprint history with patterns that are continually reenacted.[35]

In wrestling with the Akedah, he highlights the commentary of Rashbam (Rabbi Samuel ben Meir, twelfth century c.e.), who viewed the ordeal as a punishment imposed on Abraham for having made a treaty with Abimelech (Gen. 21:22-34). "After these things" (22:1) refers to the treaty. In Rashbam's view, Abraham should have had greater faith in God's promises than to make a covenant with the pagan prince.

Following Rashbam's lead, Bin Nun notes numerous linguistic and

33. Yoel Bin Nun, *Pirke ha-avot: 'Iyunim be-farashiot ha-Avot be-Sefer Bereishit* (Alon Shevut: Tevunot, 2003), pp. 100-119. Unfortunately, most of Bin Nun's biblical studies have not yet been translated into English.

34. Uriel Simon, "The Place of the Bible in Israeli Society: From National *Midrash* to Existential *Peshat*," *Modern Judaism* 19 (1999): 217-39.

35. On Bin Nun's approach to Scripture, see Hayyim Angel, "*Torat Hashem Temima*: The Contributions of Rav Yoel Bin Nun to Religious Tanakh Study," *Tradition* 40.3 (2007): 5-18. It is worth mentioning two other exegetes whose methodology is similar to Bin Nun's, Rabbis Mordechai Breuer and Menachem Leibtag. See Meir Ekstein, "Rabbi Mordechai Breuer and Modern Orthodox Biblical Commentary," *Tradition* 33.3 (1999): 6-23, and the articles (in English) on Leibtag's website, http://www.tanach.org. Like Bin Nun, Breuer and Leibtag are associated with the Israeli journal *Megadim* (= "choice fruits," Cant. 7:14). They focus on the literary and thematic ties between biblical stories and use the classic Jewish commentaries dialectically.

thematic parallels between the Abimelech story and the Akedah.[36] Nevertheless, he sees Rashbam's reading as partially flawed, and thereby expresses his disagreement with the extremists among the settlers, who have opposed all compromise with the Palestinians. Bin Nun argues that Genesis does not regard Abimelech as a completely evil figure, in contrast to Pharaoh, Hamor, and Shechem. Although Abimelech is admonished by God for taking Sarah, he vigorously protests that he knows adultery to be a "great sin" and has not touched the woman (20:4-5, 9). Unexpectedly, he makes a generous offer to Abraham: "Here, my land is before you; settle wherever you please" (20:15).

Rather than interpret the "covering of eyes" in 20:16 as Abimelech's attempt to offer cash for a "cover-up," Bin Nun suggests that he is arranging for a formal marriage of Abraham and Sarah (a "thousand pieces of silver" means a bride price, a "covering of eyes" means a veil, and "you are cleared before everyone" means that the ceremony is properly witnessed). He contrasts Abraham's subsequent oath to Abimelech (21:23-24) with God's oath to Abraham after the binding of Isaac (22:15-18). The oath to Abimelech explicitly includes a promise of land, while Abraham receives no such assurance (or rather reassurance) in the wake of his ordeal on Mount Moriah.[37]

It follows from Bin Nun's reading that Abimelech and Abraham have reached the same stage of moral/spiritual development — an average level, but not the highest — just as they are tied to each other in covenant and oath. But why then is Abraham more worthy of God's blessings than Abimelech? Bin Nun argues that the Akedah is meant to answer that very question. Contrary to Rashbam, it is not a punishment of Abraham, but rather a test that reconfirms his suitability for the divine promise, after his descent into Gerar and the land of the Philistines. Although the angel that stays Abraham's hand does not corroborate the promise of the land, it is enough that God saves Isaac's life — a kind of "second birth" even more miraculous than the first, similar to God's wondrous rescue of Ishmael by the angel (21:17-20). Moreover, the story of the Akedah leads immediately to the mention of Nahor's children, among them Bethuel, the father of

36. Gen. 20:6 and 22:16 (God spares Abimelech and Abraham does not spare Isaac), 20:8 and 22:3 (Abimelech rises early in the morning to summon Abraham, just as Abraham rises early to fulfill God's command), 20:10 and 22:17 (the phrase "you have done this thing" is repeated), 20:11 and 22:12 (Abraham rebukes Abimelech for his putative lack of the fear of God, and the angel praises Abraham for the fear of God he displays at the Akedah).

37. Compare Gen. 22:15-18 to 12:1, 24:7, and 26:3.

Isaac's future wife, Rebecca (22:20-23). Ultimately, as Bin Nun sees it, the Torah accents the consolation of national continuity.[38]

Bin Nun concludes homiletically, saying that he does not know why God continues to test Abraham's seed to this day, but he is convinced that God chose Abraham because of his deep commitment. Abraham's descendants never demand their personal deliverance as a reward for their loyalty. Rather, what they seek is the canonical promise of progeny and land — in fact, in Genesis 12:7, the land is not promised to Abram, but to his offspring. Bin Nun adds that the Akedah should serve as an inspiration for Israeli parents not "to pull their sons away from the battle for our right to exist as an independent and sovereign people in our land," an apparent reference to the ultra-Orthodox Jews who do not serve in the army.[39]

These diverse reflections on the Akedah show how the biblical text is dramatically alive and debated in Israel, as religious Jews look to the story to help them define their personal and collective identity.

IV

Today's Jewish readers have hardly anything to say about Christian understandings of the Abraham story that emphasize his faith, following Paul's emphasis on faith over works. Contrary to earlier generations of Jews, they do not seem interested in exploring that issue either textually or theologically. Perhaps this is a reflection of improved Jewish-Christian relations, but a less sanguine explanation would point to aspects of the contemporary cultural situation that impact both Jews and Christians. In a world in which the electronic media prevail, there is greater emphasis on the nonverbal. Moreover, there is a new romanticism that privileges feeling over thought. Consequently, there is far less interest in reading traditional texts, and much greater ignorance of how to read them.[40]

38. To strengthen this notion, Bin Nun turns our attention to Rashbam's understanding of the *toldot* formula in Genesis (6:9; 25:19; 37:2). According to Rashbam, whenever the Torah speaks of "generations," it emphasizes that the new generation has been saved (from the flood, the Akedah, or Laban).

39. Bin Nun, *Pirke ha-avot*, pp. 118-19.

40. My thanks to Professor Alan Berger for engaging me in discussion on this topic.

A small sample of 1000 American Jews shows that only 7 percent think that the study of Jewish texts is "essential," 35 percent describe it as "desirable," and 54 percent say it "doesn't matter." See Steven M. Cohen and Arnold M. Eisen, *The Jew Within: Self, Family and Commu-*

Because the concerns of previous generations do not resonate for them, it is only natural that many Jews today focus more on current events and the contemporary "clash of civilizations." In their theological and historical unawareness, it comes as a shock, especially to American Jews, that the Abraham story is often manipulated by extremists who use it to justify exclusivism and violence.

The title of Bruce Feiler's travelogue, *Abraham: A Journey to the Heart of Three Faiths,* a book that spent many weeks on the bestseller list, reflects the popular American assumption that Abraham serves as the bridge between Judaism, Christianity, and Islam. Feiler, who describes his Reform Jewish bar mitzvah début in Savannah and subsequent departure from home, which reminds him of God's call to Abraham to "go forth," travels to Israel in the wake of the September 11 attacks. He interviews rabbis, priests, imans, archaeologists, biblical scholars, shopkeepers, and taxi drivers, hoping to discover the underlying unity of the three traditions. Feiler gives an extraordinarily short introduction to the various permutations of the Abraham story. Perhaps he thinks his readers will find it all too complicated. He finds commonalities even in unlikely places, as when he comments that "All three monotheistic faiths force their adherents to confront the most unimaginable of human pains: losing a child. The binding, the crucifixion, and the *dhabih* — often viewed as distinguishing the monotheistic faiths — actually illustrate their shared origins."[41] But surely the devil is in the details of these different constructions of the story, as Feiler himself seems to understand, since he briefly touches on how the traditional Jewish-Christian debate focused on the theological meaning of the Akedah, while the Jewish-Christian-Muslim debates centered on the ethnic identity of the victim.

Feiler has remarkable perseverance. Even his encounter with Masoud

---

nity in America (Bloomington: Indiana University Press, 2000), p. 7. However, it should be noted that there has been a rapid growth in the number of Judaic studies courses at American colleges (although not all of the classes involve text study), and a marked increase in adult Bible study groups. In Israel, among secularists, a similar situation holds. Despite considerable estrangement from the traditional sources, a sense of cultural insufficiency has led to a modest "return to the Jewish bookshelf" since the 1990s. See Yairah Amit, "Has the Power of the Bible Decreased?" [Heb.], *Zmanim* 95 (2005); Yoram Bronowski, "Breathing New Life into the Book of Books" [Heb.], *Haaretz,* 26 March 1999; Shiri Lev-Ari, "All Study, All Night" [Heb.], *Haaretz,* 25 May 2004.

41. Bruce Feiler, *Abraham: A Journey to the Heart of Three Faiths* (New York: William Morrow, 2003), p. 108.

al-Fassed, a Jerusalem iman who tells him that "Abraham is the father of one religion, and that religion is Islam" (the cleric also says that the Holocaust and the events of September 11 fulfilled the will of God), does not deter him from looking for more temperate voices.[42] Surprisingly, the very next day, he discovers the iman of the El-Aqsa mosque, who turns out to be the soul of reasonableness.

Nevertheless, by the time the book reaches its end, Feiler recognizes that most of his interviewees have been moderate religionists. He wonders whether they are as representative of their communities as the hateful Jerusalem iman, or the Jewish settler in Hebron who tells him that the single example of Isaac and Ishmael coming together to bury their father (Gen. 25:9) is hardly enough to inspire him to seek coexistence with Muslims. In order not to lose hope, Feiler tries to imagine an Abraham who "is not Jewish, Christian or Muslim," but is "a personification of the biological need we all share to be protected by someone, something, Anything."[43] Feiler's re-created Abraham is also a risk-taker and a seeker of social unity — in short, someone who sounds a lot like Feiler himself. But why should believers feel that he honors them when he is only interested in the elements of their traditions that coincide with his vision of Abraham? Feiler's failure to adjust to the hermeneutical and theological contexts of scripture study in the three traditions undoubtedly makes his proposal a hard sell.

Reconstructionist rabbi Nancy Fuchs-Kreimer is better prepared than Feiler for the culture of dialogue. She is not interested in finding a "lowest common denominator" to unify the three faiths. She observes that it would be counter-productive for Jews, Christians, or Muslims to tell each other that the founding story on which they base their identity is only an interpretation, for that cuts both ways. It would also be foolish to try to invent a new foundation. "Our job," she writes, "is to keep telling the old stories in new ways so that our tradition continues to speak to us." She understands that having a common father "is not necessarily the best basis for unity," since Abraham's children still fight over who is the most beloved. Although it would be nice to think that the mothers could bring us together, she is also aware of the limitations of that approach, for "we actually are not full siblings — the Jews are the descendants of Sarah, the Muslims are the descendants of Hagar . . . [and] where do the Christians come in?" As for Abraham himself, she sees no

---

42. Feiler, *Abraham,* pp. 178-81.
43. Feiler, *Abraham,* p. 216.

way to reclaim him as a common forefather, because of "his favoritism, his absolutism, his murderousness."[44]

Instead, Fuchs-Kreimer suggests creating an "interreligious midrash" rooted in the stories of all three religions. She invites the parties to meditate on the angel, God's messenger, who protected Ishmael and told Abraham to lay down his hand against Isaac — the "angel of compromise, of mediation, of working things out bit by bit." She hopes that Abraham's offspring will heed the angel's advice to "Split the difference. Try a middle way. Make up a new blessing."[45] Whatever the value of Fuchs-Kreimer's new midrash, at least she recognizes the usefulness of having the three peoples read and comment on each other's stories.

The avant-garde opera "The Cave," by the husband-and-wife team of composer Steve Reich and videographer Beryl Korot, takes a unique approach to the same issues of parental favoritism and sibling rivalry.[46] Reich and Korot evoke the wounded family of Abraham by projecting video images on five large screens. Interviewees — Israeli Jews (Act 1), Palestinians (Act 2), and Americans (Act 3) — describe the Cave of the Machpelah and give their impressions of the patriarch and his family. Their words are "doubled" (re-created) by onstage musicians and singers. Reich, who has long been interested in biblical Hebrew cantillation, uses the speech melody of each interviewee to draw a kind of musical portrait of that person.[47] Texts from the Bible and Qur'an also appear on screen.

Most of the American speakers merely confirm their ignorance of history and religion (e.g., "Abraham Lincoln High School . . . that's about as far as I trace Abraham"). As Korot notes in an interview, "There is really no cave in America — there is no umbilical cord, the connections are very thin."[48] However, when the Israeli and Palestinian believers tell their stories, the "enemies" show themselves to be remarkably similar to each other. They all take the questions posed by Reich and Korot seriously and approach their texts with humility. Each side self-consciously shares much

44. Nancy Fuchs-Kreimer, "Jews, Christians and Muslims Face Modernity Together," *Journal of Ecumenical Studies* 30.3-4 (Summer-Fall 1993): 436-38.

45. Fuchs-Kreimer, "Jews, Christians and Muslims," pp. 439-40.

46. Steve Reich, *The Cave* [CD with accompanying booklet] (New York: Nonesuch, 1995).

47. Antonella Puca, "Steve Reich and Hebrew Cantillation," *The Musical Quarterly* 81.4 (Winter 1997): 537-55.

48. Jonathan Cott, "Beryl Korot and Steve Reich on *The Cave*," in *The Cave* (New York: Boosey and Hawkes, 1993), p. 13.

scripture with the other, even as it ridicules its rival. Reich and Korot do not add any editorial comments, and the audience is left to draw its own conclusions — a remarkably low-key and passive approach.

Thus, unlike "biblical calls for reconciliation" — as in Burton Visotzky's 1996 sermon that Abraham's willingness to buy the Machpelah for an exorbitant price in Genesis 23 should be a lesson to Israelis "to give and give to have security in the land"[49] — Reich and Korot prefer not to preach. The opera culminates with classical midrash, as they present the story from Pirke de-Rabbi Eliezer that Abraham ran to fetch a calf to feed his guests, but the calf escaped into the Cave of the Machpelah. Abraham followed it and saw Adam and Eve on their biers.[50] For Reich and Korot, the point of the legend seems to be that lands are defined by possession, but places are defined by myth.

Clearly, there are many different ways in which Jews are trying to come to grips with today's "theo-politics." But it appears that there is a growing awareness that resolving religiously rooted political tensions will not be achieved by avoiding public discussion of religion, but by learning how to have deeper, more meaningful *religious* conversations about the issues. This new awareness is itself a sign of hope.

V

A rapid overview like this cannot do justice to the variety and intensity of these recent reflections on the Abraham stories. In this postmodern era, when Jewish culture has become so open-ended in the West that it is almost impossible to be certain anymore what it is at all, these new readings of the ancient tales show that the Bible still retains its drawing power.

However, to call the renewed interest in Abraham a "return" to Judaism would probably be an overstatement. For many of the secular readers, there is an ambiguous sense of "going-back-where-we've-never-been" — a feeling that the Bible is their living heritage insofar as they can make use of

49. Gustav Niebuhr, "Religion Journal: A Biblical Call for Reconciliation in the Middle East," *New York Times,* 26 October 1996, sec. 1, p. 31.

50. The story is most readily available in Louis Ginzberg, *Legends of the Jews* (Philadelphia: Jewish Publication Society, 1909-47), vol. 1, p. 289; vol. 5, p. 256. Bernhard Heller, "Ginzberg's Legends of the Jews," *Jewish Quarterly Review* 24.4 (April 1934): 401, 408, suggests a relationship between the Jewish legend and Islamic storytelling. Were Reich and Korot aware of this possible connection?

its language and themes and find moral stimulation in it, but hardly a full acceptance of the biblical frame of reference. As for the religious community, which traditionally put the Torah on a pedestal but neglected it in favor of Talmud study, it appears that many believers are now approaching it in a fresh way, finding in its nuances and allusions deep echoes of the Jewish historical experience and a spiritual language to help them express their own contemporary concerns. But the believers' encounter with the Abraham stories cannot be called *teshuvah* (return) either, since they always had familiarity with the texts, at least to the extent that rabbinic literature grounds itself in Scripture.

Neither the secularists nor the believers find order in the biblical texts. On the contrary, the existential questions that they ask often draw attention to the hints of disorder and instability in the life of Abraham and in the texts that narrate his story. Yet, somehow, Abraham's insecurity becomes a source of comfort for them, as if it validated and made bearable the turbulence of the world around them.

In short, the new readers enter into the biblical narratives as people with their own personal stories and questions of faith and Jewish identity. Like Abraham, who went forth on a spiritual journey, they too seek to go to the root of their own lives.

Elizabeth Boush's "Sacrifice of Isaac": An Eighteenth-Century Object Lesson for Today's Church

LAUREN F. WINNER

In 1768 and 1769, sixteen-year-old Elizabeth Boush of Norfolk, Virginia, stitched a remarkable pictorial embroidery. Measuring 19½ by 11½ inches, the silk on silk embroidery shows a biblical scene: it is the story, found in Genesis 22, of Abraham nearly sacrificing his son Isaac. The needlework captures Genesis 22:10, the moment at which the ram, whom God has sent to be sacrificed in Isaac's stead, appears; Abraham's hand is about to be stayed and his son is about to be spared death.

In this essay, I will read Boush's needlework from two perspectives. First, I will try to read her needlework as she and her fellow eighteenth-century gentry Anglicans would have read it. I will attempt to understand how people like Boush understood both religious needlework and Genesis 22, and I will argue that making this needlework was both a spiritual act that connected her to Scripture and to God and an act that disciplined her, teaching her certain lessons about obedience, gender, and hierarchy. Second, I will ask what lessons this needlework has for us today. Specifically, I will tease out of Boush's needlework a question about the way twenty-first-century Protestants in North America currently approach the task of retrieving spiritual practices from our past.

It is a great pleasure and honor to be able to offer these reflections in honor of Marvin Wilson, whose writing on Abraham has done so much to

---

Portions of this essay are adapted from Lauren F. Winner, *A Cheerful and Comfortable Faith* (Yale University Press, forthcoming, 2010).

shape my own scholarly considerations of Abraham, and whose careful, patient, and yet passionate inquiry into the connections between Judaism and Christianity has helped me, in crucial ways, make sense of my own faith journey. Professor Wilson has been and continues to be for me a model of a generous and hospitable scholar, a wise and winsome teacher, and a devoted and humble follower of the God of Israel. My own effort to connect a rather obscure piece of history — Boush's needlework — with contemporary concerns about spiritual practice is inspired in part by Professor Wilson's refusal of falsely disinterested scholarship; it is inspired, in other words, by Professor Wilson's attention to the many connections between the history and the present practice of our faith. This essay is offered to him with deep gratitude for his work and for the friendship he has extended to me, and with a wish: *Chazak v'chazak.*

And now to Elizabeth Boush's needlework.

Elizabeth Boush's "The Sacrifice of Isaac": An Eighteenth-Century Reading of Genesis 22

When she sat down with her needle and thread to stitch a picture of Genesis 22, Elizabeth Boush was entering into a practice — needlework — with a long, ideologically fraught history. Today, we typically assume that needlework is a naturally female pursuit. But, in fact, the coding of needlework as feminine is part of the history of embroidery. True enough, by the late nineteenth century, needlework was so uniformly understood as a female undertaking that in 1895 Freud could blame women's proclivity for hysteria on "women's handiwork," since sitting with a needle and thread "gives such ample opportunity" for the "daydreams" that were the basis for the hypnoid states that were themselves the "basis and condition of hysteria."[1] But embroidery was not always the provenance of women and girls. In the Middle Ages, both men and women could aspire to be professional embroiderers, and in the fifteenth century needlework actually became more deeply associated with men, as guild regulations began to limit women's ability to achieve the status of master embroiderer.[2] During the

---

1. Sigmund Freud and Joseph Breuer, *Studies in Hysteria,* trans. Nicola Luckhurst (London: Penguin, 2004), p. 15. Cf. Rozsika Parker, *The Subversive Stitch: Embroidery and the Making of the Feminine* (London: The Women's Press, 1984), p. 11.
   2. Parker, *The Subversive Stitch,* p. 67.

seventeenth and eighteenth centuries, embroidery became thoroughly marked as "feminine." In this period, the very act of making needlework became part and parcel of how girls learned to be girls.

Typically, the first piece of needlework a girl made was a sampler. Samplers, now thought of as essentially domestic, were originally artifacts of commerce. Boasting myriad types of stitches, samplers were used as early as the thirteenth century as tools with which Egyptian embroiderers showed off their handicraft to prospective clients. Traveling west across trade routes, samplers became popular in Europe by the Renaissance. Early evidence for European samplers comes from a painting by Joos van Cleve (ca. 1485-1540): his *Holy Family* shows a linen sampler folded on a table, in front of a Madonna and child.[3] By the sixteenth century, samplers were all the rage at the English court. Edward VI owned thirteen samplers, and Shakespeare invoked samplers, with *A Midsummer Night's Dream's* Helena likening her intimacy with Hermia to the threads twinned together in a sampler, and Marcus, in Act II of *Titus Andronicus,* invoking samplers after encountering his niece Lavinia, whose tongue and hands had been cut off: "why she but lost her tongue, / And in a tedious sampler sew'd her mind."[4]

In the seventeenth century, parents and teachers began to appreciate the pedagogical potential of samplers; increasingly, sampler-making came to be seen as an economical and aesthetically pleasing way for girls to perfect their sewing skills. The hope was that making a sampler would teach a girl a dizzying array of stitches: herringbone, hem, flat, French knot, tent, eyelet, cross, and stem, among others. This understanding of samplers is reflected in eighteenth-century dictionaries. A 1730 dictionary defined "samplar" as "a Pattern or Model; also a Piece of Canvas, on which Girls learn to mark, or work Letters and Figures, with a needle."[5] Samuel Johnson's *Dictionary of the English Language* defined a sampler as "a pattern of work; a piece worked by young girl for improvement."[6]

---

3. Pamela A. Parmal, *Samplers from A to Z* (Boston: MFA Publications, 2000), pp. 7-8.

4. Betty Ring, *Girlhood Embroidery: American Samplers and Pictorial Needlework, 1650-1850,* vol. 1 (New York: Knopf, 1983), pp. 6-8; Anne Sebba, *Samplers: Five Centuries of a Gentle Craft* (New York: Thames and Hudson, 1979), p. 23.

5. William Huntting Howell, "'A More Perfect Copy than Heretofore': Imitation, Emulation, and Early American Literary Culture" (Ph.D. diss., Northwestern University, 2005), p. 167.

6. Parmal, *Samplers,* pp. 7-8; Elisabeth Donaghy Garrett, "American Samplers and Needlework Pictures in the DAR Museum, Part I: 1739-1806," in *Needlework: An Historical*

By the mid-eighteenth century, samplers and pictorial needlework were a staple of refined Southern girls' education. This was a time of heated debate about just what girls should learn. Would book-learning defeminize girls and render them "insufferable" instances of "female pedantry" that would frighten rather than attract men?[7] Alternately, would too much time devoted to ornamental "accomplishments" turn girls into coquettes? Should girls learn to dance, or would minuets and reels "allure their fond votaries from the purity and rectitude which are the chief embellishments of female character"? Should they study music, or would girls begin lusting after the praise they received after they took their turn at the piano? Although they differed about jigs and violins, moralists, pedagogues, and parents were in virtually unanimous agreement that needlework was a suitable and important component of girls' educations.[8] Needlework equipped girls with a useful skill, and unlike dancing and music, it kept them silent and immobile, in a chair, and not twirling about, on display.

So needlework was meant to teach elite girls a host of lessons: it was meant to teach them, first of all, to sew. It also taught girls lessons about proper feminine comportment: genteel girls did not show off their bodies in dance or their egos at the piano — they sat quietly and stitched. That was what the *act* of sewing taught girls: how to sew and how to be girls. The content of their needlework taught still more lessons. As map samplers and samplers featuring multiplication tables, calendars, family genealogies, and even complicated division problems suggest, some girls learned geography, arithmetic, family narratives, and timekeeping while also mastering the eyelet stitch.[9] Needlework also schooled girls in social values. As Daniel Roche and Jean Birrell have shown for pre-Revolutionary

---

Survey, ed. Betty Ring (New York: Main Street/Universe Books, 1975), pp. 94-95; Ring, *Girlhood,* p. 11.

7. James Fordyce, *Sermons to Young Women* (London, 1775), p. 33.

8. Catherine E. Kelly, "Reading and the Problem of Accomplishment," in *Reading Women: Literacy, Authorship, and Culture in the Atlantic World, 1500-1800,* ed. Heidi Brayman Hackel and Catherine E. Kelly (Philadelphia: University of Pennsylvania Press, 2008), esp. pp. 125-27, 137.

9. Bianca F.-C. Calabresi, "'You sow, Ile read': Letters and Literacies in Early Modern Samplers," in Hackel and Kelly, eds., *Reading Women,* pp. 79-104. Maureen Daly Goggin, "An *Essamplaire Essai* on the Rhetoricity of Needlework Sampler-Making: A Contribution to Theorizing and Historicizing Rhetorical Praxis," *Rhetoric Review* 21.4 (2002): 323. Cf. Laurel Thatcher Ulrich, "Creating Lineages," in *The Art of Family: Genealogical Artifacts in New England,* ed. D. Brenton Simons and Peter Benes (Boston: New England Historic Genealogical Society, 2002), pp. 9-10.

France, "In teaching how to use needles and pins, mothers, older sisters, and schoolmistresses also taught the principles of good housekeeping, the elements of a female morality, in a word, its 'ways of speaking' and 'ways of doing,' that is, its culture."[10]

And that brings us back to Boush's needlework of the sacrifice of Isaac, a stunning pictorial needlework that shows off an embroiderer who had mastered her art. "The Sacrifice of Isaac" is silk on silk — silk thread on a silk canvas — tent stitch. Tent was a common stitch that originated in Asia and may have spread to Europe as early as the Roman Empire. It is diagonal, like the first half of a cross-stitch, and was popular in the seventeenth and eighteenth centuries as a stitch for cushions and chair coverings.[11] Silk embroidery was extremely difficult. The "Sacrifice of Isaac" could have taken Elizabeth Boush well over a year to complete, and she would have made it only after making at least one sampler. In the early nineteenth century, when silk pictorial embroideries were more common, taught at girls' schools across the country, they were often regarded as "the crowning achievement" of a girl's education.[12] A piece like "The Sacrifice of Isaac" required much more skill than even the most elaborate sampler; this was not practice, but art, a painting made with a needle and thread.

Did Betsey Boush choose the subject of her embroidery herself? We can't know for sure, but it is likely that she had some say in the matter. She didn't *design* the needlework herself, of course — she worked it from a pattern. Since 1977, when needlework historians first began work on Boush's "Sacrifice of Isaac," scholars have thought that the pattern Boush used was based on Gerard de Jode's *Thesaurus Veteris Testamenti*. However, Kathleen Staples has recently determined that the print source for Boush's needlework was more likely Egbert van Panderen's engraving, ca. 1600, after Pieter de Jode's painting. Whereas Gerard de Jode's illustration shows

10. Daniel Roche, *The Culture of Clothing: Dress and Fashion in the Ancien Regime,* trans. Jean Birrell, 2nd ed. (Cambridge: Cambridge University Press, 1999), p. 266. See Ulrich, "Creating Lineages," p. 9.

11. Helen Bowen, "Tent-Stitch Work," in Ring, ed., *Needlework*, pp. 37-40. In the sixteenth century, European embroiderers used the tent stitch for cushions and hangings, and in seventeenth-century England, the tent stitch was the stitch one was likely to find in the dark, floral embroideries covering cushions of dark oak chairs. By the end of the eighteenth century, as people began to favor satin and brocade as upholstery, the fashion for the tent stitch waned.

12. Betty Ring, "Memorial Embroideries by American Schoolgirls," in Ring, ed., *Needlework,* p. 80.

Abraham's raising his left hand, the van Panderen engraving shows, as does Boush's needlework, Abraham's left hand placed atop Isaac's head.[13]

Eighteenth-century colonists had relatively easy access to needlework patterns: although patterns did not become readily available in American printer shops and milliners until after the Revolution, earlier in the century colonists could select patterns from the pages of periodicals, they could order them individually from England, or they could purchase needlework pattern books, which had been available in England and on the Continent since 1523. Catalogues of engravings and prints included patterns that could be used for needlework. According to the *Lady's Magazine,* these patterns enabled a young lady to "display the art with which she can manage her needle." Elizabeth Gardner, Betsey's teacher, did not, like Charleston schoolmistress Jane Voyer, advertise that she herself hand-drew patterns and would teach her students to as well.[14] Nor is there any clear evidence that Norfolk was home to anyone selling patterns before the 1790s, when Eliza Wallace advertised "All kinds of Lady's Fancy Patterns drawn fit for Working."[15] So when she was teaching Betsey Boush in the 1760s, Gardner almost certainly procured her patterns from England — though it is possible that Betsey selected the Isaac scene from a pattern book owned by her mother. In either case, young Betsey surely had some control over which image she would devote over a year to reproducing.[16]

Considered as part of a centuries' long tradition of Anglo girls' and women's embroidery, Genesis 22 seems at first blush an odd subject for Boush to stitch. In the Renaissance era, English girls often stitched biblical scenes featuring women, and strong, heroic women at that: Queen Esther was perhaps the most popular subject, and Judith and Jael, wielding their weapons, appeared frequently as well.[17] But considered in the context of the eighteenth-century South, Boush's choice is not so surprising. Genesis 22 was a commonplace in the visual arts that adorned elite houses in early

13. Many thanks to Kathleen Staples for sharing her yet unpublished discovery with me.

14. Kathleen Staples, "'Plain, Fine, and Fancy,'" in *Sampler and Antique Needlework* 12.1 (*A Proper and Polite Education: Girlhood Embroidery of the American South*) (Spring [March] 2006): 36.

15. Quoted in Staples, "'Plain, Fine, and Fancy,'" p. 36.

16. For a discussion of women's choosing patterns, see Parker, *The Subversive Stitch,* p. 12.

17. Ann Rosalind Jones and Peter Stallybrass, *Renaissance Clothing and the Materials of Memory* (Cambridge: Cambridge University Press, 2000), p. 158.

Virginia. Thomas Jefferson included a painting of the sacrifice of Isaac among the twenty-six biblical paintings he acquired in France (only three of which depicted Old Testament scenes).[18] Illustrated Bibles included a picture of the same scene: Abraham, hand on Isaac's neck, his hand being stayed or his vision arrested by the angel.[19] Nor was Boush the only needleworker to stitch Genesis 22: South Carolina girl Dorothy Jans worked the scene into her 1752 sampler.[20] Boush may have been inspired to work an embroidery about Abraham and Isaac by Samuel Richardson's *Clarissa*. One of Virginia girls' favorite novels, *Clarissa* mentions needlework based on the Isaac story: "'Tis true, this pretty little Miss, being a *very* pretty little Miss . . . who always minded her book, and had passed through her sampler-doctrine with high applause; had even stitched out, in gaudy propriety of colours, an Abraham offering up Isaac."[21]

But what did the image of Abraham and his son mean to Betsey, and to the many friends and relatives who would have gazed upon her handiwork? Scholars of needlework have read her subject as a political statement: Abraham's sacrifice signaled the political sacrifice made by the Boush family, patriots all.[22] Indeed, that is a fairly standard reading of the image of the sacrifice of Isaac in pre-Revolutionary and Revolutionary Virginia: Susan R. Stein, Gilder Curator at Monticello, has suggested that Thomas Jefferson may have found in the painting a symbol of his "political experiences and those of his country. . . . Jefferson and his compatriots, like Abraham, were called upon to test their beliefs and principles, and prevailed."[23]

This political reading is certainly plausible. Yet, however politically suggestive the story might have been, Revolutionary sacrifice was not, in fact, the dominant theme pre-Revolutionary Virginians found in the story

18. Susan R. Stein, *The Worlds of Thomas Jefferson at Monticello* (New York: Harry N. Abrams, 1993), p. 33.

19. See, e.g., the illustration of Genesis 22 in the Tunstall Bible (1716), Small Special Collections, University of Virginia.

20. Ethel Stanwood Bolton and Eva Johnston Coe, *American Samplers* (New York: Weathervane Books, 1973), pp. 28, 56. See also Parker, *The Subversive Stitch*, pp. 89, 96.

21. Samuel Richardson, *Clarissa Harlowe; or, the history of a young lady. Comprehending the most important concerns of private life In a series of letters. By Samuel Richardson; formerly published in eight volumes; the whole now comprised in two large octavo volumes. Embellished with elegant copper-plates* (London: Printed for Alex. Hogg, 1794), p. 728.

22. Kathleen Staples, "Tangible Displays of Refinements: Southern Needlework at MESDA," *The Magazine Antiques* 1 (2007): 200.

23. Stein, *The Worlds of Thomas Jefferson*, p. 70.

of the binding of Isaac. The story occupied a specific and central place in the early modern Anglican imagination, freighted with meanings that resonated not with the Revolutionary political aspirations of colonists determined to break free from England, but rather with the psychological and social imperatives of elite slave owners. To understand the place that Abraham and Isaac occupied in the Anglican Virginians' imagination, we can turn again to the devotional and prescriptive literature that white Anglicans in eighteenth-century Virginia read. The binding of Isaac figures in this prescriptive literature, whose authors read the story as an object lesson in obedience.

Obedience, of course, was a crucially important virtue in eighteenth-century Virginia. It was the moral backbone of the slave system, and it was socially, economically, and psychologically imperative for elite white Virginians to understand themselves both as people who owed a debt of obedience and as people to whom a debt of obedience was owed. In Virginia, each person was yoked to others through clear-cut, reciprocal chains of obedience; the obedience owed white gentry by their slaves was inseparable from the obedience white women owed white men and the obedience that white children owed white parents. Virginia girls occupied their own place in the hierarchy; they learned obedience to parents, and when they graduated from being daughters to being wives they transferred that obedience to their husbands.[24] This elaborate chain of human obedience was set inside the frame of creaturely obedience — everyone owed obedience to God, and the obedience that low-ranking Virginians owed their social betters was often described or understood as expressing that obedience owed to their Creator.

Everyone in Virginia was implicated in obedience, but obedience and duty were gendered. Virginia was a society in which everyone was subject to hierarchy, in which duty defined the lives of both master and servant, parent and child, man and woman; as scholars such as Kathleen Brown have argued, women's obedience was the ideological and domestic lynchpin of the entire social hierarchy.[25] It is not in the context of proto-Revolutionary sacrificial zeal but in the context of a social world in which

24. Martha Saxton, *Being Good: Women's Moral Values in Early America* (New York: Hill and Wang, 2004), pp. 113-14.

25. Kathleen Brown, *Good Wives, Nasty Wenches, and Anxious Patriarchs: Gender, Race, and Power in Colonial Virginia* (Chapel Hill: University of North Carolina Press, 1996), pp. 334, 339.

obedience was a virtue of signal importance and in which girls' obedience had special valence that Boush's "Sacrifice of Isaac" may best be read.

In teaching their children this most basic lesson of obedience, Anglican parents turned to Scripture, in particular to the story of the sacrifice of Isaac. To wit the popular *Plain and Easy Catechism for Children* by Isaac Watts, which draws on the story of Abraham and Isaac to explain faithful obedience in simple terms:

> Q 51. How did Abraham further, and most eminently show his obedience to God?
> A. In readiness to offer up his son Isaac in sacrifice to God's command.[26]

The sacrifice of Isaac appears in the homiletical and devotional literature Anglicans read. Richard Allestree's *The Ladies Calling,* for example, points to Abraham as a model of obedience to God: "it is not only the interest, but the duty of all that have Families, to keep up the esteem and practice of Religion in them. 'Twas one of the greatest endearments of *Abraham* to God, That he would command his household to keep the way of the Lord."[27] This theme was echoed in Anglican homiletical literature, in particular in the sermons of John Tillotson, who dramatically imagined the difficult sacrifice God asked of Abraham: "what conflict this good Man had within himself, during those three daies that he was travelling to the Mountain in Moriah; and how his heart was ready to be rent in pieces, betwixt his duty to God, and his affection to his Child; so that every step of this unwelcome and wearisome journey, he did as it were lay violent hands upon himself." All the more reason, concluded Tillotson, that Abraham is to be praised for his "remarkable," deliberate, and "glorious" obedience.[28] While Kierkegaard, not to mention the rabbis, would help us see that this total obedience reading may not be the most authentic reckoning of the binding of Isaac, it is not surprising that the patriarchs of the early South found the central meaning of the story in the son's embodying obedience to his father and the father's embodying obedience to God, in the story's appar-

---

26. Isaac Watts, *Plain and Easy Catechism for Children* (Boston: Printed by Parmenter and Norton, 1818).

27. Richard Allestree, *The ladies calling in two parts. By the author of The whole duty of man, &c.* (Oxford, 1727), p. 217.

28. John Tillotson, "A Sermon Preached at White-Hall MD CLXXXVI Before the Princess Ann" (published by Ralph Barker), pp. 50-51.

ently seamless yoking together of social, familial, and divine order, and its suggestive connections between obedience in society and obedience to the Lord.

Of course, one wishes for some direct evidence about what Betsey Boush thought about as she stitched her embroidery. How did she think about Isaac? Certainly one can think of biblical examples of daughterly duty, not least the frankly terrifying tale of Jepthe's daughter (Judg. 11:34-40), whose father sacrificed her in fulfillment of a rash vow. (Interestingly, one of Jefferson's three Old Testament paintings depicted this scene, which was also not uncommon in English needlework in the eighteenth century.[29]) Did Boush take a secret delight in seeing that boys, too, were subject to filial and divine duty? Did she even think of Jepthe's daughter? There is no evidence to answer these questions, but it is not unreasonable to suppose that Boush was familiar with the story of Jepthe's daughter, and it is intriguing to speculate that she may have drawn a connection between the two stories.

We can speculate further about one meaning that Boush may have found, years after she stitched it, in her needlework of Genesis 22. Although obedience was the most overt meaning Anglicans attached to it, they were also able to see the sacrifice of Isaac as something more than a code for filial and wifely obedience. Hester Chapone, in her popular *Letters on the improvement of the mind addressed to a young lady,* offered a reading of Genesis 22 that surely would have resonated with and offered solace to Virginia gentlewomen. Like other writers, Chapone offered Abraham as an example of the virtue of obedience. According to Chapone, Abraham's "unshaken faith and obedience, under the severest trial human nature could sustain, obtained such favour in the sight of God, that he . . . promised to make of his posterity a great nation." The tale of Abraham's climb up Mount Moriah "is affecting in the highest degree, and sets forth a pattern of unlimited resignation, that every one ought to imitate, in those trials of obedience under temptation, or of acquiescence under afflicting dispensations, which fall to their lot." This was no abstraction for the women of colonial Virginia, but a palpable encouragement, for every Virginia mother was sure to lose more than one child to illness. "If the almighty arm should be lifted up against" one's child, wrote Chapone, a mother, like Abraham, "must be ready to resign him, and all that we hold dear, to the

29. Stein, *The Worlds of Thomas Jefferson,* p. 33; Parker, *The Subversive Stitch,* pp. 89, 96.

divine will."[30] Documentary evidence suggests that two of Elizabeth's sons died in childhood.[31] Perhaps the story that she had stitched into art comforted her.

Sewing decorative needlework was one way in which girls like Elizabeth Boush learned how to be Christians — in particular, how to be Christian women in a hierarchical slave-owning society. In creating her embroidered "Sacrifice of Isaac," Boush was, at once, mastering the skill of sewing, learning how to read the Bible, and beginning to occupy her God-given station. She was learning how to comport herself with femininity, how to live in relationship to the God of Israel, and how to occupy her place in the hierarchy that eighteenth-century Anglicans believed God wove into the fabric of creation. Needlework, which engaged girls' bodies and located them, in a tactile way, in the stories of Scripture, might have been quite religiously absorbing. Elizabeth Boush likely worked on her embroidery for an hour a day, every day, for over a year — this was a ritualized practice, a time set aside during which, consciously or not, the needleworker was locating herself in a scriptural story. Each stitch may have been meditative, or even a gift to God. At the same time, the religious content of girls' needlework, with its stress on virtue and obedience, disciplined young girls, as did the very act of stitching, which kept girls not just busy but immobile. Making the needlework was an act of obedience to parents and teachers; the needlework itself conveyed lessons about obedience. Stitching Genesis 22 was thus, for Boush, a religious "discipline" in the sense that Richard Foster uses the term "discipline," but it was also a discipline or practice in Pierre Bourdieu's sense. That is, Boush was participating in an activity that regulated and maintained a socio-political structure that relentlessly disciplined the relations of men and women, of slaves and free people.[32] Looking back at Boush's needlework over the distance of centuries, it is easy to judge that her scriptural stitching is not, in fact, piety put to its best uses.

30. Hester Chapone, *Letters on the Improvement of the Mind. Addressed to a Young Lady. In Two Volumes,* vol. 1 (Dublin: Printed for J. Exshaw, H. Saunders, W. Sleater, J. Potts, D. Chamberlaine, J. Williams, and R. Moncriefte, 1773), pp. 20-21.

31. Ring, *Girlhood Embroidery,* p. 11.

32. This two-pronged notion of "discipline" is derived from Laurie F. Maffly-Kipp, Leigh E. Schmidt, and Mark Valeri, eds., *Practicing Protestants: Histories of Christian Life in America, 1630-1965* (Baltimore: Johns Hopkins University Press, 2006), especially the editors' introduction and Catherine Brekus's essay, "Writing as a Protestant Practice: Devotional Diaries in Early New England," pp. 19-34.

Object Lesson: The Spirituality of Needlework in Twenty-First-Century North America

I want to move from eighteenth-century Virginia to twenty-first-century America and tease out a cautionary word that Boush's needlework has for us today. One of the most significant trends in the landscape of American Protestant spirituality over the last thirty years has been Protestants' interest in spiritual practices or spiritual disciplines ranging from Sabbath-keeping to fixed-hour prayer. This recovery of spiritual practice has had both popular and academic manifestations. The 1978 publication of Richard Foster's *Celebration of Disciplines,* which introduced both mainline and evangelical readers to disciplines such as fasting and hospitality, was a landmark event, and it is now commonplace to meet Protestants who see a spiritual director, make spiritual retreats, and practice *lectio divina.* The Lilly Foundation has been deeply invested in this recovery of practice, funding projects like Practicing Our Faith and The History of American Christian Practice Project. On a more rarefied plane, we see this interest in spiritual practice manifested in the scholarly work of Pierre Hadot — who has described ancient philosophy not as an act of technical conceptual analysis, but as an art of living — and in all the work that has flowed from and engaged Hadot, such as Jonathan Schofer's work on rabbinic ethics, and numerous recent studies of Augustinian spirituality, like Aaron Stalnaker's "Spiritual Exercises and the Grace of God: Paradoxes of Personal Formation in Augustine."[33]

Let me give you one concrete example of the Protestant recovery of Christian spiritual practice. I recently spoke at an evangelical women's retreat in Orlando, and while there I met the women's ministry leader in a non-denominational church. She gave me a set of prayer beads. These prayer beads are a synecdoche of the Protestant rediscovery of practices of the spiritual life that thirty years ago would have been alien to Protestants. They illustrate how Protestant appropriation of spiritual practices is not static, but adaptive — you won't find too many evangelicals saying they are praying a rosary, but increasingly evangelicals are praying with the tactile aid of prayer beads. Evangelicals use prayer beads chiefly as an aid to inter-

---

33. Pierre Hadot, *Philosophy as a Way of Life: Spiritual Exercises from Socrates to Foucault* (New York: Blackwell, 1995); Jonathan Schofer, "Spiritual Exercises in Rabbinic Culture," *Association for Jewish Studies Review* 27.2 (2003): 203-25; Aaron Stalnaker, "Spiritual Exercises and the Grace of God: Paradoxes of Personal Formation in Augustine," *Journal of the Society of Christian Ethics* 24.2 (Fall/Winter 2004): 137-70.

cession — for each bead, the praying evangelical offers an intercessory prayer for a different person or global situation. These prayer beads suggest a slowly growing sense in evangelical circles that one's prayer life is not something one does just with one's head or heart or mouth, but with one's body, and with all of one's senses.

You may be wondering if anyone would seriously suggest reviving needlework as a spiritual practice. In a word: yes. In the last few years, Christian publishers have brought out no fewer than five books about the spirituality of knitting; these books offer, among other things, special prayers for casting on, for finishing a row of stitches, and for binding off. Kanuga, the Episcopal retreat center in western North Carolina, now sponsors an annual conference on knitting as a Christian practice. In 2004, thirty-two students at Calvin Theological Seminary attended a class called "Knitting: Handcraft as a Window into Domestic Culture and Religious Practice."[34] And congregations all over my hometown, including my own local church, have recently inaugurated the knitting of prayer shawls as a powerful and popular ministry. Knitting, in particular, is said to help women connect to each other and to "the Holy." "Contemplative knitting" would foster a practice of "daily mindfulness."[35] The hour a day one devoted to knitting could be "contemplative time," "conducive to . . . spiritual explorations."[36] Practitioners of spiritual knitting emphasize the contemplative peace that comes while knitting; as Melanie Fahey, a shawl knitter at St. Michael's Episcopal Church in Houston, explained, "When I am working on a shawl, I am far more at peace in my own life. Everything gets done without leaving me feeling frazzled."[37]

It would be easy to mock this. Melanie Fahey's desire to find a practice that doesn't leave *her feeling frazzled* doubtless partakes of our culture's therapeutic individualism. Indeed, just as Elizabeth Boush's needlework bears the indelible marks of the slave system in which she was embedded, so too the contemporary craze of spiritual knitting, though certainly less morally fraught, seems to bear the marks of capitalism and the disordered way

34. http://www.calvin.edu/news/releases/2003_04/knitting.htm.
35. Tara Jon Manning, *Mindful Knitting: Inviting Contemplative Practice to the Craft* (Boston: Tuttle Publishing, 2004).
36. See, e.g., Linda T. Skolnik and Janice MacDaniels, *The Knitting Way: A Guide to Spiritual Self Discovery* (Woodstock: Skylight Paths, 2005); Susan S. Izard and Susan S. Jorgensen, *Knitting into the Mystery: A Guide to the Shawl-Knitting Ministry* (Harrisburg: Morehouse Publishing, 2003).
37. http://www.beliefnet.com/story/147/story_14723_2.html.

of inhabiting time that capitalism produces. The spirituality of knitting may be New Age mishmash. Melanie Fahey's knitting spirituality *may be*, in fact, ersatz spirituality — it may represent a retreat from daily life, rather than a transformation of it; it may represent an acceptance of a fast-paced, consumerist lifestyle, rather than a Christian recalibration of time. It may risk becoming a spirituality designed not to lead the practitioner ever deeper into the paschal event, but instead designed simply to make her feel good. Or the practice may have real fruit — it is possible that knitting ministries are part of a larger practice of works of mercy, for example, in making blankets for newborn crack babies and Liberian refugees.

The recovery of spiritual practices such as contemplative prayer, the use of prayer beads, and fasting — practices that until recent years many North American Protestants had forgotten — is, in many ways, a helpful project; it has been important in my own life and in the life of my local church. For Protestants to adopt the language and habits of spiritual practices and spiritual disciplines is to move away from a rational, propositional approach to faith, and to recognize that the Christian life is not a life of being but of becoming. The appropriation of practices challenges the assumption that practice follows or reflects belief, and instead understands that practice constitutes our Christian identity. One can say, indeed, that the American Protestant recovery of spiritual practices represents a sort of mainstreaming of George Lindbeck's *The Nature of Doctrine* — when ordinary Methodists and Episcopalians and Lutherans in North America take up the category of practice they are privileging the cultural-linguistic as a way to faithfully embody the propositional and the experiential-expressive. This way of thinking about Christian becoming is nothing new, of course; it is simply our current generation's iteration of centuries' old insights about Christian formation. This is the kind of formation Bernard of Clairvaux was after when he spoke about "sowing righteousness" through practices of shedding tears, distributing alms, fasting, praying, and acts of penance. It is the kind of formation that St. Theophan the Recluse was after when he urged a correspondent to "arouse in [herself] unceasing remembrance of God" through prayer, fasting, spiritual reading, and the keeping of holy silence. For Theophan, even housework, rightly undertaken, could become a spiritual practice that draws the practitioner more deeply into a habitual recollection of Christ.[38]

38. L. Gregory Jones, "A Thirst for God or Consumer Spirituality? Cultivating Disciplined Practices of Being Engaged by God," *Modern Theology* 13.1 (1997): 3-28; St. Theophan

And yet: if the recovery of practice is a fruitful, indeed theologically vital project, it is also a project that, in its current incarnation, risks historical, moral, and theological irresponsibility. The danger is simple: that we will proceed with the task of retrieving practices from the Christian past *naively*. The church that stays stuck in this mode of retrieval risks equating spiritual practice with the "good" parts of religion — spirituality becomes the stuff of religion that we *like*, the practices and habits that *appeal* to us. Here, then, is the connection between Boush's "Sacrifice of Isaac" and our twenty-first-century landscape: today, Protestants tend to retrieve spiritual practices from the past with a naive assumption that all of these spiritual practices were good. We do not attend to the ways in which spiritual practices also sometimes wrongly disciplined people — or the ways they were embedded in social sin. Elizabeth Boush's needlework of Genesis 22 cut both ways. It rooted her physically and imaginatively in Scripture, but it also embedded her in the project of stitching together colonial Virginia's ideology of and practice of slavery.

I keep a copy of Boush's "Sacrifice of Isaac" in my office, above my computer. I find it a very helpful guide for my own studies — it reminds me to approach the study of spirituality somewhat capaciously, and to look for religious practice and spiritual formation in places I might not have expected to find it. And it is suggestive to me of a way of sitting with Scripture that feels both alien and fruitful — I think about the time needlepoint requires, and the ways in which Elizabeth Boush's sitting with the story of Isaac, hour by hour and day by day, models a kind of slow, attentive steeping in a scriptural story that most early-twenty-first-century Protestants get neither in seminary nor in Bible study. But Boush's "Sacrifice of Isaac" also chastens me. It reminds me that our most abundant symbols and stories, such as Genesis 22, can be read to death-dealing ends. It forces me to grapple with the *problematic* aspects of Scripture reading and spiritual practice as they unfolded in one particular time and place — with the ways that a spiritual practice simultaneously focused Boush's attention on Scripture and also formed her in the habits of a society strenuously interested in obedience because it was strenuously interested in slavery.

I also keep Boush's "Sacrifice of Isaac" before me as I work because it exposes the ways spiritual practices from the Christian past are not immaculate, but are in fact culturally and socially embedded. The complicity

---

the Recluse, *The Spiritual Life: And How to Be Attuned to It*, trans. Alexandra Dockham (St. Herman of Alaska Brotherhood, 1995), p. 145, and passim.

of Boush's practice in a larger system becomes a useful caution as Protestants recover a whole plethora of spiritual practices. To be faithful, those engaged in the task of recovering spiritual practices must attend to the ways in which those practices regulated the social world. Without that attention, Christian spirituality risks becoming what Rowan Williams has cautioned against — that is, spirituality as "an escape into the transcendent, a flight out of history and the flesh."[39]

Our inability to evaluate contemporary spiritual needlework — our uncertainty about whether Melanie Fahey's shawl knitting is New Age mishmash or a work of mercy — highlights the ways in which North American Protestants, in our retrieval of spiritual practices from the past, have not yet articulated the criteria whereby they can evaluate a given practice. What, after all, are the criteria by which the church can clarify and describe the "best uses" of Christian practices? How, in other words, can I even know that I am getting it right to say that Boush's needlework, with its foreshortened and ideological reading of the binding of Isaac, is chastening? Criteria for a hermeneutics of recovery and appropriation must revolve around the extent to which recovery funds authentic testimony. That is, practices are fruitful insofar as they help embed practitioners in Israel and the church's story, and they are dangerous and indeed false when they help practitioners appropriate Scripture for their own ends. The practices are worth the theological weight we give them to the extent that they are always checked — tested by the authenticity of their power of witness, by theological and scriptural tests for guarding against sociological and ideological abuses, and by the boundaries of the community, by bringing practices before the ecclesiastical environment and testing the consensus that emerges there.

It is only in the context of an adequate hermeneutics of appropriation that one can transform a historical appropriation into a spiritual appropriation such that the history is in the service of the practice, rather than the practice's simply being funded by history and justified by the patina of age. History, in other words, provides models of Christian practice from other times and places, but it also judges our current practices, both critiquing the present and pointing to other kinds of futures. A robust hermeneutics of appropriation will recognize that we cannot get Christian practice right because Christian practice is testimony about God, and tes-

---

39. Rowan Williams, *The Wound of Knowledge: Christian Spirituality from the New Testament to St. John of the Cross,* 2nd ed. (Boston: Cowley Publications, 1991), p. 49.

timony about God is inexhaustible; it is never finished. To uncritically appropriate practices from the Christian past is to suggest that someone — someone in the past who fasted or prayed with prayer beads or stitched herself into Scripture's story with silk threads and a needlework hoop — got Christian experience right. The error here is *theological:* a naive appropriation of practices from the Christian past capitalizes on a false Christian self-certainty, and ironically closes the door on the very Christian *becoming* that practices make possible. We then may find ourselves in the very spot that countless voices in the Christian tradition have sagely warned against — the spot of assuming that our Christian identity is formed chiefly through *our* having identified and adopted the right practices, rather than by God's inviting us into a pilgrimage of eschatological doxology that is always incomplete.

Our Brother Abraham: The "Sacrifice" in Films by Tarkovsky and Majidi

Mark L. Sargent

The Hebrew story of the Akedah — Abraham's "binding" of Isaac, as recounted in Genesis 22 — has a long visual heritage. Caravaggio made it a thriller, letting a boyish angel seize Abraham's arm just inches before he slices the child's throat. Rembrandt's angel is quicker to the rescue, wresting the knife from the father's grip in plenty of time, even though the aged man nearly asphyxiates his son with his free hand. But on Chagall's canvas the angel appears to arrive late.[1] A red cascade — with speckled pigment, like white cells under a microscope — falls over Abraham from a prophetic realm above. Chagall, a Russian-born Jew, turns the sacrifice into an interfaith tableau. Sarah watches from behind a tree, while Hagar, in the dreamworld overhead, rushes Ishmael away, glancing across her shoulder toward Christ bearing his cross over Mount Moriah, a precursor of Calvary. And in the midst of the ecumenical trance, Abraham's knife, aloof from the crimson rain, bears bloody stains. Isaac's sides are pierced: the patriarch of the Jewish, Christian, and Muslim faiths may have already driven his blade into his son's abdomen.

For many rabbinic scholars, especially before late antiquity, this would be an outrage. In *The Last Trial*, Shalom Spiegel notes, "the Midrash again and still again emphasizes what is specifically reported in Scripture

---

1. Specific paintings described are Michelangelo Merisi da Caravaggio, "The Sacrifice of Isaac" (1601-2), Uffizi Gallery, Florence; Rembrandt Harmensez van Rijn, "The Sacrifice of Isaac" (1634), Hermitage, St. Petersburg; and Marc Chagall, "The Sacrifice of Isaac" (1960-66), Chagall Museum, Nice. Like Rembrandt, Chagall did several versions of the Akedah, but the 1960-66 painting remains his most famous one.

too, that Abraham was categorically and in no uncertain terms forbidden from heaven so much as to touch Isaac with evil intent, or to remove from him even one drop of blood."[2] Many interpreters actually attribute the moral significance of the Akedah to its bloodlessness: the Lord intervenes to distinguish his ways from the Canaanite and Mesopotamian rites of child sacrifice.[3] But, in the Middle Ages, more strains of Christian and Midrashic exegesis depicted the Akedah not just as a test but as an expiation. Christians had long been portraying Isaac as the forerunner of Jesus; now, medieval rabbis increasingly started to claim that, although Isaac was saved, a quarter of his blood was spilt, perhaps to foretell the martyrdom of the Jewish people or to "serve as an atonement for Israel."[4] With eyes on themes of atonement, Muslims also asserted that Abraham bound his son, albeit Ishmael not Isaac. Some recent scholars even wonder if the interfaith story about child sacrifice and redemption betrays an "archaic submissiveness" at the root of modern bloodshed.[5]

Although less prominent on screen than on canvas, Abraham's trial has still been a silhouette for contemporary cinema. My thoughts here focus on two films — a Christian and a Muslim echo of the sacrifice, each with intimations of the son's wounding and death, each with intimations of God's intervention. Andrei Tarkovsky's *The Sacrifice* (1986) — the final work by the Russian Orthodox visionary — is a testament from the Cold War, a tale about a father's readiness to surrender his son to prevent a nuclear conflagration.[6] Majid Majidi's *The Color of Paradise* (1999) — one of the best-known films by a devout Muslim — blends some austere features

2. Shalom Spiegel, *The Last Trial, On the Legends and Lore of the Command to Abraham to Offer Isaac as a Sacrifice: The Akedah* (New York: Schocken Books, 1967), p. 46.

3. See John Van Seters, *Abraham in History and Tradition* (New Haven: Yale University Press, 1975), pp. 227-29. For an argument questioning the Akedah as a break from Canaanite traditions of child sacrifice, see Jon Levenson, *The Transformation of Child Sacrifice in Judaism and Christianity* (New Haven: Yale University Press, 1995), esp. pp. 12-13, 111-42.

4. Midrash quoted by Spiegel, *The Last Trial,* p. 49. For more on the Jewish interpretation of the Akedah in the Midrash, see also Levenson, *The Transformation of Child Sacrifice,* pp. 173-99.

5. Yvonne Sherwood, "Binding and Unbinding: The Divided Responses of Judaism, Christianity and Islam to the 'Sacrifice' of Abraham's Beloved Son," *Journal of the American Academy of Religion* 72.4 (2004): 821.

6. *The Sacrifice (Offret),* directed by Andrei Tarkovsky (Sweden: Svenska Filminstitutet, 1986), in Swedish, French, and English. Quotes from the film are from the subtitles provided in the DVD release by Kino International Corporation (New York, 2000).

of Iranian cinema into a populist melodrama about a blind child awaiting his father's favor.[7] The "Abraham" in each emerges less as a venerable patriarch than as one of us, our brother as it were — an insular man, skeptical, weary, confused, who must overcome inertia and self-interest to heed greater spiritual duties. While shaped by notably different aesthetics, the films both belong to a cinematic world alert to threats of global violence, and both "parables" are often read in light of modern fears. And, in both cases, when death seems inevitable, it appears that God intercedes, even if we cannot fully comprehend the poetry of his presence. Modern life, with its existential muse and economic longings, has tested our capacity for faith. The directors, by evoking Abraham's ancient sacrifice, want to reawaken it.

I

Shortly after finishing *The Sacrifice*, Andrei Tarkovsky was diagnosed with throat cancer. Within months he would be laid to rest in a Parisian graveyard, in death, as in his final days, an exile. Efforts by the Soviet leadership to prevent Tarkovsky's *Nostalghia* (1982) from receiving the *Palme d'Or* at the Cannes Film Festival did little to endear the director to his government, and while shooting *The Sacrifice* he declared that he would not return to his homeland.[8] On Tarkovsky's gravestone, the Russian artist Ernst Neizvestny — famed sculptor of Khrushchev's tomb — carved: "To the man who saw the Angel."[9]

Actually, it was during Khrushchev's rule, when artists enjoyed modest new freedoms in a post-Stalin interlude, that Tarkovsky developed his numinous style, full of spiritual yearning. With just seven features, he became one of cinema's mystics, a man who saw angels in the sunlight on swamp leaves. Swedish director Ingmar Bergman famously praised Tarkovsky as "the greatest of them all," a director "who invented a new lan-

---

7. *The Color of Paradise (Rang-e Khoda),* directed by Majid Majidi (Tehran: Varahonar Company, 1999), in Persian. DVD release by Sony Pictures Digital Inc. (New York, 2008). Quotes from the film are taken from "*The Color of Paradise,* by Majid Majidi," translated by Fouad Nahas, 2000, cinemajidi.com/color/project/script.html.

8. See *Andrei Tarkovsky: Interviews,* ed. John Gianvito (Jackson: University Press of Mississippi, 2006), pp. 155-62.

9. Albert Leong, *Centaur: The Life and Art of Ernst Neizvestny* (Lanham, MD: Rowan and Littlefield, 2002), pp. 159-60, 189.

guage, true to the nature of film as it captures life as a reflection, life as a dream."[10]

The Russian director was born in 1932, in the Volga countryside of Belarus, the son of a poet and an actress. After studying Arabic in Moscow and geology in Siberia, he enrolled in 1959 in the VGIK Moscow Film School, one of the fruits of the post-Stalin relaxation in the arts. Three years later *Ivan's Childhood* won the Golden Lion for best picture at the Venice Film Festival and introduced themes — ethereal landscapes, dreams and memories, faith and transcendence — that departed from the formulaic realism of Stalinist art.[11] But *Andrei Rublev* — his second feature, and for many his greatest — angered authorities with its medieval violence, rustic nudity, and religious desire, all of which the Soviets saw as an allegory against the state. Premier Leonid Brezhnev reportedly demanded a private screening and walked out.[12]

Shooting for *The Sacrifice* began just after Brezhnev's face-off with Ronald Reagan over nuclear arsenals and ended just before the tragedy at Chernobyl.[13] Filmed on the Swedish islands of Gotland and Faro — the latter, home to Bergman — the script echoes themes from *The Shame* (1969), Bergman's film about a lurking nuclear war.[14] *The Sacrifice* explores a single night of nuclear fear, mixed with Chekhovian themes of bourgeois disarray. But it began as something else. When he signed a contract for the film — well before he was aware of his own cancer — Tarkovsky proposed a story of a man "cured of a fatal disease as a result of a night spent in bed with a witch."[15] Only years later did "The Witch" ab-

10. Ingmar Bergman, *The Magic Lantern: The Autobiography of Ingmar Bergman* (Chicago: University of Chicago, 2007), p. 73. Also, Bergman's oft-cited remark about the "new language" appeared as the title quote of the 2003 Tarkovsky Film Festival, Pacific Film Archives (Berkeley, 2003).

11. Vida T. Johnson and Graham Petrie, *The Films of Andrei Tarkovsky: A Visual Fugue* (Bloomington: Indiana University Press, 1994), p. 8; Graham Petrie, "Andrei Tarkovsky," in *The Oxford History of World Cinema*, ed. Geoffrey Nowell-Smith (Oxford: Oxford University Press, 1996), pp. 646-47.

12. J. Hoberman, "Andrei Rublev," *The Criterion Collection: Online Cinematheque* (January 12, 1999), www.criterion.com/current/posts/43.

13. Johnson and Petrie, *Visual Fugue*, p. 8.

14. Mark Le Fanu, *The Cinema of Andrei Tarkovsky* (London: British Film Institute, 1987), p. 136. See also Gino Moliterno, "The Sacrifice," *Senses of the Cinema* (July 2001), www.sensesofcinema.com/contents/cteq/01/15/sacrifice.html.

15. Andrey Tarkovsky, *Sculpting in Time: Reflections on the Cinema* (Austin: University of Texas Press, 1989), p. 217.

sorb his version of the Akedah — a father's effort to avert atomic ruin by sacrificing his son and burning his home as an offering to God.

For all of its dark tones, *The Sacrifice* retains what Bergman's film lacks: a remnant of spiritual "hope and confidence."[16] Tarkovsky finds hope in both the atomic and the witch episodes, though the blend has riddled critics, even the director's admirers. Some who deem *The Sacrifice* "magisterial" also consider it Tarkovsky's "last great, tragically flawed film," largely because the two plots collide.[17] The conflict, however, tells a story in its own right, a tug-of-war between Christian altruism and modern spiritual freedom. According to Tarkovsky, the father's offering of his son and home to God (a "poetic parable") reflects the "Christian sense of self-sacrifice." This "idea of sacrifice, the Christian ideal of love of neighbor," is a remedy for "the endless multiplication of material goods," especially now that "the implacable march of new technology" promises not just prosperity but the threat of annihilation.[18] The witch episode, though, is a tale spun from Dostoevsky's dreams — a story about one man's "spiritual regeneration" through an occult love affair. The witch, presumably, is a "holy fool" — clairvoyant and wise, in the Russian sense of a witch, a rival to Marxists, empiricists, pragmatists, and all "normal" folk. She is a "soothsaying" Mary Magdalene who rekindles the imagination and the "unfathomable wonders of life."[19] Both atomic and witch themes invite parallels with the Akedah, not the least because their ambiguities echo the uncertain moments of Abraham's test, before the Lord intervenes.

The Abraham of the tale is a weary fifty-year-old named Alexander (played by Erland Josephson), a semi-retired actor who has moved his family into an old estate on the marshy, nearly treeless shore. Ribbed as a moody "Richardian" for his stage presence as Shakespeare's sinister king, he retains enough idealism, however dormant, to be also called a "Myshkin," after the Christ-like protagonist of Dostoyevsky's novel *The Idiot*, among Tarkovsky's favorite books.[20] His face is often half-lit. The incandescent white of dusk, which fills the marshy fields and the wind-

16. "Hope and confidence" are the last words in Tarkovsky's dedication to his son Andrejusja, which closes the film. See also Moliterno, "Sacrifice."

17. Tarkovsky, *Sculpting*, p. 209; Le Fanu, *Tarkovsky*, pp. 124, 133.

18. Tarkovsky, *Sculpting*, pp. 222, 218.

19. Tarkovsky, *Sculpting*, p. 227.

20. Tarkovsky discusses his desire to make two films of Dostoevky's *The Idiot* in an essay published at the end of *Time within Time: Diaries, 1970-1986* (London: Faber and Faber, 2002), esp. pp. 372-77.

tossed curtain lace, spreads only partially over his worn but kindly visage; half of his countenance remains shrouded by the interior of his home. He has become passive, stoic, not fully certain when his life found the shadows. His wind-swept isolation allows for rambling walks with the postman Otto, a would-be seer, and their talk is full of middle-aged rattling about God and Nietzsche. It also mirrors his domestic misery, his chilly rapport with his wife Adelaide, daughter Marta, servant Julia, and friend Victor. Alexander's one joy — a six-year-old son he calls Little Man — is mute, suffering from a throat operation. That his surgeon appears to be sleeping with the boy's mother only intimates how middle-age deceit silences the innocent.

One echo of Abraham's story comes early: *The Sacrifice* begins with a faith test for the child and the father. Medieval Christians, as well as the Midrash, often attributed to Isaac the spiritual courage to reassure his father about God's will. In the Brome play — the most famous Akedah among the medieval English mystery dramas — Isaac affirms his father's plan to slay him, asking that his mother be appeased with a fiction about his flight into another country rather than told the truth about his slaughter.[21] As *The Sacrifice* opens, Little Man helps his father plant a withered tree branch along the barren coast, as Alexander recounts the story of a Russian monk who once planted such a stem, watered it faithfully, and eventually saw it erupt with blossoms. Faith, if the test succeeds, will work miracles. But faith now belongs only to the young. An off-the-cuff existentialist, Alexander soon admits that his own relationship with God is "nonexistent," and his tongue-in-cheek reference to the bare tree as Japanese Ikebana — the traditional artistic arrangement of leaves, twigs, and blossoms — unveils more irony than hope. Little Man's silent and simple devotion to the tree is an antidote to his father's religious dryness.

The greatest antidote, though, is Tarkovsky's camera, guided this time by cinematographer Sven Nykvist, veteran of many Bergman films. When Little Man pours water on the withered trunk, he displays a spiritual hopefulness that the filmmakers also seek to bring out of the unsaturated colors, monotone palette, and natural light. Like Nykvist, Tarkovsky was suspicious of technicolor, fearful that vivid tones deaden the viewer's alertness to nuance and perspective. Redemption for Tarkovsky is always more visual than logical, an arresting shadow, an angular gaze over a barren

---

21. *The Brome Play of Abraham and Isaac* (ca. 1400-1426), in *Non-Cycle Plays and Fragments*, ed. Norman Davis (London: Oxford University Press, 1970), esp. lines 187-206.

field. The director viewed his own work as poetry rather than drama, insisting that the "poet has the imagination and psychology of a child for his ideas about the world are immediate."[22] As their lenses explore the gray tundra, tense faces, and the bare, cruciform tree, Tarkovsky and Nykvist seek an austere beauty and "unspoken elusiveness" that offset the characters' spiritual drought.[23] This visual aesthetic is a rich match for the Akedah themes, since it favors patience and trust, even in the face of terrifying and irrational options. Tarkovsky's long camera shots allow images to emerge, linger, and crystallize, a theater of visual deliberation that is neither fully realistic nor hallucinatory. It is a lyrical subjectivity — allusive, elliptical, and prayerful — that would have moved Kierkegaard.

Alexander's struggle between insularity and idealism sets the stage for a twist in the Akedah motif. In Genesis, the Lord's command to slay Isaac threatens the miracle of Sarah's late pregnancy and the promise of endless generations. In the film, though, future children may not endure without his son's death. The father's journey to his own Moriah — the top floor in his house — forces him to envision how future generations, not just the home and children to which he has retreated, can be his legacy. His own Akedah occurs shortly after media reports preempt his fiftieth birthday party, a stale, obligatory affair, with news of atomic attacks. The apocalypse emerges by visual inference: rattling champagne glasses, a shattered pitcher of milk, the TV's flickering light across strained faces. When a swell of wind overturns the boggy leaves, it is easy to imagine the centrifugal rage of an exploding warhead. Distraught by this "ultimate war," Alexander recites the Lord's Prayer, falls to the floor, and offers his son, his home, and all else that is dear to him if God will restore the world to the morning before this nuclear midnight.

What prompts this sudden bargain remains unclear, but the mystery invigorates the parable. According to Tarkovsky, Alexander "is a weak man in the vulgar, pedestrian understanding of the word. He is no hero, but he is a thinker and honest man, who turns out to be capable of sacrifice in the

22. Tarkovsky, *Sculpting*, p. 41.
23. Tarkovsky quoted in Benjamin Halligan, "The Long Take That Kills: Tarkovsky's Rejection of Montage," *Central Europe Review* 2.39 (November 13, 2000), www.ce-review.org/00/39/kinoeye39_halligan.html. His emphasis on "unspoken elusiveness" is a rejection of the ideological use of a camera by Sergei Eisenstein. Nykvist won the top honor for cinematography at Cannes for *The Sacrifice*. Nykvist discusses his work with Tarkovsky on the film at some length in his book *In Reverence of Light*, written with Bengt Forslund (Stockholm: Albert Bonniers Publishing Co., 1997), pp. 181-87.

name of a higher ideal." His "decisive action" is "in danger of not being understood" since it appears so "catastrophically destructive."[24] Indeed, it may be easiest to understand Alexander's action in metaphorical terms, rather than to search for motives. The parable does intimate that resistance to modern evil may cost innocent lives. Alexander's surrender of what he loves best signals a retreat from modern individualism and an embrace of altruism and Christ-like love. But there are enigmatic psychological layers as well. Alexander begs God to save not only the faithful, but also those, like himself, who need more time to struggle toward belief. His reactions are often visceral, subconscious: twice Tarkovsky offers dreamlike vignettes of ash and debris falling over fleeing city dwellers, a projection of nuclear victims that fuses, almost seamlessly, with the face of Alexander's sleeping child. That may be part of the "tragic conflict of his role" — the clash between the destructiveness of his immediate actions and his ability to envision, like the filmmakers themselves, even greater destruction and death lurking in the future.[25] In many respects, the eventual burning of the house — a bewildering moral act, but virtuoso cinema — is primarily an aesthetic gesture, an endeavor to awaken spiritual ruminations with the paradoxical and cruel splendor of art.[26] There may also be something of the director's own loneliness and dread in all this. During the shooting neither Tarkovsky's wife Larissa nor his son Andrejusja — to whom he dedicates the film — were allowed to leave Russia, and in Alexander's anguished monologues it is possible to hear an expatriate director's anxiety about whether he has seen the last of his own boy.[27]

Alexander's will to sacrifice is also complicated by his rush to the "benevolent witch and holy innocent" Maria. In his post-film memoir, Tarkovsky calls Maria a "gift from God," whose love redeems Alexander from the "venomous atmosphere" of his marriage.[28] It takes little to prompt the carnal escape — merely a dream by Otto, who assures Alexander that the holocaust can be averted if he will sleep with the mysterious

---

24. Tarkovsky, *Sculpting*, p. 209.

25. Tarkovsky, *Sculpting*, p. 209.

26. One of the most engaging discussions of the aesthetics of Tarkovsky, with strong interest in the climatic scene in *The Sacrifice*, is Czech critic Petr Král's "Tarkovsky, or the Burning House," *Svedectvi* 23.91 (1990): 258-68, translated by Kevin Windle, for *Screening the Past* (March 2001), www.latrobe.edu.au/screeningthepast/classics/clo301/pkch2.htm.

27. Tarkovsky's thoughts about his separation from his family appear in *Time within Time*, esp. the diaries for 1983-85.

28. Tarkovsky, *Sculpting*, pp. 225, 224.

Icelander in her nearby cottage. Once again, Alexander's tale mirrors Abraham's struggle. Throughout the film a servant, much like Hagar, is his wife's rival. As Adelaide gets lost in her own reveries, it becomes clear that Julia loves Little Man best. And Alexander's sexual engagement with the foreign servant Maria, like Abraham's encounter with Hagar, reveals doubts about his future with his wife and equivocates on his own covenant with God.

As the script moves from desperate prayer to mystic adultery, the director himself may, in inadvertent ways, imitate Abraham's doubts. Tarkovsky insists that Maria's simple love is a remedy for Adelaide's tragic soullessness and a spark for Alexander's "spiritual regeneration." The sexual tryst is a spiritual miscellany — crucifixes on Maria's wall, pictures of the Virgin, bodily levitation, and the sound of "kulning," an eerie Scandinavian music that imitates herding calls.[29] Here, as elsewhere in the director's work, Christian themes mix with occult airs, as if the modern spiritual yearning leads us to hedge our bets. It is a familiar modernist hedge, a taste for biblical wisdom reworked by Jung. Maria's role in the global drama, however, remains opaque. In his memoir, Tarkovsky speculates that only those with a "heightened sense of the supernatural" will see Maria's bed as the reason God stops the war.[30] The sexual levitation does forge a visual link between Maria's comforting of Alexander and his own fear-ridden dreams, in which he appears to levitate over panic-stricken people.[31] But the film also leaves some hints that the sexual encounter was merely a dream in itself. Otto's command may simply have been a red herring.

More conventional images of Christian redemption do appear in the film, though usually by refraction. Mirrors dominate Tarkovsky's work: faith and the human soul, it seems, are best caught at an angle. Alexander's bargain with God occurs, quite literally, under the reflections off the glass covering a "terrifying" reproduction of Leonardo da Vinci's "Adoration of the Kings." The "Adoration" was commissioned as an altarpiece for the monastery of San Donato a Scopeto near Florence, and though Leonardo left it unfinished, the completed painting might well have lacked the power of the sketch, full of ghostly, dissolving figures surrounding the Virgin and

29. The folk music of *The Sacrifice* is discussed in the blog by Ferrara entitled "Kulning: Voice of the Eternal Feminine," www.people.tribe.net/ferrarabrainpan.

30. Tarkovsky, *Sculpting*, p. 224.

31. David Gillespie discusses the flying motif in Tarkovsky in *Russian Cinema* (Harlow, England: Pearson Longman Education, Ltd., 2003), p. 183.

Child.[32] The print reappears in the mirrors and windows, as its reflections get tangled with faces and the storm-cast leaves. The camera focuses often on the infant Christ as he reaches toward the magi's chalice, by tradition a gift of embalming oil. Leonardo's sketch actually launches the film, serving as the backdrop to the credits even as we hear the "Ebarme Dich" of Bach's *St. Matthew's Passion*. From the outset, the child is set for sacrifice.

Throughout his career Tarkovosky strove to absorb the glory and legacy of Christian art — Leonardo da Vinci, Bach, Rublev's icons — into his own visions. In this last project, though, "The Adoration" intensifies the ominous mood of the parable, leaving plenty of doubt about the prospects for redemption. For some viewers, neither the sacrifice nor the mystic lovemaking earns heaven's attention; perhaps God is simply indifferent to a fear-laden fifty-year-old on the edge of the Arctic. But the famous ending of this Abrahamic parable also allows for the marvelous, for the possibility that God touches time and space. When Alexander awakens, he finds Little Man's bed vacant. At breakfast outside, Adelaide, Marta, and Victor — without talk of warplanes — are once again lost in their Chekhovian discontent. Has God indeed taken the boy and restored the world to its pre-war state? Has the nuclear threat actually been erased from history and memory? In the pale confusion of the morning, Alexander sets fire to his wood-framed dacha, fulfilling his pledge to forsake his home to atone for human failure and to ensure the world's survival. This burnt offering is now cinematic legend. No sooner was the house set afire than Nykvist's camera broke down, and Tarkovsky had the home rebuilt in three days to reshoot the catastrophe.[33]

There's a reverberation here from Tarkovsky's previous film, *Nostalghia*, in which the protagonist immolates himself by fire. "Alexander's setting fire to his house at the end of *The Sacrifice*," according to Gino Moliterno, "is merely another, and more symbolic . . . act of self-martyrdom in the service of a Christian ideal."[34] Of course, there's also reason to think Alexander psychotic. As the flames erupt, he runs frantically through the swampy grassland, at one point throwing himself at Maria, until subdued and tossed in an ambulance. More than a few critics have seen his arson and clownish antics as self-indulgent, solipsistic, and

32. See Kenneth Clark, *Leonardo da Vinci*, 2nd ed. (London: Penguin Books, 1989), pp. 71-81; Le Fanu, *Cinema*, p. 134.

33. For an account of the malfunction, see Nykvist and Forslund, *In Reverence*, pp. 183-87. For analysis, see Halligan, "The Long Take That Kills," and Král, "Burning House."

34. Moliterno, "Sacrifice."

even autobiographical, far afield of Abraham's selfless duty. "However great is Tarkovsky's mastery of mis-en-scène," Wally Hammond states, "*The Sacrifice* appears a little egocentric, and closer to a study of madness and self-delusion than . . . an illustration of the power of faith and self-sacrifice."[35] Or, as Mark Le Fanu notes, "Alexander's promise becomes complicated, from our point of view, on account of its unilateral basis: it is *his* renunciation, not his family's. Yet the flaming pyre initiates a suffering which logically is just as much theirs as his."[36]

But Alexander's resolve to scorch his home also reveals something of the subjective power that Søren Kierkegaard finds in Abraham's obedience. In *Fear and Trembling*, the Danish writer famously argues that Abraham suspends his ethical convictions for the teleological: Abraham accepts the decree to "murder" his son, not because he understands it to be "ethical" in itself, but because his "religious" faith assures him that God will always bring about an ethical end.[37] The film's denouement is not the safe aftermath of the Akedah, when theology and metaphor make retrospective and ethical sense of the Lord's test. Instead, Tarkovsky sets Alexander and sets us in the fierce moment of the blazing altar, uncertain of either the designs or the presence of God, leaving us to consider religious faith and sacrifice as great hopes for humanity even when others see them as cruel folly. The finale asks us to decide if Alexander has gone mad, has merely assuaged his own guilt, or, in Tarkovsky's phrase, has reclaimed "that higher form of spiritual life which alone is worthy of mankind and which represents man's best hope for salvation."[38]

There is at least one last refracted glimpse of salvation in the elliptical aftermath, as Little Man once more carries his water buckets to the dead trunk. Lying against the tree, the boy looks up at the stark branches and recites his only words, from the opening of the Gospel of John. Perhaps what we are seeing here is the aftermath of the fire, and Little Man has been spared and his throat healed. Or perhaps we are seeing the world as it has been restored to the previous day, just as Alexander had begged of God. If so, this flashback silences Alexander, since he cannot convey what he has seen or answer his son's questions. In the end, the narrative themes may not fully cohere, but the film's "constellation" and "conspiracy" of de-

---

35. Wally Hammond, "The Sacrifice," *Time Out London* (December 11, 2007).

36. Le Fanu, *Tarkovsky*, p. 125.

37. Søren Kierkegaard, *Fear and Trembling*, ed. C. Stephen Evans and Sylvia Walsh (Cambridge: Cambridge University Press, 2006), p. 24.

38. Tarkovsky, *Sculpting*, p. 218.

tails — to use Petr Král's memorable words — offer "a palpable fragment of mystery in the arteries of the world."[39] The lifeblood of faith, if not metaphysical clarity, has been revitalized.

It is hard, in retrospect, not to consider these final images of Tarkovsky's career as a valediction. His cancer spread quickly, and only after it had decimated his body did his family join him by his side. For all of Alexander's will to secure "world harmony" through his own actions, Tarkovsky finally concedes that he, like Abraham, longs for the intervention of God.[40] Art — yearning, painful, and beautiful — is not a way to "imitate the Creator whom we serve" but a form of faithfulness in the midst of uncertainty. "We make good our guilt before our Creator," Tarkovsky writes in his late diaries, "by using the freedom he has given us to fight against the evil within us, to overcome the obstacles lying on the path that leads to our Lord, to grow spiritually and rise above all that is base in us. Help me Lord, send me a Teacher, I have been waiting so long. I am tired."[41]

II

The Color of Paradise, a story of a blind boy scorned by his father, begins in darkness. For two minutes the screen is a black backdrop to the credits, allowing us only to eavesdrop on a young boy, Mohammad, as he quarrels with a schoolmate over the cassette tapes they must reclaim before their summer break. With this opening dark spell, director Majid Majidi tests our patience for the visual images to emerge, and in so doing replicates the deprivations of blindness. He also recalls the dark scenes in several Iranian films, including the dark chalkboard in Forough Farrokhzad's *The House Is Black* (1962), a story about a leper colony, often considered a spark for the New Wave of Iranian cinema. "There is no shortage of ugliness in the world," Farrokhazad's narrator begins. "If man closed his eyes to it, there would be even more."[42]

Majidi's dark screen foretells ugliness and willful blindness. Hashem, the severe, ironic Abraham of this story, closes his eyes to his boy's suffering to pursue an advantageous marriage. Ashamed of his son, the widower

39. Král, "Burning House."
40. Tarkovsky, *Sculpting,* p. 224.
41. Tarkovsky, *Diaries,* p. 328.
42. *The House Is Black (Khaneh siah ast),* directed by Forough Farrokhzad (Tehran, 1962), in Persian. DVD release by Facets Multi-Media (Chicago, 2005).

begs the school in Tehran to keep him for the three-month holiday, and then settles for leaving the eight-year-old with the boy's grandmother in a mountainous village, away from his own prospective bride. But the film is largely about beauty: alpine flowers, blue forest mists, brightly dyed hejabs, the wheat stalks in the wind, all part of the paradisiacal high-country village that Mohammad, quite sadly, cannot see.

This beauty can be consoling and cruel. Majidi's title, in the original Persian, literally means "The Color of God," and the story tests the old adage that the blind have an unrivaled capacity to discern the presence of the divine.[43] The film relies, riskily at times, on visual images and natural sounds to convey Mohammed's tactile and aural discoveries, as well as something of his spiritual insights. Majidi casts a blind child, Moshen Ramezani, in the lead role, and the young boy's reactions, whether to the call of a distant bird or the touch of a nearby companion, do have an authenticity most likely lost with a professional. Modern Iranian film, shaped largely by the New Wave aesthetic of the 1970s, '80s, and '90s, relies often on nonprofessionals, as the filmmakers, many of them first trained on documentaries, blur the boundaries between fiction and reality. Filmmakers often enter their own films, becoming entangled with the quandaries and social conditions they record, unable to retreat to an artist's critical distance and to extract themselves from the social and moral complexities they fashion into their fictions.[44] For all that, as Jonathan Rosenbaum notes, "Iranian cinema is becoming almost universally recognized as the most ethical in the world."[45] That aesthetic tradition raises the stakes for Majidi's work with a blind boy, since the fable cannot leave the young actor with reassuring platitudes that console the audience but insult the child. *The Color of Paradise* does face the prospect that the old adage about God's

---

43. While Arabic Muslims consistently refer to the deity as Allah, the English subtitles for Majidi's films refer to "God," a translation of the Persian "Khoda." "Just as every religion has its own special name so too does every country," Majidi observes (Corey Boutilier, "*The Willow Tree*: Exclusive Interview with Iranian filmmaker Majid Majidi and film co-writer Fouad Nahas," *IndependentFilm.com*, September 29, 2005). On release of the film to English audiences, the distributors changed the title to *The Color of Paradise*, rather than attempting a literal translation of "Rang-e Khoda." Although the translation creates some ambiguities, for consistency's sake this essay will use the English release title, the name Abraham (rather than Ibrahim), and the subtitles' translation of the Persian "Khoda" as "God."

44. Rose Issa, "Real Fictions," *House of World Cultures* (March 8, 2004), www.archiv.hkw.de/en/dossiers/iran_dossierroseissa/kapitel2.html.

45. Jonathan Rosenbaum, "The Universe in a Cellar," *The Chicago Reader* (December 8, 2000), www.chicagoreader.com/movies/archives/2000/1200/001208.html.

favor for the blind may be a delusion, false medicine given to placate the disabled, while most of us relish the sight of divinity in the wildflowers. As that dark screen opens the film — the singular moment when Mohammad and the viewers share the experience of blindness — the words of a Muslim at prayer declare the film's spiritual paradox:

> Oh, Thou, who are hidden,
> Oh, Thou, who are visible everywhere . . .

Raised in a middle-class home, Majidi is unique among Iranian directors — a dedicated Muslim with wide popularity among Western and Far Eastern moviegoers. After studying at the Institute of Dramatic Arts in Tehran, he began as an actor, soon appearing in *The Boycott*, a film by Moshen Makhmalbaf, among the leading figures in the New Wave. Majidi — who was one of five filmmakers chosen to work on a documentary for the Beijing Olympics — first drew widespread international attention as a director with *The Children of Heaven* (1997), which inspired a remake in Singapore and became the first Iranian movie nominated for an Oscar.[46] He also earned headlines in 2006 when he pulled his film *The Willow Tree* from a Danish festival to protest satirical cartoons about the Prophet Mohammad published in Denmark.[47]

Not all champions of Iranian film, though, are thrilled with Majidi's popularity. For some, he is one of the directors who, with eyes on Western viewers, settle into "formal and thematic repetition — a focus on children, village life and beautiful landscapes, reducing them to formulaic postcard Orientalist curiosities."[48] Most of the critical praise from the West is reserved for Iran's New Wave "auteurs," such as Makhmalbaf and Abbas Kiarostami, who have stayed at arm's length from the religious government and earned prizes at European festivals, notably Cannes and Venice.

But Majidi has numerous admirers among international critics, many of whom stress that one remedy for global violence could be those storytellers who can transcend their own cultures, especially as they are defined by art-house elites, and reach young and old with populist fables. Former *New York Post* reviewer Godfrey Cheshire lauds Majidi for global

---

46. Fouad Nahas and Majid Majidi, "Biography: Majid Majidi" on Majidi website, www.cinemajidi.com/biography.html.

47. "Film Festival Hit by Cartoon Row," *BBC News* (March 24, 2006).

48. Eric Egan, *The Films of Makhmalbaf: Cinema, Politics and Culture in Iran* (Washington, DC: Mage Publishers, 2005), p. 165.

accessibility, his blend of a "passionately direct melodrama" reminiscent of D. W. Griffith with an Iranian cinematic tradition that favors the natural, austere, and laconic:

> Iranians are apt to smile at the term "Judeo-Christian," which lops the Islamic branch off a tripartite monotheistic tradition that they call "Abrahamian." As with many other Iranian art works and films, including several of Kiarostami's, *The Color of Paradise* implicitly evokes the story of Abraham and Isaac. Like that ancient paradigm, Majidi's film is about a father who's willing to sacrifice his son, and a son who survives solely — make no mistake — due to divine intervention. . . . And his ultimate message, you might say, is the greatness not of the auteur, but of the Auteur.[49]

Majidi's film hints of Abraham's sacrifice as early as the initial darkness. In many of the most artistic films of the New Wave — which emerged after the Khomeini Revolution toppled the American-backed Shah in 1979 and began to shut down theaters — scenes of darkness and silence evoke human suffering even as they awaken spiritual meditation, coyly avoiding direct political dissent.[50] The "blind" screen that opens *The Color of Paradise*, in fact, anticipates the film's final cut to black, a brisk edit that leaves the spiritual denouement uncertain. The first dark screen is also a backdrop to the first words of the Basmala ("In the name of God"). These are not only the words that begins each surah, or chapter, in the Qur'an, but also the opening phrase in a supplication prayer offered during the slaughter of animals at Id al-Adha, the Festival of the Sacrifice (or Eyd e Qorbán, as it is called in Persian). Celebrated the day after The Hajj, or the annual pilgrimage to Mecca, the festival commemorates Abraham's readiness to slay his son in response to a dream from God.[51] An occasion for sacrificing the best livestock, Id al-Adha honors the time when the son was "ransomed" by God and replaced with a ram, just after Abraham had laid him "prostate on his forehead," ready for the execution.[52]

49. Godfrey Cheshire, "The Color of God," *Independent Weekly* (Raleigh, Durham, Chapel Hill, NC, May 17, 2000).

50. Hamid Naficy, "Iranian Cinema," in *The Oxford History of World Cinema*, pp. 674-75.

51. John L. Esposito, *Islam, the Straight Path,* 2nd ed. (London: Oxford University Press, 2005), pp. 92-93.

52. Qur'an 37:107, 103.

While the Hebrew Bible, the New Testament, and the Qur'an all recount Abraham's intended sacrifice, Jews and Christians differ with Muslims — often fiercely — about the name of the child set to die. The narrative in Genesis does identify Isaac as the one bound by his father, yet the Hebrew text also describes him as Abraham's "only son."[53] That, according to many Muslims, reveals that the intended victim must have been Abraham's eldest child Ishmael. It was not uncommon for Islamic apologists to claim that the name was later altered by Hebrew scribes as part of an anti-Muslim purge. By contrast, Jewish and Christian scholars, aware that much of Jewish genealogy was maternal, contend that since Hagar was an Egyptian it was certainly Isaac who was the son of a Jewish mother and the proper heir. Many modern ecumenicists, though, have downplayed the Ishmael-Isaac rivalry, stressing that the Hebrew Bible assures both men of a vibrant legacy and depicts them joining together to bury their father.[54]

Majidi's father-son fable is sufficiently generic to win ecumenical favor, but it does ring with Islamic ideals. Even though Cheshire and others can legitimately see a rough print of Isaac in the tale, the young Mohammad invites the most comparisons with Ishmael. Like Abraham's oldest son, the young boy is sent away from the father to be under a woman's care, and he thrives in the village with his grandmother and sisters, letting them pour water over him from the Imanzadeh, or shrine to the dead. As Rosa Holman observes, *The Color of Paradise* also resonates with Sufi mysticism, especially the tradition of the *ghazal*, a lyrical poetic mode that "idealized the notion of the unavailable 'Beloved,' meticulously conjuring the perfection of their physical beauty and the pain of failing to unite with them romantically."[55] Majidi, in fact, invokes an older, more classical form of Sufi romanticism, dwelling not on the more "tangible," "everyday lover" of much contemporary Iranian poetry, but on the idealized image of the eternal and unreachable love.[56] The young Mohammad aches for the world that he cannot see, all the while striving for a union —

---

53. Genesis 22:2.

54. Genesis 16:10; 25:9. For one Christian's ecumenical assessment of Ishmael and Isaac, see Hans Küng, *Islam: Past, Present and Future* (Oxford: One World, 2007), pp. 46-52.

55. Rosa Holman, "'Caught Between Poetry and Censorship': The Influence of State Regulation and Sufi Poeticism on Contemporary Iranian Cinema," *Senses of the Cinema* (2006), www.sensesofcinema.com/contents/06/41/poetry-censorship-iran.html.

56. Mohammad Reza Shafi'i Kadkani's *Advar-e Sh'r-e Farsi* (Tehran: Tus Publishers, 1980), quoted and translated in Hamid Dabashi, *Close Up: Iranian Cinema Past, Present and Future* (London: Verso, 2001), pp. 67-68.

with his father, with his grandmother, with God — that remains elusive. He gives one sister an image of a rose, a traditional Sufi symbol of the Beloved. When he runs through the wildflowers, the landscape, in the words of Holman, "appears more like the idealized paradise of the *ghazal* garden than a functioning farm" of wheat and alfalfa.[57] With both joy and struggle, Mohammad tries to discern Persian words in the texture of river stones and wheat buds, to read the world with his fingers as if the language of God was Braille.

Nature's Braille offers a global scripture: part of the film's cross-cultural appeal is this vision of God discernable in nature and available to all sectarian traditions. But Majidi does not allow an easy, ecumenical pantheism to resolve the most sorrowful theological questions. There is always in young actor Moshen Ramezani's face some pain for what his fingers cannot fully read in the stones. "Our teacher always says that God loves the blind more than other people," a sobbing Mohammad tells a blind woodcutter. "She said that He is invisible and we can feel Him everywhere. She said that we can reach Him with our hands. Now . . . I search for God everywhere and one day when my hand will reach Him, I will tell Him everything, all my thoughts, even my most secret ones." The woodcutter's terse response to the broken child — "she spoke the truth" — burns more than it heals. He too knows the pain of yearning after an unseen God. *The Color of Paradise* is still a story about an Ishmael banished from a patriarch's future, awaiting the intervention of God.

By contrast, the father Hashem reads only the ominous language of nature — thunderclaps, disorienting fogs, the weightiness of the sod. His cold eye on rural life no doubt strikes shrill notes in Iran. With greater freedom for artists in the post-Khomeini 1990s, filmmakers flooded to the countryside, in part because of lower production costs, but also to reclaim the landscape as a source of imagination and community. While the cries of ringdoves and woodpeckers awaken joy in Mohammad, the sharp sounds of the woods startle Hashem, causing him to cut himself severely while shaving, as he drops and shatters his mirror on the river rocks that Mohammad read with elation. Mirrors, like the rose, are Sufi emblems of love. By shattering his glass, Hashem gets a foresight of his own eventual romantic failure, drawing blood from his own neck, as if he has become the reflection of the child he would sacrifice. In Islam, neglect for the blind often comes in for strong censure. Even the Prophet Mohammad was

---

57. Holman, "Caught Between."

scolded for ignoring a sightless man. Once, intent on converting some polytheist nobles and persecutors, the Prophet shunned the blind Abdullah ibn Umm Maktum, who had come to him to hear a verse of scripture read. According to the Qur'an, the Prophet is reproached for devoting his full attention to those who ignored faith and for disregarding a man "full of eagerness and in awe of God."[58]

Majidi's strongest echo of Abraham's tale occurs in the mystical final scene, when Hashem will find his son, lying prone like Ishmael in the margins between life and death. By now Hashem has lost nearly all. His mother, grieved by his selfishness, has died, and his prospective bride's family has returned his gifts, claiming that the marriage would be a "bad omen." Forlorn, Hashem reclaims his son and begins a long homeward journey, until a bridge collapses, tossing the boy and his horse into a river. For a few moments, Hashem freezes in indecision, but he will soon leap after him, his one note of courage. He has, though, no chance against the fury of the current. After a fierce descent down the rapids, he will awaken under a gray sky on the still shores of the Caspian Sea, his face and clothes ravaged, his lifeless son just a few paces away. As Majidi's camera rises, the body of Mohammad is at first almost indistinguishable from the dark, writhing roots of the fallen trees, making the boy part of the scene of debris and driftwood. Yet, when the weeping father gathers his son into his arms, he does not see the color of God — a bright, orange-white glow — as it softly illuminates his son's hand. These are the fingers that have long, and often sadly, tried to touch the invisible God, whether by stroking a bird's feathers or squeezing chaff in a field of wheat. But now at the moment of death God appears to have reached him. For an instant, before the screen turns dark, we see Mohammad's fingers twist slightly, as if reading Braille, and then turn upward, an open palm toward heaven.

Such visual evidence of the divine divides viewers. For everyone who sees a "lachrymose" and "wrong-note final image," there are others who admire Majidi's refusal to suspend belief, who find this brisk cinematic epiphany genuinely moving.[59] The Abrahamic finish does allow both literal and mystical readings. Even though there is no angel, the call of a distant ringdove — which often alerts Mohammed to higher things — breaks the squeals of geese and gulls with a premonition of grace. God, it appears,

58. Qur'an 80:116.
59. Dana Stevens, "'The Color of Paradise': Iran's Way with Nature and a Blind Boy," *New York Times* (March 31, 2000).

has literally restored Mohammad's life. Some Iranians, even those not drawn to transcendent themes, note that the conclusion reveals political optimism. Cinema historian Hamid Dabashi claims that *The Color of Paradise* "reflects the hopeful spirit of resurrection that immediately followed Khatami's election" to the presidency. Elected two years before the release of Majidi's film, Seyyed Mohammad Khatami soared into office with a huge popular vote, initially stirring confidence that his leadership could offset the repression of the Khomeni years, the anguish of the war with Iraq, and the tragedy of the great 1990 earthquake in Gilan and Zanjan. Dabashi sees that resurrection spirit in several Iranian films of the late 1990s, even in Kiarostami's *Palme d'Or*–winner *A Taste of Cherry* (1997), a suicide story that, strangely enough, "illuminates the value of life" and tells of "a rich urban life about to resurface."[60]

Yet *The Color of Paradise* ends with enough mystery to allow us to see the final scene as a luminous death, especially when the film breaks briskly from Mohammad's twisting fingers into darkness. Throughout the scene, the serene light on the small waves, as well as the overcast tone of this final montage, contrasts with the sunlit colors of village life; it is easy to imagine this to be a dreamlike interval between life and death. The orange-glow on Mohammad's hand that intrudes into the gray cinematography may signal that God is taking the lost, broken child into paradise. That same shade of light appears once earlier, when it illuminates the face of Mohammad's grandmother on the verge of her own passing. Perhaps Mohammad's tender soul has finally led him to touch his Beloved, the God to whom he has told his secrets. It is a beautiful but perilous finale. Majidi's ending leaves Mohammad in the transcendent, though he can do less, of course, for the young actor Moshen. With its radiant finish, the film departs from the New Wave aesthetic of entangling filmmakers and actors in the ongoing thread of human struggle, and we are left to decide if we have seen a clumsy *deus ex machina* or a real presence. Perhaps to avoid charges of escapism, Majidi returns soberly once more to the theme of blindness in *The Willow Tree* (2005), where he undercuts a happy ending by depicting a middle-aged professor who recovers his sight only to discover the gap between his inner life and the sordidness of the world he now can see.[61]

---

60. Hamid Dabashi, "Persian Blues," *Sight & Sound* 12.1 (January 2002): 33.

61. *The Willow Tree (Beed-e Majnoon)*, directed by Majid Majidi (Tehran: Soureh Cinema Development, 2005), in Persian. DVD release with English subtitles by New Yorker Video (New York, 2005).

III

Andrei Tarkovsky succumbed to cancer three years before the Berlin Wall fell. He did not live, as his peer Bergman did, to see the greatest fears of the West shift from the threat of a nuclear apocalypse to the rise of Islamic jihadism. History can dull a film's edge. Today *The Sacrifice*, despite many Tarkovsky revivals, is often deemed the self-conscious, seldom-seen art film from the end of a Cold War era. By contrast, Majidi's more sentimental fable has flourished in Western festivals, not the least because its Persian colors and compassion offset Iran's Western image as a desert haven for terrorism. But the world's nuclear angst has risen recently, in large measure due to Western anxieties about Soviet nostalgia in Russia and uranium plants in Iran. And there are strong voices in the public square lamenting that the faithful of all monotheistic traditions are becoming the dark alter egos of Kierkegaard's Abraham — believers who accept violence against the innocent as an obligation from God, not because it is ethical, but because they believe that God will make all things just in their eschatons.

That's why Tarkovsky's "poetic parable," even with all its unresolved riddles, remains compelling. It resists an eschatology not tied to the Christian ethic of self-sacrifice and love. In its echoes of Abraham, it portrays a modern skeptic who chooses a difficult faith but with empathy rather than pride. If the film concedes some existential doubts, even a preference for the "holy fools" and refracted icons, it never confuses ambiguity with despair, but finds beauty in the sodden landscape and midnight glimmers. And, if Alexander's faith test in this film leads to flames, it also ends in hope, with the possibility that God can preserve future generations despite human madness. More conventionally pious, Majidi's finale celebrates the clear intervention of God. But God's unbinding of Mohammad from his sorrowful life primarily underscores Hashem's tragic self-absorption. The film's final image, in fact, shares the tense design of Chagall's painting: a father holds a child who has been wounded, largely by the father's hand, even before heaven intercedes. The atonement must cover the father's own sins, as vivid in the film as in the red cascade over Chagall's Abraham. In Islam, as in many Jewish and Christian interpretations of the Akedah, Abraham's sacrifice is often viewed as a paradigm for the surrender of base instincts for a higher purpose.[62] Even if God has spared his son Mohammad, Hashem must look inward for renewal. He may be the dark father of

---

62. Küng, *Islam*, p. 138.

this fable, but his pride, social longing, and depression mirror the human condition, as much as we may prefer to keep our distance.

For the Abraham of both films, the epiphanies are belated, mournful, and incomplete, a reminder that faith requires the courage to face future sorrows. After all, as some Midrash taught, when the angels saw God's mercy toward Isaac they were so moved that they wept, their tears falling upon Isaac's eyes and, with time, making him blind.[63]

63. See Marc Bergman, "Aqedah: Midrash as Visualization," *Journal of Textual Reading* 10 (2001): 245-51, for a discussion of how the Midrash depicts the blinding of Isaac during the sacrifice as a visual, and possibly cinematic, motif.

Evangelicals and Jews: The Unfinished Agenda

Rabbi A. James Rudin

Marvin Wilson is a true original.

As a member of the American Jewish Committee's Interreligious Affairs Department, I first encountered Marvin in the early 1970s when we jointly planned, developed, and promoted a series of pioneering national academic conferences involving leaders of the Jewish and Evangelical communities. Marvin and I quickly became close personal friends and professional colleagues, but in those early years of our work it was not always easy to bring our two communities together in a purposeful way. Mutual suspicions and inaccurate information about "The Other" were in plentiful supply as Jews and Evangelicals warily eyed one another.

But we persisted, and from our relationship sprang a series of ground-breaking meetings and several books on Evangelical-Jewish relations that Marvin and I coedited. Over the years, he has led countless groups of Christians on intensive life-changing missions to modern Israel, and he has established strong bonds of trust and esteem within the American Jewish community. And, of course, Marvin's "magnum opus," *Our Father Abraham: Jewish Roots of the Christian Faith,* a perennial best-seller, has taken its well-deserved place as a landmark in Christian-Jewish relations.

However, as Marvin and I discovered, Evangelical-Jewish relations came rather late to the American scene. The first post–World War II interreligious meetings in the United States generally involved members of "mainline" Protestant churches: United Methodists, Presbyterians, Episcopalians, American Baptists, non–Missouri Synod Lutherans, Congregationalists (the United Church of Christ), and the Disciples of Christ. But even those early contacts were frequently limited to joint Thanksgiving services in a synagogue or church and a myriad of rabbi-minister contacts involving local community issues, especially civil rights.

However, the pace of Christian-Jewish relations accelerated in 1965 following the conclusion of the Second Vatican Council in Rome when the world's Catholic bishops overwhelmingly adopted the historic *Nostra Aetate (In Our Time)* declaration that rejected the infamous deicide or "Christ killer" charge that had been hurled at Jews for centuries. *Nostra Aetate* also condemned anti-Semitism and called for "mutual respect and knowledge" between Catholics and Jews. The Vatican Council Declaration resulted in an enormous proliferation of Catholic-Jewish meetings, dialogues, programs, and consultations. Indeed, there have been more positive contacts between Catholics and Jews since the conclusion of the Second Vatican Council than there were in the first 1,900 years of Christianity.

But in 1965 the building of serious and constructive Evangelical-Jewish relations was not yet part of that interreligious mix. The reasons for this lacuna were both geographical and theological.

Until recently, most American Jews lived in large numbers in either the Northeast or the Upper Midwest: think New York City, Philadelphia, Boston, Baltimore, Pittsburgh, Cleveland, Chicago, and Detroit. The largest Christian groups Jews encountered in those urban centers were frequently Catholics with family roots in Italy, Ireland, and Poland, and Eastern Orthodox Christians from Russia, Romania, and the Balkans.

In those years, Evangelicals, mainly the descendents of immigration from Great Britain and other western European countries, lived as the majority in the South and Southwest, which had only small Jewish population centers.

As a result of these distinctive demographic patterns, the formative American experiences for both Jews and Evangelicals took place in different regions of the country. I have written elsewhere that until the early 1970s our two faith communities were akin to the proverbial "ships that pass in the night," barely aware of one another and never truly encountering one another as vibrant and unique spiritual communities.[1]

This geographical distance was one reason why many Evangelicals and Jews dealt in caricatures and stereotypes about the unknown "Other."

---

1. A. James Rudin and Marvin R. Wilson, eds., *A Time to Speak: The Evangelical-Jewish Encounter* (Grand Rapids: Eerdmans; Austin: The Center for Judaic-Christian Studies, 1987), p. xi.

Evangelicals back then were often perceived by many Jews as unenlightened "Elmer Gantrys," even bigoted anti-Semites. Conversely, many Evangelicals defined Jews as "Christ killers," "deniers of Jesus," and "scribes and Pharisees."

Marvin Wilson began his unique teaching ministry of reconciliation amidst those bleak realities that plagued and diminished the encounter between Jews and Evangelicals. That he has succeeded so well in building human bridges of mutual respect and understanding between our two faith communities is a credit to Marvin's intellectual prowess and his remarkable interpersonal skills.

Today, the strengthening of positive Evangelical-Jewish relations shows no sign of abating, even though ambivalences, ambiguities, and differences remain. Overarching those relations are several important issues that must be addressed.

Are Jews and Evangelicals domestic adversaries because of longstanding differences on a host of "at home" issues, including prayer and Bible reading in public schools, gun control, stem cell research, choice in abortion, and a deep-seated concern that some Evangelical extremists seek to create a legally mandated "Christian America"?

In addition, the Jewish community rejects the often strident efforts to convert Jews to Evangelical Christianity. The term "completed Jews," used by many Evangelicals to describe converted Jews, is especially odious and spiritually insulting since it implies that Judaism is somehow an "incomplete" religion — a belief, of course, that Jews vigorously reject.

At the same time, are these two important religious groups international partners, especially as they relate to the survival and security of the State of Israel and enhancing human rights and religious liberty throughout the world?

The remainder of this article will examine these questions.

Whenever Evangelicals and Jews encounter each other, five central issues or themes are inevitably part of such conversations:

1. anti-Semitism
2. the State of Israel
3. the Holocaust/Shoah
4. mission, witness, teshuvah, conversion
5. the Religious Right in American politics

Anti-Semitism

Anti-Semitism is the hatred of both Jews and Judaism. This pathology of the human spirit can take on political, social, cultural, and religious coloration. However, I have always believed the tap root of anti-Semitism is theological. That is one reason why Marvin Wilson's efforts are so important; he attacks the long-held Christian belief that the new religion superseded the old, leaving Jews and Judaism bereft of meaning, spirituality, and purpose.

Anti-Semitism is reflected in the Christian teaching that the "Old Israel" (the Jewish people) and its "Old Testament" (the Hebrew Bible) have been replaced/fulfilled by the "New Israel" (the Church) and the "New Testament." In some cases a "wrathful Jewish God" is unsuccessfully pitted against a "loving Christian God."

Anti-Semitism was an integral part of the centuries-long Christian "teaching of contempt" tradition that was used to defame and delegitimize Judaism and its followers.[2] In such a toxic religious climate, Judaism was pictured as merely a theological "retro rocket" to be speedily discarded once triumphant Christianity emerged or "went into eternal orbit."

Nostra Aetate was a response to the "teaching of contempt" aspect of Christianity, and even though it is clearly a Catholic teaching document it has had a profound effect upon Protestants, including many Evangelicals. Part of that Vatican Council document declared:

> [Jesus'] passion can not be charged against all the Jews, without distinction, then alive, nor against the Jews of today. . . . The Church, moreover, rejects every persecution against any person. For this reason and for the sake of the patrimony she shares with Jews, the Church decries hatreds, persecutions, and manifestations of anti-Semitism directed against Jews at any time and by anyone.[3]

Many Evangelical leaders, including Marvin Wilson, have affirmed these teachings. The recent surge in anti-Semitic acts and language, especially in parts of Europe and within many Islamic nations, is a cause for great concern that will hopefully bring Evangelicals and Jews closer together as part of a coalition that opposes hatred of Jews and Judaism and all other forms

---

2. Jules Isaac, *The Teaching of Contempt: Christian Roots of Anti-Semitism,* trans. Helen Weaver (New York: Holt, Rinehart and Winston, 1964).

3. A. James Rudin, *A Jewish Guide to Interreligious Relations* (New York: The American Jewish Committee, 2004), pp. 3-5.

of religious bigotry and prejudice. Because Christianity is extant in almost every part of the world, it is imperative that Evangelicals forcefully speak against "hatreds, persecutions, and manifestations of anti-Semitism."

The State of Israel

During the last decades of the twentieth century, Evangelicals and Jews were active international partners as they demanded religious liberty and freedom of conscience for Jews and Christian believers — often Evangelicals — residing within the former Soviet Union. Evangelicals were highly supportive of the campaign to allow Soviet Jews to immigrate to Israel, the U.S., and other lands of freedom.

It was a successful effort. During the past twenty years, more than 1,000,000 Jews have left the former USSR for Israel, the United States, and other lands of freedom. However, many Jews have chosen to remain in the former Soviet Union, especially in the three Baltic republics of Estonia, Latvia, and Lithuania as well as Russia, Belarus, and Ukraine. While their situations are much improved from the grim days of the former USSR, they frequently remain victims of anti-Semitism and discrimination. Today, another coalition of Evangelicals and Jews is again required to monitor and actively oppose the continued persistence of anti-Semitism.

Another vital area of international partnership between Evangelicals and Jews is working to protect the security and survival of an independent Jewish state in the Middle East. It is safe to say that neither faith community regards modern Israel as simply another nation that achieved its independence since 1945 following the end of World War II. Not surprisingly, Israel has been an important leit-motif in the teachings of Marvin Wilson:

> the concepts of "land of promise" and "return to Zion" are deeply grounded in biblical literature. The very last word in the Hebrew Bible (2 Chron 36:23) is a call to "go up" to Zion. . . . I also believe that the remarkable preservation of Israel over the centuries and her recent return to the land are in keeping with those many biblical texts which give promise of her future.[4]

Marvin and millions of other Evangelicals are keenly aware that the land of Israel was where Jesus taught, where he was executed by the Roman Em-

4. Rudin and Wilson, *A Time to Speak*, pp. 171-72.

pire, and where, they believe, he was resurrected. For them, modern Israel is a powerful combination of biblical landscape plus the sense that Israel reborn is part of a divine economy that calls for a Jewish ingathering of exiles as a prerequisite for the Second Coming of Jesus.

That is, of course, a broad brush to paint the Evangelical beliefs and attitudes vis-à-vis the State of Israel. But I believe it accurately describes many of Marvin's students, colleagues, and members of his numerous study groups who regularly visit Israel.

Marvin Wilson especially knows that the creation of modern Israel has placed Evangelicals and Jews in new theological and psychological territory. Hoary Christian teachings about the cursed "wandering Jew" must be permanently "deleted" from Christian consciousness and replaced by an affirming belief in the reestablishment of Jewish independence on its ancient biblical homeland.

I have written that Christian support for the security and survival of the Jewish State often divides along moral and eschatological lines:

> One Christian response is rooted in the many biblical verses that speak of a Jewish restoration in the land of Israel. . . . For such Christians, Israel is God's chosen people (Deut. 7:6-8), the state of Israel is the fulfillment of prophecy (Isa. 43:5-6, Ezek. 37), Israel occupies a special place in God's kingdom (Ezek. 36:30, 33-38, Amos 9:1-15, Zech. 8:22-23, Romans 9–11), and Israel has a God-ordained right to the land (Deut. 28–30, Acts 7:5). . . . A second major Christian response is also highly supportive, but it is not directly linked to biblical prophecy or eschatology. This position is primarily based on the twin concepts of justice and morality for the Jewish people. . . . Solidarity with Israel, however, is one concrete and compassionate way to begin the Christian process of eradicating anti-Semitism and of building a healthy and respectful relationship with the Jewish people who have been wronged by Christians for so long.[5]

Naturally, Evangelicals and Jews will differ with one another and among themselves over specific policies of the Israeli government. That is to be expected. But Marvin Wilson for the past fifty years has insisted that Evangelicals affirm Israel reborn with love and passion.

---

5. A. James Rudin, *Israel for Christians: Understanding Modern Israel* (Philadelphia: Fortress Press, 1983), pp. 122-23.

The Holocaust/Shoah

It is not possible to overstate the importance of the Holocaust ("Shoah" in Hebrew) in relations between Christians and Jews. It is of historic significance that public interest in the Nazis' mass murder of 6,000,000 Jews continues to intensify even though the Holocaust ended in 1945. Films, plays, books, works of art, religious liturgies, museums, academic conferences, university and college courses, and visits to Holocaust sites in Europe have all increased in recent years.

The Nazi German "War against the Jews" between 1933 and 1945 continues to be a central focus of contemporary Evangelical-Jewish relations.

Let me be clear on a critical point. Today's Evangelicals, most of whom were born after 1945, should not feel any personal "guilt" for the horrific events that were carried out in the heart of Christian Europe by the Nazis and their collaborators in many countries. Rather, Evangelicals, especially their leaders and teachers, must take "responsibility" to educate church members about the Shoah and the widespread collapse of Christian morality and ethics in the face of radical evil.

In 1995 the Alliance of Baptists issued a statement on Christian-Jewish relations recognizing that the Shoah was made possible only by

> centuries of Christian teaching and church-sanctioned action directed against the Jews simply because they were Jews. As Baptist Christians we are the inheritors of and, in our turn, have been the transmitters of a theology which lays the blame for the death of Jesus at the feet of the Jews . . . a theology which has valued conversion over dialogue, invective over understanding, and prejudice over knowledge.[6]

The Alliance also confessed sins of "complicity . . . of silence . . . of indifference and inaction" amid the horrors of the Holocaust. The Holocaust took place in Europe and was carried out by men and women who overwhelmingly were baptized Christians. Many Evangelicals no longer perceive the mass murders as divine punishment inflicted upon Jews because they "rejected" Jesus, and they also deny the traditional Christian belief that the Roman destruction of the Holy Temple in Jerusalem in the year 70 is proof of God's rejection of the Jews. Rather, such Evangelicals see the Shoah as

---

6. http://64.233.169.104/search?q=cache:bbHdrsFccJcJ:www.allianceofbaptists.org/ statementsonChristian-Jews.html+alliance+of+baptists+sta.

the lethal culmination of centuries of negative Christian teachings and practices aimed at Jews.

Mission, Witness, Teshuvah, Conversion

"Mission" is a term used by both Jews and Evangelicals, but it is interpreted in vastly different ways by the two communities. The traditional Jewish understanding of "mission" means that the message of the one God of the universe — ethical monotheism — should be extended to the entire world. "On that day the Lord shall be One and God's name shall be One" (Zech. 14:9) is a basic synagogue prayer. In addition, Jews are commanded to be *ohr l'goyim* — a "light unto the nations" (Isa. 42:6).

However, this self-understanding of the Jewish mission precludes coercion, religious triumphalism, or a sense of spiritual "victory." People who are not Jewish are required only to follow the seven classic laws of Noah as developed by the ancient rabbis: the establishment of courts of justice, and prohibitions against blasphemy, idolatry, incest, bloodshed, robbery, and the eating of flesh torn or cut from a living animal.

While many Evangelicals and Jews are unfamiliar with Franz Rosenzweig's *Star of Redemption* (1921), they are probably aware of the German Jewish theologian's oft-quoted assertion that Jews do not spiritually require Christianity for salvation since they are "already with the Father" thanks to the *brit* or covenant made by the ancient Israelites at Mt. Sinai. Thus, the New Testament verse that "no one comes to the Father but by the Son" (John 14:6) does not apply to the Jewish people.

Jews have experienced the Christian mission or "Great Commission" throughout the centuries. It has usually been a bitter, painful, and theologically insulting experience filled with forced conversions, fraudulent medieval disputations, expulsions, and frequently death — all at the hands of Christians who sought to "bring the Jews to Christ."

For over a thousand years in Europe, Jews were an oppressed minority living without religious freedom. Even today, Jews are still confronted by coercive Christian missionaries, often Evangelicals, who perceive Jews as targets for conversion and who continue to perpetuate the lie that Judaism is an incomplete religion devoid of intrinsic spiritual value.

It is no wonder that "Christian mission," whatever its earliest benign meaning, has become a pejorative, an attack upon Jewish sacred history and upon Jews themselves as a covenanted people of God.

But happily, a growing number of Christian theologians, including some Evangelicals, are repudiating this definition of "mission." Instead, Marvin Wilson and others are emphasizing the Jewish roots of their Christian faith. It is no accident that the subtitle of *Our Father Abraham* reflects this belief.

In 1973, during the Evangelical-sponsored "Key 73" conversion campaign, Billy Graham sharply criticized the excesses of some missionaries:

> I believe God has always had a special relationship with the Jewish people. . . . In my evangelistic efforts, I have never felt called to single out Jews as Jews. . . . Just as Judaism frowns on proselytizing that is coercive, or that seeks to commit men against their will, so do I.[7]

Today many Evangelicals define "mission" and "witness" far differently than in the past. They stake out a clear distinction between the two terms; mission is an act of insensitivity directed to the adherents of another faith community, while witness is the actual living out of one's religious beliefs without attempting to proselytize another human being, a child of God. There are no hidden agendas, no subliminal messages. Instead, such Evangelicals cite the biblical verse: "You are my witnesses, saith the LORD" (Isa. 43:12).

The late Krister Stendahl, the former Lutheran Bishop of Stockholm and Dean of the Harvard Divinity School, spoke about members of each faith community making others in different religions "jealous" of one's spiritual life. Stendahl, who died in 2008, was a friend and colleague of Marvin Wilson, and he urged Jews and Christians to "compete" with one another in the quality of our family lives, our ethics, and our prayer life. That, for Stendahl and for many Evangelicals and Jews, is the authentic meaning of "witness."

Aiding this effort is the ancient Jewish concept of *teshuvah* (Hebrew for "turning" or "repentance"). Teshuvah is open to all people who have made a sincere effort to mend their unethical ways and to seek atonement for errors of judgment and action. Teshuvah, by definition, is free of religious triumphalism, with no spiritual "winners" or "losers."

I am well aware that there will always be individual acts of conversion, sometimes from Judaism to Christianity, and sometimes the reverse process also takes place. But Jews deeply resent and are angered by system-

---

7. See "Billy Graham on Key 73," *Christianity Today,* March 16, 1973, p. 29.

atic Christian public campaigns, whatever their source, that specifically target Jews *qua* Jews as potential converts.

Clearly, Evangelicals and Jews will continue to discover opportunities for future dialogue when they openly address the critical themes of mission, witness, conversion, and teshuvah.

The Religious Right in American Politics

The emergence of the Religious Right in the United States has important implications for the Evangelical-Jewish encounter. My studies show that it is the white Evangelical community that supplies much of the religious and political ideology as well as the "foot soldiers," a.k.a. voters, who fuel the current "culture war."

In my recent book, I note that

> evangelicals do constitute the largest group of Christians who are actively involved in politics and piety, and they lead the current effort to baptize America. But not all evangelicals seek to permanently alter the historic communal fabric of American life. Such evangelicals may, in fact, be devout Christians, but they do not want to shatter or even weaken the long-held American principle of church-state separation, nor do they desire the legal establishment of any religion, even their own, in today's America.[8]

For that reason, I strongly believe Evangelicals and Jews need to recognize that, at its heart, the Religious Right believes America has lost its moral compass as a nation. There are some Religious Right leaders who continually invoke "Divine authority" to buttress their political policies and platforms and who characterize their opponents as "sinful" or "ungodly."

Behind the catchy rhetoric of "family values" and "moral tradition," the Religious Right remains committed to changing America as we have known it since its creation in the late eighteenth century. Some zealots actually speak of establishing a "Christian America" that will embody the Religious Right's particular and exclusivist theological beliefs.

Nor should anyone be deceived because many Religious Right leaders are strong public supporters of Israel. Evangelical-Jewish relations, in-

8. See James Rudin, *The Baptizing of America: The Religious Right's Plans for the Rest of Us* (New York: Thunder's Mouth Press, 2006).

deed interreligious relations in general, is not a kind of *quid pro quo* game in which Jews are willing to overlook the disturbing domestic agendas of the Religious Right in return for support of the Jewish State. Because the Evangelical-Jewish agenda is a broad-based one, support on one key issue does not guarantee agreement or consensus on other vital questions. Authentic dialogue presupposes both agreement and disagreement.

Instead, Jews and Evangelicals should continue their efforts to build mutual respect and understanding while fully recognizing that the Religious Right is seeking to impose its agenda at a time in our nation's history when recent population studies indicate the U.S. is becoming increasingly a multireligious, multiethnic, and multiracial society. Americans are becoming more, not less, diverse in their religious identities. The attempt — so far unsuccessful — by the Religious Right to create an exclusive and constricted "Christian America" flies directly in the face of these facts.

In 1984, during a historic Evangelical-Jewish meeting held at Gordon College, Marvin Wilson and I jointly issued a ten-point "Conference Call." A quarter century has passed since then, but I strongly believe the words of our original "Call" are as relevant today as when they were first issued:

1. *We are united in a common struggle against Anti-Semitism. We are outraged by the continued presence of this evil and pledge to work together for the elimination of Anti-Semitism and all other forms of racism. We are committed jointly to educate this present generation and future generations about the unspeakable horror of the Holocaust.*

2. *We categorically reject the notion that Zionism is racism. Zionism, the Jewish people's national liberation movement, has deep roots in the Hebrew Scriptures, no less than in the painful history of the Jewish people.*

3. *We are committed to support Israel as a Jewish state, within secure and recognized borders. We also recognize that Palestinian Arabs have legitimate rights. We pledge our joint efforts in behalf of a just and lasting peace not only between Jews and Arabs but among all peoples of the Middle East.*

4. *No government is sacred, and no government's policies are beyond criticism. But we strongly object to the practice of holding Israel to a different standard of conduct and morality from that applied to all other nation-states, especially those committed to Israel's destruction.*

5. *We affirm the eternal validity and contemporary relevance of the Hebrew Scriptures as a primary source of moral, ethical, and spiritual val-*

ues. And we pledge to work together to uphold and advance these biblical values in our society and throughout the world.

6. We pledge to uphold the precious value of religious pluralism in our society. We strongly condemn those who would use unethical, coercive, devious, or manipulative means to proselytize others. Witness to one's faith must always be accompanied with great sensitivity and respect for the integrity of the other person lest religious freedom and pluralism be threatened.

7. We will seek to overcome any popular stereotypes, caricatures, and images that may contribute to one faith community falsely perceiving the other. To further this end, we pledge to continue to examine the rich spiritual legacy that Judaism and Evangelicalism hold sacred together as well as their profound differences of belief.

8. We share a common calling to eliminate inhumanity and injustice among all humankind. We also jointly resolve to work together to prevent nuclear annihilation and to pursue the path of world peace.

9. We share a joint commitment to uphold the principle of separation of church and state in the United States.

10. We pledge to deepen our joint involvement in the struggle to achieve human rights and religious liberty for our coreligionists in the Soviet Union and elsewhere in the world.[9]

In the Jewish tradition, we wish beloved friends and colleagues a lifespan of *me-ah v'esrim,* the Hebrew term for 120 years of productivity and achievement. That is my hope and prayer for Marvin Wilson as he celebrates fifty years of brilliant teaching and pioneering leadership. May God grant him many more!

9. Rudin and Wilson, *A Time to Speak,* pp. xi-xiii.

Following Abraham into the Twenty-First Century: Building Christian-Jewish Relations Today

JoAnn G. Magnuson

I am honored by the invitation to contribute to this Festschrift in celebration of the life and work of Dr. Marvin R. Wilson on the occasion of his seventy-fifth birthday. I am certain that each of the contributors to this book has a unique relationship with Dr. Wilson. In addition to his many intellectual and scholarly gifts, Dr. Wilson has a rare gift for friendship and a generous manner of weaving his friends into his larger circle of associates. I have been the recipient of this generosity in more ways than I can calculate.

I am probably the only contributor to these pages who is not a professional academic. My work has been primarily in the trenches of Jewish-Christian relations — with the Israel pilgrims, the amateur Bible students, the political and religious enthusiasts, the Vacation Bible School teachers, and the committee members for the annual Yom Hashoah and Yom Ha'atzmaut observances. I am eternally grateful to Dr. Wilson, who, as a fellow night owl, is often willing to engage with me in late-night phone conversations ranging from current crises in Jewish-Christian relations to interpretations of obscure biblical texts.

Had I organized my academic career more carefully I might be teaching the fine points of Jewish-Christian relations to students in ivy-covered buildings instead of sharing my accumulated insights with jet-lagged tourists while bumping along the highways and byways of Israel and Eastern Europe. However, I would not have wanted to miss my lifetime of unique adventures: leading over sixty tours to Israel since 1977; working on a plethora of projects with the Jewish Community Relations Council of

Minnesota and the Dakotas (a great group of folks); serving for many years as the only Evangelical on the Minnesota Council of Churches Jewish-Christian Relations Committee; lobbying on Capitol Hill with my dear friend Esther Levens and a variety of pro-Israel activists; bringing American Christians to Auschwitz on March of the Living; serving as U.S. Coordinator for Christian Friends of Yad Vashem. I have to admit that my life has been not been dull.

What Is Christian Zionism?

I am an Evangelical Christian with a life-long interest in the relationship between Christians and Jews. I grew up in a Jewish neighborhood and have been blessed with a long list of Jewish friends. While not a trained scholar, I am a serious student of the Bible. I read Hebrew slowly and Greek even more slowly. Over a lifetime of Bible reading I have been impressed with the amount of space given in the sacred text to our father Abraham, his family, their relationship with God, and the attention paid to the details of their connection to a small strip of land along the eastern coast of the Mediterranean Sea.

Dr. Wilson described his book *Our Father Abraham* as "an exposition on what it means for today's Church to be part of Abraham's spiritual family."[1] What would the church look like if it were truly aware of its connection to Abraham's family tree?

I am pondering this question on the fourth Sunday in Advent, when the liturgical readings in church this morning included portions from 2 Samuel 7, where God promises King David that "Your house and your kingdom shall endure forever before me; your throne shall stand firm forever." On the Jewish calendar this Shabbat includes a reading from the prophet Amos, chapter 9, verses 14-15, which says, "'I will bring back my exiled people Israel; they will rebuild the ruined cities and live in them. They will plant vineyards and drink their wine; they will make gardens and eat their fruit. I will plant Israel in their own land, never again to be uprooted from the land I have given them,' says the LORD your God."

The long-term relationship of the Jewish people to their ancient homeland is a major theme in Scripture and is often referred to as "Zion-

---

1. Marvin R. Wilson, *Our Father Abraham: Jewish Roots of the Christian Faith* (Grand Rapids: Eerdmans; Dayton: Center for Judaic-Christian Studies, 1989), p. xvi.

ism." There are many aspects of this concept, but let us try to define "mere" Zionism, the most basic notion of Zionism that seems to be suggested in the Bible.

Zionism supports the return of the Jewish people to Zion, to the land of Israel, to the land promised by God to Abraham and his descendants forever. This promise appears often in Scripture, but we find the first reference in Genesis 12:1-3, enlarged upon by Genesis 15:7: "God said unto Abraham, I am the LORD who brought you out of the land of Ur of the Chaldees to give this land to you to inherit it."

The first reference in the Bible using the word "Zion" is in 2 Samuel 5:7: "Nevertheless David took the stronghold of Zion, that is, the city of David." From that point on, the word is used 154 times in the Hebrew Scriptures. The basic meaning of the root word seems to be "a dry place" or "a fortress." In biblical usage it may refer to the City of David, the Temple Mount, all of Jerusalem, and in some cases all of the land of Israel.

The term *Zionism* was coined in 1891 by the Austrian publicist Nathan Birnbaum. It describes anyone who believes the Jews have a right to return to their ancient homeland. Birnbaum played a prominent part in the First Zionist Congress (1897), where Theodor Herzl called for the founding of a Jewish state.

If Zionism is the support of the return of the Jewish people to the land of Israel, Christian Zionism is simply Christian support for the return of the Jewish people to the land of Israel. Not every Christian who cares about the Jewish people wants to be called a Christian Zionist, and the terminology is not crucial. Our real question is, where should Christians see the Jews fitting into God's ongoing plan for the world? Is there still a place for the Jews as God's covenant people? If so, how should Christians relate to their Jewish neighbors?

Background of Jewish-Christian Relations

A doctrine, later known as "supersessionism" and sometimes referred to as "replacement theology," rose up early in church history and has complicated Jewish-Christian relations ever since. As the church moved away from Israel and its Jewish matrix, Christian theologians began to see Christianity not just as an extension but as a replacement of Israel. A few references will illustrate the attitude that developed in the time of the church fathers:

(1) Justin Martyr (c. 160 C.E.) wrote: "For the true spiritual Israel . . . are we who have been led to God through this crucified Christ."

(2) Eusebius of Caesarea (265-339), the first historian of the Christian church, claimed that Jews in every community crucified a Christian at their Purim festival as a rejection of Jesus. He also made a distinction between Hebrews [whom he saw as "good men of the Old Testament"] and Jews [whom he characterized as evil.]

(3) Origen (c. 250 C.E.) wrote: "Jews have suffered because they were a most wicked nation, which although guilty of many other sins, yet have been punished severely for none as for those that were committed against our Jesus." His thought was important to the development of supersessionism. He taught that Israel was permanently rejected by God and that the church was the new Israel.

It is important for Christians to remember what Jesus himself said of his suffering and death: "No one takes my life from me, I lay it down of myself" (John 10:18). Christianity teaches that Jesus came to be the sacrificial Lamb of God. Christians are encouraged to be thankful for this gift, not to search for someone to blame for the crucifixion.

Most of the earliest Christians were Jewish, but the church gradually lost interest in its Jewish roots and heritage as it moved into the pagan world. While there was certainly some persecution of the early Christians by the official Jewish leadership, most Christians in the first generations saw themselves as Jews. By the third century C.E., however, few Christians thought of Jesus as a Jewish teacher or rabbi. Still fewer thought of God's prophets, priests, kings, and apostles as Jews. Some medieval Christian pilgrims remembered the ancient, biblical Jews while traveling to the Holy Land, but few felt connected to the contemporary Jews they met along the way.

By the fourth century the prevailing view was that the church had totally replaced Israel and the Jewish people as a carrier of God's covenant. This view prevailed, with few dissenting voices, until the dawn of the Reformation period. As ordinary people began to have access to the Bible in their own languages, many readers noticed a fairly obvious fact: much space in the sacred text is given to the relationship between God and the land and the people of Israel. This led many Christian readers of the Bible to conclude that God intended the Jewish people to come back to their ancient land in the latter days of human history. This view is sometimes called "Restorationism," and in recent times it has been known as Christian Zionism.

The word "restore" implies the act of giving something back that has been lost or stolen, a return to a former or a normal condition. Isaiah tells us to "Look to the rock from which you were cut and to the quarry from which you were hewn; look to Abraham, your father, and to Sarah, who gave you birth" (Isa. 51:1-2). The Christian church has neglected her relationship with our spiritual parents, Abraham and Sarah, as well as their descendants and their worldview, for so long that it has been nearly lost and mostly forgotten.

As we have noted, early in Christian history, as church leadership moved away from the land of Israel, many began to ignore and in some cases to despise the biblical storehouse that contained the Hebraic treasures of our faith. The Old Testament was part of the canon, but it was viewed through a very Christian filter.

I am not suggesting that the effort of the church fathers to bring Christian understanding to the Jewish texts was totally wrong and misguided. New ideas and understandings often cause pendulum swings in history. However, this particular swing has had some very unfortunate side effects.

Restoration Efforts

There have been several points in history when Christians endeavored to restore their connection to their Hebrew heritage. A fascinating account of various Christian efforts to discover the quarry from which we Christians were hewn is found in Barbara Tuchman's *Bible and Sword, An Overview of Christian Zionism,*[2] subtitled *England and Palestine from the Bronze Age to Balfour.* This book traces the path of an interesting assortment of Christians who, for one reason or another, looked to the quarry from which they were hewn, to the olive tree into which they were grafted (Rom. 11:17-21).

Studying the history of those who believed that the descendants of Abraham, Isaac, and Jacob would return to the land the Lord promised to them is a study in the amazing grace of God — grace because it is quite clear that many of the individuals involved took wrong turns and usually made progress by accident. Radio host and Jewish theologian Dennis Prager refers to Genesis as "an account of the world's first recorded dys-

2. Barbara Tuchman, *Bible and Sword, an Overview of Christian Zionism: England and Palestine from the Bronze Age to Balfour* (New York: Ballantine Books, 1984).

functional family" (not that we've seen many fully functional families since the angel barred the gate to Eden). In both the Christian and the Jewish branches of the family, the lovers of Zion have been a rather eccentric crew. Tuchman comments on this phenomenon: "It is a curious fact that so many notable English eccentrics have been drawn irresistibly to the East. Perhaps it was because most of them, like T. E. Lawrence, the archetype, were voyaging on some private religious or metaphysical quest of their own and, like Disraeli's Tancred, sought spiritual rebirth in the place where three great religions were conceived."[3] Or perhaps it is simply that those seeking God, however confused their motives, tended to search in the land where it all began.

As history continued, anti-Semitism became quite well entrenched in Christian thought. We modern Christians need to study this history in order to understand why Jews often fear Christians in positions of power.

Most of today's Evangelical Christians have no intention to force their beliefs on others. Our biblical call is to persuade others, not pummel them into submission. However, the Jewish community does have a basis for concern. We need to realize that the Jewish experience under Christian governments has not been positive. German Christians had the right to pray in schools in the 1930s. Unfortunately few who prayed had the wisdom or the courage to perceive and oppose the rise of Nazism. Too few asked themselves the questions: "Where am I?" and "What is happening to my Jewish neighbors?"

Since World War II, as the shocking details of the Holocaust became public knowledge, church leaders began to wake up to the damage caused by theological anti-Semitism. In the post-war years, significant progress was made in Jewish-Christian relations. The birth of modern Israel has given the Jewish people a home base in which to rebuild after centuries in dispersion. This homeland has also given Jews and Christians the opportunity to meet together and to encounter each other as equal partners in the study of, among other things, archeology, geography, biblical languages, and biblical texts.

The ensuing dialogue has been rich. Catholic scholars deserve a great deal of credit for this movement. The Second Vatican Council was instrumental in producing the document called *Nostra Aetate (In Our Time)*. This led to many positive changes within Catholic circles concerning their relationship with the Jewish community. Individually, Catholic leaders

---

3. Tuchman, *Bible and Sword*, p. 270.

such as Sister Rose Thering[4] and Father Edward Flannery[5] led the movement toward dialogue with the Jewish community in the United States.

Evangelical Christians showed less interest in Jewish-Christian dialogue in the early post-war years. Evangelicals have generally been better at proclamation than at dialogue. There was a mixture of opinion in the Evangelical world after the founding of the State of Israel in 1948. Some believed that the restoration of Israel was a fulfillment of biblical prophecy, while others questioned such a view. After the 1967 Six-Day War and the reunification of Jerusalem under Israeli control, more Evangelicals became actively supportive of Israel. Organizations such as the International Christian Embassy, Jerusalem; Bridges for Peace; Christian Friends of Israel; and the International Fellowship of Christians and Jews sprang up during the 1970s and 1980s. The movement now often identified as Christian Zionism became a popular cause in the Evangelical world.

One of the serious efforts to bring Evangelicals and Jews together for dialogue was initiated by our friend Dr. Marvin Wilson. Between 1975 and 1984 Dr. Wilson organized three gatherings that served to break new ground in this field. It is my hope that much more work will be done in this area. Today we have a new cast of characters who would profit greatly from this experience. In addition to public presentations of papers, I believe the current scene would benefit from some form of "round table" discussions between Jewish and Evangelical leaders in a venue with enough privacy so the participants could discuss sensitive issues without an audience — the sort of discussion Jews refer to as talking "tachlis."

I am concerned that many leaders of the pro-Israel Christian community today have little experience in actual dialogue with Jews. Often they are people who bring large groups of Christians to travel in Israel, and their main source of Jewish friendships is limited to Israelis involved in the tourism industry. This often guarantees that our Christian leaders never have the benefit of constructive criticism from Jewish friends. I know that both Dr. Wilson and I are thankful today for the Jewish friends in our early years, who were more concerned with honest communication and less concerned with the protection of our fragile egos.

---

4. Oren Jacoby, *Sister Rose's Passion* (DVD Storyville Films, 2004).

5. Edward H. Flannery, *The Anguish of the Jews: Twenty-Three Centuries of Antisemitism,* 2nd ed. (Mahwah, NJ: Paulist Press, 2004).

Does Christian Zionism Require Dispensationalism?

I seem to confuse people when I say that I am a Christian Zionist but not a dispensationalist. At present there appears to be a common perception that Christians who believe that the Jewish people are back in their ancient land by divine appointment must also share a view of eschatology that includes a rigid plan for the end of days and an expectation of a pre-tribulation "rapture" of the church[6] — as well as a number of events supporting Christian triumphalism.

While I am a life-long Protestant, I have learned a great deal from my Catholic friends. There seems to be more room in Catholic theology for the category of "mystery." Not every theological concept fits neatly into our file cabinets. I believe that God created the world without my advice, and he will wrap up the current phase of human history in his own good time — again without my advice. In between those events I am called to "do justly, love mercy and walk humbly with God" (Mic. 6:8).

Therefore I do not find it contradictory to believe that the Scriptures which indicate that the Jewish people will be back in their ancient homeland in the "latter days" do not require me to have clear expectations about details of the those days. John Nelson Darby's notions of the "end" are not the only biblical possibilities.

One of my favorite hymns is "Holy God We Praise Thy Name." The fourth verse ends with these words: "And adoring bend the knee, while we own the mystery." I am very content to "own the mystery."

How Can We Follow Abraham on Pilgrimage Today?

A significant segment of Evangelical Christians has developed an interest in Israel and the Jewish people through reading books on end-time prophecy. But the impact of this emphasis looks different when you spend time in Israel. A friend who once worked on a kibbutz in the Jezreel Valley remarked, "It is harder to get enthused about blood running up to the horses' bridles in the Valley of Armageddon when you have breakfast every morning with people who live there." Some Evangelicals have made Israel and the Jewish people into museum pieces to support their interest in the

---

6. Hal Lindsey and Carole C. Carlson, *The Late, Great Planet Earth* (Grand Rapids: Zondervan, 1970); Tim LaHaye and Jerry B. Jenkins, *Left Behind* series (Carol Stream, IL: Tyndale House, 1995-2007).

past and the future. However, the oft-heard criticism that "Evangelicals are only interested in Israel because they think the Jews need to be there so the final battle can occur and Jesus will come again" is really an oversimplification of Evangelical and Christian Zionist views.

After thirty years of leading Christian groups on tours of Israel, I have seen a pattern of thought and behavior develop. At first, most tourists want to see the biblical sites and are fascinated by visualizing how Jesus will come again. But as they get to know local people (I make sure they meet a variety of them), as they hear about the challenges of daily life and learn about the family backgrounds of various Israelis — Holocaust survivors, American, Iranian, Moroccan, Yemenite immigrants, families who have been there for generations, and folks who came last year from Russia — the plot thickens. Our tourists become more empathetic and interested in the here and now and less fixated on eschatology.

It is important to remember that Jewish-Christian relations, at least in any positive sense, are a relatively new experience. Since the fourth century of the common era Christians alternately ignored or persecuted Jews, and Jews tried to stay out of the path of Christians. In the years since the Holocaust, many Christians — from the left to the right and in the center — have realized that while the Holocaust was a physical tragedy for the Jews it was a moral tragedy for the church. We Christians must work to educate our community about the past and build relationships for the future.

I hope that both Jews and Christians can be patient with each other while we get acquainted again after nearly 2,000 years of separation. For those among us who hope for a fulfillment of Robert Burns's famous desire to "see ourselves as others see us," I suggest a recent book by a Jewish author, Zev Chavets, *A Match Made in Heaven*,[7] which is subtitled *American Jews, Christian Zionists, and One Man's Exploration of the Weird and Wonderful Judeo-Evangelical Alliance*. It is a breezy, humorous, and insightful look at the Evangelical community through the eyes of a Jewish friend who is trying to explain the Evangelical world to his fellow Jews.

Encouragement from Father Abraham

While contemplating some of the eccentricities of modern Christian pilgrims, we can draw encouragement from our father Abraham, who also

---

7. Zev Chavets, *A Match Made in Heaven* (New York: HarperCollins, 2007).

journeyed with some difficult fellow travelers. Nephew Lot, for instance. Often on the lookout for his own advantage and finding a scenic spot to settle, Lot built his house near the Dead Sea and discovered he had moved into a bad neighborhood. When Lot was taken captive, Abraham, without complaint, mounted an army and hiked up to the Golan Heights to rescue nephew Lot.

Down through history there have been many times when our Jewish family members have been in desperate need of rescue, and the Christian grafted-in branches went by on the other side of the road. In the post–World War II years, when the Iron Curtain fell over Eastern Europe, both Jewish and Christian dissidents needed rescue.

I recently heard the story of a wedding held in Jerusalem in January 2008. Rachel, the daughter of Natan and Avital Sharansky, was the bride. Natan and Avital — Russian Jews who wanted to immigrate to Israel — were married in the Soviet Union in 1974. Avital's exit visa was about to expire, so she left immediately for Israel. Natan was denied exit, and three years later the KGB hauled him away to prison, leaving a young Avital to lead the struggle for his freedom. After nine miserable years in the Gulag, Natan was reunited with Avital in Jerusalem and they began to build their family.

As I read about Rachel Sharansky's lovely wedding, wiping away a few tears, I was also remembering a day in the early 1980s when a small group of Jews and Christians gathered on the campus of the University of Minnesota to protest on behalf of Soviet refusniks — both Jewish and Christian prisoners of conscience. At the time my son was working in London supporting the "Campaign to Free the Siberian Seven," an effort to rescue two Russian Pentecostal families who, after years of persecution, had made it to Moscow and had sought refuge in the U.S. Embassy. They lived in the basement of the Embassy for five years, causing much diplomatic embarrassment. To the shame of most U.S. churches, this situation was generally ignored here. When we tried to lobby for Christian dissidents, our main colleagues were the Soviet Jewry activists. Indeed, some of the Evangelical Christian support for Israel today is built on friendships born in the "bad old days" of the Soviet persecution and the collegial relations developed at that time, rather than current "end of the world" theology.

How well I remember that day at the University of Minnesota campus. We all brought signs with pictures of Soviet prisoners of conscience. The Jews carried pictures of Natan Sharansky and Ida Nudel and many others. The Christians carried pictures of the Siberian Seven. The bus carrying the Russian Trade Delegation was late in arriving. The intent of the meeting was to hear from the Russians who came to talk about all that our nations had in common and how important it was to have commercial trade and positive relations and to ignore our differences. Our little group of dissidents was not welcome in this happy celebration of détente. Suddenly it began to rain, and we headed for the bus shelter and piled our signs in the corner. After a long wait, suddenly the sun came out, the bus with the Russians pulled up, and we ran out waving our signs — to the great annoyance of the trade organizers. As we began to lift our signs I looked around and realized that most of the Jews were waving pictures of the Christians and most of the Christians were waving pictures of the Jews. I glanced heavenward and had a feeling that God was smiling on us. I believe that the positive relationships between Evangelical Christians and the Minnesota Jewish community began a new growth spurt from that day.

Years later I met Rabbi Leonid Feldman, another former refusnik and a Russian prisoner of conscience. I asked him a question. We who wrote postcards naming prisoners about whom we were concerned were often told by "experts" that calling attention to individuals could make their situation worse. We worried about that, but we wrote the postcards anyway. Leonid assured me that the opposite was the case. When the Communists knew that people in the West knew your name, they were less likely to simply get rid of you and more likely to eventually release you. Leonid said he didn't know how many postcards it took to make one's plight a public issue, but one day a Communist guard came to his cell and turned the key. Leonid was free.

I was glad to receive the report of the wedding of the Sharanskys' daughter. All of us who participated in large or small ways in the Soviet resistance movement can rejoice in the privilege of playing a small part in a significant moment of history. Perhaps we, like Queen Esther, came into the world for such a time as this.

The Holocaust in Jewish-Christian Understanding

There is an old rabbinic story about the rabbi whose young disciple was assuring him of his love and commitment. The young man kept saying, "Rabbi, I love you!" The rabbi looked at him sadly and said, "Don't tell me you love me if you don't know what causes me pain."

Many Evangelical Christians who are starting their pilgrimage into the Jewish world are quick to assure their new Jewish friends of the depth of their love for the "Chosen People." While such Christian enthusiasm is well meant, this display of affection usually makes their new Jewish friends nervous and uncomfortable. Jews are also unlikely to be impressed with Christians blowing shofars or wrapping themselves in prayer shawls. When I teach seminars on Jewish-Christian relations, I often tell my students that, shocking as it may seem to them, after seventeen hundred years of persecution most Jews would be content if Christians simply left them alone.

Before we begin proclaiming our love, it would be helpful if Christian Zionists spent a day at Yad Vashem, the museum and Holocaust education center in Jerusalem — or at least made a visit to the nearest Holocaust museum in the U.S. I would also recommend a trip to Poland and the remains of the Nazi death camps, as well as the multitude of obscure sites in towns and forests where millions of ordinary Jewish families were massacred by Hitler's demonic hatred while most of the Christian world looked away.

Several years ago I traveled through parts of Poland with my American friend, Ron Cantrell, and our Slovakian friend, Jozef Janits. Jozef drove, Ron navigated, and I sat in the back seat and read aloud from Martin Gilbert's book *Holocaust Journey*.[8] We visited five of the six "death factories" — Auschwitz-Birkenau, Belzec, Majdanik, Sobibor, and Treblinka. Standing on these sites while reading Gilbert's powerful text was an unforgettable experience. However, it was a bit difficult to answer the predictable question asked by friends when I returned to the States, "Did you have fun on your summer vacation?"

I share the sentiment of Jan Karski, the Polish army officer who was smuggled into the Warsaw Ghetto and then tried to rally support from the Western Allies for the endangered Jews. He said in reference to the Holocaust, "This sin will haunt humanity to the end of time. It does haunt me. And I want it to be so."[9]

I want this tragedy to haunt me. It's not that I'm a masochist — I'm not trying to suffer. But our Jewish friends need to know that Christians — who say they are friends — are willing to put their shoulders under this burden. Many Christians tell me that they couldn't possibly visit such hor-

8. Martin Gilbert, *Holocaust Journey* (New York: Columbia University Press, 1997).

9. Michael Berenbaum, *A Promise to Remember: The Holocaust in the Words and Voices of Its Survivors* (Boston: Bulfinch Press/AOL Time Warner Book Group, 2003), p. 68.

rible, painful places. I realize this is not everyone's calling. But we need enough Christians, with strong hearts and stomachs, to visit these sites, hear these stories, and tell them to the next generation.

Because I want Christians to remember and relate to Jewish history and experiences, I began leading tours to Eastern Europe in 1995. My first trip was with a group of Protestant, Catholic, and Jewish women from a study group in the Minneapolis–St. Paul area. This introduction brought me into contact with a variety of folk in the former Soviet Union who were trying to build positive Jewish-Christian relations. This led me into a new set of adventures.

While traveling in Ukraine with a group of Christian humanitarian aid workers from Poland, we visited the town of Drohobycz, where a major massacre took place in 1943. When we visited in 2006 we met the last remaining Jewish resident of Drohobycz, Alfred Shrayer, a survivor of the massacre. He took our group of Christians to the memorial site in the forest where hundreds of Jews were murdered by the Nazis. Alfred played original music on his violin while we knelt to leave flowers and memorial stones at the gravesite. He then accompanied us to their local soup kitchen, which is supported by our Polish and Slovakian Christian friends. Alfred insisted that we eat our soup while he and his friends serenaded us with tunes from *Fiddler on the Roof.*

In Poland one will also meet a growing number of younger Christians who are studying the Holocaust, attending seminars at Yad Vashem, trying to come to grips with their own national past, and hoping to build a better future. They hold summer conferences where speakers address enthusiastic audiences of Eastern Europeans. Anti-Semitism is losing its hold in the former Soviet bloc. Meeting these brothers and sisters and encouraging their work would go a long way in broadening our Christian horizons.

Much work remains to be done in the area of Holocaust education. The next generation of Christians needs to hear the stories of the few heroic rescuers, as well as the painful stories of perpetrators and bystanders. All churches in the English-speaking world should conduct showings of Pierre Sauvage's beautiful film, *Weapons of the Spirit*,[10] the story of a major Christian rescue effort in the French town of LeChambon. When the Nazis demanded that Pastor André Trocmé give them lists of local Jews, he replied, "We don't know what a Jew is, we only know men." Professor Patrick Henry's recent book about rescuers quotes Pastor Trocmé and carries the

---

10. Pierre Sauvage, *Weapons of the Spirit* (Chambon Foundation, 1989).

title, *We Only Know Men*.[11] David Gushee's book *Righteous Gentiles of the Holocaust*[12] should also be required reading for Christian educators. It will introduce the next generation of Christians to role models who chose the path of costly discipleship.

I am currently working with a joint project of Yad Vashem and the International Christian Embassy Jerusalem, which is sponsoring a Christian Desk at Yad Vashem. Our director there, Dr. Susanna Kokkonen, is available to meet with Christian groups touring the museum and to arrange special activities and meetings to enrich the experience for Christian visitors. We are also working to bring the educational resources of Yad Vashem to Christian educators around the world.

Looking to the Rock from Which We Were Carved

Christian Zionists are often accused of holding the opinion that Israel can do no wrong. No serious person thinks that Israel dwells in a condition of sinless perfection. Like all political entities it has a mixture of heroes, villains, and a lot of ordinary human sinners. But Israel is not the cause of all the troubles in the Muslim world. It is not the cause of all the problems in the Palestinian community. A major part of the work of most Christian Zionist organizations is to report good news about Israel, to tell the positive story of a thriving — albeit beleaguered — democratic state in the Middle East.

But my plea is not merely to encourage Christian support for a plucky little democracy. The reason we must speak out for Israel and the Jewish people is a far deeper one. It is rooted in the commandment to "Honor your father and mother [which is the first commandment with a promise] that it may go well with you and that you may enjoy long life on the earth" (Exod. 20:12; Eph. 6:2-3).

"Look to the rock from which you were cut and to the quarry from which you were hewn; look to Abraham, your father, and to Sarah, who gave you birth. . . ." Less than seventy years since the onset of the Anschluss (the beginning of Hitler's march across Europe), vile anti-Semitic materi-

---

11. Patrick Henry, *We Only Know Men* (Washington, DC: The Catholic University of America Press, 2007).

12. David P. Gushee, *Righteous Gentiles of the Holocaust: Genocide and Moral Obligation* (St. Paul: Paragon House Publishers, 2003).

als are appearing in major newspapers in Europe and the Arab world. Supposedly civilized people still believe that Jews kidnap and kill Christian children to use their blood to make Passover matzah. Blood libels die hard. Our spiritual parents are still under attack. I know that God loves everyone, and I'm glad that there are Christians standing up for the Christian Arabs, the Muslims, and endangered people groups everywhere. I hope no one will be offended when I choose to stand up for the Jews. I've read enough Holocaust history to know that I do not want to be a bystander.

I realize that the public perception of Christian Zionism has been framed in a way that makes those of us who are pro-Israel look like right-wing fanatics, salivating over eschatological expectations. My response is simply that, after more than thirty years of involvement in the pro-Israel movement, I know that most of my colleagues are far more influenced by moral and historical issues than by end-time concerns. We can see significance in biblical prophecies without painting a clear and definite picture of the end or suggesting that public policy must support Christian expectations.

In summary, I believe that God has a hand in history and a continuing relationship with the descendants of Abraham. I believe that the church for many years has disconnected from its Jewish roots — and is the poorer for it. I believe that modern Christians and Jews will benefit from reconnecting and listening and learning from each other. I am thankful to Dr. Wilson for blazing a trail, and I am thankful for having had a chance to share some of the adventures on that trail. It is my prayer that many in generations to come will join in this pilgrimage and build the trail into a highway.

My personal history in this field began during World War II, when my grandmother and I developed an evening ritual, parking ourselves in front of the old Silvertone radio to listen carefully to the "war news." Several older cousins were in the army, and prayers were raised on their behalf. Gram always read from the Bible, particularly from the prophet Jeremiah, often the portion which says, "This is what the LORD says, he who appoints the sun to shine by day, who decrees the moon and stars to shine by night, who stirs up the sea so that its waves roar — the LORD Almighty is his name: 'Only if these decrees vanish from my sight,' declares the LORD, 'will the descendants of Israel ever cease to be a nation before me.' This is what the LORD says: 'Only if the heavens above can be measured and the foundations of the earth below be searched out will I reject all the descendants of Israel because of all they have done,' declares the LORD" (Jer. 31:35-37).

She would say to me, "God has a covenant with the Jews that will last as long as the sun, the moon, and the stars. This is a terrible war, but Hitler will be defeated and the Jews will be back in their ancient land. We must pray for that."

She died in May of 1947, leaving behind her old Bible underlined at many of the points recording the promises to restore Israel. So I was impressed, but not too surprised, when I came home from school a year later to find the Minneapolis *Tribune* headline shouting, "State of Israel Declared."

I thought, "Wow, Gram knew this was going to happen because she read the Bible." That definitely affected my view of the Bible and world events — and set me on a path that led to life-long involvement with Israel and the Jewish people.

The last time I looked, the sun, moon, and stars are still out there.

"The Other Woman": A Collaborative Jewish-Christian Study of Hagar

David J. Zucker and Rebecca Gates Brinton

Few narratives in the book of Genesis are devoted to Hagar the Egyptian, but her presence is significant in the early accounts of the patriarchs and matriarchs. Hagar also appears in the Christian Scriptures and in writings of the rabbis and the church fathers. As "the Other Woman" in the life of Abraham, Hagar is often viewed as an "Other" or an "Outsider" in a variety of ways and at multiple levels.

Hagar appears only briefly in the Hebrew Bible (the Christian Old Testament), primarily in Genesis chapters 16 and 21, with a short historical note in Genesis 25:12. Later sources, however, provide a wide array of additional perspectives on her role and significance within the Genesis narrative.

For example, in the Christian New Testament Paul utilizes Hagar as an allegorical symbol when writing to the Galatian church. Somewhat later, Hagar appears in classical Rabbinic literature. During roughly this same period, the church fathers — the Patristic writers — discuss Hagar in a distinctly different manner.

This chapter focuses primarily on the biblical (Hebrew Bible and Christian Scriptures), Rabbinic, and Patristic views of Hagar, though brief note is taken of some contemporary writing, which often considers her through the lenses of literary, feminist, and/or other forms of biblical commentary. Though each of these sources refers to the same person, they provide differing and sometimes (though not necessarily) competing perspectives on the figure of Hagar.

Hagar's presence in the Hebrew Bible and the Christian New Testament may be limited; however, a closer study of her role in these primary sources and later Rabbinic and Patristic writings demonstrates that Hagar's impact is considerable and long-lasting.

Hagar in Genesis

Genesis 16

Hagar appears

Hagar is first mentioned in the opening line of Genesis 16. "Now Sarai . . . had an Egyptian slave-girl whose name was Hagar" (Gen. 16:1).[1]

The Bible does not indicate how Hagar the Egyptian slave-girl entered Sarah's entourage. Abraham and Sarah had sojourned in Egypt, and they had prospered there. When in Egypt, Abraham acquired "male and female slaves" (Gen. 12:16). Presumably, Hagar was one of these women.

Hagar and Sarah: the early encounters

The Bible indicates that Sarah was barren. "Sarai, Abram's wife, bore him no children" (Gen. 16:1; cf. 11:30). Sarai then says to her husband, "You see that the LORD has prevented me from bearing children." This is not a casual statement. In the ancient world both barrenness and fertility were ascribed to God, and "childlessness was regarded as a virtual sign of divine disfavor (see [Gen.] 16:2; 30:1-2 [33:5; 1 Sam. 1:6])."[2] Consequently, she designates Hagar to serve as a surrogate womb for her. "[Sarai said:] go in to my slave-girl; it may be that I shall obtain children by her" (Gen. 16:2).

This concept of surrogate motherhood was enshrined in Near Eastern law and tradition. If a wife, especially of the upper classes, was unable to bear children, she could designate someone to serve in her place. This woman would bear the husband's child and that child would become the official heir.[3] Given the importance of having an heir of quality, the surro-

---

1. Translations used for this chapter (unless specifically otherwise noted) come from the New Revised Standard Version (NRSV). This Bible version was chosen because it presents both a modern translation and inclusive, gender-neutral language.

2. Susan Niditch, "Genesis," in *The Women's Bible Commentary*, ed. Carol A. Newsom and Sharon H. Ringe (London: SPCK; Louisville: Westminster John Knox, 1992), p. 17.

3. For the cultural context of such legalized surrogate motherhood, see E. A. Speiser, *Genesis*, The Anchor Bible (New York: Doubleday, 1964), pp. 119-21; Nahum M. Sarna, *Understanding Genesis* (New York: Schocken, 1970), pp. 127-29; Nahum M. Sarna, ed., *Genesis,*

gate mother would likely be someone of a good family, though impoverished. The concern here is not romantic love. Rather, the issue refers to business, property, and inheritance. There may also be a religious or ritual aspect to this matter of surrogate motherhood.[4]

What did Hagar think about this arrangement? Did Sarai consult Hagar in the matter? Was Hagar upset? Was she attracted to this man, or was she repelled? Did Hagar see this as a change in her status, or as a humiliation? What was her relationship with Sarai before this? Was Hagar expected — indeed, did Hagar expect — to have a long-term, ongoing sexual relationship with her new husband, bearing more children? Did Hagar even have a voice in these issues? No, the Bible is completely silent on these matters.

What Genesis narrates is that "Sarai, Abram's wife, took Hagar . . . and gave her to her husband Abram as a wife" (Gen. 16:3). The Hebrew for "wife" is *'ishah*. Yet, was Hagar really a wife or just a concubine? Robert Alter notes that several "English versions, following the logic of the context render this as 'concubine.' The word used, however, is not *pilagesh* [the normal Hebrew word for concubine] but *'ishah* [wife], the same term that identifies Sarai at the beginning of the verse."[5] In quick succession, the Genesis narrative emphasizes Sarai's "wife-hood" (Gen. 16:1, 3), which simply highlights the fact that there are now going to be two "wives" in the picture, doubtless foreshadowing the problems to come!

The next verse in the text explains, "He went in to Hagar, and she conceived" (Gen. 16:4).[6]

The JPS Torah Commentary (Philadelphia: Jewish Publication Society, 1989), comment on verse 2, p. 119.

4. Savina J. Teubal, *Hagar the Egyptian: The Lost Traditions of the Matriarchs* (New York: HarperSanFrancisco, 1990). Teubal suggests that Sarah is a priestess and that this act of surrogate motherhood is part of a formalized ritual. See Teubal's earlier work, *Sarah the Priestess: The First Matriarch of Genesis* (Athens: Swallow/Ohio University Press, 1984). Teubal refers to "a prior understanding — an oral or written agreement — between the participants in the ritual, which both Sarah and Hagar were duty-bound to honor and which was witnessed by the divinity" (*Hagar*, p. 78).

5. Robert Alter, *Genesis* (New York: Norton, 1996), p. 68. Speiser (*Genesis*, p. 117) and Sarna (*JPS-Genesis*, p. 119) make the case that Hagar is a concubine, not a wife. Alter's comment notwithstanding, many well-regarded English translations also use the term "wife." Cf. the NRSV, NEB, NIV, JB. See also *The Schocken Bible*, vol. 1, *The Five Books of Moses*, trans. Everett Fox (New York: Schocken, 1995). Nahmanides (Ramban), the thirteenth-century Spanish commentator on the Bible, also suggests that the correct term is "wife," not "concubine." As shall be explained further on in this chapter, the rabbis consider Hagar to be Abraham's wife.

6. According to Teubal, the "immediacy of conception as described in the text sup-

Once Hagar is pregnant, her relationship with her mistress and her husband irreparably changes. The biblical text explains that when Hagar "saw that she had conceived, she looked with contempt on her mistress" (Gen. 16:4).[7]

Sarai is furious, and she reproaches, not Hagar, but her husband.[8] She says to him, "May the wrong done to me be on you! I gave my slave-girl to your embrace, and when she saw that she had conceived, she looked on me with contempt. May the Lord judge between you and me!" (Gen. 16:5).

Abraham then chooses to abdicate his responsibility for Hagar's welfare. He refuses to stand up to Sarai.[9] Denying his own relationship with Hagar, Abraham even refuses to mention Hagar by name, but rather refers to her as Sarai's property. He tells her, "Your slave-girl is in your power; do to her as you please." In her anger and frustration, Sarai does just that. Sarai "dealt harshly with her, and she [Hagar] ran away from her" (Gen. 16:6).

Jo Ann Hackett observes that "Abram responds [to Sarai] with apparent calm, although with no sensitivity whatsoever to Hagar's plight, and he tells Sarai that Hagar is in her power, 'in her hand' literally. . . . Sarai proceeded to oppress Hagar . . . and the Hebrew verb generally carries the connotation of physical harm: it can mean . . . to oppress . . . as well as simply to humble or humiliate."[10]

Hagar's reaction is to run away from the Abrahamic encampment, ultimately arriving at an oasis in the nearby desert.

Hagar and the angel of the Lord

In the desert wilderness, Hagar has a divine encounter that is quite remarkable. "The angel of the Lord found her by a spring of water in the wilderness, the spring on the way to Shur" (Gen. 16:7). This is the first

ports the notion that this was, indeed, a ritual union rather than the beginning of a lengthy period of concubinage." Teubal, *Hagar*, p. 77.

7. ". . . her mistress was lowered in her esteem" (New Jewish Publication Society — NJPS/*TANAKH* [Philadelphia: Jewish Publication Society, 1985]). It is unclear what Sarai has done to aggravate and alienate Hagar. For a discussion of this issue, see the chapter in this volume, "Sarah: The View of the Classical Rabbis," above.

8. Cf. Teubal, *Hagar*, pp. 77-81.

9. In Genesis 21 Abraham will repeat this behavior, betraying his responsibilities for Hagar and their mutual child. David J. Zucker, "Betrayal (and Growth) in Genesis 22," *CCAR Journal* 46.2 (Spring 1999): 60-72.

10. Jo Ann Hackett, "Rehabilitating Hagar: Fragments of an Epic Pattern," in *Gender and Difference in Ancient Israel,* ed. Peggy L. Day (Minneapolis: Fortress, 1989), p. 14.

mention of such a divine messenger in the Bible. Robert Alter points out that this "'angel' (Hebrew, *mal'akh*, Greek, *angelos*) . . . [is someone] who carries out a designated task . . . the divine speaker here begins as an angel but ends up (verse 13) being referred to as though he were God."[11]

The angel clearly knows who Hagar is and what her status is. He addresses her as "Hagar, slave-girl of Sarai."[12] The angel then poses two questions to her. "Where have you come from and where are you going?" Phyllis Trible notes that the "questions embody origin and destiny."[13] They do, but those questions also have a dimension that is both literal and existential.[14] Hagar acknowledges her status, but then gives an open-ended answer when she replies to the angel, "I am running away from my mistress Sarai" (Gen. 16:8-9). Either Hagar has no specific idea to where she is going, or she chooses not to address the second part of the angel's query.

The dialogue between the angel and Hagar is measured; it is not rushed. The literal Hebrew text intersperses spoken words with descriptions of who is speaking. The specific phrase "the angel of the LORD" appears four times within five sentences. The angel speaks, posing statements in a thoughtful manner, and then there is a pause. He tells her to return to her mistress and to submit to her. The angel speaks gently, not mentioning Sarai again by name. Only after Hagar has had some time to think about this does the angel continue. He balances the news that she does not wish to hear (that she must return and submit) with a powerful and empowering announcement: "I will so greatly multiply your offspring that they cannot be counted for multitude" (Gen. 16:10). Hagar will be the mother of numerous descendants. Further, God has noted her affliction. In addition, she will be reminded of this wondrous encounter in the very name she is to call her son, Ishmael ("God hears").

"And the angel of the LORD said to her, 'Now you have conceived and

---

11. Alter, *Genesis*, p. 69. A similar movement in status of the speaker(s) takes place in Genesis 18 and 19. In Genesis 18, Abraham and Sarah's visitors appear first as humans, and then later God is speaking. In Genesis 19, the visitors to Lot's home are first called men and later angels.

12. The angel addressing Hagar as "slave-girl of Sarai" underscores her precarious position. On one hand, she is Abram's "wife" [*'ishah*], but undoubtedly at the same time she is Sarai's servant, which allows Sarai to humiliate Hagar.

13. Phyllis Trible, *Texts of Terror: Literary-Feminist Readings of Biblical Narratives* (Philadelphia: Fortress, 1984), p. 15.

14. "Where have you come from?" and "where are you going?" certainly have a literal level of meaning. Existentially, the angel is asking Hagar, Where are you on your own spiritual life journey?

shall bear a son; you shall call him Ishmael, for the LORD has given heed to your affliction'" (Gen. 16:11).

The angel makes it clear that Ishmael will not have a life of ease. "He will be a wild ass of a man, with his hand against everyone, and everyone's hand against him; and he shall live at odds with all his kin" (Gen. 16:12). The final words of this NRSV translation, "at odds with all his kin," place Ishmael in an adversarial relationship with others around him. NJPS/ TANAKH, however, translates the same phrase "He shall dwell alongside of all his kinsmen." Dwelling alongside one's kin often means forming alliances; it hardly suggests a relationship of continuous conflict.[15]

Hagar draws comfort from the angel's explanation. She believes that she may have seen God. Yet, Hagar is aware of a tradition that one cannot see God and remain alive. She draws attention to this in her reply.

"So she named the LORD who spoke to her, 'You are El-roi'; for she said, 'Have I really seen God and remained alive after seeing him?' Therefore the well was called Beer-lahai-roi; it lies between Kadesh and Bered" (Gen. 16:13-14).

The angel/Hagar encounter in the wilderness is remarkable for several more reasons. This is the first instance of an angelic annunciation. This annunciation is to an outsider, to someone who is not, and will not be, part of the Abrahamic line. Hagar is the only person in the Bible, male or female, to "name" God.

The birth of Ishmael

Though not specifically stated, it is clear that Hagar returns to the familial encampment. It is there that she gives birth to Ishmael. She likely shared her encounter with at least her husband, for when the child is born, Abram "named his son, whom Hagar bore, Ishmael" (Gen. 16:15). Isaac will become the link to the Jewish people, and therefore to Judaism and Christianity. Ishmael, according to Muslim tradition, is the link to Islam. That important connection, while of great interest in its own right, is beyond the scope of this chapter.

---

15. David J. Zucker, "Conflicting Conclusions: The Hatred of Isaac and Ishmael," *Judaism* 39.1 (Winter 1990): 39.

Genesis 17

Ishmael and Abraham

Ishmael, but not Hagar, appears in Genesis 17. God speaks to Abram and changes his name to Abraham, as well as changing Sarai's name to Sarah (Gen. 17:5, 15). God then addresses Abraham and expands on the information formerly given to Hagar. Ishmael will father twelve princes and will be a great nation (Gen. 17:20). Further, the covenantal sign between Abraham and his descendants is to be circumcision. Abraham then circumcises Ishmael, age thirteen, all his household males at whatever age they were, and he himself at age ninety-nine (Gen. 17:23-27).

Genesis 21

The Hagar section of Genesis 21 is a recasting of the Hagar narrative in Genesis 16. The lead characters are the same: Sarah, Hagar, and Abraham. There appears to be tension between the two women. Sarah complains to Abraham. Abraham defers to Sarah. Hagar leaves the encampment and finds herself alone in the wilderness. Hagar meets an angel by a spring of water, and that angel speaks to her. Particularly striking is that, in both episodes, the text presents Hagar and her situation quite sympathetically. Further, in both narratives the angelic visitor tells Hagar that, through her son, she will be the mother of a great nation.

Hagar and Sarah: the later encounters

Chapter 21 begins with the announcement that Sarah conceived and gave birth to Isaac. When Isaac was about three years of age, he was weaned.[16] A great feast celebrates this milestone.

At the weaning festivities, or more likely some time later, Sarah sees Ishmael *playing*, perhaps with Isaac.[17] She suddenly goes to her husband and demands that he exile Hagar and Ishmael. Her specific words are,

16. Sarna, *JPS-Genesis*, p. 146.

17. The Hebrew (Masoretic Text) has Ishmael "playing." The Septuagint, the Greek Vulgate, and many Christian translations add the words "with her son Isaac" (Gen. 21:9). For more on this episode and possible interpretations of Sarah's actions, see the chapter "Sarah: The View of the Classical Rabbis," in this volume.

345

"Cast out this slave woman with her son; for the son of this slave woman shall not inherit along with my son Isaac" (Gen. 21:10).

Sarah's demand deeply disturbs her husband. "The matter was very distressing to Abraham on account of his son" (Gen. 21:11). What of Hagar's hapless situation? Susan Niditch raises an important point when she writes, "This passage is a difficult one in biblical ethics. Abraham cares not at all about the maid he has bedded and Sarah is contemptuous of mother and child and would expose them to death. The author works hard to rationalize and justify the emotions and actions of Abraham and Sarah (21:12-13)."[18] God, however, intervenes and explains to the patriarch that he need not be concerned. Unlike Abraham, God is concerned with both Hagar and Ishmael. God says to him: "Do not be distressed because of the boy and because of your slave woman; whatever Sarah says to you, do as she tells you, for it is through Isaac that offspring shall be named for you. As for the son of the slave woman, I will make a great nation of him also, because he is your offspring" (Gen. 21:12-13).

In chapter 16, Hagar *ran away.* In chapter 21, Hagar and Ishmael, at Sarah's insistence, are *sent away* from the encampment. In this latter instance, God actively supports Sarah's demand. Phyllis Trible describes Hagar as befriended and protected neither by Abraham nor by God. "God supports, even orders [Hagar's] departure to the wilderness, not to free her from bondage but to protect the inheritance of her oppressors."[19] Trible's comment is not without merit. Nonetheless, it is too narrow a reading of the Hagar passages. God consistently explains to both Hagar and Abraham that Ishmael will prosper and become a great nation (comments to Hagar: Gen. 16:10; 21:18; comments to Abraham: Gen. 17:20; 21:13). The Bible itself celebrates Ishmael's successes. It specifically names Hagar as his mother (Gen. 25:12-18). As Paul Borgman notes, "this thrusting out of mother and child [in Gen. 21:14-21] — becomes . . . the opportunity for Ishmael's line to distinguish itself and thrive."[20]

Early the next morning, Abraham takes some bread and a skin of water, puts them on Hagar's shoulder, and sends mother and child away. She departs and wanders around in the wilderness surrounding Beer-sheba.

18. Niditch, "Genesis," p. 18.

19. Trible, *Texts of Terror*, p. 25.

20. Paul Borgman, *Genesis: The Story We Haven't Heard* (Downers Grove: Inter-Varsity, 2001), p. 55. For a discussion of Hagar's destination and destiny in the desert, see David J. Zucker, "The Mysterious Disappearance of Sarah," *Judaism* 55.3-4 (Fall/Winter 2006): 30-39.

That Hagar and Ishmael are sent away with such meager provisions, and without a pack animal, suggests that she was directed to go to a specific place, one that is nearby. (Contrast this with chapter 22, in which Abraham and Isaac, accompanied by a couple of servants, head off on a three-day journey. On that occasion, they take along a pack animal.) The Bible does not indicate the location of Hagar and Ishmael's destination. One valid possibility is the oasis at Beer-lahai-roi, which lies between Kadesh and Bered, for it was there years before that Hagar had found refuge.

Unfortunately, apparently Hagar loses her way. She eventually runs out of water. Distraught, she finds some shelter for Ishmael. Then she moves some distance away. She cannot bear to look upon what she expects will be her son's death. Hagar is distressed, as is Ishmael. Hagar's anguish concerning her son's welfare moves her to pray on his behalf.[21] "She lifted up her voice and wept. And God heard the voice of the boy, and the angel of God called to Hagar from heaven, and said to her, 'What troubles you, Hagar? Do not be afraid; for God has heard the voice of the boy where he is. Come, lift up the boy and hold him fast with your hand for I will make a great nation of him.' Then God opened her eyes and she saw a well of water. She went, and filled the skin with water, and gave the boy a drink" (Gen. 21:16-19).

Genesis's Final Remarks on Hagar

Though Hagar is simply referred to as "his mother," the Bible explains that Ishmael dwelled in the wilderness of Paran and that "his mother got a wife for him from the land of Egypt" (Gen. 21:21). Hagar's final mention in Genesis is when, once again, she is identified as the mother of Ishmael. "These are the descendants of Ishmael, Abraham's son, whom Hagar the Egyptian, Sarah's slave-girl, bore to Abraham" (Gen. 25:12).

Genesis 23 records Sarah's death. In Genesis 25 Abraham remarries.

---

21. Hagar models behavior that has contemporary application. "When Hagar cries out in anticipation of her son, Ishmael's death, God hears and heeds Ishmael's cries. Interestingly, Ishmael does not pray aloud on his own behalf; Hagar prays for him. In the language of Clinical Pastoral Education (CPE), she lends her voice to his unspoken prayer to live. I suggest that those of us who accompany suffering people can do this as well." Bonita E. Taylor, "The Power of Custom-Made Prayer," in *Jewish Pastoral Care: A Practical Handbook,* 2nd ed., revised and expanded, ed. Dayle A. Friedman (Woodstock, VT: Jewish Lights, 2005), p. 151.

This is to a woman named Keturah [Qeturah], who then bears him six more sons (Gen. 25:1-6). Rabbinic tradition, as shall be noted below, suggests that Hagar is the same person as Keturah.

The Rabbinic views of Hagar form the next major section in this chapter.

The Hagar of the Rabbis

As we have seen, while Hagar appears as a figure only in Genesis 16 and 21, she also is the subject of post-biblical Rabbinic writing.

The definitions of the rabbis, Rabbinic literature, and midrash are covered more thoroughly in the chapter in this volume dedicated to Sarah, "Sarah: The View of the Classical Rabbis." The interested reader is invited to peruse those explanations. What follows is a précis of those descriptions.

Some Definitions

Rabbis

The classic Rabbinic period is about three hundred years, c. 200-500 C.E. in the land of Israel and in the area of Babylonia at that period. The rabbis of antiquity were teachers and expositors of Jewish tradition who developed a whole set of laws and commentaries, often based on the Hebrew Bible. Whenever the Bible was not explicit or specific, or when conditions in the post-biblical world demanded new answers, the early interpreters of the post-biblical world (i.e., the Rabbinic period, and their successors as well) sought to provide new insights as to what might be meant in a given context. Consequently, there developed alongside the Bible a supplement, an additional way to understand what God desires of humans and what it means to lead a Jewish life.

In broad terms, Rabbinic literature is composed of the multi-volume Talmud and various collections of Midrash.[22]

---

22. See Marvin R. Wilson, *Our Father Abraham: Jewish Roots of the Christian Faith* (Grand Rapids: Eerdmans, 1989), p. 31.

Midrash

"The Bible is a laconic, elliptical, and at times ambiguous text; thus it is open to a variety of interpretations of any one [word, phrase, or] verse."[23] The generic term for this exegesis or interpretation of biblical texts is "midrash" (plural: "midrashim"). The Hebrew for "sermon," *derasha*, is based on the word "midrash."[24]

Through midrash, the rabbis fill in gaps and offer new insights. According to Rabbinic tradition, each word in the Torah has seventy possible interpretations.[25] Midrash involves many genres: tales, allegories, ethical reflections, epigrams, and legends.

The rabbis use midrash to instruct the Jewish world about Rabbinic values such as the nature of God, opposition to idolatry, proper modesty, the importance of studying sacred texts, generosity, hard work, chastity, and loyalty, as well as commenting on differences between the Jewish community and other communities.

The rabbis often were not of one mind on a given passage or word. To say that something is a Rabbinic view, or even the Rabbinic view, does not mean that all rabbis support that position or that interpretation.

There are traces of midrash prior to the beginning of the third century in the Common Era, but the flowering of midrash as a unique genre began around 200 C.E. It continued as late as the twelfth and thirteenth centuries C.E. The development of midrash occurred around the same time that the early Christian writers were setting down the traditions of the Christian Scriptures, often quoting from the Hebrew Bible.

An Overview of Rabbinic Interpretation: Hagar as "the Other Woman"

As noted at the beginning of this chapter, Hagar was "the Other Woman" in the life of the first Patriarch. This fact negatively colored what the rabbis thought of her. She was this "Other" woman in several ways.

Ancient peoples in the biblical world — Israelites no less than others

---

23. Leilah Leah Bronner, *From Eve to Esther: Rabbinic Reconstructions of Biblical Women* (Louisville: Westminster John Knox, 1994), p. xv.

24. Naomi M. Hyman, *Biblical Women in the Midrash: A Sourcebook* (Northvale, NJ: Jason Aronson; Lanham, MD: Rowman and Littlefield, 1998), pp. xxvii-xxxiii.

25. *Shiv'im panim ba-Torah:* "The Torah has 70 faces." *Midrash Numbers Rabbah* 13.15.

— thought in terms of "us" and "them."[26] Subsequently, later Rabbinic Judaism considered all non-Jews to be the "Other" and portrayed them in a negative light. "All foreign peoples were portrayed in a negative light; for example, in the Greco-Roman world the Roman satirists depicted Egyptians, Syrians, Jews and other non-Romans" in an unflattering light. This demonizing of "Others" was standard fare, not a uniquely Jewish trait. It was, in fact, "totally consistent with pre-modern thinking in the West and Middle East."[27]

Hagar was an "Other" because she was not an Israelite. She was an Egyptian. She was an "Other" for a further reason. She was the mother of Ishmael. In time Ishmael's descendants, the Ishmaelites, became a generalized symbolic figure for Israel's neighbors (Moabites, Ammonites, Edomites, Midianites, etc.). For example, the caravan that takes Joseph to Egypt is led by Midianites. The text also describes them as Ishmaelites (Gen. 37:25, 27-28).

This biblical and later Rabbinic antipathy toward Ishmael reflects the realpolitik tensions between Israel and her neighbors. Ishmael becomes synonymous with various Semitic and/or Arab tribes with whom Israel is in competition.[28] "The ancient Israelites were keenly aware of their geographic, linguistic and cultural kinship with Arab peoples." Though they were conscious of a close affinity between Israelites and Arabs, the biblical writers tried to maintain a discreet distance. While peoples with Arabic

26. Egyptians were very conscious of their being different from their neighbors (cf. Gen. 46:34); Amorites and Moabites distrusted Israelites (Num. 21:23; 22:1-4); Philistines did not trust Hebrews (1 Sam. 29:1-5); Moses instructed the Israelites to clear away the native population of Canaan (Deut. 7:1-2). These facts, naturally, did not preclude biblical leaders from making military or political alliances with former enemies, when it was in their perceived self-interest to do so.

27. Reuven Firestone, personal communication, January 17, 2000.

28. Following the birth of Islam, the historical progenitor of which is Ishmael, calumnies increase. Indeed, after c. 650 c.e., Ishmael becomes a code word for Islam. The *Pirke De Rabbi Eliezer,* composed c. 725 in the land of Israel, during the closing days of the Umayyad dynasty, even contains Arab legends. *Pirke de Rabbi Eliezer,* trans. Gerald Friedlander (New York: Sepher-Hermon, 1981). For example, in *Pirke De Rabbi Eliezer* (chapter 30) Abraham's son Ishmael is featured as having two wives, whose names are respectively Ayesha and Fatima. Both are the names of wives of Mohammed, who will live two millennia in the future. These are not coincidental references. Later territorial disputes between Israel and Arabs, or, in the case of Islam, territorial and religious disputes, are retrojected to the time of the Patriarchs and Matriarchs in Genesis so that it appears that Isaac and Ishmael had a long-standing history of conflict. For a discussion about the artificiality of this "conflict" between Isaac and Ishmael, see David J. Zucker, "Conflicting Conclusions: The Hatred of Isaac and Ishmael."

names continued to interact with Israelites, those relations were "inevitably portrayed with little love lost." In the post-biblical world, in the Hellenistic and the Roman periods, relations between Jews and Arabs continued. "Arabs continue to be mentioned in the Talmud . . . where they are sometimes referred to as Ishmaelites."[29]

Rabbinic Commentary on Genesis 16

Hagar as Pharaoh's daughter

"Rabbi Simeon bar Yohai said: Hagar was Pharaoh's daughter. When Pharaoh saw what had been done on Sarah's behalf in his own house [cf. Gen. 12:17] he took his daughter and gave her to Sarah, saying 'Better let my daughter be a handmaid in this house than a mistress in another house.'"[30]

Why was she named Hagar?

The word for "stranger" in Hebrew is *ger*, so it is possible that the name Hagar hints at the words "the stranger" (*ha-ger* = "the stranger"). In *Midrash Genesis Rabbah*, there is a pun on the word "Hagar." When Pharaoh presents Hagar to Sarah, he says, "Here is your reward (*agar* = reward)."[31] *Agar* is an Aramaic word, similar to the biblical Hebrew word *agorah* (payment).

Hagar and Abraham

Sarah, according to the rabbis, persuaded Hagar that it was in her (Hagar's) interest to become Abraham's wife.[32] "[Sarah] persuaded her [Hagar] with words, 'Happy are you to be united with such a holy man.'"[33]

The biblical text explains that Abraham "went in to Hagar, and she

---

29. Reuven Firestone, *Journeys in Holy Lands* (Albany: State University of New York Press, 1990), pp. 3-4. For an example of Arabs as Ishmaelites portrayed in a negative light, see *Midrash Lamentations Rabbah* 2.2.4. Egyptians and Ishmaelites are both denigrated in *Midrash Esther Rabbah* 1.17.

30. *Midrash Genesis Rabbah* 45.1; *Pirke de Rabbi Eliezer,* chapter 26.

31. *Midrash Genesis Rabbah* 45.1.

32. Hagar is Abraham's wife, not his concubine. A midrash proclaims, "TO BE A WIFE, but not a concubine." *Midrash Genesis Rabbah* 45.3. See also Abraham's remarks to Sarah that once Hagar was given higher status she could not be enslaved again. *Midrash Genesis Rabbah* 45.6.

33. *Midrash Genesis Rabbah* 45.3.

conceived" (Gen. 16:4). She conceived on their initial attempt at intimacy, suggests a rabbi. His view is challenged by a colleague who says that "A woman never conceives by the first intimacy." A counter-argument, however, is then raised that refers to the episode of Lot and his daughters. In this episode, each daughter lay with her father but one night and immediately conceived (Gen. 19:36).[34] This example referring to Lot and his daughters, and their incestuous relationship, subtly suggests that Hagar likewise is of questionable moral character.

Rabbi Hanina ben Pazzi offers an agricultural analogy. "Thorns are neither weeded nor sown, yet of their own accord they grow and spring up, whereas how much pain and toil is required before wheat can be made to grow."[35] His point is that something valuable takes nurturing; it does not take place immediately. Just as Lot's daughters immediately conceived and then bore children who would be Israel's adversaries (the Moabites and Ammonites), so Hagar's quick conception foreshadowed that Ishmael and his descendants, the Ishmaelites, would be in an adversarial role with Israel.

Not specifically stated but inferred by this statement is that since it took so many years to conceive Isaac, he must therefore be a special and a righteous person.

Unwise Hagar; Consequences

The biblical text explains that when Hagar knew she was pregnant, she held Sarah in contempt. A midrash speculates about what happened.

Hagar flaunts the fact that she conceives so quickly. She compares her limited experience with Abraham to the many years Abraham and Sarah had been married. Without giving particulars, Hagar subtly refers to the ancient idea that fertility meant divine favor and infertility meant divine disfavor. Hagar's unspoken but implied message was unambiguous: I, Hagar, am a "virtuous" person. I conceived immediately. According to a section in *Midrash Genesis Rabbah*, female visitors would come to talk to Sarah. Sarah in turn referred them to Hagar. Then "Hagar would tell them: 'My mistress Sarai is not inwardly what she is outwardly: she appears to be a righteous woman, but she is not. For had she been a righteous woman, see how many years have passed without her conceiving, whereas I conceived in one night!'"[36]

---

34. *Midrash Genesis Rabbah* 45.4.
35. *Midrash Genesis Rabbah* 45.4.
36. *Midrash Genesis Rabbah* 45.4; *Midrash ha Gadol*, ed. Mordecai Marguiles (Jerusa-

Sarah is infuriated at Hagar's impudence. She rails at her husband, suggesting to him that this is entirely his fault. Sarah wants him to revoke Hagar's status as second wife. She tells him to make her a slave again. He explains that he cannot do this. He suggests that if a woman has been sold as a slave and then given higher status, such as becoming a wife to the master, she cannot be re-enslaved, even if she has displeased her master. He then quotes the words, "he shall have no right to sell her to a foreign people" (Exod. 21:8).[37]

> How can Abraham quote a verse from Scripture that, on the face of it, has not yet appeared? The legislation he quotes comes from Exodus! This is not a problem for the midrashic tradition. According to the rabbis, there is no such thing as linear time when it comes to the Torah. Past, present, and future time merge. They are all part of one seamless continuum. Abraham simply knew about this future statute.[38]

Abraham then defers to Sarah and says, "Your slave-girl is in your power; do to her as you please" (Gen. 16:6). Sarah mistreats her. According to midrashic tradition, Sarah prevents Hagar and Abraham from engaging in sexual relations. Additionally, Sarah slapped Hagar and made her perform menial tasks.[39]

Hagar and the angel of the Lord

In her plight, Hagar runs away to the wilderness. There an angel of the Lord encounters her. Not just one angel, say the rabbis, but multiple angels! "Rabbi Hama bar Rabbi Hanina said: Five, for each time 'speech' is mentioned it refers to an angel. The Rabbis said: Four, this being the number of times the word 'angel' occurs." The midrash asks the question, was

---

lem: Mossad haRav Kook, 1947), Genesis 1.244. Another midrash avers that the "earth shudders at . . . a slavegirl who supplants her mistress, this is Hagar." *The Midrash on Proverbs,* trans. Burton L. Visotsky (New Haven and London: Yale University Press, 1992), Proverbs 30, comment on Prov. 30:21-23.

37. *Midrash Genesis Rabbah* 45.6. Cf. *The Midrash on Proverbs,* Proverbs 26. The midrash puts these words into Abraham's mouth to prove a moral point. This is not necessarily an accurate (or inaccurate) evaluation of Near Eastern laws and traditions at the time of Abraham.

38. "*Ayn muqdam um'uhar baTorah* — There is neither later nor previous time in the Torah." Babylonian Talmud *Pesahim 6b.*

39. *Midrash Genesis Rabbah* 45.6.

not Hagar frightened at seeing these angels? No. In "Abraham's household there were prophets [lit. watchers, understood as angels], so she [Hagar] was accustomed to them."[40] In an adjacent midrash, Hagar expresses delight that she could see the angel in her own right. Previously she had been in the company of her mistress when she saw such figures. For a non-Israelite to see an angel, much less converse with one, is a very rare event.[41]

After the angel speaks to Hagar, the text explains, "So she named the LORD who spoke to her, 'You are El-roi'; for she said, 'Have I really seen God and remained alive after seeing him?'" (Gen. 16:13). God did not speak to her directly, the midrash explains. It was through the medium of an angel.[42]

Rabbinic Commentary on Genesis 21 and 25

Hagar (and Ishmael) following Isaac's weaning

Genesis 21 details Sarah's response when she sees Ishmael "playing." According to one midrashic source, Sarah insists that Abraham divorce Hagar, and he does give her such a document.[43]

The net result is that Hagar is sent away from the Abrahamic encampment. From the Genesis text itself, it is clear that the Patriarch has mixed feelings about this request. "The matter was very distressing to Abraham on account of his son" (Gen. 21:11). Though it only mentions "his son," it is likely that he was equally concerned about Hagar. She was his second wife and the mother of his firstborn son.

With dismay, Abraham does send Hagar away, but, according to one Rabbinic source, Abraham wants to know where she is going, presumably to know that she is safe and probably to visit her. Consequently, he ties some kind of sash around her, which will leave a mark in the sand that he can subsequently follow.[44]

As noted earlier in this chapter, Hagar apparently loses her bearings. She believes she is lost in the wilderness. The biblical text says that the "water in the skin was gone" (Gen. 21:15). That is not how it was, explains a midrash. "By the merit of our father Abraham the water did not fail in the

---

40. *Midrash Genesis Rabbah* 45.7; 75.4. Cf. *Midrash Exodus Rabbah* 3.16.
41. *Midrash Genesis Rabbah* 45.10.
42. *Midrash Genesis Rabbah* 20.6; 45.10.
43. *Pirke de Rabbi Eliezer*, chapter 30.
44. *Pirke de Rabbi Eliezer*, chapter 30.

bottle, but when she reached the entrance of the wilderness, she began to go astray after the idolatry of her father's house; and forthwith the water in the bottle was spent."[45]

Another midrash suggests that Sarah had put a spell on Ishmael. Therefore he was feverish and drank a lot, exhausting the water supply.[46]

Hagar then settles Ishmael down under some bushes. She moves some distance away. The rabbis speculate that she may even have gone a mile's distance from Ishmael.[47]

Hagar's plaint

Hagar bewails her fate. "[She] said, 'Do not let me look on the death of the child' . . . she lifted up her voice and wept" (Gen. 21:16). To whom is Hagar speaking when she says these words? The midrash understands that in speaking out and raising her voice, Hagar has addressed her plaint to God. "Yesterday you promised me, 'I will greatly increase your seed' [Gen. 16:10] and now my son is dying of thirst!"[48]

God immediately answers Hagar through the medium of an angel. In those verses, it is clear that Ishmael also has protested his situation. The text says, "God heard the voice of the boy; and the angel of God called to Hagar from heaven, and said to her, 'What troubles you, Hagar? Do not be afraid; for God has heard the voice of the boy where he is." This is followed by a further iteration that Ishmael will father a significant group. "I will make a great nation of him" (Gen. 21:17-18).

45. *Pirke de Rabbi Eliezer*, chapter 30.

46. *Midrash Genesis Rabbah* 53.13.

47. *Midrash Genesis Rabbah* 53.13 end; *Midrash Numbers Rabbah* 2.9.

48. *Midrash Genesis Rabbah* 53.13 end. Hagar's plaint to God that aforetime God had promised that Ishmael would prosper, and now Ishmael is on the edge of death, is in contrast to a midrash where we might have expected Abraham to say the same thing in terms of Isaac on Mt. Moriah. In that midrash, amazingly, Abraham says to God, Even though you asked me to sacrifice Isaac I was willing to do this. I, Abraham, did not say to you, earlier on you had promised that through Isaac I would have descendants. *Pesikta Rabbati (Discourses for Feasts, Fasts and Special Sabbaths)*, trans. William G. Braude (New Haven and London: Yale University Press, 1968), Piska 40.6; *Pesikta de-Rab Kahana: Rabbi Kahana's Compilation of Discourses for Sabbaths and Festal Days*, trans. William G. Braude and Israel J. Kapstein (Philadelphia: Jewish Publication Society, 1975), Piska 23.9; *Midrash Leviticus Rabbah* 29.9.

Hagar as Keturah [Qeturah]

Following Sarah's death, Abraham married again. "Abraham took another wife, whose name was Keturah [Qeturah]. She bore him" six sons (Gen. 25:1-2). Though Hagar does not appear — as a living figure — past Genesis 21, there is a well-established Rabbinic tradition that Hagar and Keturah are the same person.[49]

Punning on the name Keturah, the midrash explains why she had that specific name. She was named Keturah because "she united *(qitrah)* piety and nobility." An additional reason is that "she was like one who seals up a treasure and produces it with its seal" (based on the word *qatar*, "to tie," hence "to seal up"). The words *qitrah* and *qatar* share the same root letters as Keturah *(quf-tet-resh)*.[50] "Her name was Keturah, because she was perfumed with all kinds of scents . . . and her actions were beautiful like incense" *(qetoret* is incense, cf. Exod. 30:1). Here again, the word shares the same root letters as Keturah.[51]

Not only was Hagar the same person as Keturah, but Isaac brought Hagar/Keturah to Abraham so that they could marry. "THEN ABRAHAM TOOK A WIFE AGAIN. It is simply that when Isaac took Rebekah, Isaac said: Let us go and bring a wife to my father. Hagar and Keturah are the same person."[52]

There also is a tradition that Hagar/Keturah bore Abraham a daughter.[53]

---

49. *Midrash Genesis Rabbah* 61.4; *Midrash Tanhuma, Genesis,* vol. 1, S. Buber Recension, trans. John T. Townsend (Hoboken, NJ: Ktav, 1989), *Hayye Sarah* 5.9 Genesis 25:1 ff., Part III; *Pirke de Rabbi Eliezer,* chapter 30.

50. *Midrash Genesis Rabbah* 61.4.

51. *Pirke de Rabbi Eliezer,* chapter 30; *Midrash ha Gadol,* Genesis 1.244.

52. *Midrash Tanhuma, Genesis, Hayye Sarah* 5.9 Genesis 25:1ff., Part III; *Midrash Genesis Rabbah* 60.14; *Midrash Tanhuma-Yelammedenu, Genesis and Exodus,* trans. Samuel Berman (Hoboken, NJ: Ktav, 1996), Genesis 5.8, p. 163.

53. Babylonian Talmud *Baba Batra* 16 b. *Midrash Genesis Rabbah* 59.7. The text says that "God blessed Abraham in all things" (Gen. 24:1). All things is interpreted by the rabbis to mean a daughter. Since that statement comes in Genesis 24 and Sarah had died at the beginning of Genesis 23, the rabbis credited this daughter to Hagar/Keturah. That Abraham did not marry Keturah until Genesis 25 was not a problem for the rabbis. As explained earlier in this chapter (see n. 38 above), for the rabbis, when it comes to biblical matters, strict linear time is not relevant.

Summary on the Rabbis and Hagar

As noted in the section that defined midrash, there is no one singular Rabbinic view. There are Rabbinic views. The rabbis often were not of one mind on a given passage or word.

The goal of the rabbis was to influence their community: to teach Jewish culture, to bring people closer to their religious traditions and to the presence of God. They sought to enhance Jewish life. Through midrash, they taught Rabbinic values. The Rabbinic "sages utilized every sort of literary and rhetorical technique to make this material attractive and compelling to their audience."[54]

There are midrashim that are sympathetic to Hagar and support her, though there are many more midrashim that see her as the "Other," and therefore cast her in a negative light.

Hagar is credited with royal lineage, as being Pharaoh's own daughter. She prays to God and angels speak to her, as does God, even if it is through the mediation of these angels. Yet Hagar is an "Other," someone who comes from outside of the community.

Further, Hagar is the mother of Ishmael. In time Ishmael's descendants, the Ishmaelites, became a generalized symbolic figure for Israel's neighbors (the Midianites, Ammonites, Edomites, etc.), with whom there often were territorial and religious disputes. This biblical and later Rabbinic antipathy toward Ishmael/Ishmaelites reflects the realpolitik tensions between Israel, and later post-Exilic Judean tension, with neighboring entities. Ishmael becomes synonymous with various Semitic and/or Arab tribes with whom Israel is in competition.

The rabbis have a strong predilection to favor Abraham and to feature him in a positive light. When in chapter 21 Abraham sends Hagar away, according to the rabbis he ties a sash to her to mark her way in the desert so that he can find her and make sure she is safe. Secondarily, the rabbis admire Sarah and generally present her favorably. Sarah encourages Hagar to marry Abraham, that righteous man.

Yet Hagar's pagan origins are never far from the minds of the rabbis. When Hagar is banished from the Abrahamic encampment in Genesis 21, the water that Abraham provided evaporates. This is because she began to go astray after the idolatry of her youth when she reached the entrance of

---

54. Joseph Heinemann, "The Nature of the Aggadah," in *Midrash and Literature*, ed. Geoffrey H. Harman and Sanford Burdick (New Haven: Yale University Press, 1986), p. 47.

the wilderness. Danger is always lurking at the edge of the society. If one leaves the protection of the community, apostasy is possible.

In the mind of the rabbis, in addition to biblical statements about the life of Hagar there was more to her persona. This is the Hagar portrayed by the rabbis in classical Jewish texts, the Talmud and many collections of midrash. The Rabbinic view of Hagar develops out of the biblical texts. The rabbis, for the most part, are wary of Hagar. With their expanded portraits they offer a broader and deeper picture and additional ways for people to understand and probably to mistrust her.

Hagar in the New Testament: The Letter to the Galatians

The treatment of the figure of Hagar in the New Testament is markedly different from that which is seen in the Hebrew Bible. In the Hebrew Bible, she is featured as a character within the context of a historical narrative. In the New Testament, she instead is used allegorically within a letter intended to exhort and admonish those to whom it was addressed. Hagar appears in a scant eleven verses within the fourth chapter of the letter to the Galatians (Gal. 4:21-31). The brevity of this passage, however, belies its importance. Drawing upon Genesis, Paul uses Hagar (and Sarah) to form an allegory addressing the Galatians' apparent acceptance of, in Paul's mind, "erroneous" instructions regarding the law[55] (including specifically circumcision) and its role in the lives of the believers in Galatia. This section of Galatians is just one part of a larger argument Paul makes in the epistle, the importance of which, as Bruce Metzger notes, "is hard to overestimate. In it Paul sets forth, with impassioned eloquence, the true function of the Mosaic law and its relation to God's will revealed in Jesus Christ. . . . The declaration of the principles reiterated in these six brief chapters made Christianity a universal, world religion, instead of a sect within Judaism."[56]

Prior to examining how Paul presents Hagar, it is helpful to consider the context of this letter.

---

55. In NRSV and many other Christian translations, "Law" (i.e., Torah/normative Jewish teaching) is not capitalized.

56. Bruce M. Metzger, *The New Testament: Its Background, Growth and Content*, 2nd ed. (Nashville: Abingdon, 1983), pp. 222-23.

The Composition of the Early Christian Community

The synagogue of the first century was not monolithic. It included both Jews by birth and circumcised converts to Judaism, as well as Gentile God-fearers who remained uncircumcised but who nevertheless followed Jewish practices and participated in the synagogue. It was in this Jewish milieu that the Christian church was born. Historically, Christianity is deeply rooted in Judaism. The very early Christian church was comprised solely of Jews who believed that Jesus was the Jewish Messiah. Christianity, then, was initially a *Jewish* community, and these Jewish Christians continued to regard themselves as Jews.[57]

The controversial question faced by the early church was not whether *Jews* could be part of the church. The question was whether *Gentiles* and *Gentile God-fearers* could enter the church without first becoming full Jewish converts, undergoing circumcision.[58] Soon, this early Jewish church witnessed events that forced it to wrestle with the nature of its own identity. The Holy Spirit, which first had been poured out on the Jewish Christians at Pentecost (Acts 2:1-47), was also now being poured out on Gentile Christians without requiring their prior conversion to Judaism.

This understanding that Gentile Christians were also recipients of the Holy Spirit was more than simply a human decision on the part of the early church leaders. Rather, the book of Acts records it as revelation from God through dreams and visions to men such as Ananias, Peter, and Paul (Saul), as well as others who witnessed firsthand the signs of the Holy Spirit being poured out upon Gentile followers of Christ (Acts 9:10-16; 10:1-48; 15:1-35).

Because of this new understanding of the church as a community of both Jewish and Gentile believers, practical and theological questions immediately surfaced. How were these two distinctly separate groups to maintain fellowship? What did this mean for the traditional Jewish understanding of cleanliness versus uncleanliness? Did Gentile Christians need to undergo circumcision? How were Gentile Christians to relate to the Jewish law? What theological significance did this have for understanding the gospel message?

It is in this context that Paul, one "entrusted with the gospel for the uncircumcised" (Gal. 2:7; cf. Rom. 11:13), writes his letter to the Galatian church.

---

57. Wilson, *Our Father Abraham*, pp. 41-43.
58. Wilson, *Our Father Abraham*, p. 43.

The Background of the Letter to the Galatians

Paul's authorship of this letter is rarely debated. In fact, the book is often viewed as a standard by which to measure the integrity of other works attributed to Paul.[59]

The church in Galatia was "no doubt predominantly Gentile."[60] This was largely due to the opposition that Paul and Barnabas faced from synagogues in the region, an opposition that brought about Paul's subsequent turn to the Gentiles (Acts 13–14). The letter to the Galatians, then, is addressing Gentile Christians who, Paul believes, have gone astray from the gospel message he had preached.[61] These members of the Galatian church were Gentiles who had become followers of the gospel of Christ during a previous visit by Paul to their region.[62] Paul himself reiterates within the letter his call to preach this gospel to the Gentiles, just as Peter had preached to the Jews (Gal. 2:6-10). He makes it clear that the Galatians first received the Holy Spirit through belief in the gospel message he had preached to them, and only after that began to consider a turn to law observance (Gal. 3:1-5). This movement toward the law on the part of these Galatians was the result of mistaken teachings that distorted the gospel message taught by Paul.

Who had propagated this incorrect interpretation of the gospel? The New Testament book of Acts indicates that Paul and his companions ini-

59. See, for example, James Montgomery Boice, *Galatians,* The Expositor's Bible Commentary 10 (Grand Rapids: Zondervan, 1976), pp. 420-21; Ernest D. Burton, *A Critical and Exegetical Commentary on the Epistle to the Galatians,* International Critical Commentary (New York: Charles Scribner's Sons, 1920), pp. lxv-lxvii; and Richard N. Longenecker, *Galatians,* Word Biblical Commentary (Dallas: Word Books, 1990), pp. lvii-lviii.

60. D. A. Carson, Douglas J. Moo, and Leon Morris, *An Introduction to the New Testament* (Grand Rapids: Zondervan, 1992), p. 295.

61. The ethnicity of the audience of the epistle is, however, disputed. Was the letter addressed strictly to those who were ethnic Galatians (i.e., those residing in North Galatia) or to the southern region of the larger Roman province of Galatia at that time, which was comprised of mixed ethnic groups? Likewise, and hinging in part on the destination of the letter, the date of Galatians is somewhat disputed. Should it be dated to just after Paul's first journey (prior to the Council of Jerusalem in Acts 15) or to his third journey? For a concise summary of the debate surrounding the intended destination and possible date of Galatians, see Carson, Moo, and Morris, *Introduction,* pp. 290-93.

62. Acts 13–14 demonstrates that in southern Galatia Paul followed the pattern of speaking first to the Jews and God-fearers in the synagogues, but that he turned to the Gentiles when Jewish opposition to his work arose (cf. Carson, Moo, and Morris, *Introduction,* p. 295).

tially were welcomed by many Jews and converts in the synagogues of Galatia (Acts 13:43; 14:1). However, the apostles soon faced opposition from other Jews, God-fearers, and Gentiles (Acts 13:45, 50; 14:2, 4-5, 19), and their message was rejected by certain members of each of these groups both for theological reasons (Jesus' identity and ability to forgive) and because of jealousy (Acts 13:45; 14:1-2).

It is not likely, however, that the "different gospel" (Gal. 1:6) described in the book of Galatians originated from those in the region of Galatia who had outright rejected the gospel of Christ. Rather, it was promoted by those who saw themselves as followers of Christ, and yet taught that "those who embrace the Christian salvation must submit to the Jewish law, the Torah."[63] Their teaching was not a direct rejection of the gospel message; rather, they were, in Paul's mind, perverting this message, proclaiming "half-truths" mixed with incorrect teaching in a manner that was in many respects far more insidious and detrimental to the churches than outright rejection would have been (Gal. 1:6-7). Their emphasis on the law suggests that they were most likely Jewish Christians, and they probably originated from areas outside the region of Galatia.[64] Though himself a zealous Jew (Gal. 1:14), Paul believed that their understanding of the gospel was so misconstrued and in such opposition to the gospel of Christ that he called for them to be accursed (Gal. 1:8, 9; 5:10). As evidence of his convictions, Paul even opposed Peter (termed Cephas in some translations), a Jewish Christian and apostle to the Jews. He did so because Peter had begun to compromise the gospel message under pressure from Jewish Christians who insisted that circumcision was necessary for Gentile Christians (Gal. 2:11-13; see also Acts 15).

As noted earlier, the early church was facing critical questions regarding the role of the Jewish law in the lives of Gentile believers. Even more fundamentally, how was that law to be understood within the theological framework of the gospel? Was the Christian gospel message opposed to the law, or did it require observance of the law? Paul may not have been aware of the exact identity of the "misguided teachers" in Galatia (Gal. 5:10). Nonetheless, one thing was clear: in an attempt to avoid persecution (Gal. 6:12), these teachers were zealous in their teaching that observance of the law (and specifically circumcision, cf. Gal. 5:2-3) was an essen-

---

63. Carson, Moo, and Morris, *Introduction*, p. 295.

64. These teachers may have originated from Judea, where Paul reportedly had a sharp dispute with a "circumcision group" of believers (Acts 15:5; cf. Gal. 2:11-13).

tial prerequisite for receiving the Holy Spirit. Paul was equally adamant that their teaching was false and contrary to the gospel that he preached (Gal. 1:6-9; 3:2).

> Before a [person] could become a Christian, they [the group claiming that observation of the law was a prerequisite to becoming a Christian, i.e., the Judaizers] maintained, he had to undergo the rite of circumcision, keep the Sabbath and other Jewish days, eat only kosher food, and observe the other ceremonial laws of the Old Testament. In short, the Judaizers declare that a [person] is saved by faith and works, whereas Paul held that a [person] is saved through faith alone. Paul saw that the controversy was not a minor one. . . . He knew that salvation is God's free gift to those who have faith in Christ, not something to be earned by keeping certain rules.[65]

Paul's outrage against this "incorrect teaching" is evident at the outset of the letter. His appeal to the Galatians, while carefully and rationally constructed, unabashedly exhibits Paul's deep emotional anguish over the matter (Gal. 1:6, 9; 3:1; 4:11-20; 5:12). He had great concern for the fledgling congregation in whose birth he had played such an important role. How, then, did Paul frame his argument against these "erroneous teachings"?

The Content of the Letter to the Galatians: An Overview

Paul's calling and authority (Gal. 1:1–2:10)

Paul's letter opens with a customary greeting, indicating first its sender and then its addressee. This greeting itself reveals the nature of the content to follow. Unlike other canonical Pauline epistles, Paul uses it to establish that the source of his apostolic authority is not derived from fellow humans, but that it is in fact derived from "Jesus Christ and God the Father, who raised him from the dead" (Gal. 1:1; see also 1:11-12).

The law and justification (Gal. 2:11–4:20)

Having described his opposition to Peter, Paul uses the incident as a springboard for a detailed exploration of the law and of "justification by faith" in Jesus Christ. What is meant by justification?

---

65. Metzger, *The New Testament,* p. 222.

According to John R. W. Stott, "'Justification' is a legal term, borrowed from the [legal system]. It is the exact opposite of 'condemnation'. 'To condemn' is to declare somebody guilty; 'to justify' is to declare him not guilty, innocent or righteous. In the [Christian] Bible it refers to God's act of unmerited favour by which He puts a sinner right with Himself, not only pardoning or acquitting him, but accepting him and treating him as righteous."[66]

Paul presents his case by guiding his readers through a series of questions (Gal. 2:14; 3:2-5). Each of these rhetorical questions points to the fact that the Galatians received the Spirit apart from their observance of the law, solely because of their belief in the apostolic gospel message. "Just as Abraham believed God, and it was reckoned to him as righteousness," Paul insists, righteousness has always been the result of faith (Gal. 3:6). Christ, he explains, redeemed us from the curse of the law by becoming a curse for us (Gal. 3:13). That is, in legal terms, we who were condemned under the law are justified (made righteous) because Jesus Christ, who alone was without sin, redeemed us by paying the penalty of death for us. Those who believe in Christ are children of Abraham, for as Genesis teaches, "all nations will be blessed in [Abraham]" (Gal. 3:8; cf. Gen. 12:3; 18:18; 22:18).

Just as a covenant cannot be changed once it is established, Paul argues, so God's covenant of promise with Abraham and his offspring is not set aside by the covenant of the law established with Moses years later. The inheritance and covenant were given to Abraham through a promise. Through his offspring, which is Jesus Christ (Gal. 3:16), Abraham's blessing came to the Gentiles also.

Paul anticipates his readers' next question: "Is the law then opposed to the promises of God?" (Gal. 3:21). Absolutely not, he answers emphatically! Rather, the law was a guide, intended to lead us to Christ (by indicating our sin) so that we might be justified by faith in Christ.

In light of all this, Paul now returns to the crisis he is facing in Galatia. In short, Paul says, you Galatian Christians once were slaves but now you are children, with the full rights of children, heirs according to the promise given by God to Abraham. Why return to your former slavery by living as if you are justified by the law (Gal. 4:3-9)?

This leads to the culmination of Paul's discussion, an argument drawn from the law itself, an analogy based on Hagar.

---

66. John R. W. Stott, *The Message of Galatians*, The Bible Speaks Today (Downers Grove: InterVarsity Press, 1986), p. 60.

Paul's use of Hagar (Gal. 4:21-31)

Paul asks his readers: "Tell me, you who desire to be subject to the law, will you not listen to the law? For it is written that Abraham had two sons, one by a slave woman and the other by a free woman. One, the child of the slave, was born according to the flesh; the other, the child of the free woman, was born through the promise" (Gal. 4:21-23). As he did earlier in the letter with a reference to Abraham, Paul uses the very law that his readers are embracing to challenge their understanding of that law. Even before reading any further, one hears echoes of the themes Paul has addressed to this point in his letter: *law, promise, slavery, freedom, children.*

Paul then writes: "Now this is an allegory: these women are two covenants" (Gal. 4:24).

Allegory is a "literary device which attempts to express immaterial truths in pictorial forms. . . . The device employs a point-for-point comparison between the intangibles under discussion and specified representations which are recognizable to the intended audience."[67] Allegory is essentially an extended metaphor used to explain an idea or group of ideas. Paul felt confident his readers in Galatia would understand the allegory he presents here and would be persuaded through its use.

In his allegory, Paul uses Hagar (and Sarah, who remains unnamed) to represent two covenants. Hagar represents the covenant made through Moses on Mt. Sinai between God and his people (the Israelites who were recently freed from slavery in Egypt). This is the covenant of the law, the Torah. Meanwhile, Sarah represents the covenant of the promise, made first with Abraham long before the covenant of the law, and now fulfilled in Christ.

Likewise, Paul continues, Hagar is in slavery with her children, and she corresponds to the present city of Jerusalem. Meanwhile, Sarah represents the Jerusalem that is above, the heavenly Jerusalem, the free city.

It is clear why Sarah would be connected with the covenant of the promise, that is, the covenant made by God with Abraham in which God promised that the patriarch miraculously would be the father of many nations through a son born of Sarah (Gen. 17:4-16). It is not as immediately clear why Paul allegorically connects the covenant of the law, the Mosaic cov-

---

67. S. E. McClelland, "Allegory," in *Evangelical Dictionary of Theology* (Grand Rapids: Baker, 1984), p. 33.

enant, with Hagar, a slave-woman. After all, Hagar is an "other," an Egyptian *outsider,* and she predates the giving of the law by hundreds of years.[68]

However, Hagar is more than simply an outsider or foreigner. By the first century, Philo describes her as a Jewish proselyte, a foreigner who had become a member of the community by choice and by rule of life.[69] Thus, as one who was understood to be a proselyte, Hagar was a fitting symbol for the covenant of the law of Moses. "Against the background of ideas like those in [Philo's *de Abrahamo*], this covenant [of the law of Moses] meant that gentile Christian converts should comply to the Laws of Moses and become Jews."[70] Hagar was a "figure on the borderline,"[71] a foreigner and yet a member of the community. Moreover, Mt. Sinai, where Moses received the law, was in Paul's day viewed as part of Arabia. And to further explain Paul's symbolic choice, the Jerusalem of Paul's day was the center for the law[72] and was experiencing a slavery of its own under Roman occupation and oppression.[73]

Therefore, within the framework of Paul's thought already established to this point in Galatians, the Hagar/Mt. Sinai/covenant-of-the-Law-of-Moses/present-Jerusalem connections all make perfect sense. They all share the same feature: slavery. In Paul's allegory, this element of slavery, typified by Hagar, is set in opposition to the concept of freedom, typified by the Sarah/covenant-of-the-Promise/heavenly-Jerusalem connections and is central to Paul's overall argument in the epistle. "In this way, Paul has made two important points of argument against the Judaizers: they were making slave-proselytes out of the Christian gentile converts, and these slave-proselytes were the result of the Law of Sinai, which similarly came into being on a mountain in a pagan country."[74]

Paul then presents his climactic point. Building on his argument in

68. G. W. Hansen, "Letter to the Galatians," in *Dictionary of Paul and His Letters* (Downers Grove: InterVarsity Press, 1993), p. 333.

69. See *De Abrahamo,* in *The Works of Philo,* trans. C. D. Yonge (Peabody, MA: Hendrickson Publishers, 1993), p. 251; and P. Borgen, "Some Hebrew and Pagan Features in Philo's and Paul's Interpretation of Hagar and Ishmael," in *The New Testament and Hellenistic Judaism* (Peabody, MA: Hendrickson Publishers, 1997), pp. 153-56.

70. Borgen, "Some Hebrew and Pagan Features," p. 158.

71. Borgen, "Some Hebrew and Pagan Features," p. 154.

72. Borgen, "Some Hebrew and Pagan Features," p. 159; Hansen, "Galatians," p. 333; K. A. Matthews, "Hagar," in *New Dictionary of Biblical Theology* (Downers Grove: InterVarsity Press, 2000), p. 532.

73. Matthews, "Hagar," p. 532.

74. Borgen, "Some Hebrew and Pagan Features," p. 161.

Galatians up to this moment, Paul claims that, "Now you, my friends, are children of the promise, like Isaac. . . . But what does the scripture say? 'Drive out the slave and her child; for the child of the slave will not share the inheritance with the child of the free woman.' So then, friends, we are children, not of the slave but of the free woman" (Gal. 4:28, 30-31; cf. Gen. 21:10). Paul thereby accomplishes two primary goals through this allegory: illustration and exhortation.

First, he illustrates his claim that the "outsiders" in the early Galatian church (that is, the uncircumcised Gentile believers) are children of Sarah just like Isaac, because they are the children of the promise. They are *not* children of the "outsider" slave-woman Hagar. Unlike Hagar's son, who was born in the "ordinary" way by the power of human beings, the believers at Galatia are like Sarah's son: promised by God, born in an extraordinary way, and born by the power of the Spirit (Gen. 17:15-22; 18:11-12; Gal. 4:29). If the Galatians belong to Christ Jesus, then they are children of God through faith in Christ Jesus. They are Abraham's offspring, and they are heirs according to the promise given by God to Abraham (Gal. 3:26-29).

Second, Paul exhorts the Galatians to follow the teachings of the law that they so eagerly desire to be under. They are to "drive out the slave and her child" (Gal. 4:30) just as the law states. That is, they are to reject the teaching of those who argue that adherence to the law is necessary for justification. They are to reject the belief that Gentiles must first become Jewish proselytes if they desire to become Christians.

Living as children of the free woman (Gal. 5:1–6:18)

The conclusion of the letter to the Galatians draws together the various threads of Paul's argument and lays forth the practical implications of the Hagar allegory. Freedom is Paul's overarching theme. The Galatians are free just as their mother is free, and they are not compelled to return to the burdensome yoke of the law by living as if the law can provide justification (Gal. 5:1).

Rather, they are to live by the Spirit in righteousness. They are to avoid immoral acts such as fornication, impurity, idolatry, and sorcery (Gal. 5:19-21). They are to embrace acts such as love, peace, patience, kindness, and generosity (Gal. 5:22-23). These teachings reflect broadly the Ten Commandments and Leviticus 19, a chapter from which Paul explicitly quotes: "For the whole law is summed up in a single commandment, 'you shall love your neighbor as yourself'" (Gal. 5:14; cf. Lev. 19:18). According to Paul, "in Christ Jesus neither circumcision nor uncircumcision counts for anything; the only thing that counts is faith working through love" (Gal. 5:6).

A Final Note on Galatians: Paul's Purpose and Intent

At this point it is important to note that, contrary to the way some of the church fathers later understood this text (see below), Paul did not intend his allegory to set Christians and Jews in opposition to one another.

As has been argued above, the purpose of the allegory was in fact to illustrate that, contrary to the teaching of some Christians, Gentile Christians did not first need to become circumcised Jews in order to be Christians. They were children of Abraham in the same way as Isaac, children through miraculous promise, not through the usual laws of nature. In Paul's writing, the children of Hagar were *not* the Jews of the synagogue; they were those Christians who returned to the slavery of the law by seeking justification through a law that they could never successfully keep.

Paul's allegory centered on the concepts of freedom versus slavery, *not* Christian versus Jew. Its purpose was to unify the Jewish Christians and Gentile Christians within the early church under Jesus Christ. Paul concludes by saying that if you belong to Christ, you are Abraham's offspring, whether Jew or Greek (Gal. 3:28-29). Its purpose was *not* to sever the Christian church from its Jewish roots in an "us-versus-them" contrast. Paul makes this clear in Romans 11. Paul does *not* intend to exalt the Christian church over the Jews as a "replacement" for a rejected Israel.

Hagar in Patristic Literature

In the centuries immediately following Paul and the first generation of Christians, the early Christian theologians wrestled with theological themes that were foundational to the identity of this new religious community. At the forefront of their discussion were issues such as sin, grace, soteriology, Christology, the doctrine of the Trinity, the relationship between Christianity and Judaism, and how the church was to understand and interpret the Old Testament (Hebrew Bible) in light of the New Testament.

Interestingly, many of these defining issues figure prominently in the references to Hagar in the Patristic literature. The following section will examine Patristic references to Hagar, and how the context of the early church in turn influenced the church fathers' understanding of Hagar as a historical figure and allegorical symbol.

The Church Fathers and Hagar in Genesis

The most significant and influential Patristic writings on Hagar centered on Paul's allegorical use of her in Galatians. Nevertheless, the texts related to Hagar in Genesis also engaged the interest of the church fathers. "Scripture," to the early church, originally referred to the Old Testament, or Hebrew Bible, though canonical authority soon was assigned to the writings of the New Testament as well. Therefore, the study of the Hebrew Bible was an important endeavor in the minds of the church fathers.

Allegorizing: Hagar and wisdom

Often when the early church grappled with the Hebrew Bible, they did so through the lens of Christianity in an effort to understand the relationship between the Hebrew Bible and the New Testament. At times, the method of allegorizing was used to accomplish this. In these cases the interpreter sought to find deeper, obscure meanings in the text that were not otherwise readily apparent.[75]

Allegorizing differs from the use of allegory. Allegory, as exemplified by Paul in Galatians, is a method of communication. It is a means of expressing abstract ideas through metaphor. On the other hand, allegorizing is a method of interpretation. Allegorizing finds hidden meaning in the text beyond that of its original purpose or sense.

To understand an allegory, one must understand the original *authorial* intent. Allegorizing, on the other hand, is highly subjective and reflects the *reader's* interpretation. Allegorizing was not a new hermeneutic at the time of the church fathers. It had originated in sixth-century B.C.E. Greece and entered into Jewish thought through Philo, a Jewish philosopher during the first century C.E. who sought to harmonize his faith with the thought of Greek philosophers. However, it did become a common practice of the early church (though by the Reformation it was denounced as an unacceptable form of interpretation).[76]

75. McClelland, "Allegory," p. 33.
76. McClelland, "Allegory," p. 33. In the Christian tradition, allegory and allegorizing

As an example, Ambrose, Bishop of Milan in the latter half of the fourth century (c. 375 C.E.), applied allegorizing to Hagar's encounter with the angel in Genesis 16. According to Ambrose the wells dug by the patriarchs as they traveled throughout the land held a spiritual significance beyond simply their earthly purpose. "They were fountains of the human race, and specifically fountains of faith and devotion. For what is a well of living water but a depth of profound instruction?"[77] His point is exemplified in the experiences of notable figures such as Isaac, Jacob, and Moses, all of whom were strengthened by the waters of wisdom they drank. Isaac, for example, practiced wisdom and foresight by reopening his father's wells and digging new ones (Gen. 26:18-33), while Jacob and Moses both met their wives beside a well (Gen. 29:10-12; Exod. 2:15-21).

Alongside these noteworthy characters, Ambrose cites Hagar, who was visited by the angel of the Lord beside a well. She is one to whom profound instruction was given, a recipient of godly wisdom. Her directive from the angel in Genesis 16:9 ("Return to your mistress, and submit to her") was only part of that wisdom, for this directive is followed by the promise of the angel to increase Hagar's descendants beyond measure, and it is concluded with the prophecy regarding Ishmael, her yet-to-be-born son (Gen. 16:10-12).

As a result of this angelic encounter, Hagar gives a name to the figure who spoke to her: "You are the God who sees." Moreover, the well at which the event occurred becomes known as Beer-lahai-roi, that is, "well of the Living One who sees me" (Gen. 16:13-14). This well, according to Ambrose, represents wisdom, and this wisdom was life-giving water to Hagar during her time of thirst.

Another example of allegorizing is found in the writings of Clement of Alexandria. Like Ambrose, Clement (c. 150 C.E.) was influenced by Philo. In book one of his *Stromateis* ("Miscellanies"), Clement addresses

---

may seem foreign in the post-Reformation era, which in particular rejects allegorizing as a means of interpretation (cf. Geerhardus Vos, *Biblical Theology* [Edinburgh: The Banner of Truth Trust, 1975], pp. 352-54). However, to Paul's first-century Greco-Roman audience these were hardly unusual literary or hermeneutical devices. Philo of Alexandria, for example, was a Hellenistic Jewish author and contemporary of Paul and Jesus, and is perhaps the best-known example of suggesting allegorical interpretations of the Law of Moses.

77. *Isaac, or the Soul*, in *St. Ambrose: Seven Exegetical Works*, ed. Bernard M. Peebles, trans. Michael P. McHugh (Washington, DC: The Catholic University of America Press, 1972), p. 24.

the relationship between secular philosophy and Christian truth. He builds directly on Philo's own thoughts regarding the connection between philosophy and wisdom, recorded in Philo's *De Congressu Quaerendae Eruditionis Gratia* ("On Mating with the Preliminary Studies").

Here, Philo correlates Hagar the handmaid with "intermediate instruction" (the preliminary branches of education) and Sarah her mistress with "virtue" or "wisdom."[78] Sarah graciously and wisely gives her handmaiden to her husband, so that he might later "enjoy a connection with her mistress, tending to the procreation of legitimate children."[79] In Philo's interpretation, Sarah recognizes that the preliminary branches of education, whether they be music or rhetoric or dialectic science, are necessary for attaining true wisdom.[80] As such, Philo is able to conclude: "Whoever, therefore, has acquired wisdom from his teachers, would never reject Hagar. For the acquisition of all the preliminary branches of education is wholly necessary."[81]

The influence of Philo can clearly be seen in Clement's interpretation of Hagar. For Clement, "Before the Lord's coming, philosophy was an essential guide to righteousness for the Greeks. At the present time, it is a useful guide towards reverence for God."[82] He argues, "Just as the educational curriculum conduces to its lady Philosophy, so Philosophy herself contributes to the acquisition of wisdom."[83]

As evidence of this, Clement turns to Hagar and Sarah in Genesis 16. Just as Sarah entrusted Hagar to her husband Abraham, "so wisdom, who makes her home with the man of faith — Abraham was accounted faithful and righteous — was still barren and without child in that generation and had not yet conceived a child of virtue for Abraham. She sensibly thought it best that the man who had at the time a suitable opportunity for progress should begin by going to bed with secular education [Hagar's homeland of Egypt is representative of the secular world], and later come to her to father Isaac in accordance with divine Providence."[84]

---

78. *On Mating with the Preliminary Studies,* in *The Works of Philo,* trans. C. D. Yonge (Peabody, MA: Hendrickson Publishers, 1993), pp. 304-6.

79. Philo, *On Mating,* p. 305.

80. Philo, *On Mating,* pp. 305-6.

81. Philo, *On Mating,* p. 306.

82. *Stromateis, Books 1-3,* in *Clement of Alexandria,* ed. Thomas P. Halton, trans. John Ferguson (Washington, DC: The Catholic University of America Press, 1991), p. 41.

83. Clement, *Stromateis,* p. 43.

84. Clement, *Stromateis,* p. 44.

Interestingly, in their attempts to harmonize secular philosophy with their faiths, both Philo and Clement comment on the "in-between" status of Hagar as both a wife and a sojourner among the Hebrews, but also as an Egyptian foreigner.[85] For both, Hagar is an essential figure, and highly valued, but is nevertheless subservient to Sarah. Therefore, for both men, secular philosophy has great honor in education but is only a bridge to the greatest truth, that of wisdom.

As Clement states, "That is why Abraham, when Sarah was jealous at Hagar's comparatively honorable status, choosing only the utilitarian element from secular philosophy, said to her, 'Look, your maid is in your power; treat her as you want,' [Gen 16:6] meaning, 'I welcome liberal education as young and fresh, and as your servant, but I revere and honor your scientific knowledge as mistress in the fullest sense.'"[86]

Studying the text: Hagar and Ishmael

Despite the prevalence of allegorizing, it is evident that reading and understanding the Hebrew Bible in its own right remained a valued enterprise during the Patristic period.

Bishop Braulio of Saragossa (died c. 650 C.E.) entertained the following textual question from a certain man, Fructuosus, regarding the flight of Hagar from her mistress: "He [Jerome] added of Agar [Hagar] that, while fleeing her mistress, she carried on her back Ismael [Ishmael], who was a full-grown young man. I want to know how that is explained."[87]

Braulio's response draws from the writings of Jerome, and he demonstrates a close knowledge of the Hebrew text, as well as the variety of scholarly opinions regarding Fructuosus's question. Braulio replies to Fructuosus, "We for our part, choosing the shorter time, have reckoned that Ismael [Ishmael] was cast out with his mother after 18 years and that it is not likely that an adolescent sat on his mother's back. There is a genuine idiom of the Hebrew language whereby every son by comparison with his parents is called infant and small. . . . Therefore, Abraham set bread and a bottle upon the shoulder of Agar [Hagar], and when he had done so, gave the boy to his mother, that is, put him in her hands, entrusted him, and so

---

85. Philo, *On Mating,* pp. 305-6; Clement, *Stromateis,* p. 44.

86. Clement, *Stromateis,* p. 45.

87. Letter 43, in *Iberian Fathers: Braulio of Saragossa and Fructuosus of Braga,* ed. Roy Joseph Deferrari, trans. Claude W. Barlow (Washington, DC: The Catholic University of America Press, 1969), p. 97.

sent them away from home."[88] Though Ishmael was a young man, not a child, at the time of his mother's flight from Sarah, Braulio explains, his mother "carried" him in the sense that she continued to provide parental care for him.

Homilies and exhortations: learning from Hagar

For the church fathers, interpretation of the Hebrew Bible often went hand-in-hand with exhortation. What could be learned from the text?

One such exhortation can be seen in the writing of John Chrysostom, Bishop of Constantinople (c. 400 C.E.). In Chrysostom's homily on the Hagar narrative in Genesis, he expresses a high regard for Sarah and Abraham. He has a far more negative opinion of Hagar:

> Now, however, on the contrary, see the ingratitude of the maidservant and the frailty of woman's nature. . . . "She saw that she was pregnant," the text goes on, "and her mistress was shown scant respect by her." This, you see, is the way with servants; if they happen to gain some slight advantage, they can't bear to stay within the limits of their station but immediately forget their place and fall into an ungrateful attitude. This is what happened to this maidservant, too: when she saw the change in her figure, she gave no thought either to her mistress's ineffable forbearance, nor her own lowly station, but became arrogant and self-important, scorning the mistress who had shown such great regard for her as even to bring her to her husband's very marriage bed.[89]

Hagar therefore is held up to Christians as a warning against arrogance and ingratitude, while Abraham and Sarah are exalted as positive role models.

Likewise, Augustine, Bishop of Hippo (c. 400 C.E.), utilized Hagar in his debate with the Donatists. The Donatists were a splinter group of the church, which felt that in the wake of persecution bishops who had lapsed in their faith were no longer part of the church and could no longer validly administer the sacraments. Contrary to this, Augustine and the Catholic

---

88. Letter 44, in *Iberian Fathers*, p. 107.

89. Homily 38, in *Chrysostom: Homilies on Genesis 18–45*, ed. Thomas P. Halton, trans. Robert C. Hill (Washington, DC: The Catholic University of America Press, 1990), p. 364. See note 36 above for a similar sentiment in *The Midrash on Proverbs*.

Church in general believed that a repentant minister could be restored to his authority in the church.[90]

Citing Genesis 16, Augustine draws a parallel between the Donatists and Hagar. Just as Hagar was sent by God back to Sarah, Augustine exhorts the Donatists to repent of their schismatic ways and return to the Catholic Church:

> So then, when God wishes to stir up the authorities against heretics, against schismatics, against the disintegrators of the Church, against the rejecters of Christ, against the blasphemers of baptism, let them not be astonished, because God urges that Agar [Hagar] be beaten by Sara [Sarah]. Let Agar recognize herself, let her bow her neck, because when she departed in humiliation from her mistress, an angel met her and said, "What is the matter, Agar, bondwoman of Sara?" When she complained about her mistress, what did she hear from the angel? "Return to your mistress." For this reason, therefore, is she harassed, that she may return. And would that she return; for her child, like the sons of Jacob, will hold the inheritance with his brothers. . . . And if you have suffered, O party of Donatus, bodily affliction from the Catholic Church, you are Agar, having suffered at the hands of Sara. "Return to your mistress."[91]

Doctrinal debates: Hagar and the Trinity

The Hagar narrative in Genesis proved to be fruitful to the church fathers in one final way. The early church, as we have mentioned, focused heavily on doctrinal formation. That is, based on the witness of the canonical Scriptures of the church, key beliefs were debated by the early fathers and finally set down in formal creeds.

One such doctrine was belief in the three persons of the Trinity (God the Father, God the Son, and God the Holy Spirit), that is, the doctrine of God. Closely tied to the doctrine of the Trinity was the doctrine of Christ,

---

90. The debate was highly significant. On a pragmatic level it directly impacted the validity of the Catholic Church as a body. One such apostate had been allowed to consecrate the bishop of Carthage, thereby casting doubt on the purity of the church as a whole. On a theological level, the Donatist controversy forced the early church to wrestle with the doctrine of the church. What was the church, and in what sense was the church holy?

91. *Tractate 11: On John 2.23-25 and 3.1-5*, in *Augustine: Tractates on the Gospel of John 11–27*, ed. Thomas P. Halton, trans. John W. Rettig (Washington, DC: The Catholic University of America Press, 1988), pp. 16-26.

for the identity and nature of Jesus Christ directly impacted the church's understanding of the nature of God.

Against those in the church who argued that Christ was an angel (or messenger), but not God, Novatian in his treatise on the Trinity draws heavily from the Hagar narrative. He states:

> When Hagar, Sarah's maidservant, had been banished from her home and put to flight, she was met at a spring of water on the road to Shur by an angel, who questioned her and learned the reason for her flight. She was advised to humble herself, with the hope that she would later bear the title of mother. Furthermore, the angel vowed and promised that the progeny of her womb would be numerous. Not only was Ishmael to be born of her but the angel also made known to her, among other things, the place of Ishmael's abode and described his manner of life. Now scripture portrays this angel as both Lord and God, for He would not have promised the blessing of progeny if He had not been both angel and God.[92]

Novatian continues at length, drawing from various passages in the Hagar narrative to support his claim that the angel of the Lord in those instances must be both God and an angel. How can he be both? Novatian states, "if we examine both sides of the question, truth itself drives us to this conclusion: we must acknowledge that He was the Son of God."[93]

He explains, "Because He is of God, He is rightly called God, since He is the Son of God; and because He is subject to the Father and herald of the Father's will, he is proclaimed 'Angel of the Great Counsel' [see Isa. 9:6 (5 H)]. Therefore, if this passage is not appropriate to the person of the Father, lest He be called an angel, nor to the person of an angel, lest He be called God, it does, however, suit the person of Christ, since He is not only God, inasmuch as He is the Son of God, but also an angel, inasmuch as He is the herald of the Father's dispensation."[94]

With this, Novatian draws his conclusion regarding the nature of Jesus Christ: "For if John says that this Word, who lays bare the bosom of the Father, was also made flesh [see John 1:14], so that He could lay bare the

---

92. *The Trinity*, in *Novatian*, ed. Bernard M. Peebles, trans. Russell J. DeSimone (Washington, DC: The Catholic University of America Press, 1974), p. 68.

93. Novatian, *The Trinity*, p. 69.

94. Novatian, *The Trinity*, p. 69. Cf. Hilary of Poitiers, *The Trinity*, which makes a similar argument based on the angel of the Lord in the Hagar narrative.

heart of the Father, it follows that Christ is not only man but also an angel. And the Scriptures show not only that He is an angel but also that He is God. This is what we too believe. For, if we will not admit that it was Christ who then spoke to Hagar, we must either make an angel God or reckon God the Almighty Father among the angels."[95]

The church fathers and Hagar in Galatians

Having examined the church fathers' use of the Hagar narrative in Genesis, let us now consider their discussion of Hagar in the New Testament. Paul's use of Hagar in the New Testament highlights two critically important and closely interwoven issues in the early church. Because of the nature of the church as a child of the synagogue, originally developing as a sect within Judaism but soon departing from those Jewish roots, two controversial subjects required immediate attention. What was the relationship between Jews and Christians, and likewise, what was the relationship between the New Testament (or "New Covenant") and the Hebrew Bible ("Old Testament" or "Old Covenant")?

The relationship between Jews and Christians: a deepening schism

As stated above, the church in its infancy was wholly Jewish. Its members were Jews who believed that Jesus was the Messiah proclaimed in the Hebrew Scriptures. They viewed themselves as Jews. Likewise, in spite of the friction that developed early on between followers of Jesus and other Jews, the synagogue and the Roman leadership initially viewed the church as merely a sect within Judaism.[96]

However, by 64 C.E. the Jewish Christians had developed an identity distinct from other Jews, as is evident in the actions of Nero, who singled out the Jewish Christians from the others following the fire in Rome.[97] By the second century C.E., the Christian sect had become almost thoroughly Gentile in its makeup and increasingly Hellenistic in its outlook. The church recast itself as the "New Israel" in place of Israel and in doing so effectively severed itself from its Jewish roots.[98]

---

95. Novatian, *The Trinity,* p. 72.
96. Acts 24:5; see also Wilson, *Our Father Abraham,* p. 41.
97. Tacitus, *Annals* 15.44; see also Wilson, *Our Father Abraham,* p. 74.
98. Wilson, *Our Father Abraham,* p. 89.

Meanwhile, the loss of the Temple and the fall of Jerusalem in 70 c.e. resulted in a modified, post-Temple Judaism known as Rabbinic Judaism, which was distinctly separate from Christianity. With the Second Jewish Revolt (132-35 c.e.), the widespread acceptance of Bar Kokhba's messianic claim drove a permanent wedge between the two groups.[99]

Bishop Ambrose of Milan (c. 375 c.e.) offers a glimpse of this schism in his reflections on Paul's use of Hagar in Galatians. In answer to Horontianus's question regarding the inheritance of a divine legacy, Ambrose states that all Christians will indeed receive such an inheritance, "and it is hoped for by promise, not by the Law. This is proved by the parable of the Old Testament [Hebrew Bible] in the words of Sara [Sarah]: 'Cast out this slave-girl with her son; for the son of this slave-girl shall not be heir with my son Isaac' [Gen. 21:10]. . . . We [Christians], in comparison with Isaac, are sons by promise; the Jews, in comparison with the flesh, are sons of the slave-girl."[100]

Notice the correspondence Ambrose makes here. Paul's allegory in the letter to the Galatians, Ambrose claims, demonstrates a distinction between Christians as sons of the promise (i.e., sons of Sarah) in contrast to Jews, who are sons of Hagar the slave-woman.

Ambrose does not explicitly direct his Christian readers toward an attitude of arrogance toward Judaism, though that may well have been the consequence of his writing. As he states at the conclusion of this passage, their attitude should be one of love: "The promise was ours [the Christians] before they [the Jews] had the Law. . . . But although the promise is before the Law, as we have said . . . love is according to the Law and love is greater than freedom."[101] However, as Ambrose's reading of the Hagar allegory in Galatians illustrates, by the fourth century the church *had* largely severed its connection to its Jewish roots and therefore could easily read a "Christian-versus-Jew" mind-set into an allegory that was originally aimed at competing factions *within* Christianity.

By the first half of the sixth century c.e., this erroneous interpretation of Galatians 4:21-31 was reiterated in a sermon of Caesarius of Arles (c. 550 c.e.). Caesarius states:

99. Wilson, *Our Father Abraham*, pp. 88-89.

100. Letter 47: Ambrose to Horontianus, in *Ambrose: Letters 1-91*, ed. Roy Joseph Deferrari, trans. Mary Melchior Beyenka (New York: Fathers of the Church, Inc., 1954), p. 245.

101. Ambrose, Letter 47, pp. 245-46.

The fact that the synagogue first existed and then later the church, and that the church would have greater glory than the synagogue, is very clearly contained in all the books of Scripture. Moreover, this idea is known to have been shown, not once or twice or three times, but very frequently in the writings of the Old Testament [Hebrew Bible]. Therefore, even if a man be simple and unlearned, he can recognize it clearly and plainly. At the very beginning of the world, of those two sons who were born of Adam, Abel the younger is chosen, while as a figure of the Jewish people Cain the older one is condemned. Afterwards, in the time of Abraham, the same figure is fulfilled in Sara [Sarah] and Agar [Hagar]. Sara was sterile for a long time as a type of the Church, while Agar as a figure of the synagogue bore a son at once. Hence, it is that the younger son Isaac is received into the inheritance, but Ismael [Ishmael] who was older is driven away.[102]

Like Ambrose, Caesarius figuratively correlates Ishmael, the son of Hagar, with the Jews, pressing Paul's analogy beyond its original intent. In doing so, Caesarius openly demonstrates a belief in the exaltation of the church and the condemnation and rejection of the Jews, a belief that clearly contradicts Paul's teaching in Romans 11.

Sadly, the figure of Hagar as used by Paul was often misused by the church fathers and reflects the growing schism and antagonism between Christianity and Judaism during the Patristic period.

The relationship between the Hebrew Bible and the Christian New Testament

Though the relationship between Christians and Jews grew increasingly antagonistic, the faith of the church was reliant on and in fact grew out of the Hebrew Bible. This tension created challenges for the church fathers, for even as their antagonism toward Judaism increased, they could not reject the Hebrew Scriptures. One Patristic solution to this dilemma involved allegorizing. Through allegorizing, as we have seen, elements of the Hebrew Bible could be removed from their original context and instead be redefined within the (often anti-Jewish) context of the early church. These allegories misrepresented the original context and intent of

---

102. Caesarius of Arles, Sermon 104, in *Sermons 81-186*, ed. Roy Joseph Deferrari, trans. Mary Magdeleine Mueller (Washington, DC: The Catholic University of America Press, 1964), p. 113.

the author, and many times encouraged an antagonistic attitude toward the synagogue.[103]

Not all Patristic solutions to this tension, however, reflected this antagonism. Church fathers such as Augustine of Hippo laid the groundwork for standards of biblical interpretation that are now commonly accepted in the Western church. Relying in part on the teaching of Galatians 4:21-31, Augustine's statement, "The New Testament is hidden in the Old; the Old is made accessible by the New," succinctly encapsulates his belief in the unity of the Hebrew Bible and the New Testament.[104] The two were not at odds with one another at all; on the contrary, they were organically unified and interconnected.

Building on the teaching of Ambrose, Augustine argues for two senses of Scripture: a literal/historical sense, and an allegorical/spiritual sense.[105] Passages of Scripture could refer to either sense or to both simultaneously.

An allegorical interpretation of a passage, according to Augustine, does not in any way deny its historicity. As he states:

> There are some who have allegorized the entire Garden of Eden. . . . The trees and fruit-bearing shrubs are turned into symbols of virtues and ways of living, as though they had no visible and material reality and as if Scripture had no purpose but to express meaning for our minds. The assumption here is that the possibility of a spiritual meaning rules out the reality of a physical Paradise. That is like saying that Agar [Hagar] and Sara [Sarah], the mothers of the two sons of Abraham, "the one by a slave-girl and the other by a free woman," had no historical existence simply because the Apostle has said that "by way of allegory . . . these are the two covenants."[106]

Rather, the historic realities in the Hebrew Bible reflect actual persons and events, but also were shadows of that which was to come, symbols of the spiritual reality that was to be.

To illustrate this point, Augustine turns to Galatians 4:21-31. Here, Augustine argues that one sees the portrayal of two cities: an earthly city

---

103. Wilson, *Our Father Abraham*, pp. 96-97.

104. Alister E. McGrath, *Historical Theology: An Introduction to the History of Christian Thought* (Oxford: Blackwell Publishers, 1998), p. 144.

105. McGrath, *Historical Theology*, p. 144.

106. St. Augustine, *City of God*, ed. Roy Joseph Deferrari, trans. Gerald G. Walsh and Grace Monahan (New York: Fathers of the Church, Inc., 1952), pp. 330-31.

that is a shadow of the heavenly city to come. According to Augustine, Hagar symbolizes the earthly Jerusalem that is in bondage, while Sarah symbolizes the heavenly Jerusalem that is free. Hagar symbolizes a shadow, for the earthly Jerusalem is a shadow of the reality that is to come in the heavenly Jerusalem.

As Augustine explains, "It was because shadows were to cease when the light came that the free woman, Sara, symbol of the free City . . . uttered the words: 'Cast out this slave-girl with her son' (Gen. 21:10). . . . In the world community, then, we find two forms, one being the visible appearance of the earthly city [i.e., Hagar] and another whose presence serves as a shadow of the heavenly City [i.e., Sarah]."[107]

Continuing this analogy, Augustine asks, who are the citizens of these two cities? These citizens are symbolized by the two sons of Abraham, the son of the flesh (Hagar's son) and the son of the promise (Sarah's son). Augustine states: "Of course, both were sons of Abraham, but he begot the one by a law suggesting the order of nature, while the other was born in virtue of a promise which pointed to the order of grace. What is clear in the one case is human action; in the other, divine favor."[108] Those citizens of the earthly community symbolized by Hagar are those who are born of human nature, marred by sin. Only "grace, which frees nature from sinfulness, can bring forth citizens of the heavenly city"[109] symbolized by Sarah.

Augustine concludes: "This exegesis [of Galatians 4:21-31], which comes to us with apostolic authority, opens up for us a way to understand much that is written in both Testaments, the Old and the New."[110] Through these symbols, Augustine demonstrates his understanding that the Hebrew Bible and the New Testament "bear witness to the same faith, even if its mode of expression may be different."[111] The New Testament is the fulfillment of the Hebrew Bible, and there is a unity between the two.[112]

107. Augustine, *City of God*, p. 417.

108. Augustine, *City of God*, p. 417.

109. Augustine, *City of God*, p. 417.

110. Augustine, *City of God*, p. 416.

111. McGrath, *Historical Theology*, p. 144.

112. This same argument from Galatians 4:21-31 is contained in Augustine's remarks concerning the views of his contemporary, Pelagius. Pelagius believed that the reward of God was based on human merit (i.e., following God's commandments), a belief that was denounced by the church as heresy. Against Pelagius, Augustine argues that the merit of God is dependent on God's promise of divine grace. Expounding on the citizens of the earthly city and the heavenly city, Augustine asks how children of the promise could fail to be disturbed

Augustine's belief that the New Testament is the fulfillment of the Hebrew Bible, and that unity exists between the two, is reiterated in his work, *The Advantage of Believing*. There, Augustine argues against the beliefs of the Manicheans, whom he claims "tear apart" and "mangle" the Old Testament (Hebrew Bible).[113] Against their claim that the Old Testament is now void for Christians, Augustine points to Paul's allegory in Galatians as evidence that Christ has not done away with the Old Testament but has in fact made clear its fullest significance, which was concealed until Christ. Augustine states:

> What is made void in Christ is not the Old Testament, but its veil; that through Christ there may be understood and, as it were, laid bare, that which without Christ is obscure and covered over. And at once, to be sure, the same apostle adds [in 2 Cor. 3:16], "But when you shall be converted to Christ, the veil will be taken away." But he does not say, "The Law will be taken away" or "The Old Testament." These, then, have not been taken away through the grace of the Lord as though they concealed useless things; rather, there was removed their covering by which useful things were hidden. This is the treatment followed in the case of those who studiously and faithfully, not turbidly and rashly, seek the sense of the Scriptures. A careful demonstration is made of the order of things, and of the causes of deeds and words, and of the harmony of the Old Testament with the New, so pervading that no tittle is left in disagreement.[114]

Summary on the Church Fathers and Hagar

The classical rabbis did not put forth a single, homogenized opinion on Hagar. Likewise, as a figure in both the Hebrew Bible and the New Tes-

---

by Pelagius's attempt to make Hagar (human merit) the equal of Sarah (grace). Though the law (human merit) and the promise (grace) are not equals, Augustine is not suggesting that they are mutually exclusive or in opposition to one another. Rather, the former is a shadow of the latter, and the latter is the ultimate fulfillment of the former. See Augustine, *On the Proceedings of Pelagius*, in *St. Augustine: Four Anti-Pelagian Writings*, ed. Thomas P. Halton, trans. John A. Mourant and William J. Collinge (Washington, DC: The Catholic University of America Press, 1992), pp. 125-26.

113. St. Augustine, *The Advantage of Believing*, ed. Ludwig Schopp, trans. Luanne Meagher (New York: CIMA Publishing, 1947), p. 395.

114. Augustine, *The Advantage of Believing*, p. 402.

tament, Hagar is understood by the church fathers in wide variety of ways.

In some cases, Hagar is honored. Though she is never given the status that Sarah receives, Hagar is often understood to be a valuable contributor to Abraham's household. Sarah may represent wisdom and virtue, but Hagar represents the knowledge and secular philosophy that are necessary for acquiring that Christian truth, and as such she is seen as a vital part of Sarah's accomplishments. And while Hagar is not equated with wisdom, she is portrayed as a recipient of divine wisdom, the first to be visited by the angel of the Lord.

On the other hand, Hagar is also viewed negatively by certain church fathers. She is portrayed as arrogant, boastful, and proud. She becomes self-important upon the discovery of her pregnancy and scorns her mistress. As such, she is denounced and held up as a negative role model and an example of how Christians should not act.

Hagar is connected with schismatics in the early church, who, like Hagar, fled their mistress the church and are now being called to return to her as the angel of the Lord commanded. And as a reflection of the growing schism between the church and the synagogue, Sarah's call to cast out Hagar and her son is often used in support of the erroneous view that God had rejected the Jews.

The church fathers' reading of Hagar is impacted by the immediate concerns of a church forging its own identity distinct from the synagogue. They wrestle with understanding the nature of Jesus Christ and the Trinity, and Hagar's encounter with the angel of the Lord becomes part of that conversation. They struggle to understand the connection between the Hebrew Bible and New Testament, and Paul's use of Hagar in Galatians sheds light on that subject.

At the same time, however, the church was deeply rooted in the synagogue, and the influence of Jewish thought is evident in the church's understanding of Hagar. Like the rabbis, the church fathers are also wary of Hagar (although unlike the rabbis, who associate her with competing Semitic/Arab tribes, the church fathers are inclined to associate her with the Jews of the synagogue). Like Philo, the Patristic writers view Hagar as a route to acquiring wisdom, even though she herself is not wisdom. And with the rabbis, Paul understands Hagar to be "the Other Woman," an outsider even though a member of the community, a slave and a proselyte even while a wife.

From this survey of the Patristic writings on Hagar, one fact is readily apparent. The church fathers understand Hagar through a decidedly *Christian* lens. Often they demonstrate an intimate connection with and knowledge of their Jewish roots, while at other times their writings reflect or contribute to the severing of these roots. But in either case, their interpretations are influenced by the Christian New Testament, Christian theology, and the needs and challenges facing the early church. While these influences stand to reason, they are nevertheless no small matter. They indicate that at the inception of the church, a distinctly *Christian* theological perspective developed that distinguished the Christian church, originally a sect within Judaism, as an entity all its own.

"The Other Woman": Concluding Remarks Regarding Early Jewish and Christian Perspectives on Hagar

There are limited narratives devoted to Hagar the Egyptian in the book of Genesis, but her presence is significant in the early accounts of the Patriarchs/Matriarchs, and her influence can later be seen in the Christian Scriptures and in writings of the rabbis and the church fathers.

In the Hebrew Bible and the New Testament, Hagar is often viewed as an "Other" or as an "Outsider," but her impact is considerable and long-lasting. Despite her status as a foreign slave-woman, she is in Genesis the mother of Abraham's first son, who by God's word would be the eponymous ancestor of many people. She is, moreover, the first person in the Bible to encounter an angel, and also the first person to receive an annunciation. Her "Otherness" is carried with her into the first century c.e., where Paul presents her as a figure "on the borderline," that is, both part of Abraham's family and yet once again in many ways an "Other" or "Outsider." While the Gentile Christians of the early church community are likewise "on the borderline," Paul argues that through faith they are not the children of Hagar, the symbol of slavery and of the unnecessary burden of circumcision. They are, rather, children of Sarah just like the Jewish believers, children of the symbol of freedom and of the promise of a covenant that is fully realized in the figure of Jesus. Paul's message welcomes the Gentile Christians into the Jewish church with open arms.

The Rabbinical Hagar is a double "Other" or "Outsider." She is an Egyptian; consequently she is a reminder — even subliminally — of the oppression during the hundreds of years of slavery to Pharaoh. Hagar likewise bears the burden of being the mother of the Ishmaelites, who come to represent many of Israel's close Semitic neighbors such as Edomites and Arabs (and later Muslims), with whom there often were political/territorial as well as religious disputes. While many rabbis denigrate Hagar, marginalizing her as the Other/Outsider, there were rabbis who praised her as well. In the view of some rabbis, Hagar is of royal lineage, the very daughter of Pharaoh. Hagar immerses herself so well within the Abraham-Sarah household that when she sees angels, she is not surprised; she is conversant with such figures. There also is a well-established Rabbinic tradition that Hagar is the same person as Keturah (Qeturah), the woman Abraham marries after Sarah dies, and that Isaac himself brought Hagar to Abraham.

In like manner among the church fathers, Hagar is often seen as the Other/Outsider. For Augustine, Hagar is a fitting figure for the schismatics of his days, those who broke away from the church, the Donatists. As Hagar had fled into the wilderness from the encampment of Abraham and Sarah and was told to return and submit, so Augustine urged the Donatists to return and submit to the mother church. Regrettably, in other cases the church fathers at times misused the figure of Hagar as "Other," reflecting the growing schism and antagonism between Christianity and Judaism during the Patristic period. Yet, just as there were rabbis who praised Hagar, so likewise there were those among the Patristic writers who regarded Hagar in a positive light. She is the recipient of wisdom through her encounter with the angel, and as a symbol of secular philosophy she is a bridge to the greatest truth of wisdom. Embedded within these interpretations is the understanding that Hagar, while seemingly insignificant, is a path to something quite significant indeed.

A cursory reading of the Hagar texts suggests that she is an unimportant character. The small role she plays, however, can be misleading. Though often cast as a borderline figure, Hagar's role in her own right, and then as the mother of Ishmael, becomes significant in the unfolding biblical drama. Through Paul's letter to the community at Galatia, as well as through Rabbinic teachings and Patristic writings, Hagar has had a lasting impact on Judaism and Christianity.